Apples and Ashes

Series Editors

Jon Smith, Simon Fraser University

Riché Richardson, Cornell University

Advisory Board

Houston A. Baker Jr., Vanderbilt University

Jennifer Greeson, The University of Virginia

Trudier Harris, The University of North Carolina, Chapel Hill

John T. Matthews, Boston University

Tara McPherson, The University of Southern California

Apples and Ashes

Literature, Nationalism, and the Confederate States of America

 COLEMAN HUTCHISON

The University of Georgia Press   Athens and London

© 2012 by the University of Georgia Press
Athens, Georgia 30602
www.ugapress.org
Set in Sabon by Graphic Composition, Inc.,
   Bogart, Georgia
Printed and bound by Thomson-Shore
The paper in this book meets the guidelines for
permanence and durability of the Committee on
Production Guidelines for Book Longevity of the
Council on Library Resources.

Printed in the United States of America
16 15 14 13 12 P 5 4 3 2 1

Library of Congress Cataloging-in-Publication Data

Hutchison, Coleman, 1977–
   Apples and ashes : literature, nationalism, and the Confederate States of
America / Coleman Hutchison.
       p. cm. — (The new Southern studies)
   Includes bibliographical references and index.
   ISBN-13: 978-0-8203-3731-9 (cloth : alk. paper)
   ISBN-10: 0-8203-3731-5 (cloth : alk. paper)
   ISBN-13: 978-0-8203-4244-3 (pbk. : alk. paper)
   ISBN-10: 0-8203-4244-0 (pbk. : alk. paper)
   1. American literature—Southern States—History and criticism. 2. Politics and
literature—Southern States—History—19th century. 3. Confederate States of
America—Intellectual life. 4. Regionalism—Southern States—History—19th
century. 5. Group identity—Southern States—History—19th century. 6. United
States—History—Civil War, 1861–1865—Social aspects. I. Title.
   PS261.H88 2012
   810.9'35875—dc23   2011037743

British Library Cataloging-in-Publication Data available

In memory of Betty and Jim

For the South to neglect to employ every instrumentality appertaining to the production of a vigorous, healthy, native, loyal and beneficent literature; for her to depend almost exclusively upon foreign sources for her reading, and, outside of local politics, for her thinking, would be to manifest a fatal hesitation—to throw away a magnificent future—to doom herself to dwell amid the defilements and abominations of a detested past, and famishing in arid plains, to feed upon apples of ashes.

quoted in the *Southern Literary Messenger*, October 1861

The voices of reaction have to be encountered in all their complexity and not assumed to be self-evident or dismissed as too offensive.

Jay Fliegelman, "Anthologizing the Situation of American Literature"

Contents

Figures

Apples and Ashes

Great Expectations

The Imaginative Literature of the
Confederate States of America

For nearly 150 years there has seemingly been a critical consensus that Confederate imaginative literature is not worthy of extensive consideration. Despite consistent, even obsessive interest in the most obscure aspects of American Civil War culture, literary historians have largely ignored the poetry, fiction, drama, music, and criticism produced in the Confederate States of America between 1861 and 1865. When literary historians have engaged this literature, it has often been in a comparative mode, with Confederate literary culture read in relation to a much more developed U.S. literary culture. Not surprisingly, such a methodology has led to two conclusions about the literature of the Confederate States: There wasn't much of the stuff, and in any case it wasn't very good.

For instance, the two best-known literary studies of the American Civil War, Edmund Wilson's *Patriotic Gore* (1962) and Daniel Aaron's *The Unwritten War* (1973), both assume the meagerness of Confederate literary culture. As a result, Wilson and Aaron base their discussions of the Confederacy almost entirely on postwar, retrospective southern publications. While Wilson finds flashes of brilliance in writers like Mary Chesnut (whose diaries were heavily revised after the war and not published until the early twentieth century), Aaron remains unconvinced, declaring that "[v]ery little fiction or poetry written in the South during the War came to much" (234).[1]

Unfortunately, Confederate literature has not fared much better when placed in broader literary contexts. It has garnered only scant attention from southern literary studies, the disciplinary field perhaps best positioned to give an account of it. This has led one Civil War historian to conclude that Confederate literature is the "perennial poor relation of Southern literature" (Muhlenfeld 178). If southern literary studies has neglected its Confederate cousin, then nineteenth-century American literary studies has disowned it outright. With a handful of notable exceptions, the literature of the South during the American Civil War is simply not on the "C19" map.[2]

One can imagine a number of reasons that Confederate literature has eluded both southern and nineteenth-century American literary studies. First and foremost, the assumption that critics like Wilson and Aaron make about the paucity of Confederate literature is a sensible one. The Confederacy lasted for four short years, during which time its littérateurs were perpetually beleaguered. Among the persistent and structural problems faced by Confederate writers and publishers were severe shortages of paper, ink, type, skilled labor, and printing presses—"in short, everything needed to produce a successful publishing industry" (Fahs 5).[3] These material hardships were exacerbated by economic and logistical hardships, including rampant inflation, a shoddy interstate mail system, and the omnipresence of Yankee troops on southern land. This is to say nothing of relatively low literacy rates in the new Confederate nation. In truth, many southerners remained dubious about the prospects of a southern literature before, during, and after the American Civil War.[4]

Faced with such challenges, the emergence of a literary culture in the Civil War South would have been no small wonder. And yet, as this book demonstrates, the Confederacy gave rise to a robust literary culture. The war had thrown the South for the first time "upon its own literary resources" (Hubbell, *South* 454); among other things, the federal blockade denied southern readers access to northern literature. This, in turn, provided southern, white elites with an opportunity to claim cultural autonomy from the North. As Michael T. Bernath argues persuasively in his recent intellectual history of Confederate cultural nationalists, their success in creating a "native literature" was "startling, almost unbelievable," particularly in light of the difficulties outlined above (152). Although this book largely avoids recursive debates about literary quality, one of its organizing principles is that the Confederacy produced a *quantity* of literature that warrants closer examination.[5]

Military defeat may provide another reason for the ongoing critical neglect of Confederate literature. The Confederate States of America failed, and failed spectacularly. Perhaps literary historians see little reason to study in depth an abortive literature. To be sure, the Confederate national moment was whirligig, and scholars have few models for thinking about the emergence and collapse of a nation over the course of a mere fifty-one months. Moreover, in light of the eventual failure of Confederate nationhood, it is all too easy to read Confederate literary nationalism either proleptically or palinodically. Knowing what we know about the future that was to come, how can we engage the Confederate past in all its complexity and contingency? That is, how can we return to a moment when both a Confederate nation and a Confederate national literature were possibilities, not merely lost causes? As the first epigraph of this book suggests, many wartime writers worked in earnest to achieve a "magnificent future" for their new nation. We need to think creatively—if not counterfactually—about such literary nationalism, emphasizing its great expectations rather than its stultifying disappointments.[6]

The difficulties inherent in such thinking bring us to a final reason for Confederate literature's "poor relations." Perhaps literary historians have eschewed the literature of the Confederacy because of what Gary Gallagher calls the "aroma of moral disapprobation" that surrounds any serious, scholarly conversation about Confederate nationalism (*Confederate* 70). To write about the Confederate nation is to risk being seen as endorsing its right to exist. Let me be clear: This book is by no means an apology for the Confederacy or Confederate nationalism. I find almost nothing that is admirable in the politics and culture of the Civil War South. Much of Confederate literature was deeply conservative. Emerging from a fiercely nationalistic milieu, it resounds with both racist and racialist rhetoric and makes the case again and again for an antidemocratic republic. Thus, the story told in the following pages is that of both the losers and the "bad guys." No matter how unsavory that story proves, I think it is important that it be told. Per Jay Fliegelman, the reactionary voices of Confederate literature—in all their complexity—have a great deal to teach literary studies.[7]

It is the broad claim of *Apples and Ashes* that Confederate literature allows us to trace the development of a national literature both in process and in miniature. Several themes emerge from the texts of this nation struggling to write itself into existence: the messiness of history (literary and otherwise); the provisional nature of American nationalism during this period; and a less exceptionalist account of the United States, its southern other, and their purportedly civil war. Confederate literature was an essential vehicle for Confederate nationalism, a sinewy and multifarious phenomenon that historians have begun to take seriously. Confederate literature was also in intimate conversation with other nineteenth-century literary cultures, especially those of Britain and the United States. Finally, Confederate literature has profound implications for our understanding of American literary nationalism and the relationship between literature and nationalism more broadly.[8]

In the wake of Benedict Anderson's ubiquitous study *Imagined Communities: Reflections on the Origin and Spread of Nationalism* (1983, 1991), literary studies of the 1980s and 1990s championed the textual nature of nationalism. Perhaps flattered by Anderson's emphasis on newspapers and novels, literary and cultural critics like Homi K. Bhabha redefined "nationness as a form of social and textual affiliation" (201). In more recent years, literary and cultural critics have labored to "think and feel beyond the nation," to write, that is, postnational, transnational, hemispheric, and global literary histories (Cheah and Robbins). Despite an immense amount of productive scholarship in these modes, we seem no closer to a full understanding of the relationship between literature and nationalism. A wide range of scholars agree that there is something fundamentally "literary" about the construction of nationality, but details remain vague.[9]

Although this book does not offer a theory of literary nationalism per se, it does tout the usefulness of the Confederate example for thinking about the role of literature in the imagining of political communities. Indeed, Confederate literature provides an urgent case study because it represents a literary nationalism that was not only internationally minded but also more durable than its state apparatus. Thus, the literature produced in the South during the war offers an endorsement of Ernest Gellner's influential dictum that "[i]t is nationalism which engenders nations, and not the other way round" (54). *Apples and Ashes* identifies, in turn, a number of specific mechanisms by which literary nationalism helped to engender the Confederate States of America.[10]

"Ethnogenesis": Thirteen Ways of Looking at Confederate Literature

At the risk of being too programmatic, I want to introduce the dominant features of Confederate literature using a familiar example: Henry Timrod's poem "Ethnogenesis." In early 1861, Henry Timrod was a promising young poet and critic from South Carolina. He had just published his first collection of poems after gaining acclaim as a regular contributor to *Russell's Magazine* (1857–1860), the Charleston-based literary journal edited by Paul Hamilton Hayne. With the secession of the southern states, Timrod's romantic and formal poems would take on a decidedly Confederate nationalistic cast.[11]

Like so many Confederate poems, "Ethnogenesis" circulated through a number of media. It first appeared in an issue of the *Charleston Daily Courier* dated 23 February 1861 as "Ode on Occasion of the Meeting of the Southern Congress"; a broadside version of the poem, "Ode on the Meeting of the Southern Congress," followed shortly thereafter. The poem was also heavily reprinted throughout the war in newspapers, magazines, and anthologies (Parks and Parks, *Collected Poems* 180–81). As its early titles suggest, "Ethnogenesis" celebrates the convening of the Provisional Confederate Congress, which met in Montgomery, Alabama, beginning 4 February 1861.

Ethnogenesis.
Ode on Occasion of the Meeting of the Southern Congress.

I.

Hath not the morning dawned with added light?
And will not evening call another star
Out of the infinite regions of the night,

To mark this day in heaven? At last, we are
A nation among nations; and the world
Shall soon behold in many a distant part
            Another flag unfurled!
Now, come what may, whose favor need we court?
And, under God, whose thunder need we fear?
            Thank Him who placed us here
Beneath so kind a sky—the very sun
Takes part with us; and on our errands run
All breezes of the ocean; dew and rain
Do noiseless battle for us; and the year,
And all the gentle daughters in her train,
March in our ranks, and in our service wield
            Long spears of golden grain!
A yellow blossom as her fairy shield
June flings our azure banner to the wind,
            While in the order of their birth
Her sisters pass, and many an ample field
Grows white beneath their steps, till now, behold
            Its endless sheets unfold
The Snow of Southern Summers! Let the earth
Rejoice!—beneath those fleeces soft and warm
            Our happy land shall sleep
            In a repose as deep,
            As if we lay intrenched behind
Whole leagues of Russian ice and Arctic storm!

                        II.
And what, if mad with wrongs themselves have wrought,
            In their own treachery caught,
            By their own fears made bold,
            And leagued with him of old,
Who long since in the limits of the North
Set up his evil throne, and warred with God—
What if, both mad and blinded in their rage,
Our foes should fling us down their mortal gage,
And with a hostile step profane our sod!
We shall not shrink, my brothers, but go forth
To meet them, marshalled by the Lord of Hosts,
And overshadowed by the mighty ghosts
Of Moultrie and of Eutaw—who shall foil
Auxiliars such as these? Nor these alone,
            But every stock and stone
Shall help us; but the very soil,
And all the generous wealth it gives to toil,

And all for which we love our noble land,
Shall fight beside, and through us, sea and strand,
      The heart of woman, and her hand,
Tree, fruit, and flower, and every influence,
        Gentle or grave or grand.
      The winds in our defence
Shall seem to blow: to us the hills shall lend
   Their firmness and their calm;
And in our stiffened sinews we shall blend
   The strength of pine and palm!

III.

Look where we will, we cannot find a ground
   For any mournful song:
Call up the clashing elements around,
   And test the right and wrong!
On one side, pledges broken, creeds that lie,
Religion sunk in vague philosophy,
Empty professions, pharisaic leaven,
Souls that would sell their birthright in the sky
Philanthropists who pass the beggar by,
And laws which controvert the laws of Heaven
And, on the other—first, a righteous cause!
      Then, honor without flaws,
Truth, Bible reverence, charitable wealth,
And for the poor and humble, laws which give,
Not the mean right to buy the right to live,
      But life, and home, and health.
To doubt the issue were distrust in God!
If in his Providence he hath decreed
That to the peace for which we pray,
Through the Red Sea of War must lie our way,
Doubt not, O brothers, we shall find at need
      A Moses with his rod!

IV.

But let our fears—if fears we have—be still,
And turn us to the future! Could we climb
Some Alp in thought, and view the coming time,
We should indeed behold a sight to fill
      Our eyes with happy tears!
Not for the glories which a hundred years
Shall bring us; not for lands from sea to sea,
And wealth, and power, and peace, though these shall be;
But for the distant peoples we shall bless,
And the hushed murmurs of a world's distress:

For, to give food and clothing to the poor,
    The whole sad planet o'er,
And save from crime its humblest human door,
Our mission is! The hour is not yet ripe
When all shall see it, but behold the type
Of what we are and shall be to the world,
In our own grand and genial Gulf Stream furled,
Which through the vast and colder ocean pours
Its waters, so that far-off Arctic shores
May sometimes catch upon the softened breeze
Strange tropic warmth and hints of summer seas! (Shepperson 63–66)

From its first cajoling question through its last rosy exclamation, this is a poem of exuberant rhetorical nationalism. Despite its occasional frame, "Ethnogenesis" makes few references to the actual work of nation building that occurred in Montgomery during February 1861, which included drafting a constitution, establishing a government, electing Jefferson Davis as president, and authorizing the first Confederate flag. Instead, Timrod emphasizes the communal and cultural elements of this new nationality, paying particular attention to the Confederacy's place in the world and the endorsements of "Nature," if not "Nature's God."

One of the poem's most striking characteristics is its sense of urgency and inception. Even before Timrod retitled the poem "Ethnogenesis" in January 1862, this was clearly a poem of beginning, of new morning "dawned with added light." The speaker, who favors the collective utterance "we" throughout, moves elegantly among the present, future, and future conditional tenses: "At last, we are / A nation among nations; and the world / Shall soon behold in many a distant part / Another flag unfurled!" The preposition "At last" reveals the first feature of Confederate literature: It was *belated*. The literary historian Gregory Jusdanis argues that nationalism "emerges out of comparisons people make regarding the relative standing of nations" (*Necessary* 102). He sees "belated societies" as those that feel keenly the "angst of lagging behind" others: "Nations differ in the extent of their development and devise strategies to narrow the gap between themselves and their neighbors or colonizers" (*Necessary* 108, 102). Southern elites before, during, and after the American Civil War were constantly considering the "relative standing of nations." They were anxious to "catch up" and convinced that the war had finally ("At last") provided an opportunity to do so. Literature bore a great deal of this nationalist burden. Confederates needed to invent a national literary tradition, and in a hurry.[12]

A sense of lagging behind and needing to catch up introduces a second feature of Confederate literature: Nearly all of it was *written for a vanishing present*. Inception and urgency often resulted in hasty composition and a rush to the printer. While many Confederate literary texts bear the marks of such feverish, even sloppy production, I am more or less uninterested in the quality of their versification, character development, or printing practices. For instance, Timrod's is a more or less a lapidary poem that evinces a great deal of formal and rhetorical control. However, the tight window of time between the convening of the Provisional Congress and the poem's publication (that is, less than three weeks) suggests a hurried effort to get this poem out into the world. More often than not, Confederate writers like Timrod were trying desperately to connect their texts "to a political immediacy," namely the chaos of a war-torn world and the hopes of a new nationality (Deleuze and Guattari 18). This brings to mind Gilles Deleuze and Félix Guattari's description of the composition of a "minor literature"—"[w]riting like a dog digging a hole, a rat digging its burrow" (18). These rough figures elegantly describe much of the literature produced in the South during the war, a fact that many southern littérateurs openly confessed. For instance, the 24 September 1863 issue of the London-based, pro-Confederate journal *The Index* offered a survey of "Confederate Books." Its conclusion is frank and revealing: "What is now written, though necessarily hurried and imperfect, gives promise of a brilliant future, when the people of the Confederate States will have a literature worthy of their glory in arms and of their descent" (347).[13]

   The Index's "promise of a brilliant future" sounds a great deal like the *Southern Literary Messenger*'s "magnificent future." This rhetoric of futurity brings us to three related features of Confederate literature: It reads as *a literature of aspiration*; it practiced *a near perpetual process of deferral*; and it was *future oriented.* Many Confederates were admirably clear-eyed about the time and effort it would take to found a national literature. They were also painfully aware of the material challenges they faced. Thus, in aspiring to a national literature, they were more than willing to wait, to defer the realization of their literary nationalist desires and designs until some unspecified, future date. This dynamic pervades the ways Confederates talked about their literary culture in the making. A representative example comes from William Gilmore Simms, who demanded patience from readers and writers alike: "All our thoughts resolve themselves into the war. We are now *living* the first grand epic of our newly-born Confederacy. We are *making* the materials for the drama, and for future songs and fiction; and, engaged in the actual event, we are in no mood for delineating its details, or framing it to proper laws of art, in any province" (*Southern Illustrated News* 11 October 1862: 2). Although Simms was throughout his life an outspoken advocate for an autonomous southern literature, he defers here, arguing that Confederate literature will not be born fully formed, especially during a time of war.[14]

   It is not surprising, then, that "Ethnogenesis" reverberates with the rhetoric of aspiration, deferral, and futurity. Again, Timrod's use of the future and future conditional tenses is telling. The word "shall" appears a remarkable fourteen times in the poem. The world "Shall soon behold . . . Another flag unfurled!"; Confederates "shall find at need / A Moses with his rod!" Indeed, in the opening lines of the poem's final section, the speaker directs all attention to a quasi-messianic future:

> But let our fears—if fears we have—be still,
> And turn us to the future! Could we climb
> Some Alp in thought, and view the coming time,
> We should indeed behold a sight to fill
>   Our eyes with happy tears!

The provisionality of these lines ("Could we climb . . . We should indeed behold") speaks to the contingency of the Confederate national moment, as does the evocation of unarticulated Confederate "fears." The trick, the poem suggests, is in seeing beyond the immediate moment, of gaining enough perspective to see what comes after Confederate independence is achieved. Later lines are even more explicit about this temporality: "The hour is not yet ripe / When all shall see it, but behold the type / Of what we are and shall be to the world." Although the speaker emphasizes the charitable aid that the Confederacy will eventually bring to the world, the poem's final turn to the future also reflexively figures the benefits of a robust Confederate literary culture— benefits that will not be realized until the hour is ripe.[15]

The poem's articulation of Confederate national purpose is jarring: "For, to give food and clothing to the poor, / The whole sad planet o'er, / And save from crime its humblest human door, / Our mission is!" The promise to "give food and clothing to the poor" is a quiet allusion to the agricultural riches that the South possessed on the eve of the American Civil War. It is also tantamount to a King Cotton argument: that the Confederacy should be recognized as an independent nation because circa 1861 it was responsible for approximately two-thirds of the world's cotton production. Thus, Timrod's humanitarian gesture is, I argue, of a piece with Confederate literature's tendency to make *agro-literary appeals*. Much of Confederate literature refers not simply to cotton and plantations but also to the pastoral and the agrarian. These references appealed to two audiences. For foreign readers, such allusions helped to associate the new nation with agricultural plenty; for domestic readers, they helped to normalize desires for an autonomous southern literature by yoking the literary to the region's dominant economic interests.[16]

Such an appeal recurs throughout Timrod's ode. A good deal of the poem's first section figures God and nature as fighting on the side of the Confederacy: "on our errands run / All breezes of the ocean; dew and rain / Do noiseless battle, for us." Even time and the seasons muster with the Gray: "and the year, / And all the gentle daughters in her train, / March in our ranks, and in our service wield / Long spears of golden grain!" This marshalling of nature results in agricultural bounty—the very stuff on which Confederate diplomacy was based. Although the word *cotton* does not appear anywhere in "Ethnogenesis," it is figured in Timrod's odd, alliterative image "THE SNOW OF SOUTHERN SUMMERS!" Extending this metaphor, the speaker has unshakable faith in what "those fleeces soft and warm" portend for the Confederate States of America: perpetual peace, "As if we lay intrenched behind / Whole leagues of Russian ice and Arctic storm!"

Another word that does not appear anywhere in Timrod's ode is *slave*— a present absence if ever there was one. Before Confederate cotton can help secure the new nation and "bless" "distant peoples," someone has to tend, pick, and gin all that "SNOW." Although Timrod cannily avoids direct mention of the peculiar institution, it is nonetheless a given in the poem's closed circuit of meaning.[17] This is in keeping with a signal feature of Confederate literature: It was *the literature of a slaveholding republic*. As Stephanie McCurry argues forcefully, the Confederacy was in this regard suï generis: "What secessionists set out to build was something entirely new in the history of nations: a modern proslavery and antidemocratic state, dedicated to the proposition that all men were not created equal" (1). In both its inclusions and its exclusions, through both clear declarations and subtle insinuations, Confederate literature bears out McCurry's claim. As a result, Confederate literature offers us an uncommon opportunity to trace the relationship between "slavery and the literary imagination"—a relationship that was, in the Confederate context, exceedingly complicated. For every poem like "Ethnogenesis," which seems to avoid or beg the "slavery question," there is a poem like *The Old Plantation* (1862), which ardently depicts and defends slavery. In a brief preface, the poet, Joseph Addison Turner, acknowledges that "it might have been best for me to avoid the question of slavery altogether"; however, he concludes, "negro slavery is the south, and the south is negro slavery. . . . And you had as well attempt to depict Swiss scenery without mentioning the Alps, as to attempt to describe the south without referring to negro slavery" (Turner 4). While individual texts oscillate between these representational extremes, there is no denying slavery's dominant presence in the Confederate literary imagination.[18]

One expression of this presence comes through racialist rhetoric, which is everywhere in Confederate literature. It was a Confederate habit of mind to make clear racial and ethnic demarcations, not only between white and black but also between "Norman and Saxon" and "Cavalier and Yankee." This brings us to the final title of Timrod's ode, "Ethnogenesis," which the *Oxford English Dictionary* defines as the "formation or emergence of an ethnic group within a larger community." As part of a nation-building process, Confederate literature labored to *imagine southerners as a fictive ethnicity*.

The phrase "fictive ethnicity" comes from Étienne Balibar, whose definition has urgent implications for the Confederate national moment: "No nation possesses an ethnic base naturally, but as social formations are nationalized, the populations included within them, divided up among them or dominated by them are ethnicized—that is, represented in the past or in the future *as if* they formed a natural community, possessing of itself an identity of origins, culture and interests which transcends individuals and social conditions" (Balibar and Wallerstein 96).[19] Part of the cultural work of this literature was, then, to render a diverse people as a coherent and natural community. For instance, in renaming his poem "Ethnogenesis," Timrod consolidates the community imagined by the poem's insistent rhetoric of the first-person plural. His is no mere occasional ode but instead a declaration of ethnic emergence and solidarity. It should come as no surprise that by the conclusion of section 3, Confederates have become "Providence's" chosen people: "Through the Red Sea of War must lie our way, / Doubt not, O brothers, we shall find at need / A Moses with his rod!"[20]

This extended metaphor comes at the end of a section that contrasts explicitly North and South: "On one side, pledges broken, creeds that lie / Religion sunk in vague philosophy. . . . And, on the other—first, a righteous cause! / Then, honor without flaws." Such comparisons recur throughout the literature of the Confederacy, which repeatedly *defined itself against northern/American literature.* As the sociologist Sarah Corse notes, aspirational national cultures often take pains to distinguish themselves from other, extant national cultures: "In order to proclaim cultural independence, a nation-state must produce and identify a literature that differentiates it from other states, particularly the most relevant others—e.g., 'Mother England' for the United States and both England and the United States for Canada" (9). Given that it was fighting a war for independence from the United States, the Confederate States' "most relevant" other was just to the north.[21]

The process of Confederate national differentiation was not limited to a North-South axis, however, just as the American Civil War was not confined to a provincial "House Divided." For instance, many Confederates called for a national literary culture that would embrace rather than eschew European models and traditions. The result was a dialectic of cultural separatism and cosmopolitanism: Confederates sought a national literature that would be both distinct from northern literary culture and sympathetic to European literary traditions. Thus, Confederate literary nationalism was *a triangulated phenomenon.* An essay on the "Literature of the South" from a May 1862 issue of *The Index* is unequivocal about such triangulation: "The two sections of the late Republic spoke the same language, and lived under the same government; but in all other respects there was no community, nay, not so much as between the Confederate States and England, or, indeed, almost any other European nation" (8 May 1862: 23).[22] In this articulation, the Confederate States is clearly not the United States; indeed, according to the propaganda of *The Index*, it may not even be part of the "new world." This play between repulsion and attraction helps us to address a question posed by Douglas Southall Freeman, one of the earliest historians of the Confederacy: "Southerners of that period were original in their conversation; why did so many of them find no better way of expressing their poetic impulses than in palpable attempts to imitate Byron, Macaulay, and lesser men?" (14). The triangulation of Confederate literary nationalism provides a partial answer. Although cultural independence and autonomy were important parts of the nation-building process, Confederate Euro- and Anglophilia in fact helped to differentiate the new nation from its most relevant other. The United States might not deign to listen to the courtly muses of Europe, but the Confederate States was all ears.[23]

Deference to British and European literatures brings us to back to "Ethnogenesis," an ode obviously indebted to the poetry of Coleridge and Wordsworth. Timrod's poem also betrays broadly international investments, beginning with its opening paean. To reiterate, the Confederate States is now "A nation among nations; and the world / Shall soon behold in many a distant part / Another flag unfurled!" Later, the poem emphasizes not just "what we are" but also what "we shall be to the *world*" (emphasis mine). As these lines suggest, Confederate literary nationalism was *global in its purview and imperial in its ambitions*. This feature of Confederate literature took a number of forms, including ubiquitous descriptions of a worldly Confederacy, debates about the extension of reciprocal international copyright, and even "literary soldiers of fortune" in England and Europe. This is consistent with Jusdanis's understanding of nationalism as "nothing other than a syncretic and cosmopolitan process by which a group differentiates itself from other groups and builds a republic on the basis of this difference" (*Necessary* 101). In building their republic, Confederates remained painfully aware of their sudden emergence on a global stage and deeply desirous of international recognition—political and otherwise.

For instance, the final five lines of "Ethnogenesis" promise international commerce and exchange with the far reaches of the world:

In our own grand and genial Gulf Stream furled,
Which through the vast and colder ocean pours
Its waters, so that far-off Arctic shores
May sometimes catch upon the softened breeze
Strange tropic warmth and hints of summer seas!

Carried along by an ocean current—that most transnational of flows—the Confederacy promises to spread southern culture and goods across the Atlantic and beyond. Such an awareness of a world outside of North America expands the mental map on which the American Civil War is played out, allowing us to tell the story of this conflict in less exceptionalist, more cosmopolitan terms.[24]

In closing this anatomy of Confederate literature, I want to return to the form of Timrod's poem. With its long duration and elevated tone, the ode is one of the most ceremonious of poetic forms. By choosing to commemorate the Provisional Congress in an ode, Timrod makes a quiet claim about the intellectual capacity and refined tastes of the Confederate people. (Among other things, they know their literary traditions: Timrod's is an irregular or Cowleyan variation on the Pindaric ode.) À la Timrod, many southern littérateurs lobbied for a *polite* Confederate literature—that is, a literature that would be "refined, elegant, scholarly; exhibiting good or restrained taste" ("Polite," def. 2a.). As we will see, however, a great deal of the literature actually produced during the war was *popular* in orientation—that is, "intended for and directed at a general readership" ("Popular," def. 4a.). Thus, Confederate literature is characterized by an at-times *uneasy fit between polite and popular forms*. Even when Confederates managed to produce polite texts, they often circulated across popular media. For instance, much of Timrod's poetry found readers via broadsides and newspapers. The resulting admixture of "high" and "low" cultures, of "elite purpose and popular influence" (Faust, *Creation* 16), obscured stark class differences in the new nation and helped to resolve a socioeconomically diverse populace into a coherent national community. Put another way, such are the strange bedfellows engendered by nationalist movements.[25]

To summarize, Confederate literature was both belated and written for a vanishing present. As a result, it remained throughout its short life an aspirational literature, distinguished by a near perpetual process of deferral and a steadfast orientation toward the future. It made repeated agro-literary appeals and confirmed its status as the literature of a slaveholding republic. In imagining southerners as a fictive ethnicity, Confederate literature was constantly defining itself against northern/American literature. And in looking abroad for literary models and traditions, Confederate literary nationalism became a triangulated phenomenon, one that was global in its purview and imperial in its ambitions. Finally, the form that much of the resulting literature took shows an uneasy fit between the polite and the popular.

The following pages develop and complicate all of the above features, which, to be clear, did not carry equal ideological weight in the Confederacy. (In truth, Confederate literature's belated status and global purview prove far more important than its agro-literary appeals.) Yet all were implicated in the process of Confederate nation building. Finally, although a few of these features are idiosyncratic to the Confederacy, the majority appear in other literary nationalistic contexts as well. It is my hope, then, that what follows will help to illumine the still-shadowy relationship between literature and nationalism.

Method and Scope

Confederate literature, broadly conceived, has received sustained attention from a pair of intellectual and cultural historians: Alice Fahs, in *The Imagined Civil War: Popular Literature of the North and South, 1861–1865* (2001), and Michael T. Bernath, in *Confederate Minds: The Struggle for Intellectual Independence in the Civil War South* (2010). By emphasizing the social life of literature and constellating an impressive range of sources, both make invaluable contributions to our understanding of intellectual and cultural life in the Civil War South. This book, however, addresses a very different set of questions from those of Fahs and Bernath. It also focuses more closely on individual examples of Confederate literature. This is in keeping with a literary-historical—rather than an intellectual-historical or cultural-historical—methodology. Put simply, I ask literary questions of the literary texts of the Confederacy.

The Shakespeare scholar Marjorie Garber defines literary questions as "questions about the *way* something means, rather than *what* it means, or even *why*." She continues: "It is not that literary studies is uninterested in the what and the why. . . . But literariness, which lies at the heart of literary studies, is a matter of style, form, genre, and verbal interplay, as well as of social and political context—not only the realm of reference and context but also intrinsic structural elements like grammar, rhetoric, and syntax; tropes and figures; assonance and echo" (12). Although I hesitate to use a term as abstract or tautological as "literariness," this book does pay close attention to the formal and rhetorical structures of Confederate texts. This is not to suggest that the literary is somehow separate from the historical or the social. Like Larzer Ziff, I understand literature to be "a particular concentration of cultural forces continuous with, rather than apart from, society" (xii). As a result, this book shuttles back and forth between individual readings of texts and the broader social contexts of their production, circulation, and reception.[26]

As the range of references in my reading of "Ethnogenesis" suggests, the tools of literary and postcolonial theory, the comparative history of nationalisms, and the sociology of culture are also central to this study. When used in tandem with close reading, these tools can help to explain how literary texts helped to imagine the Confederate States of America. Because of this interest in the cultural work of Confederate literature, my emphasis is on texts that actually circulated, whether in print, manuscript, or oral performance forms. Despite their allure, I do not treat unpublished memoirs or diaries such as those of Mary Chesnut. Finally, the following pages also show a keen awareness of the materiality of the Confederate text. Particularly in light of the challenges that southern writers and publishers faced, we need to look at, not see through, the material forms by which Confederate literary discourse entered social worlds (de Grazia and Stallybrass 257).

The chapters of this book are organized by literary genre, and each uses a single text or a small set of texts to limn a broader aspect of Confederate literary culture. The first and final chapters tell a story about what happened before and after the Confederacy. The middle chapters focus on "proper" Confederate literature, by which I mean imaginative literary texts produced in the Confederate States of America between early February 1861 and early May 1865. I am not, however, doctrinaire about this definition of Confederate literature. I also discuss several nationalistic poems and songs from border states and occupied areas of the Confederacy. Finally, because I hope that it will be the first of many literary historical engagements with Confederate literature, *Apples and Ashes* does not aim to be comprehensive. This is not a definitive literary history of the Confederacy, nor does it treat all genres of Confederate literature. For instance, although I consider two closet dramas in chapter 3, I do not devote a chapter to Confederate drama. I also largely neglect oratory.[27]

Apples and Ashes opens with "A History of the Future," a contextual chapter focused on the three decades prior to the American Civil War. These "cold war" years, with their fierce debates over slavery and federalism, gave rise to an increasing literary sectionalism, one that pitted southern literature against northern, "American literature." This chapter reads literary criticism that appeared in the *Southern Literary Messenger*, a periodical that was, I demonstrate, an important venue for pre-Confederate southern literary nationalism. I argue that the *Messenger*'s convoluted literary nationalist discourses mark an early and crucial moment in a process of cultural integration—the first of many struggles for the achievement of what would become a Confederate literary culture. The chapter also reveals a southern obsession with literary futurity. Southern literary nationalists may not have agreed on much, but they did share an interest in what sort of futures their imaginative literature both projected and engendered.

Chapter 2, "A New Experiment in the Art of Book-Making," shifts to the midpoint of the American Civil War to consider the unlikely rise of the Confederate novel (singular): Augusta Jane Evans's *Macaria; or, Altars of Sacrifice* (1864). The signal publishing achievement of the Confederacy, Evans's novel had, I argue, an intimate and dynamic relation to the Confederate national moment. Exploiting a series of deft textual effects, the novel elegantly manages tensions between the local and the national by presenting a delocalized, resolutely nationalistic narrative with a decidedly international set of intertexts. In turn, with its precise timeliness, *Macaria* also captures the sacrifices demanded and the upheavals brought on by the war. This is particularly the case with Evans's representation of wartime "Womanly Usefulness," a phenomenon she thought essential to the hopes of Confederate independence. In reading *Macaria* in these terms, I weigh the problems that Evans—one of the nineteenth century's bestselling authors—faced in writing a nationalistic novel for a vanishing present, and offer a new, speculative account of *Macaria*'s frenzied composition.

Chapter 3, "Southern Amaranths," tends the ruined garden of Confederate verse. Leaving largely untouched the Confederacy's most familiar poets laureate (for example, Henry Timrod, Paul Hamilton Hayne, and Sidney Lanier), I stress here Confederate poetry's popular orientation, occasional character, and multimedial circulation. Through readings of poems published in volumes of verse, broadsides, newspapers, and anthologies, the contours of a vigorous poetic culture come into view. That culture had as its sine qua non, I argue, a vexed poetics of place, one that represented well both local southern communities and tensions among the "sovereign and independent" Confederate states. Read in its original material forms, the poetry of the Civil War South both affirms the fervency of Confederate literary nationalism and betrays the provisional nature of a Confederacy made up of seceding states.

Chapter 4, "The Music of Mars," expands definitions of the literary by examining popular song, which, I argue, was a privileged way for southerners to imagine a new nation. The circulation of popular song was not limited to a public sphere of print, as songs circulated simultaneously in oral, manuscript, and printed forms. These complementary modes of circulation helped to negotiate the material problems faced by the Confederate States of America. In fact, Confederate production of popular song actually rivaled that of the United States. And such a rivalry produced no small amount of anxiety in the North. Here I use "Dixie," the de facto Confederate national anthem, as a case study, charting its complicated textual history and recurrent movement across the Mason-Dixon line. By exploring "Dixie" as a malleable, even promiscuous cultural object, this chapter identifies a process of revision that enabled this "sweet and inspiring air" to fit local, regional, and national agendas and helped the people of both the United and Confederate States of America to manage the existence of competing nationalisms.

This book's final chapter, "In Dreamland," shifts to the years immediately following the cessation of Civil War hostilities and considers a belated genre of Confederate literature: the postwar memoir. As the conflict shifted from the field of battle to the field of cultural memory, autobiographical texts sought to memorialize the Confederate States of America in print. Having lost a physical struggle for independence, former Confederates sought to win a new, ideological struggle over the causes and costs of the war, its legacies and meanings for a newly re-United States. This chapter reads one of the most idiosyncratic of Confederate memoirs, *The Woman in Battle* (1876), an account of the chaotic life and times of Loreta Janeta Velazquez, a Cuban-born, cross-dressing Confederate sympathizer, soldier, and spy. I argue that the Velazquez narrative is a restless text, one that remaps the American Civil War within a global system of immigration, foreign intervention, and trans-national capital and imagines a Confederacy in and of the world. In doing so, I also consider one of Velazquez's fellow travelers, the Swiss-born editor, writer, and propagandist Henry Hotze, who worked tirelessly to win European hearts and minds to the southern cause via a nascent Confederate literature.

In discussing literary criticism, fiction, poetry, popular song, and memoir, *Apples and Ashes* draws out the intricacies and ambivalences of Confederate literary discourse. It also reminds us of Confederate literature's once-great expectations. Before their defeats and abjections—before apples turned to ashes in their mouths—many Confederates thought they were in the process of creating a nation and a national literature that would endure. To return to the epigraph that gives this book its title, Confederates employed "every instrumentality" possible to produce a "vigorous, healthy, native, loyal and beneficent literature." The fact that their "magnificent future" never came to pass—that they were so clearly on the wrong side of history—is, finally, beside the point. The literature of this failed nation has a great deal to teach literary studies, and literary studies should have a great deal to say about that literature.

CHAPTER ONE

A History of the Future

Southern Literary Nationalism
before the Confederacy

The particular legacy (if not genius) of the Confederacy
is that it was able to convince an entire nation to look
toward the future for events that had already taken place
in the past, to believe that emancipation would result in
rampant miscegenation.
—Sharon P. Holland, "The Last Word on Racism"

I've seen the future, brother: it is murder.
—Leonard Cohen, "The Future"

I begin with a pithy, pretty piece of apocrypha, one retold with some regularity in literary histories of the pre-Confederate South: that the 1856 Southern
Commercial Convention in Savannah passed the following resolution: "*Resolved*, That there be a Southern Literature. *Resolved*, That William Gilmore
Simms, L.L.D., be requested to write this literature" (qtd. in Hubbell, "Literary Nationalism" 195). Alas, there is no surviving material record of such
a resolution. (And would that a national or even sectional literary culture
could be accomplished by decree or fiat. The course of cultural nationalism
rarely runs so true.) Nonetheless, this anecdote reveals a great deal about
the status and stakes of southern literary nationalism in the lead-up to the
American Civil War, and, more broadly, about the vicissitudes of literary nationalist desires.

This resolution takes us back to a moment when the nascent literary culture of the southern United States was being asked to bear a great deal of
ideological weight and to do a great deal of protonationalist work—back
to a moment when such a resolution was not at all outside the realm of pos-

sibility. The Savannah Convention did in fact appoint a committee whose charge it was to prepare for the southern states "a series of books in every department of study, from the earliest primer to the highest grade of literature and science." And William Gilmore Simms, widely considered the most accomplished of antebellum southern writers, was "doing his best" to single-handedly write such a southern literature during this period (qtd. in Hubbell, "Literary Nationalism" 195).

By 1856, readers in the South and beyond would have been well acquainted with—perhaps even inured to—calls for an "indigenous," distinctively southern literature. As early as the late 1820s, a number of southern cultural elites began advocating for a literature that would, variously, represent southern experiences; be produced "at the south"; and help to make the region a more culturally autonomous entity, one free from reliance on northern publishers, northern writers, and northern literary influence. During these years, many of the same elites were simultaneously calling for an American literature, one to which the South would make a strong, sectional contribution. In doing so, these writers participated in a complicated and controversial "campaign" for a national literature. The phrase "southern literary nationalism" had multiple and at times conflicting significations during this period; one particular problem lies in determining which nation these nationalists hoped to imagine, the United States of America or some alternative thereof.[1]

In this chapter, I reconsider the problem of pre-Confederate southern literary nationalism, in particular its aims and accomplishments. In doing so, I offer a history of the future, as it were. That is, I am interested in limning the ways the convoluted literary nationalist discourses of the three decades prior to the American Civil War provided a context for the literary productions of the Confederacy. I demonstrate that pre-Confederate southern literary nationalism was a much more complicated and multifarious phenomenon than has been acknowledged. Contingent and at times surprisingly cosmopolitan, this nationalism found expression in a pliable and ingenious rhetoric, one that requires some explication. As rhetoric, it performed real cultural work; it was not merely so much bluster, as several critics have surmised. The ways southerners talked about their literary culture was every bit as important as the literature itself. As a result, this chapter treats literary nationalist rhetoric as a form of literary rhetoric; that is, I read the writings of literary nationalists closely, with an attention to imagery, metaphor, direct address, and the like.[2]

In attending to this rhetoric, I approach pre-Confederate southern literary nationalism not as a unified, monolithic phenomenon but as a series of uncoordinated and diverse efforts. Furthermore, I hold that developmental or teleological accounts of the "growth" of southern literary nationalism subsume radical differences and historical contingencies, making it all too easy to tell a simple story about the inevitability of literary and political secession. As Robert S. Levine has recently cautioned, literary historians should be wary of such a simple story of American "national literary development and fulfillment": "In a very basic way, the historical premises of such a story are invariably anachronistic, the result of the needs, interpretative models, and desires of a relatively small number of literary nationalists being imposed retrospectively and all too neatly on literary debates that were much messier at the time than subsequent literary critics have generally allowed" (3). Like Levine, I want to recover "a sense of the provisional and contested nature of American literary nationalism," not only through my subject—an alternative American literary nationalism—but also through my methodology (1).[3]

This chapter does not offer a broad, chronological survey of pre-Confederate southern literary nationalist rhetoric. Instead and per Levine, I take a more episodic approach, offering close readings of three moments of intellectual crisis and creation. The resulting discussion focuses almost exclusively on the nationalist rhetoric that appeared in the pages of the *Southern Literary Messenger*, a literary periodical based in Richmond, Virginia, that was published continuously from 1834 to 1864. Described variously as "the South's one serious literary journal" (Craven 155), "the jewel of Southern periodicals" (McCardell 171), and "the mouthpiece of southern culture" (Mott 1: 630), the *Messenger* was a crucial clearinghouse for a diverse set of literary nationalist writings.[4]

More to the point, as Terence Whalen has recently demonstrated, both the *Messenger*'s writers and audience were "much less homogenous than generally assumed, at least in regard to political affairs"—especially on the crucial issue of slavery ("Average" 13, 15–16.) Suffice it to say that the periodical offers an uncommon opportunity to read southern literary nationalist discourse both article by article and year to year.[5] The publication dates of the *Southern Literary Messenger* also encompass conveniently a period of intense debate over the prospect of a national literature. As Benjamin T. Spencer demonstrated a half century ago, "there developed between 1837 and 1855 what one may well call the controversy over a national literature in place of the generally approved movement toward it" ("National" 143–44). Such controversy was on full display in the pages of the *Messenger*.[6]

Pre-Confederate southern literary nationalism has been underestimated as a cultural force. A close examination of the rhetoric of this nationalism reveals a national literary culture in aspiration. Recent comparative histories of nationalism suggest that the struggle to found a national culture is in many ways every bit as important as its achievement or failure. Such histories also emphasize the privileged and peculiar relationship between the social construction of nationality and time. For instance, the literary historian Gregory Jusdanis has theorized the experiences of both national belatedness and national culture in aspiration. As he argues, "culture does not abruptly become nationalized as soon as patriots discover the tardiness of their societies. Nor is it somehow invented upon declaration of independence from a colonial ruler. The process of cultural integration usually occurs decades before independence. Intellectuals simply give political expression to this culture" (*Necessary* 112).[7]

I argue that the pre-Confederate southern literary nationalism treated in this chapter marks an early and crucial moment in a process of cultural integration—the first of many struggles for the achievement of a Confederate literary culture. One defining feature of this literary nationalistic rhetoric is its obsession with literary futurity. Like most literary nationalists, the pre-Confederate writers treated in this chapter wrote for what Gayatri Spivak calls a "vanishing present"; however, their writings return perseveratively to a not-too-distant future, one in which southern literature is a central component of a national culture. Southern literary nationalists may not have agreed on much—including, crucially, to which national culture southern literature would be central—but they did share a keen interest in what sort of futures their criticisms, fictions, and poems both projected and engendered.

O Pioneers!

In 1834, Thomas Willis White, a self-deprecating and ingratiating Richmond printer with little background in literature, undertook what he would later call a "rash and perilous enterprize": the founding of a southern literary periodical (*Southern Literary Messenger* 6 [January 1840]: 1). Since, by his own admission, "[n]o literary periodical on our side of Mason's and Dixon's line, had been able to survive a sickly infancy," the outlook for White's "enterprize" seemed grim (*SLM* 6: 1; see also Jacobs 66–68). Yet, despite the cautions of his friends and colleagues, White threw his capital and his ample energies into the quixotic endeavor, publishing in August 1834 the first issue of the *Southern Literary Messenger*.

When critics and historians discuss that first issue, they invariably remark on James Ewell Heath's fervent opening editorial, "Southern Literature." From its declarative title to its closing call for a great southern "awakening," the essay ably captures the at times conflicting desires of pre-Confederate southern literary nationalism. It also leaves little doubt about its status as rhetoric:

> It is understood that the first number of the "Messenger," will be sent forth by
> its Publisher, as a kind of pioneer, to spy out the land of literary promise, and to
> report whether the same be fruitful or barren, before he resolves upon further action. It would be a mortifying discovery, if instead of kindness and good will, he
> should be repulsed by the coldness and neglect of a Virginia public. Hundreds of
> similar publications thrive and prosper north of the Potomac, sustained as they
> are by the liberal hand of patronage. *Shall not one be supported in the whole
> south?* (1)

The metaphor of surveyor-cum pioneer was a common one for both American and southern literary nationalists during the 1830s. Here it is used deftly to acknowledge the precariousness of the *Messenger*'s endeavor ("whether fruitful or barren") and quietly evoke the agrarian (all those uncultivated fields of "literary promise")—a rhetoric with particular appeal to a planter class. With the metaphor in place, the editorial moves quickly to its arts of persuasion. The emergence of a dour diction ("mortifying," "repulsed," "coldness," "neglect") and direct address ("Virginia public") immediately heighten the emotional stakes of the essay. Tellingly, by his third sentence, Heath has set the South in full—if friendly—competition with the North. This is, at bottom, a literary arms race. And, according to Heath, as of August 1834, the North was clearly winning that race.[8]

Heath is bewildered by this state of affairs, since he holds that Virginia (and the South as a whole) has all the makings of a successful republic of letters: "Is it not altogether extraordinary that in this extensive commonwealth, containing a white population of upwards of six hundred thousand souls—a vast deal of agricultural wealth, and innumerable persons of both sexes, who enjoy both leisure and affluence—there is not one solitary periodical exclusively literary?" (1–2). To Heath's mind, Virginia's robust agricultural economy makes it particularly well situated to produce a literary periodical. Of course, Heath more or less elides a crucial element of that economic system: slave labor. Heath's phrase "a white population" is elegantly circumlocutionary, indicating as it does which "souls" count and which do not. These enjoyments of "both leisure and affluence" are enabled by the labor that helps to produce such a "vast deal of agricultural wealth." Following Heath's argument to its logical conclusion, the unnamed slave labor is yet another reason the South should have great expectations for an "exclusively literary" periodical.

Heath slyly shifts the terms of debate from patronage and subscription to vassalage and character—particularly charged terms during the period: "Are we to be doomed forever to a kind of vassalage to our northern neighbors— a dependence for our literary food upon our brethren, whose superiority in all the great points of character,—in valor—eloquence and patriotism, we are no wise disposed to admit?" (1). Once again, the rhetoric of dependence suggests an anxious process of cultural comparison-cum-competition. The masters of slaves must not be the slaves of anyone. The slight return of an agricultural metaphor ("literary food") further sets up the work of differentiation that is to follow. Heath will not concede the North's moral superiority. Indeed, in one of the editorial's many rhetorical questions, Heath asks, "We are not willing to borrow our political,—religious, or even our agricultural notions from the other side of Mason and Dixon's line," and so why be willing to do so with literary notions (2)?

Ever the rhetorician, Heath conjures and negates a potential critique of his argument: "Shall it be said that the empire of literature has no geographical boundaries, and that local jealousies ought not to disturb its harmony?" (2). This was a pressing question for both southern and American literary nationalists during this period, yet Heath does not tarry with it. At stake for Heath (who was in 1834 a Virginia state auditor) is a simple logic of quasi-economic exchange: "To this there is an obvious answer. If we continue to be *consumers* of northern productions, we shall never ourselves become *producers*. We may take from them the fabrics of their looms, and give in exchange without loss our agricultural products—but if we depend exclusively upon their *literary* supplies, it is certain that the spirit of invention among our own sons, will be damped, if not entirely extinguished" (2). Rhetorically and logically, the passage sets in play a failed chiasmus. The South provides agricultural products to the North; the North, in turn, produces fabric "of their looms." Although Heath does not say the word *cotton* here, the latent text/textile pun ensures that his readers would be thinking about the South's primary export—if not about the tariff debates of the 1820s. However, this model for purportedly fair exchange—again, it occurs "without loss"—is not translatable to literary production. Extending Heath's metaphor, this is a warning to readers that the "spirit of invention" is a resource that needs tending and renewing; an overreliance on northern literary goods threatens its very extinction.

Thus, in its first few passages, "Southern Literature" brings into close conversation the literary and the agricultural. In a move often repeated in southern and then Confederate literary nationalist discourse, the agricultural products of the South are yoked to its once and future literary products. The concurrent rhetoric of literary scarcity translates the potentially obscure and elite desire for a distinctive literary culture to a more familiar register: the agricultural. By quietly asserting a casual if not quite causal relationship between agriculture and literature, pieces such as Heath's "Southern Literature" familiarize or even naturalize literary desires. The resulting agro-literary appeal expands significantly the purview of and audience for a nascent southern literature.[9]

Having rendered literature familiar, Heath must next make a positive argument for the "value of a *domestic* publication." Said value lies, tautologically, in its domesticity. A southern literary periodical would encourage all "who choose to venture into the arena as rivals for renown" to do so, precisely because it would be "accessible": "It imparts the same energy, and exercises the same influence upon mental improvement, that a rail road does upon agricultural labor, when passing by our doors and through our estates" (2). This is an odd but quite timely analogy. The implication is that the immediate presence of a railroad—which connected rural producers and products to a broader world of commerce and exchange—had a stimulatory effect on labor, perhaps inspiring a sense of purpose and resolve. To tease out the analogy, a domestic literary periodical would, similarly, act as a constant reminder to literary producers that there is a broader world of letters to which the South could contribute and that its tracks run just "by our doors and through our estates."

Returning with a vengeance to the issue of cultural competition, Heath notes that whatever literary successes the North had achieved to date were due to its domestic periodical culture: "The literary spirit which pervades some portions of New England and the northern cities, would never have existed, at least in the same degree, if the journals and repositories designed to cherish and promote it, had been derived exclusively from London and Edinburgh" (2). We see at work in this passage a literary nationalist relay of sorts. Heath takes for granted that by 1834 there was an identifiable "literary spirit" at work in the North, no small claim in this period of "controversy" over a national literature. Furthermore, he suggests that because that spirit was engendered by domestic periodicals, it can be understood as a product of a nascent cultural independence from England and its literary metropoles.

The rhetoric of national differentiation that Heath draws on here would have been familiar to contemporary readers both North and South. Returning to Sarah Corse's discussion of the "most relevant others" (quoted in the introduction), what is remarkable about Heath's editorial is how quickly he moves to differentiate the South not from Mother England but from the North. "In like manner," Heath notes tartly, "if we look to Boston, New York or Philadelphia . . . we must content ourselves with being the readers and admirers of other men's thoughts, and lose all opportunity of stirring up our own minds, and breathing forth our own meditations" (2). If the South is to have a literary spirit—and, Heath insists, a modicum of self-reliance and self-respect—it must be independent from northern literary hubs. To Heath's mind, the North is the South's most relevant other. Just as northern literary culture needed to be independent from London and Edinburgh, so southern literary culture needs to be independent from Boston, New York, Philadelphia, and "some portions of New England." This is a swaggering claim, one that places southern and northern literary cultures in direct competition and quietly connects the struggle for U.S. cultural independence from England to an incipient struggle for southern cultural independence.

But, having raised the specter of cultural secession, Heath judiciously and performatively steps back from this critique of northern cultural imperialism: "It is not intended to be intimated that the aristarchy of the north and east, cherish any unkind feelings towards the literary claims of the south. Oh no!" (2). Instead Heath observes ironically that northern publishers who are eager to maintain southern patronage of northern periodicals are more than willing to "pocket our money and praise us as a very generous and chivalrous race." He suggests that "in order to preserve the monopoly of the southern market," these publishers may even respond to literary products of the South with "a modicum of praise, and render some faint tribute to rising merit." This skeptical depiction of northern periodical culture is apposed with another assurance of intention and good will: "Without therefore intending any thing invidious, or without cherishing any unkind or unmanly sentiment towards our political confederates, we ought forthwith to buckle on our armour, and assert our mental independence" (2). The tension between Heath's first two dependent clauses and the third and fourth independent clauses is palpable. The former suggest kind, manly affection with the North; the latter urge martial action and a forceful declaration of independence.

Heath exults in such kind, manly affection as he lists the names of several "lofty and generous spirits" in the North who would "approve the resolution, and be among the first to welcome the dawn of a brighter era in a region of comparative twilight" (2). Included among these "spirits" are Washington Irving, James Fenimore Cooper, Fitz Greene Halleck, William Cullen Bryant, Catharine Maria Sedgwick, and Lydia Sigourney, all of whom, Heath assures his readers, "will rejoice in the emancipation of the south, from the shackles which either indolence, indifference, or the love of pleasure, have imposed upon us." The rhetoric of emancipation on these pages may be jarring for twenty-first-century readers. After all, this editorial was published just months after the first meeting of the American Anti-Slavery Society in Philadelphia in December 1833. Yet it figures the lettered South as a shackled vassal whose plight is monitored intensely by sympathetic northerners. The profound paradox and hypocrisy of such figuration is well worth noting; however, I am also interested in that litany of sympathetic northerners. Heath names a veritable who's who of early American literature, and he speaks on their behalf in favor of an independent southern literary culture.[10]

In projecting a sense of literary kinship between writers of the North and South, Heath is in the main currents of literary nationalist thought during this period, even as his rhetoric seems to vex that very kinship. "Southern Literature" begins in the second column of the first issue of the *Southern Literary Messenger*. The first column and a half of the issue are devoted to a "Publisher's Notice" that excerpts "a few passages from the letters of several eminent literary men" who support, in name if not in deed, White's ambitious literary project (1). The first of these men is Washington Irving, who gives his "highest approbation and warmest good wishes" to White's enterprise: "I cannot but feel interested in the success of a work which is calculated to concentrate the talent and illustrate the high and generous character which pervade that part of the Union" (1). Likewise, "J. Fenimore Cooper" notes that the South is "full of talent, and the leisure of its gentlemen ought to enable them to bring it freely into action." Other supporters include John Pendleton Kennedy, John Quincy Adams, and Peter A. Browne. The longest excerpt is from James

SOUTHERN LITERARY MESSENGER.

VOL. I.] RICHMOND, AUGUST, 1834. [No. I.

T. W. WHITE, PRINTER AND PROPRIETOR. FIVE DOLLARS PER ANNUM.

PUBLISHER'S NOTICE.

In issuing the first number of the "SOUTHERN LITE-RARY MESSENGER," the publisher hopes to be excused for inserting a few passages from the letters of several eminent literary men which he has had the pleasure to receive, approving in very flattering terms, his proposed publication. Whilst the sentiments contained in these extracts illustrate the generous and enlightened spirit of their authors, they ought to stimulate the pride and genius of the south, and awaken from its long slumber the literary exertion of this portion of our country. The publisher confidently believes that such will be the effect. From the smiles of encouragement, and the liberal promises of support received from various quarters—which he takes this opportunity of acknowledging,—he is strongly imboldened to persevere, and devote his own humble labors to so good a cause. He is authorised to expect a speedy arrangement either with a competent editor or with regular contributors to his work,—but, in the mean time, respectfully solicits public patronage, as the only effectual means of ensuring complete success.

FROM WASHINGTON IRVING.

"Your literary enterprise has my highest approbation and warmest good wishes. Strongly disposed as I always have been in favor of 'the south,' and especially attached to Virginia by early friendships and cherished recollections, I cannot but feel interested in the success of a work which is calculated to concentrate the talent and illustrate the high and generous character which pervade that part of the Union."

FROM J. K. PAULDING.

"It gives me great pleasure to find that you are about establishing a literary paper at Richmond,—and I earnestly hope the attempt will be successful. You have abundance of talent among you; and the situation of so many well educated men, placed above the necessity of laboring either manually or professionally, affords ample leisure for the cultivation of literature. Hitherto your writings have been principally political; and in that class you have had few rivals. The same talent, directed to other pursuits in literature, will, unquestionably, produce similar results,—and Virginia, in addition to her other high claims to the consideration of the world, may then easily aspire to the same distinction in other branches that she has attained in politics.

*   *   *   *   *

"Besides, the muses must certainly abide somewhere in the beautiful vallies, and on the banks of the clear streams of the mountains of Virginia. Solitude is the nurse of the imagination; and if there be any Virginia lass or lad that ever seeks, they will assuredly find inspiration, among the retired, quiet beauties of her lonely retreats. Doubtless they only want a vehicle for their effusions,—and I cannot bring myself to believe that your contemplated paper will suffer from the absence of contributors or subscribers.   *   *   *   *

"If your young writers will consult their own taste and genius, and forget there ever were such writers as Scott, Byron, and Moore, I will be bound they produce something original; and a tolerable original is as much superior to a tolerable imitation, as a substance is to a shadow. Give us something new—something characteristic of yourselves, your country, and your native feelings, and I don't care what it is. I am somewhat tired of licentious love ditties, border legends, affected sorrows, and grumbling misanthropy. I want to see something wholesome, natural, and national. The best thing a young American writer can do, is to forget that any body ever wrote before him; and above all things, that there are such caterpillars as critics in this world."

VOL. I.—1

FROM J. FENIMORE COOPER.

"The south is full of talent, and the leisure of its gentlemen ought to enable them to bring it freely into action. I made many acquaintances, in early youth, among your gentlemen, whom I have always esteemed for their manliness, frankness, and intelligence. If some, whom I could name, were to arouse from their lethargy, you would not be driven to apply to any one on this side the Potomac for assistance."

FROM J. P. KENNEDY.

"I have received your prospectus, along with your letter of the 1st instant. It gives me great pleasure to perceive so just an estimate of the value of literary enterprise as that indicated by your announcement of the 'Southern Literary Messenger.' A work of this kind is due to the talents of your noble state, and I doubt not will be received with a prompt encouragement."

FROM JOHN QUINCY ADAMS.

"Your design is so laudable, that I would gladly contribute to its promotion; but the periodical literature of the country seems to be rather superabundant than scanty. The desideratum is of quality rather than quantity."

FROM PETER A. BROWNE.

"Although you could not have chosen one less able to assist you, owing to my numerous professional engagements, which deprive me of the pleasure of dipping into the other sciences, or literature, I am willing to contribute my mite, and sincerely wish you success."

For the Southern Literary Messenger.
SOUTHERN LITERATURE.

It is understood that the first number of the "Messenger," will be sent forth by its Publisher, as a kind of pioneer, to spy out the land of literary promise, and to report whether the same be fruitful or barren, before he resolves upon future action. It would be a mortifying discovery, if instead of kindness and good will, he should be repulsed by the coldness and neglect of a Virginia public. Hundreds of similar publications thrive and prosper north of the Potomac, sustained as they are by the liberal hand of patronage. *Shall not one be supported in the whole south?* This is a question of great importance;—and one which ought to be answered with sober earnestness by all who set any value upon public character, or who are in the least degree jealous of that individual honor and dignity which is in some measure connected with the honor and dignity of the state. Are we to be doomed forever to a kind of vassalage to our northern neighbors—a dependance for our literary food upon our brethren, whose superiority in all the great points of character,—in valor—eloquence and patriotism, are we no wise disposed to admit? Is it not altogether extraordinary that in this extensive commonwealth, containing a white population of upwards of six hundred thousand souls—a vast deal of agricultural wealth, and innumerable persons of both sexes, who enjoy both leisure and affluence—there is not one solitary pe-

Southern Literary Messenger 1 (August 1834): 1. Courtesy of the Harry Ransom Humanities Research Center, The University of Texas at Austin.

Kirke Paulding, whose enthusiastic letter urges the South's young writers to "consult their own taste and genius, and forget there ever were such writers as Scott, Byron, and Moore." Paulding, a staunch literary nationalist who was passionately committed to the idea of an indigenous American literature, continues, "Give us something new—something characteristic of yourselves, your country, and your native feelings, and I don't care what it is" (1).

Taken together, these endorsements bear out Heath's confident assertion that northerners as well as southerners supported southern literary culture. Indeed, many American literary nationalists during this period hoped that strongly sectional contributions from the South and West would enliven a broader American literature. As Eugene Current-Garcia notes, "It had long been felt that the nation's area was too great and its social elements too diverse to be expressed in any single, homogenous literary pattern" (326). Thus, heterogeneous sectional literary cultures could prove a boon to a nascent national literature. During the three decades before the American Civil War, northerners and southerners alike seem to have agreed on as much. As historian John McCardell notes, many writers living in the South had "a dual purpose": "On the one hand they were fervent disciples of American literary nationalism; on the other they were strong in the belief that a Southern sectional literature was a necessary component of the American national literature they envisioned" (144). In the context of the early 1830s, we need not think of the sectional and the national as being antithetical.[11]

For William Gilmore Simms, the sectional and the national were inextricably linked. Writing in the same year as the Savannah Convention, which may or may not have charged him with producing a southern literature, Simms claimed that the subject of his collection of "border tales," *The Wigwam and the Cabin*, "is local, sectional—and to be *national* in literature, one must needs be *sectional*. No one mind can fully or fairly illustrate the characteristics of any great country; and he who shall depict *one section* faithfully, has made his proper and sufficient contribution to the great work of *national* illustration" (4). The division of literary labor Simms describes here is well represented on the pages of the inaugural issue of the *Southern Literary Messenger*. That is, some twenty-two years before Simms's pronouncement, Heath was making the case for a strongly sectional literary culture.[12]

That said, it is not at all clear that Heath (circa 1834) and Simms (circa 1856) share the same literary theories or literary nationalist aims. Among other things, there is a remarkable rhetorical remainder in Heath's editorial. Previous critics have suggested that the early years of the *Messenger* were characterized by "sectional good feeling" and the promotion of goodwill between South and North (Jacobs 73). Yet the sectional literary culture Heath describes seems at times fiercely independent of, if not outright antagonistic to, northern literary culture. Sentence by sentence, and even clause by clause,

Heath vacillates between begrudging acknowledgments of northern literary precedence and desperate calls for southern literary ascendance. This is not to say that Heath was in 1834 calling for a southern literary secession; it is, however, to suggest that his rhetoric embodies a far more conflicted set of literary nationalist desires than has been previously acknowledged. Such vacillations and conflicted desires are a much more apt characterization of pre-Confederate southern literary nationalism than any developmental or teleological narrative of the phenomenon. If, following Robert D. Jacobs, we read Heath's initial editorial as "the beginning of the campaign for a Southern literature, a campaign initiated in the spirit of friendly rivalry with the North," we might ask, how friendly was that rivalry and at what point in time (68)? More broadly, when and for whom does a sectional literary culture become a separatist literary culture?

Perhaps not surprisingly, the final paragraphs of Heath's editorial make scant mention of northern literary culture. Instead, Heath closes his argument for a domestic periodical (and by extension for a distinct "Southern Literature") with a direct appeal to both subscribers and contributors. To support "one poor periodical, devoted to letters and mental improvement," would, Heath argues, essentially transform southern society, contributing toward the "building up a character of our own, and providing the means of imbodying and concentrating the neglected genius of our country" (2). As in Thomas Jefferson's *Notes on the State of Virginia*, the rhetoric of "country" is both overdetermined and indeterminate. Does "country" refer to Virginia, the South as a whole, or the United States? Given the context—that is, a sustained argument for a "Southern Literature"—the first two possibilities seem more likely than the third.

Begging the questions of which and whose country, Heath's rhetoric again grows martial, even protonationalistic: "Let the hundreds of our gifted sons, therefore, who have talents and acquirements, come forth to this work of patriotism, with a firm resolution to persevere until victory is achieved" (2). If we understand "patriotism" to be the "love of or devotion to one's country" ("Patriotism"), we again confront the slippery problem of "country." Of course it is possible that Heath is citing what W. J. Cash later described as that "old local patriotism and particularlism native to the South" (218)— that is, love of, or devotion to, one's state or locality first. Alternatively, this might represent an early example of a nested southern nationalism, a phenomenon I discuss in greater detail in chapter 3. In either case, the accompanying rhetoric of perseverance and bold statement of purpose grants the titular cause of "Southern Literature" a certain grandiosity, suggesting that he has in mind something more than mere local literature. Again, I hesitate to say that Heath is calling for a separatist, southern national literature; however, his rhetoric leaves open the possibility for such a call in the future.

As we might expect, Heath's final paragraph is laced with impassioned, performative language. Working in a quasi-jeremiadic mode, Heath marshals the language of heraldry and honor as he proffers the *Messenger* as a central means by which to "redeem our country's escutcheon from the reproach which has been cast upon it" (3). In doing so, Heath produces a diverse set of imagined readers and subscribers:

> Let the miser open his purse—the prodigal save a pittance from his health-wasting and mind-destroying expenditures—the lawyer and physician, spare a little from their fees—the merchant and mechanic, from their speculations and labor—and the man of fortune, devote a part, a very small part of his abundance, towards the creation of a new era in the annals of this blessed Old Dominion. It may possibly be the means of effecting a salutary reform in public taste and individual habits; of overcoming that tendency to mental repose and luxurious indulgence supposed to be peculiar to southern latitudes; and of awakening a spirit of inquiry and a zeal for improvement, which cannot fail ultimately to exalt and adorn society. (3)

The first long, staccato sentence calls into being several southern types, each drawn from a different socioeconomic class and each charged with doing their part to "exalt and adorn society." As with the earlier railroad analogy, the final clause of the sentence deftly merges the new with the old, suggesting how elegantly the products of literary "creation" would complement already existing "annals." The second, more verbose sentence underscores the potentially profound influence a shared literature could have on southern society. Indeed, in his discussion of "mental repose and luxurious indulgence," Heath hazards calling southern literature a panacea. If the first sentence cites southern types, the second constitutes those types as a community, granting them shared "public taste," as well as "peculiar" habits and tendencies—what Benedict Anderson calls "the image of their communion" (6).

As my reference to Anderson should make clear, I am suggesting that Heath's editorial imagines a literary community, one with shared interests, traditions, and, crucially, a new domestic periodical. Although that community need not be dubbed national in character, its "nationness" should be gauged, especially the forms of "deep, horizontal comradeship" that it images (Anderson 7). To this end, I am particularly interested in Heath's use of the phrase "awakening a spirit of inquiry and a zeal for improvement." Anderson has identified the trope "awakening from sleep" as among the most widely used metaphors in second-generation European nationalist movements (194–95). Explaining the "astonishing popularity" of this trope during the period, Anderson observes that it "took into account the sense of parallelism out of which the American nationalism had been born and which the success of the American nationalist revolutions had greatly reinforced in Europe. . . . Read as late awakening, even if an awakening stimulated from afar, it opened up an immense antiquity behind the epochal sleep" (195–96). This trope found great use in nationalist movements because it made available for nationalist ends two seemingly at-odds orders of time: an inaccessible prenational antiquity and a quasi-messianic national future. In marshaling this figurative language, nationalist movements were able, with a deft, "modular" turn of phrase, to invent a nationalist tradition and project a nationalist future, all the while keeping their eyes trained on other "successful" nationalist movements.

In the case of "Southern Literature," Heath's deployment of the trope brings into closer relation the "annals" of the "Old Dominion"—his use of this sobriquet works to produce a sense of Virginian-cum-southern antiquity—and the "new era" he hopes the *Messenger* will herald. Ever confident of the power of a distinct southern literature, Heath avers that a domestic periodical would be the agent of change that stirs the South from its sleepy "mental repose and luxurious indulgence." To return to Jusdanis's terminology, Heath spends the first part of the editorial proclaiming the tardiness of southern literary culture; here, the work of catching up to "friendly" rivals begins in earnest with a literary awakening.

I have been emphasizing a single word in Heath's capacious text. White's "Publisher's Notice" in the first issue of the *Messenger* is much more explicit in its use of the trope: "Whilst the sentiments contained in these extracts illustrate the generous and enlightened spirit of these authors, they ought to stimulate the pride and genius of the south, and awaken from its long slumber the literary exertion of this portion of our country. The publisher confidently believes that such will be the effect" (1). White's "long slumber" sounds a great deal like Anderson's "epochal sleep," and the rhyming coexistence of White and Heath's tropes on the same periodical pages grants this rhetoric a sense of coherence, if not coordination.[13]

If, per Anderson, the trope "awakening from sleep" was a privileged site of cultural work during this period, one that helped give rise to a "modular, 'continuous' awakening from a chronologically gauged, A.D.-style slumber" (195), we might ask what sorts of cultural work it performed on the first pages of the *Southern Literary Messenger*. Not inconsequentially, Heath's editorial was published at the midpoint of what Anderson calls the "second generation" of European nationalism, 1815–1850. While Anderson confines the trope to Europe—he asserts confidently that it was "wholly foreign to the Americas" (195)—its presence on the pages of a Virginia literary periodical raises a number of questions: about the translation of nationalist tropes across the Atlantic and to non- or extranationalist settings; about the intelligibility of such tropes to readers in both the southern and northern United States in the mid-1830s; and about the relationship of nascent southern literary cultures to European literary cultures.

Bracketing those questions for the time being—they are, in fact, central and recurrent questions for this book as a whole—I want to observe that the presence of the trope "awakening from sleep" on these pages grants the inaugural issue of the *Southern Literary Messenger* a quasi-nationalistic feel. Again, while neither Heath nor White seems to be agitating for a separate southern nation, their use of nationalist rhetoric and projection of a brilliant, not-too-distant literary future for the South is certainly suggestive of the forms of "cultural integration" that Jusdanis and others prime us to look for in the lead-up to struggles for national independence.

Poe Poe Poe Poe Poe Poe Poe (and Others)

Edgar Allan Poe's tumultuous time with and contributions to the *Southern Literary Messenger* represent further efforts at cultural integration and provide another important pre-Confederate literary nationalist episode. Poe managed the editorial duties of the *Messenger* from December 1835 to January 1837, but he made significant and regular contributions to the monthly beginning in March 1835. This encompasses a period of critical importance for both the periodical and the country as a whole. During these years, the *Messenger* established itself as a highly visible literary journal—no mean feat for a southern periodical of its day. Likewise, these years gave rise to increasingly strained sectional relations, with the abolitionist pamphlet campaign of 1835, the presidential election of Martin Van Buren, and the onset of the Great Panic of 1837 exacerbating tensions between South and North.

As Terence Whalen notes, "Poe did not take over a foundering magazine; the *Messenger* was in fact doing quite well when Poe arrived in Richmond" (*Edgar Allan Poe* 68). Nonetheless, Poe's contributions to the periodical were conspicuous, in every sense of that word. Poe had come to the attention of Thomas W. White through John Pendleton Kennedy, the plantation novelist and historical romanticist who served as one of Poe's important early mentors. Poe, who was merely twenty-six years old when he arrived in Richmond in August 1835, succeeded Heath (August 1834–April 1835) and Edward Vernon Sparhawk (May 1835–July 1835), a minor poet and journalist from Maine, as de facto editor of the *Messenger*. His tenure was famously contentious, with Poe taking at least one leave of absence from his duties, and with White constantly worrying about Poe's drinking and fussing over his incendiary, attention-grabbing reviews. As one recent critic concludes dryly, White had "the singular misfortune to put a young Edgar Allan Poe on his payroll for about fifteen months" (L. Jackson 128).[14]

Poe's time at the *Messenger* has garnered extensive critical attention, and with good reason. In addition to numerous reprints of Poe's previously published poems and tales, the *Messenger* offered first printings of his tales

"Berenice," "Morella," "Lion-izing," and "Hans Phaal," among others; his poems "To Mary," "Lines Written in an Album," "Ballad," and "Sonnet. To Zante," among others; scenes from his closet drama "Politan"; the two-part hoax "Autography"; and excerpts of his sole novel, *The Narrative of Arthur Gordon Pym*. Moreover, the *Messenger* was the first of four periodicals with which Poe would work during his career as a magazinist. As a result, its issues offer an uncommon view of his "literary apprenticeship." For the purposes of this chapter, I am most interested in locating Poe's caustic and capacious editorial reviews in the context of both the career of the *Southern Literary Messenger* and pre-Confederate southern literary nationalist discourse more broadly. Viewed with fresh eyes, Poe's and his colleagues' reviews during this period demonstrate that literary criticism was a vibrant part of a process of southern cultural integration and differentiation. Their criticism aimed to locate the South and the *Southern Literary Messenger* at the center of an emergent American literary culture.

Although Poe's editorship did not officially begin until December 1835, "Berenice" appeared in the March 1835 issue, and his reviews began peppering the *Messenger* in April 1835, nearly four months before he relocated to Richmond (Pollin and Ridgely 3–4). In a notice "To Readers and Contributors" in the August 1835 issue, White wrote: "We avail ourselves of this opportunity again to solicit contributions, especially from our Southern acquaintances. While we shall endeavor to render the Messenger acceptable to all, it is more particularly our desire to give it as much as possible a *Southern* character and aspect, and to identify its interests and associations with those of the region in which it has taken root" (1: 716). While this solicitation does not mark a significant shift in editorial policy—from its first issue, the *Messenger* underscored its regional interests and associations, even and especially as it addressed a northern audience—it is a prolegomenon of sorts for Poe's time at the *Messenger*. This is especially appropriate given that the solicitation was immediately followed by a refutation of "one or two criticisms in relation to the Tales of our contributor, Mr. Poe" (716). The apposition of these two notices, one calling for contributions of "*Southern* character and aspect," the other defending the contribution of a southern "acquaintance," suggests a fierce regionalism at work on the editorial pages of the journal at the precise moment Poe began his on-site work with the *Messenger*.

It was the December 1835 issue that announced resoundingly Poe's arrival at the editorial table. That issue's "greatly expanded review section" included twenty-five reviews (twenty-four of which are generally attributed to Poe) and stretched across twenty-seven two-column pages (Pollin and Ridgely 46–47). Avid contemporary readers of the *Messenger* would have noted not only the remarkable growth of the review section but also the diversity of its topics and the generally biting tone of its editorial voice. The issue reviewed William Godwin's *Lives of the Necromancers* (about which Poe was breathless); a biography of George Washington written entirely in Latin; Sarah Josepha Hale's *Traits of American Life* (1835); two books concerned with life in the "western" United States, James Hall's *Sketches of History, Life, and Manners in the West* (1835) and Chandler Robbins Gibbons's *Legends of a Log Cabin* (1835); eulogies of Chief Justice John Marshall; *Nuts to Crack: or, Quips, Quirks, Anecdote, and Facete of Oxford and Cambridge Scholars*; as well as a number of gift books and annuals; two religious biographies; an almanac; and four rival periodicals, the *Edinburgh, Westminster, London Quarterly,* and *North American Reviews.*[15]

Poe's December 1835 review of Robert Montgomery Bird's *The Hawks of Hawk-Hollow* is in many ways characteristic of his reviews of contemporary American fiction for the *Messenger*. In short order the review engages forthrightly with the text at hand; includes a lengthy plot summary that nearly reveals too much of the concluding action; emphasizes the "style" of the piece; pays particular attention to matters of typography and punctuation; places the text in the broader context of American literature (for instance, Poe praises Bird's style as "at least *equal* to that of any American writer whatsoever" [2: 45]); pulls no literary critical punches (here Poe concludes that Bird's novel, "is, in many respects, a bad imitation of Sir Walter Scott" [46]); and yet takes pains to say what Poe finds of value in the author's oeuvre (Poe thought very highly of Bird's previous novels *Calavar* [1834] and *Infidel* [1835]). Such an editorial approach resulted in a criticism that was thorough and serious, if far from polite.

The apex of Poe's unpolite (and perhaps unpolitic) career as a critic came early, with his infamous savaging of Theodore Fay's novel *Norman Leslie* in the December 1835 issue. Sidney Moss considers the review to be "the first shot in what was to become one of the major battles of American periodicals" (38). While Moss's research on Poe's "literary campaign" is foundational, his emphasis on Poe's "career" and his "singlehanded" rhetoric obscure the broader context of the battle. This storied spat was not merely a battle between Poe and the New York literati; it was also a battle over the place of southern literary criticism in an American republic of letters. If this was indeed "one of the major battles of American periodicals," it is significant that the upstart *Southern Literary Messenger* fired the first shot and that its pages proved the battleground for the better part of a year.[16]

Poe begins his review with great verve and pith: "Well!—here we have it! This is *the* book—*the* book *par excellence*—the book bepuffed, beplastered, and be-*Mirrored*. . . . For the sake of every thing puffed, puffing, and puffable, let us take a peep at its contents!" (2: 54). As Poe's alliteration suggests, the object of his sarcastic tone is the prepublication puffing of Fay's novel. Between July and October 1835, Fay's own newspaper, the *New York Mir-*

ror, had published five lengthy excerpts from, and laudatory endorsements of, *Norman Leslie*. Poe will not—in this context at least—countenance such self-puffery: "Norman Leslie, gentle reader, a Tale of the Present Times, is, after all, written by nobody in the world but Theodore S. Fay, and Theodore S. Fay is nobody in the world but 'one of the Editors of the New York Mirror'" (55). To Poe's mind, naming the anonymous author of the novel draws back the curtain on the machinations of "literary fraud" (L. Jackson 226).

Although puffery is the initial object of Poe's scorn, it is Fay's seeming ineptitude as a novelist that bears the brunt of his critique. *Norman Leslie*'s character development is, Poe avers, particularly wretched, with Fay's style and grammar "unworthy of a school-boy" (56). As this suggests, Poe takes no prisoners in his review; indeed, he seems hell-bent on keeping readers away from the novel. In a lengthy and sardonic retelling of the plot, which he describes as "a monstrous piece of absurdity and incongruity" (56), Poe predictably gives away the ending of the novel, thus compromising any sense of readerly suspense (Pollin and Ridgely 77). Indeed, it is with the rhetoric of literary protectionism that Poe concludes his review of *Norman Leslie*, calling the novel "the most inestimable piece of balderdash with which the common sense of the good people of America was ever so openly or so villainously insulted" (56). With no small amount of hyperbole, Poe renders this American novel, written by an eminent American littérateur, not merely bad literature but also an affront to the American reading public.

To give Poe's withering criticism of *Norman Leslie* some context, the very next review in the December issue addressed *The Linwoods*, a new novel by Catharine Maria Sedgwick. Poe feels much more comfortable entrusting "the good people of America" to "Miss Sedgwick," whom he believes is "fully deserving of all the popularity she has attained" (57). Although Poe later confesses that *The Linwoods* "cannot, however, be considered as ranking with the master novels of the day," he does rank her first among "American *female* writers" (57). Poe's grandiloquent assessment resounds with American literary nationalism. In apposing Sedgwick and Fay, Poe is clearly drawing a line between the "best of our native novelists" and the worst (57). Crucially, Poe returns again to the problem of puffery, beginning the review by claiming that Sedgwick is "one among the few American writers who have risen by merely their own intrinsic talents, and without the *a priori* aid of foreign opinion and puffery" (57). The bald assertion that puffery is endemic to American literary publishing further casts Poe the editor in the role of Jeremiah, a broken-hearted prophet whose tirade may not find an audience.[17]

Yet Poe and the *Messenger* did find an audience, with the *Norman Leslie* jeremiad garnering a great deal of contemporary attention. The furor over Poe's review took hold immediately: The January 1836 number of the *Messenger* concluded with a remarkable eight-page, two-column "Supplement" that attested to the review's fame. The supplement opens with a "Publisher's Notice": "We are very proud in being able to afford our friends so many and so great evidences of the Messenger's popularity" (2: 133). White then quickly specifies that it is the December 1835 issue that has drawn the lion's share of this attention: "We hazard little in saying, that *never before in America has any Journal called forth so unanimously, testimonials so unequivocally flattering, as the First Number of the Second Volume of our 'Southern Literary Messenger'*" (133). While White is surely trying to sell subscriptions with his over-the-top bluster, the *Messenger* was in fact drawing a great deal of notice from other periodicals, both southern and northern, in early 1836. The supplement included reviews from all over the United States. In addition to predictable plaudits from southern periodicals—the *Richmond Whig* (133), *Petersburg Intelligencer* (134), *Norfolk Herald* (135), *Charlottesville Jeffersonian* (136), *Grand Gulf Advertiser* (137), *Charleston Courier* (138), *Lynchberg Virginian* (139), and *Petersburg Constellation* (140), among others—the supplement also quotes at length from northern periodicals, all of which comment on Poe's reviews in general and the *Norman Leslie* review in particular.[18]

For instance, the *New York Courier and Enquirer* calls the review section "the boldest, the most independent, and unflinching, of all that appears in the periodical world." Singling out the reviews of Bird's, Fay's, and Sedgwick's novels, the *Courier and Enquirer* opines, "This is as it should be—over-levity towards rising writers is a more real sin than over-sternness; and we are sorry to say, it is a sin, into which most of our magazines are wont to fall" (135). In a similar vein, the *Philadelphia Saturday Evening Post* observes, "[T]he editorial criticisms and reviews appear to be written in a spirit of candor quite unusual for the American Press" (137). The Washington, D.C., *National Intelligencer* concurs that the "tone of the criticisms differs widely from puffery, and is perfectly independent" (135). Calling the *Messenger*'s "Critical Notices" "the fullest *Review* in the country," the *Intelligencer* goes on to note that the *Messenger* "has, very unexpectedly, left its Northern competitors behind in the race for fame, and assumed all at once a pre-eminent rank among American periodicals" (135). Finally, the *New Yorker* concludes quite dramatically, "The Editor examines with impartiality, judges with fairness, commends with evident pleasure, and condemns with moderation. May he live a thousand years!—or at least to have five thousand gratified, substantial and 'available' patrons" (140).

Although we need be suspicious of the representativeness of the notices White and Poe cherry-picked for the supplement, the unanimity of praise for the "independence" and "candor" of the *Messenger*'s "Critical Notices" section suggests that Poe's reviews were quickly becoming the distinguishing feature of the South's preeminent literary periodical. More to the point, independent and candid literary criticism was, for better of worse, becoming associated with the South (Jacobs 77). In the months that followed the publication of this supplement, the *New York Mirror, New York Commercial Advertiser, Knickerbocker,* and *Philadelphia Gazette* would all take Poe to task for his "slashing" of Fay's novel and others. The *Southern Literary Journal, Newbern Spectator,* and *Richmond Courier and Daily Compiler* also got in on the action, urging the *Messenger* to adopt a more measured editorial tone going forward (S. Moss, esp. 38–62).[19]

Predictably, Poe eschewed moderation in the issues that followed; he offered sneering criticism to any piece that violated his at times obscure standards for American literature. For instance, the February 1836 review of Morris Matt-son's *Paul Ulric* found the critic once again functioning as an arbiter of, and watchman for, American literary quality. In the review, which cemented Poe's reputation as the "greatest literary gladiator of his time" (H. Allen 390), Poe depicted himself as protecting the country from the "grievou[s]" threat of subpar "native" literature, especially that published by major houses such as Harpers: "Such are the works which bring daily discredit upon our national literature" (2: 180). As a result, Poe spares no pains in "exposing fully before the public eye" *Paul Ulric*'s "four hundred and forty-three pages of utter folly, bombast, and inanity" (173). Over the course of nearly fifteen columns, Poe decimates the novel, concluding that it is "despicable in every respect" (180).

Just two issues later, in April 1836, Poe published his most important *Messenger* review, one that laid bare what he considered the stakes of literary criticism in mid-1830s America. The Drake-Halleck review, as it has come to be known, begins with "a few words in regard to the present state of American criticism" (2: 326). By its conclusion, some ten two-column pages later, it comprised a defense of the *Messenger*'s editorial practices; a stinging dismissal of two popular American poets, Joseph Rodman Drake and Fitz Greene Halleck; and the fullest articulation to date of Poe's poetics. Not surprisingly, Poe begins with the problem of undue puffery:

> In a word, so far from being ashamed of the many disgraceful literary failures to which our own inordinate vanities and misapplied patriotism have lately given birth, and so far from deeply lamenting that these daily puerilities are of home manufacture, we adhere pertinaciously to our original blindly conceived idea, and thus often find ourselves involved in the gross paradox of liking a stupid book the better, because, sure enough, its stupidity is American. (326)

This stirring rebuke makes a compelling argument for a discerning nationalist literary criticism, one that is neither "blind" nor "vain," neither "indiscriminate" nor "arrogant." Poe then states flatly, "it has been our constant endeavor, since assuming the Editorial duties of this Journal, to stem, with what little abilities we possess, a current so disastrously undermining the health and prosperity of our literature" (327). The accomplishment of this ingenious rhetoric is twofold: First, it retroactively gives coherence to the *Messenger*'s desultory and at times idiosyncratic reviews, suggesting that the "Critical Notices" had always had a single purpose and program. Second, and more urgently for our purposes, the review establishes the *Southern Literary Messenger* as the last bastion for a literary criticism that draws clear distinctions between "admirable" and "despicable" products of American literature. Thus, the Drake-Halleck review ratifies the southern periodical's position as the once and future home of a responsible "American criticism"— one willing to call a stupid American book stupid.

By way of further ratification, the April 1836 issue of the *Messenger* concluded with another eight-page, two-column supplement of "flattering evidences of public favor" (341). Per the Drake-Halleck review, these "evidences" resound with the rhetoric of discernment. Announcing that "The *Messenger* is no longer a query, it has earned a proud name," the *Norfolk Herald* effuses: "Popular opinion has placed the Messenger in a very enviable position as regards the Literature of the South. We have no hesitation in saying that it has elevated it immeasurably. To use the words of a Northern contemporary 'it has done more within the last six months to refine the literary standard in this country than has been accomplished before in the space of ten years'" (343). The *Natchez Christian Herald* concurs, albeit with an odd mixed metaphor: "American prose writers and novelists are led under this keen critic's knife, as sheep to the slaughter. In the name of literature we thank Mr. White for his criticisms, that must purify the literary, as lightning does the natural atmosphere" (344). The *New Yorker* even offers up the *Paul Ulric* review as a prophylactic against future literary vapidity: "If any young gentlemen shall find himself irresistibly impelled to perpetrate a novel, and all milder remedies prove unavailing, we earnestly advise him to read this criticism" (348).[20]

Taken together, these gaudy "foreign" endorsements seem to affirm the very critical practice that Poe propounds in the Drake-Halleck review. Indeed, the April 1836 issue as a whole makes the case for discerning literary criticism as correctly applied patriotism. By "refin[ing] the literary standard," remaining "alive to the literary reputation of the country," "purify[ing] the literary," and keeping inept novelists from "perpetrat[ing]" bad novels, the *Messenger*, is, we are told, encouraging the growth of a nascent American literature by refusing to "puff" "good, bad, or indifferent" texts. This is not to suggest that the *Messenger* was above puffery. In fact, the first review in the December 1835 issue was a first-rate piece of puffery for one of White's private publishing endeavors, a new edition of Eaton Stannard Barrett's *The Heroine* (1813). White had taken care to list his son-in-law, not himself, as the publisher of the piece, thus allowing Poe to "give it that praise in the Messenger to which it is so eminently titled" (qtd. in Pollin and Ridgely 75). Poe, it seems, had no problem puffing his employer's publication in the very same issue in which he eviscerated Theodore Fay's.

A more complicated example of Poe and the *Messenger*'s relation to puffery and American literary nationalism comes with John Pendleton Kennedy's Revolutionary-era historical romance, *Horse-Shoe Robinson* (1835). Writing his first long review for the *Messenger*, Poe placed Kennedy in "the very first rank of American novelists" (1 [May 1835]: 522) and praised the novel, which sets its action in Virginia and the Carolinas during the Revolutionary War, for its signal originality. Poe opines, "[T]he novelist has been peculiarly fortunate in the choice of an epoch, a scene, and a subject" (523). That epoch, scene, and subject were of great interest to both American and pre-Confederate southern literary nationalists. While Kennedy was a well-regarded southern novelist, and while *Horse-Shoe Robinson* was indeed an important early American novel, it is difficult to abstract Poe's affectionate review from the great personal and professional debt he owed his mentor. After all, without Kennedy, Poe would not have been reviewing for the *Messenger* (Pollin and Ridgely 17).

Poe was also not above using his editorial table to collect on debts he perceived others as owing him. For instance, another of Poe's famous, spleen-venting reviews is that of William Leete Stone's *Ups and Downs in the Life of a Distressed Gentleman* in the June 1836 issue. Poe is wholly dismissive of the slight volume, calling it "a public imposition" (2: 455) and concluding that it should have been "printed among the quack advertisements, in a spare corner" of the *Commercial Advertiser*, the New York newspaper Stone edited (457). Poe's interest in dismissing Stone's *Ups and Downs* may not have been wholly "patriotic." As Pollin and Ridgely note, "This is Poe in full cry, gleefully avenging himself on Colonel Stone, who had earlier savaged him in the New York *Commercial Advertiser*" (223). Thus we find Poe marshalling his discerning criticism in the cause of personal retribution, not on behalf of the prospect of an American literature.

In making sense of Poe's vexed relationship to puffery, we might say that, while Poe seems very much committed to the practice of an exacting, disinterested literary criticism, he is never able to lose sight of personal, local, and regional interests. In tending first to such interests, Poe was very much in line with the *Messenger*'s stated editorial desires: again, "to give [the periodical] as much as possible a *Southern* character and aspect, and to identify its interests and associations with those of the region in which it has taken root" (1: 716).[21] Not surprisingly, several works about the South or by "Southern acquaintances" fared very well in the *Messenger*'s "Critical Notices" section. For instance, the March 1836 review of Augustus Baldwin Longstreet's *Georgia Scenes: Characters, Incidents, &c., in the First Half Century of the Republic* beams with regional pride: "The author, whoever he is, is a clever fellow, imbued with a spirit of the truest humor, and endowed, moreover, with an exquisitely discriminative and penetrating understanding of *character* in general, and of Southern character in particular" (2: 287). As one of the first published pieces of "southwestern humor," *Georgia Scenes* was replete with local color and dialect. For all its horse humor and bawdy jokes, Longstreet's book aspired to a protoliterary realism, one Poe found convincing.

Poe imagines a cosmopolitan audience for this deeply regional book. Noting that "if this book were printed in England it would make the fortune of its author," Poe wonders aloud how these southern scenes would be received across the Atlantic: "imagine what a hubbub they would occasion in the uninitiated regions of Cockaigne. And what would Christopher North [a pseudonym for *Blackwood's Magazine* contributor John Wilson] say to them?—ah, what would Christopher North say? that is the question. Certainly not a word. But we can fancy the pursing up of his lips, and the long, loud, and jovial resonnation of his wicked, and uproarious ha! ha's!" (2: 287). Such prognostications grant an emergent regional literature a global purview. Poe believes that, as an uncommon representative of southern character, *Georgia Scenes* has the potential to travel not merely north but also abroad.[22]

As his fanciful rhetoric and conditional tense suggests, the British reception of *Georgia Scenes* is fabulated by the reviewer. Indeed, Poe remains dubious about the self-published and self-circulated book's prospects for success, "in the bookselling sense of the word": "Thanks to the long indulged literary supineness of the South, her presses are not as apt in putting forth a *saleable* book as her sons are in concocting a wise one" (287). This critique of the southern publishing industry (such as it was) notwithstanding, Poe reads this intrepid and "wise" book as a literary harbinger of sorts. He concludes, "Altogether this very humorous, and very clever book forms an aera in our reading. It has reached us per mail, and without a cover. We will have it bound forthwith, and give it a niche in our library as a sure omen of better days for the literature of the South" (292).

Poe's use of "aera" is crucial. The *Oxford English Dictionary* defines *aera* as a "date, or an event, which forms the commencement of a new period in the history of a nation, an institution, individual, art or science, etc.; a memorable or important date" ("Aera," def. 3a.). With no small amount of dramatic flair, Poe suggests that *Georgia Scenes* has produced something like an epistemic shift. Now begins a new period in the history of the "literature of the South"; "better days" are to come. The promise to have the book bound and preserved in a library underscores the review's interest in literary posterity. It also offers an elegant figure for the ways a modest regional production—one that arrives anonymously, "per mail, and without cover"—can become, with the aid of an enterprising editor, a permanent part of a distinct and distinctive literature.

Such an insistence on literary posterity was not unusual for Poe during this period of increasing literary sectionalism. When Poe praised a book, northern or southern, it was often in terms of originality and with an eye toward literary futurity. For instance, in the May 1836 issue Poe reviewed Paulding's life of George Washington—a literary nationalist project if ever there was one. Worrying that in a market flooded with Washington biographies the contemporary public might overlook the book's "rare merits," Poe places his confidence in future readers: "We have no fears, however, for the future. Such books as these before us, go down to posterity like rich wines, with a certainty of being more valued as they go. They force themselves with the gradual but rapidly accumulating power of strong wedges into the hearts and understandings of a community" (2: 396). Similarly, in the September 1836 issue Poe praises Bird's *Sheppard Lee* for its willingness to break from tradition: "[T]his novel is an original in *American* Belles Lettres at least; and these deviations, however indecisive, from the more beaten paths of imitation, look well for our future literary prospects" (2: 662).[23]

Poe's breathless review of Nathaniel Beverley Tucker's southern romance *George Balcombe* (1835) similarly praises that novel's rambles off the "more beaten paths of imitation." Poe believes that the anonymous author shows "that rarest of all qualities in American novelists, and that certainly most indispensable—*invention*" (3: 51). Indeed, to hear Poe tell it, *George Balcombe* is "*the best* American novel" to date: "There have been few books of its peculiar kind, we think, written in *any* country, much its superior. . . . Its most distinguishing features are invention, vigor, almost audacity, of thought—great variety of what the German critics term *intrigue*, and exceeding ingenuity and finish in the adaptation of its component parts" (58). Poe is uncharacteristically effusive here; the terms of that effusiveness are, however, characteristic. Tucker's novel succeeds, Poe claims, because of its inventiveness and originality. The fact that this novel was southern in both origin and sensibility certainly did not hurt its cause, at least not on the pages of the *Southern Literary Messenger*.[24]

Burton R. Pollin and Joseph V. Ridgely have noted that Poe's lengthy review slights the politics of Tucker's novel, which offers a number of "quintessentially Southern disquisitions on such topics as slavery, states' rights, and the lofty role of the Virginia gentleman" (362). While he does not pursue those disquisitions directly, Poe does embrace ardently the overall philosophy of its titular character: "Balcombe, frank, ardent, philosophical, chivalrous, sagacious—and, above all, glorying in the exercise of his sagacity" (57). In fact, it is on the basis of that philosophy that Poe bases his attribution of authorship: "The mind of the chief personage of the story, is the transcript of a mind familiar to us—an unintentional transcript, let us grant—but still one not to be mistaken. George Balcombe thinks, speaks, and acts, as no person, we are convinced, but Judge Beverley Tucker, ever precisely thought, spoke, or acted before" (58).

And Poe was exceedingly familiar with Tucker's mind. By January 1837 Tucker had published in the *Messenger* several lengthy dissertations, including two notorious defenses of domestic slavery, "Remarks on a Note to Blackstone's Commentaries" (January 1835) and "Slavery" (April 1836); nearly a dozen poems and translations; and countless reviews. As editor, Poe worked extensively with Tucker's prose and poetry, reading them closely and making emendations, and the two men carried on a correspondence.[25] As a result, Tucker, a law professor at the College of William and Mary and scion of an important Virginia family, was among the most intimate friends of the *Messenger*: a prolific contributor, sometime assistant editor, and close confidante of Thomas W. White. The January 1837 issue was something of a tribute to Tucker: It included four of his poems, his review of a play by Edward Bulwer-Lytton, and lengthy discussions of his novels *George Balcombe* and *The Partisan Leader*. Given Tucker's close relationship with the *Messenger*, we might think of Poe's gonzo assessment of *George Balcombe*—again, "*the best* American novel"—in terms of those regional "interests and associations" White so privileged and prized.[26]

This is not to suggest that Poe responded to every southern book as an "omen of better days for the literature of the South." His January 1836 review of Simms's *The Partisan* is notable for its willingness to critique the southern novelist par excellence on the pages of a southern periodical. Citing "manifest and manifold blunders and impertinences," Poe suggests that Simms would have done better to write a history about the Revolutionary War rather than a multivolume historical romance (2: 121). Here, whatever local or regional interests the *Messenger* held were subordinated to candid and independent literary criticism. However, turning just a single page in the same issue, we have to question the disinterestedness of Poe's praise of Joseph Holt Ingraham, the Yankee behind the travel-narrative-cum-slavery-apologia *The South-West* (1835). This troubling review toes the *Messenger*'s avoidant editorial line on slavery and exhibits what Terence Whalen has rightly called Poe's "average racism":

The traveler from the North has evinced no disposition to look with a jaundiced eye upon the South—to pervert its misfortunes into crimes—or distort its necessities into sins of volition. He has spoken of slavery as he found it—and it is almost needless to say that he found it a very different thing from the paintings he had seen of it in red ochre. He has discovered, in a word, that while the *physical* condition of the slave *is not* what it has been represented, the slave himself is utterly incompetent to feel the *moral* galling of his chain. Indeed, we cordially agree with a distinguished Northern contemporary and friend, that the Professor's

strict honesty, impartiality, and unprejudiced common sense, on the trying subject which has so long agitated our community, is the distinguishing and the most
praiseworthy feature of his book. (2: 122)[27]

In this relatively brief review—less than three paltry columns, a pittance
for the prolix Poe—the reviewer figures slavery as both a misfortune and a
necessity and goes out of his way to defend the South and its peculiar institution from the North's "general prejudices," jealousies, and misconceptions.
While this does not constitute a "positive good" argument for slavery (à la
Tucker or Thomas Roderick Dew), Poe's rationalization about the slave being
"utterly incompetent to feel the moral galling of his chain" does place him in
the main currents of racialist thought in the South. Moreover, the fact that
Poe finds the treatment of slavery "the distinguishing and the most praiseworthy feature" of this capacious, two volume, 568-page doorstop betrays a
great deal about his regional affiliations. Finally, the fact that Poe describes
the divisive and "trying subject" of slavery via a rhetoric of "community"
should come as little surprise. It is difficult to think of any of Poe's reviews
for the *Messenger* outside of the communities—southern and northern—
they puffed, critiqued, addressed, and helped to imagine.

Poe's employment at the *Southern Literary Messenger* came to a sudden
but perhaps inevitable end on 3 January 1837, when White excused him from
his editorial duties. White's reasons for firing Poe were at least threefold: Poe's
continuing struggles to remain sober; honest editorial disagreements about
the content and direction of the periodical; and grave concerns about the
"editorial assaults on the *SLM* engendered by Poe's caustic reviews" (Pollin
and Ridgely 324). It was this final concern that seems to have most troubled
White. In a 24 January 1837 letter to Tucker, White wrote, "[T]he Messenger
is safe. It shall live—and it shall outlive all the injury it has sustained from
Mr. Poe's management" (qtd. in Thomas and Jackson 241). Needless to say,
the *Southern Literary Messenger* survived Edgar Allan Poe, and vice versa.[28]

Injurious or not, Poe's time at the *Messenger* proved momentous for both
the periodical and the national literary culture in aspiration this chapter describes. As its three puffy supplements ably suggest, the *Messenger* achieved
a startling fame in its first two years of existence. For better or worse, Poe's
caustic reviews were part and parcel of that fame. Through Poe's conspicuous "Notices," White's extensive outreach, and an increasingly impressive
roster of contributors, the *Messenger* garnered a great deal of attention from
periodicals in both the South and the North. As a result, this southern literary periodical came to be seen as both a viable publishing endeavor and an
important venue for a thoroughgoing, if not unbiased, literary criticism. By
July 1836 the *Louisville City Gazette* could figure the *Messenger* staff as the
stewards of American literature, "vigilant sentinels" whose criticisms work

to "preserve the vigor of American Literature" and keep various barbarians at the gates (2: [July 1836]: 523). The suggestion that the duty of safeguarding American literature had fallen to an upstart southern literary periodical was both radical and oft-repeated during this period.[29]

The emergence of a southern literary criticism—one that would engage regional, national, and international texts—constituted an important act of prenational cultural integration and differentiation. After all, literary and cultural criticism is often a key early participant in "the nation-building process," since it allows people to make comparisons regarding the relative standing of national literatures (Jusdanis, *Belated* 1; *Necessary* 102). In the decades that followed Poe's tenure at the *Messenger*, the terms with which such comparisons were made grew increasingly stark and fanatical. Thus, the *Southern Literary Messenger*'s emergence in the 1830s as a viable venue for literary criticism proved portentous given the sectional cold war that would break out in the 1840s and 1850s.

Uncle Tomitudes

In the years immediately following Poe's departure from Richmond, White worked tirelessly as proprietor and editor to keep the *Messenger* in the first rank of American periodicals. In early 1840 he brought in as associate editor Matthew Fontaine Maury (a veteran of the U.S. Navy who would later become an important early oceanographer), and the two collaborated until White suffered a paralytic stroke at the Astor House in New York in 1842. White died on 19 January 1843, and that July the *Southern Literary Messenger* was sold to Benjamin Blake Minor, an inexperienced, twenty-five-year-old lawyer, who ran the periodical until August 1847. As owner and editor, Minor made southern history the dominant subject of the journal, complementing and at times overshadowing its earlier, nominally belletristic interests (Jacobs 65; Mott 648).

During these years, Minor also dialed up the *Messenger*'s sectional rhetoric and made the defense of slavery official editorial policy. For instance, in the January 1845 issue, Minor printed and responded at length to a letter from "S——," a steadfast northern subscriber who wrote to cancel his subscription. Noting that under White the journal had been "always neutral on exciting subjects" (fair and balanced, as it were), "S——" decries the *Messenger*'s unwillingness to publish antislavery essays alongside its "rabid" defenses of slavery (11: 61). Minor replies with gusto: "Neutral on exciting subjects! What a yea-nay—no-opinion affair, such persons would have the Messenger to be! It never was 'neutral on exciting subjects.' It has abstained from the exciting struggles of mere party politics, and religious controversy. On every question affecting the rights and institutions of the South it never was and never will be 'neutral'" (61). Minor goes on to cite several proslavery pieces published during White's tenure (Jacobs 83; Pollin and Ridgely 365).

Most urgently, Minor uses this heated exchange—the subscriber concludes, "go your own way; hug your barbaric arguments; sleep over a volcano; prepare for a revolution that shall shake your *sunny hills* to their aristocratic centres" (61)—to limn the *Messenger*'s editorial aims and aspirations: "Southern yet National, Literary yet philosophical, light yet solid and useful, discussing Public affairs, yet espousing no party" (62). Lest these equivocations leave the reader confused, Minor states forcefully the *Messenger*'s regional sympathies: "But we are a *Southerner*, and mean to maintain Southern institutions, rights, and interests. . . . But we will vindicate Southern interests from assault, Southern manners from aspersion and Southern Literature from disparagement" (62).[30]

After Minor found other, nonliterary opportunities, John Reuben Thompson, an even younger, even less experienced literary man, purchased and took over the editorial duties of the *Messenger*. In an introductory piece, "The Editor to His Patrons" (November 1847), Thompson reiterated Minor's confusing declarations of both national commitment and regional affiliation. Regarding the "excitement of faction as eminently pernicious to the graces of literature," Thompson nonetheless affirms the *Messenger*'s increasingly sectional worldview: "But as the prefix of *Southern* to the name of the Messenger has always had a peculiar significance in pointing it out as the guardian of Southern rights and interests, we shall ever be prompt to defend those rights and interests, when they are made the object of ruthless assault. To this extent it will be political and sectional and no farther" (13: 644).

In truth, slavery was a constant presence on the pages of the *Messenger* in the years following Poe's editorship, and the periodical's coverage of the "exciting subject" was far from neutral. In addition to Tucker's writings on slavery, White also published Simms's review essay "Miss Martineau on Slavery" (November 1837); William Harper's "positive good" lecture "Memoir on Slavery" (October 1838); Abel P. Upshur's treatise "Domestic Slavery" (October 1839); Conray Robinson's pseudo legal brief "Slavery and the Constitution" (January 1840); the anonymous and much discussed "White and Black Slavery" (March 1840); a long discussion of Francis Wayland and Richard Fuller's correspondence, "Domestic Slavery, Considered as a Scriptural Institution" (September 1845); and the review essay "Slavery as a Moral Relation" (July 1851). Thus, as both a purported right and a deeply held interest of southerners, the defense of slavery became a central component of the *Messenger*'s message during these years.[31]

This is not to say that the *Messenger* lost sight entirely of its literary interests following Poe's departure; far from it, in fact. During the late 1830s and throughout the 1840s, the *Messenger* continued to position itself as an arbiter of American literary quality and criticism, publishing lengthy piece after lengthy piece on the prospects and pitfalls of a nascent American literature. In review essays such as George Tucker's "Discourse on American Literature" (February 1838), the anonymous "The Inferiority of American Literature" (September 1840), and William Cowper Scott's "American Literature: The Present State of American Letters, the Prospect and Means of Their Improvement" (July 1845), the *Messenger* kept its eyes on the prize of a distinct national literature. It also served as an important venue for debates about international copyright law, publishing a four-part series by William Gilmore Simms in 1844.[32]

Under Thompson's management, the *Messenger* also returned to—or promised to return to—principles of literary criticism resembling Poe's. In a header to the January 1848 "Notices of New Works" section, Thompson reaffirmed the need for an independent literary criticism: "Perhaps there is no duty more important in a Literary Magazine than that of presenting impartial critical notices of new publications" (14: 59). Couching his discussion of literary criticism in the inopportune rhetoric of slavery (that is, "lash" and "whip"), Thompson echoes Poe by noting that "we have fallen into the habit of extravagantly praising every thing American and looking through a perverted and pleasing medium at all American productions" (60). Instead, Thompson promises, the *Messenger* "shall endeavor in a humble way to render an impartial judgment" (60).

As Minor's and Thompson's anxious editorials suggest, the devil was in the details of reconciling the *Messenger*'s self-assigned roles as both warden of "impartial judgment" and "guardian of Southern rights and interests," of keeping the "graces of literature" separate from the "excitement of faction." Such reconciliation became all the more dicey during the mid-1840s, as debates raged about the annexation of Texas and the Wilmot Proviso and as schisms emerged in the Methodist and Baptist denominations over the issue of slavery (Varon 165–98). Of course, the Crisis of 1850 further excited factionalism, both South and North. But it was the book publication of Harriet Beecher Stowe's *Uncle Tom's Cabin; or Life among the Lowly* (1852) that heralded the collapse of any and all difference between these willful categories. The *Southern Literary Messenger* responded to Stowe's novel with a series of essays and reviews that aimed to protect the "rights and interests" of the South via a ferocious literary criticism, one that brought together the "graces of literature" with the "excitement of faction," and transformed a proud literary regionalism into a steadfast literary separatism.

The first of these responses appeared in the October 1852 issue, with (literary historians believe) editor-proprietor Thompson offering a thorough and impassioned rebuke of Stowe. The more than ten-thousand-word review took up nine of the eleven two-column pages devoted to "Notices of New Works," forcing Thompson to append the following apology. "Notices of many new works and collegiate addresses are unavoidably deferred till the next number of the Messenger from want of room" (18: 640). As "an immediately recognizable metonym for the anti-slavery position," Stowe's new work clearly demanded notice and precedence in the preeminent southern literary periodical (C. Weinstein 42).

The review opens with a disquisition on the ethics and efficacy of criticizing a "lady author," thus framing gender as one of the review's key anxieties. After a couple of scholarly paragraphs on the proper behavior of women, the review concludes that, given her "shameless disregard of truth and of those amenities which so peculiarly belong to her sphere of life," Stowe "has forfeited the claim to be considered a lady, and with that claim all exemption from the utmost stringency of critical punishment" (630). And let the punishment begin.

Using the dual rhetorics of literary nationalism and moral uplift, the review concedes many of the features of Stowe's writing that subsequent critics have celebrated: keen descriptive acuity, an accessible prose style, and an uncommon ability to elicit and manipulate reader sympathy. But, the reviewer avers, Stowe has used "such talents" for evil, not good:

> [S]he might, in the legitimate exercise of such talents, have done much to enrich the literature of America, and to gladden and elevate her fellow beings. But she has chosen to employ her pen for purposes of a less worthy nature. She has volunteered officiously to intermeddle with things which concern her not—to libel and vilify a people from among whom have gone forth some of the noblest men that have adorned the race—to foment heart-burnings and unappeasable hatred between brethren of a common country, the joint heirs of that country's glory—to sow, in this blooming garden of freedom, the seeds of strife and violence and all direful contentions. (630)

In laying out the charges against Stowe—the review tries to build a quasi-legal case against the author for having "shockingly traduced the slaveholding society of the United States" (631)—the reviewer is extravagant with his accusations. In addition to intermeddling and libeling, the author of *Uncle Tom's Cabin* is accused of treasonous acts: fomenting "heart-burnings and unappeasable hatred between brethren of a common country" and sowing "the seeds of strife and violence and all direful contentions." Thus, long before Lincoln purportedly gave this "little woman" credit for starting the American Civil War, the *Southern Literary Messenger* acknowledged the potential for *Uncle Tom's Cabin* to exacerbate sectional tensions and speed the spread of disunion.[33]

As the review proceeds, concerns about the representations of women and about what it means to have a woman produce socially conscious, representative art become paramount. At stake for the reviewer are the dictates of proper white womanhood, which, he suggests, are subject to regional difference:

> We know that among other novel doctrines in vogue in the land of Mrs. Stowe's nativity—the pleasant land of New England—which we are old-fashioned enough to condemn, is one which would place woman on a footing of political equality with man, and causing her to look beyond the office for which she was created—the high and holy office of maternity—would engage her in the administration of public affairs; thus handing over the State to the perilous protection of diaper diplomatists and wet-nurse politicians. (631)

This passage suggests great anxiety about the full incorporation of women into the body politic. The reviewer takes aim at both the audacity of Stowe's act of feminine impropriety—writing a novel that looks "beyond the office for which she was created"—and her female characters. For instance, commenting on Mrs. Selby's attempts to aid and abet the escape of Eliza Harris, the reviewer says snidely, "[A]s obedience to one's husband is not recognised by the new school of Woman's Rights, perhaps there is no departure herein from ethical consistency" (631). Later, describing the domestic lives of Senator and Mrs. Byrd, the reviewer adds a biting parenthetical comment about Mrs. Byrd ruling their household "as completely as any Women's Rights Orator could desire" (632). The reviewer finds in these three women, Mrs. Selby, Mrs. Byrd, and Mrs. Stowe, a shared impudence and lack of respect for masculine authority, traits that can be blamed on their proximity to or full enrollment in the "school of Woman's Rights."

As we might expect, the reviewer takes particular umbrage at the representation of Marie St. Clare, who is described as "a gross and stupendous libel. And this libel is all the more unpardonable because Marie St. Clare is represented as a member of a Christian Church" (635). The reviewer suggests that, "as a portraiture of Southern female character," the twinned representation of Marie St. Clare's hateful behavior and Christian faith are among the novels most egregious sins, since they seek "to bring into contempt the entire communion of the Southern States" (635). It is one thing, the review asserts, to call into question the moral character of slave traders, but quite another to impugn that of southern white women, who are the ultimate representative of southern civilization.[34]

In defending white southern womanhood from Stowe's "libels," the reviewer laments more broadly "the cruel disparity, both intellectual and physical, which our authoress makes between the white and black races, to the prejudice of the former" (633). Stowe is something of a race traitor, a novelist who "can thus 'see Helen's beauty in a brow of Egypt,'" but "is unable to look upon a white face without tracing in it something sinister and repulsive. The fairest of her Southern ladies retain some ugly marks of their descent from the erring mother of our race." In a telling nod to European literary traditions, the reviewer moves from the Garden of Eden to the netherworld of the *Inferno*, noting that "Dante fell into some rather bad company when he descended with Virgil to the realms of the lost, but the demons of the Inferno are amiable and well-behaved gentlemen in comparison with Marks and Loker. On the other hand, Beatrice, soaring to the loftiest circles of the glorified, is but a common-place damsel by the side of Eliza" (633). The reviewer's sarcasm veils a deep indignation at Stowe's representational politics. It also suggests that the reviewer read the novel closely and with great attention to issues of characterization and development. Among many other things, this review locates *Uncle Tom's Cabin* in a global literary tradition and context.

Sarcasm gives way to glee as the reviewer turns his attention to the "head-devil" of the novel, Simon Legree. Once again, the reviewer is willing to "perform an act of justice to Mrs. Stowe"—to remain impartial and independent in his criticism of the novel, as Poe might have it—and commend her characterization of the novel's villain: "Legree is a darker, a more perfect, a more consistent, a more symmetrical piece of diabolism than the literature of any language within the limited sphere of our knowledge can furnish" (635). Of course this high praise is conditioned by the fact that Simon Legree is a northerner, not a southerner, by birth. This fact allows the reviewer to dilate on the "greater humanity of Southern men in the administration of corporal punishment." Remarkably, the review then quotes "a Northern writer who brought forth, two years ago, a volume, the object of which was the abolition of flogging in the Navy" (636). Said "Northern writer" was Herman Melville, who wrote: "It is a thing that American man-of-war's-men have often observed, that the Lieutenants from the Southern States, the descendants of the old Virginians, are much less severe, and much more gentle and gentlemanly in command, than the Northern officers, as a class" (Melville, *White-Jacket* 141). Here are two northern writers, Stowe and Melville, who seem to concur that northerners are more severe in their corporal punishment than are southerners. As a result, Legree becomes part of a fierce interregional competition for moral authority. If this southern reviewer can discover northern inconsistencies or hypocrisies like this, then the force of Stowe's damning novelistic critique can be lessened or even obviated.

Such discussions of gender and race—again, discussions grounded in the forms and conventions of antebellum literary criticism—are in the foreground of the review; in the background is a persistent concern for accuracy, particularly with regard to slave law. In its opening paragraphs, the review declared its purpose: "[W]e desire to be understood as acting entirely on the defensive, when we proceed to expose the miserable misrepresentations of her story" (631). The rhetoric of defensiveness is deployed here to suggest a society besieged by ill feeling and defamed by inaccurate characterizations. Although acknowledging the "very torrent and tempest of our wrath," the reviewer suggests that this will be a temperate assessment of Stowe's novel, one based on fact and impartial judgment (631).[35]

In its final pages, the review labors methodically to refute the three points "upon which the authoress rests her abuse of the Southern States": "the cruel treatment of the slaves, their lack of religious instruction, and a wanton disregard of the sacred ties of consanguinity in selling members of the same family apart from each other" (637). In doing so, the review marshals legal precedent to make the case against Stowe. For instance, the reviewer spills a great deal of ink over the murder of Prue and St. Clare's defensive, laissez-faire statements to Miss Ophelia that slaveholders "have absolute control; they are irresponsible despots. There would be no use in interfering; there is no law that amounts to anything practically, for such a case. The best we can do is to shut our eyes and ears, and let it alone. It's the only resource left us" (Stowe 328). Citing the "statute-book of Louisiana . . . Civil Code of that State, Chapter 3rd, Article 173," the reviewer concludes that the law is "thus watchful of the negro's safety in life and limb, [and] confines not its guardianship to the inhibitory clauses, but proscribes extreme penalties in case of their infraction" (634). In St. Clare's Louisiana, there are laws, we are told, which would have protected Prue from her abusive master. The review then goes on to cite legal cases from Tennessee and Virginia where masters were punished for abusing their slaves.[36]

Similarly, Stowe is lambasted for her poor understanding of "the Law of Contracts, as it affects Slavery in the South" (632). The review is incredulous about George Harris's master taking him from the factory without the consent of the factory's proprietor: "George, by virtue of the contract of hiring had become the property of the proprietor for the time being, and his master could no more have taken him away forcibly than the owner of a house in Massachusetts can dispossess his lessee, at any moment, from mere whim or caprice" (632). Suggesting a common ground between southern slave law and New England real estate law, the reviewer makes an unexpected address to northern readers. Such a move is repeated later as the reviewer rejects as "manifestly absurd and preposterous" the idea that a slaveholder would offer a reward for an escaped slave "with the alternative of 'dead or alive'" (632):

> What man of Vermont, having an ox or an ass that had gone astray, would forthwith offer half the full value of the animal, not for the carcass which might be turned to some useful purpose, but for the unavailing satisfaction of its head? Yet are the two cases exactly parallel. With regard to the assumption that men are permitted to go about, at the South, with double-barrelled guns, shooting down runaway negroes in preference to apprehending them, we can only say that it is as wicked and wilful as it is ridiculous. (632)

In rendering equivalent—"exactly parallel," even—an escaped slave and an astray beast of burden, the reviewer betrays a great deal about his racial poli-

tics. But his rhetorical question performs additional work as well. Taken together, these references to life and law in New England quietly imagine an
uneasy confederacy of a homeowner in Massachusetts, a farmer in Vermont,
and a southern slaveholder. If the Melville quotation tweaks sectional differences, these attempts to translate the peculiar institution for other audiences
and to other settings seem to elicit sympathy, suggesting connections among
what the reviewer earlier called "brethren of a common country, the joint
heirs of that country's glory" (631). Needless to say, such a confederacy is
predicated on whiteness.[37]

Unsurprisingly, the review concludes by returning to the purportedly dire
threats Stowe's novel posed to sectional and national interests. In a startling
piece of prophecy, the reviewer suggests that a failure to criticize *Uncle Tom's
Cabin* will result in civil war:

> Justice to ourselves would seem to demand that [the novel] should not be suffered
> to circulate longer without the brand of falsehood upon it. Let it be recollected,
> too, that the importance Mrs. Stowe will derive from Southern criticism will be
> one of infamy. Indeed she is only entitled to criticism at all, as the mouthpiece of a
> large and dangerous faction which if we do not put down with the pen, we may be
> compelled one day (God grant that day may never come!) to repel with the bayo-
> net. (638)

This haunting passage underscores both the earnestness with which the
Southern Literary Messenger approached this literary criticism and the reviewer's deft use of rhetoric. The revision of Bulwer-Lytton's 1839 quip, "the
pen is mightier than the sword," conjures and negates the specter of civil
war. In turn, the passivity of the conditional tense ("may be compelled") and
menacing indeterminacy of the date ("one day") makes this a particularly
ominous prophesy (*ominatio*). Likewise, the parenthetical interjection "(God
grant that day may never come!)" functions as *deprecatio*, a prayer against
the coming of such strife. Continuing to train the reader's eyes on the future,
the review promises that the *Messenger* will return to the novel in subsequent
issues. In the meantime, its final sentence dramatically urges Stowe to take
seriously the ninth commandment: "THOU SHALT NOT BEAR FALSE WITNESS
AGAINST THY NEIGHBOUR" (638).

Readers of the *Messenger* did not have to wait long for a further engagement with Stowe's barnburner of a novel. In December 1852, another nearly
ten-thousand-word essay on *Uncle Tom's Cabin* appeared over eleven two-
column pages. The review, penned by George Frederick Holmes, a professor of history and law at William and Mary, was unsigned. Of the vehement
piece, Holmes is quoted as saying, "I would have the review as hot as hellfire,
blasting and searing the reputation of the vile wretch in petticoats who could
write such a volume" (Craven 155). And as hot as hellfire it was. Among many

other things, Holmes goes so far as to cast the novel as a series of Decalogic offenses. Stowe, we are told, violates "frequently and systematically" "all the commandments relative to the duties of mankind to each other." Most urgently she bears false witness against her neighbors (in publishing a novel so openly hostile to the South); blasphemes (in her description of southern Christianity); and even murders ("murder is distinctly prescribed and applauded both by the precept and example of this book") (18: 730–31). Above all else, Holmes's review condemns "the folly, the presumption, and the unchristian spirit, which used [the details of the novel] to fan the flames of discord, and to stir up the embers of civil war" (730).

This prolix review engages less with the text than did the first review; indeed, its attention to the novel's plot and characterization suggests at best a quick perusal of its contents. Instead, the review offers a more or less philosophical meditation on *Uncle Tom's Cabin* as a representative of the degradation of literary art in the antebellum United States; an incitement to, and indictment of, southern literary culture; and a way to understand the inequality of the races. The resulting review is profoundly rhetorical, with Holmes deploying one rhetorical question after another. It is also strangely dilatory, with the reviewer referring again and again to the difficulty of the task before him and the impossibility of a proper response to Stowe's by then hugely popular novel.

Holmes begins with the problem of genre and literary tradition:

> But, in these late and evil days, the novel . . . has descended from its graceful and airy home, and assumed to itself a more vulgar mission, incompatible with its essence and alien to its original design. Engaging in the coarse conflicts of life, and mingling in the fumes and gross odours of political or polemical dissension, it has stained and tainted the robe of ideal purity with which it was of old adorned. Instead of remaining the ever welcome companion of an idle hour, which turned to profit by its sweet alchemy the loose moments devoted to intellectual reverie, it has entered upon a sterner career, and one which requires us to question the visitant before admitting it to our confidence or listening to its tale. (721)

He is correct in describing the novel's engagement in "the coarse conflicts of life." After all, *Uncle Tom's Cabin* had clear "designs on its readers," to crib a phrase from Jane Tompkins: Stowe wanted her readers to first "feel right" and then help abolish slavery. Holmes prefers a literature of "amusement," "leisure," "fancy," "imagination," and "intellectual reverie" over that of gritty social realism and advocacy. As a result, he positions Stowe's novel at the fore of a literary culture in decay. In these "late and evil days," Holmes suggests, novels like Stowe's force the reader to be wary and suspicious, for fear that she or he fall prey to "proselytism" during their "loose moments."

Holmes's attention shifts quickly from fiction in general to the fictionality of Stowe's novel in particular. Using *ploce* to great effect, Holmes ensures that his readers will not miss the point:

> We have said that Uncle Tom's Cabin is a fiction. It is a fiction throughout; a fiction in form; a fiction in its facts; a fiction in its representations and coloring; a fiction in its statements; a fiction in its sentiments; a fiction in its morals; a fiction in its religion; a fiction in its inferences; a fiction equally with regard to the subjects it is designed to expound, and with respect to the manner of their exposition. It is a fiction, not for the sake of more effectually communicating truth; but for the purpose of more effectually disseminating a slander. It is a fictitious or fanciful representation for the sake of producing fictitious or false impressions. Fiction is its form and falsehood is its end. (722)

Whereas gender trouble seemed to haunt the first *Messenger* review, genre trouble produces terrific anxiety here. Holmes seems to take great offense at the fact that Stowe used a novel, "a fiction in form," as the vehicle for her "proselytism." Like the earlier reviewer, Holmes sees Stowe as exploiting the conventions of the novel—using fiction "for the sake of more effectually communicating truth"—to excuse its "misrepresentations" and "lies." For Holmes, Stowe's treasonous aims in doing so are clear: "Every fact is distorted, every incident discolored, in order to awaken rancorous hatred and malignant jealousies between the citizens of the same republic, the fellow countrymen whose interests and happiness are linked with the perpetuity of a common union, and with the prosperity of a common government" (723).

Holmes also acknowledges the impossibility of responding to a novel that had already circulated widely and sold well, both in the North and in England. In worrying over how to secure "a dispassionate hearing for our defence," to administer "the antidote where the poison has spread," he decries a "literary atmosphere which is fatal to the dissemination of unpopular truths." Holmes describes a South beset on all sides by the "whole phalanx of Abolition literature," which is, he shudders,

> completely turned against us: and an aggregation of hostile tendencies is brought to bear upon us so as to deny to our complaints, our recriminations, or our apologies, either consideration or respect. The potency of literature, in this age of the world, when it embraces all manifestations of public or individual thought and feeling, and permeates, in streams, more or less diluted, all classes of society, can scarcely be misapprehended. (724)

At a moment of profound sectional and national crisis, the South is being attacked, not by invading armies but by literature broadly conceived. This remarkable endorsement of literature's power to influence opinion and enact social change pits the vibrancy of abolitionist literary culture against the relative lassitude of southern literary culture.

Indeed, Holmes returns to the rhetoric of the very first issue of the *South-*

ern Literary Messenger, suggesting that the proverbial chickens have come home to roost:

> But the illiberal, unjust, and unwise course of Southern communities, has deprived them of the aid of this potent protection, by excluding themselves and their views almost entirely from the domain of literature. The Southern population have checked and chilled all manifestations of literary aptitudes at the South; they have discouraged by blighting indifference, the efforts of such literary genius as they may have nurtured: they have underrated and disregarded all productions of Southern intellect; and now, when all the batteries of the literary republic are turned against them, and the torrent of literary censure threatens to unite with other agencies to overwhelm them, it is in vain that they cry in their dire necessity, "Help me, Cassius, or I sink." (724–25)

It is because of the lack of a strong, unified, and well-supported literary culture that the South now faces such trials. A "silly and fatal indifference to the high claims of a native and domestic literature"—an indifference that the *Messenger* had loudly lamented since 1834—has left the South unprotected against the "batteries of the literary republic" (725). In extending his martial metaphor, Holmes effectively collapses vehicle and tenor. By 1852 it was possible that the *military* phalanxes and batteries of the republic would be turned against the South.

Using personification, Holmes even figures the region as a self-destructive woman who has left herself defenseless: "[S]he is now exposed, unarmed and unprotected. . . . She has invited and merited her own fate: she has wooed the slander which she is almost powerless to repel" (725). This stinging indictment aimed no doubt to play off pervasive fears about the susceptibility of southern white womanhood. Having rendered the South ripe for ravishment, Holmes can make his case for the "only true defence of the South against this attack": "to create and cherish a true Southern literature." Sounding a great deal like both Heath and White, Holmes calls for a strongly separatist literary culture: "Let the South honestly and cordially sustain her own periodicals, and her own writers, and such productions will cease to alarm or annoy her. . . . Let her fail to do this, and no one can complain if she is slandered, without contradiction and maligned without defence" (725).[38]

Holmes has a specific type of literature in mind for the South. Conceding the "insufficiency" of anti-Tom texts like "Aunt Phillis's Cabin, and similar apologies" (727), he urges the South to produce a literature that would represent the horrors of northern and European labor. This cosmopolitan and almost Marxian critique of "the incidents of life" (728) returns us to Holmes's initial provocation that *Uncle Tom's Cabin* substitutes "the real thraldom of free labor for the imaginary hardships of slavery" (722–23). To be clear, Holmes is a racialist; he believes that the "joys and the sorrows of the slave are in harmony with his position" (729). He is also of the belief that slavery has "peculiar advantages" for slaves themselves (729). As a result, Holmes holds that "the average condition of the slave at the South is infinitely superior, morally and materially, in all respects, to that of the labouring class under any other circumstances in any other part of the world" (730). If Holmes's region had a literature of its own to make this case—a literature of counterproselytism, as it were—then the South would be protected.[39]

We can understand Holmes's review as an attempt to reify what Jusdanis calls cultural belatedness. A comparison with "Abolition literature" suggests that southern literary culture is terribly behind its northern other. The process of "catching up" must, Holmes avers, begin immediately. As both reviews suggest, the popularity of Stowe's novel represents a moment of profound crisis for the southern literati. That crisis, Holmes hopes, might very well lead to a concomitant moment of creation, if southerners will only rally to the call of the *Messenger* and patronize a "true Southern literature." To be clear, the periodical was not without self-interest in calling for such patronage. The publication of these reviews followed closely a period of financial difficulty for the *Southern Literary Messenger*. Arousing sectional spirit was one way to ensure southern subscriptions—a chief concern for both Minor and Thompson as proprietors (Jacobs 84–89, 94–97; cf. Whalen, *Edgar Allan Poe* 122). Both of these reviews use the incendiary publication of *Uncle Tom's Cabin* to arouse sectional spirit in the service of a southern literature; however, they also recycle and recast rhetoric that had appeared in previous issues of the *Messenger*. These urgent calls for a "true Southern literature" were very much of a piece with the eighteen years of southern literary agitation that had come before.[40]

John McCardell has called the publication of *Uncle Tom's Cabin* "the catalyst in transforming Americanism into Southern literary nationalism" (166; cf. Hubbell, "Literary Nationalism" 189). McCardell suggests that as sectional tensions intensified in the years following the publication of the novel, "Southern sectionalism soon became Southern nationalism" (143). The years from 1853 to 1861 certainly bear this out. To take but one example, the lead essay in the October 1856 issue, "The Duty of Southern Authors," was resolutely nationalistic in its rhetoric. Quoting extensively from James P. Holcombe, the pleading essay urges southern authors to take up the "varied forms, of poem, drama, novel, history and essay" (243) and make a defense of domestic slavery, which the author calls "a great social, moral and political blessing—beneficial alike to us and to the slave" (241). Southern authors should, he urges, "deluge all the realms of literature with a flood of light upon this subject" (23: 242). The author of the piece, "W.R.A.," argues that through such a literature the South could attain protonational status: "It is the literature of a country that gives her people a position among the nations of the earth, and to this source must she look for the place she is destined to fill in the eyes of future generations" (241). This, then, is a call for a southern literary culture that is wholly separate from, not a merely a strongly sectional contribution to, American literary culture. Emphasizing yet again literary futurity, this rhetoric also places the pre-Confederate South "among the nations of the earth," a particularly bold claim amid the fraught presidential campaign of 1856 and ongoing violence in "Bleeding Kansas."[41]

Thus, the publication of Stowe's novel does seem of utmost importance to the realization of a pre-Confederate southern literary nationalism. However, I want to take seriously McCardell's catalytic metaphor. *Uncle Tom's Cabin* may well have provided the "catalyst" for such a realization, but the work of prenationalist cultural integration began long before Stowe first serialized her novel. After all, a catalyst merely "increases the rate of a chemical reaction or process" ("Catalyst"); the component parts of that reaction or process must be in place at the time of the introduction of the catalyst. The component parts of southern literary nationalism were on full display in the pages of the *Southern Literary Messenger* as early as 1834.

Coda: Back to the Future

In one of the first systematic assessments of pre-Confederate southern literary nationalism, Jay B. Hubbell remained dubious about the accomplishments of the "ceaseless Southern agitation of the literary question" ("Literary Nationalism" 219):

> The demand for a Southern literature resulted in the establishment of numerous short-lived periodicals, and it stimulated some persons to write or at least to publish what had been written with no thought of publication. It perhaps also made Southern writers less likely to imitate popular Northern authors. But it did not serve to make Southern literature *Southern* except in a rather superficial sense of the word. ("Literary Nationalism" 218)

Hubbell, the founding editor of *American Literature* and one of the first serious scholars of antebellum U.S. southern literature, tries to account for something that may well be unaccountable. What *were* the "literary harvests" of calls for a distinct southern literature, of an "impartial and independent" southern literary criticism, of the vigorous response to *Uncle Tom's Cabin*? Hubbell seems to judge the results on the basis of the southernness of the texts produced in response to such "agitation." Yet, as Benjamin T. Spencer rightly suggests, literary nationalism is "concerned rather with literary intention than result; it is a record of the course of the national literary will rather than a reckoning of the full achievement of the American imagination" (*Quest* vii). Indeed, during the 1830s, 1840s, and 1850s, the intentions and wills of southern literary nationalists were protean and at times contradictory. As a result, no single Whiggish or developmental narrative captures fully the complexity of southern literary nationalist thought or rhetoric during the lead-up to the American Civil War.

Yet, the comparative history of nationalisms—a set of texts and tools neither Hubbell nor Spencer had entirely at hand when they wrote their pioneering studies—suggests that intentions and wills can in fact give rise to material results. As the cultural sociologist Sarah Corse observes perspicaciously, "National literatures, like nations, are created by the cultural work of specific people engaged in an identifiable set of activities" (7). In focusing on a few moments of crisis and creation in the history of a single periodical, I have emphasized the "identifiable set of activities" of specific people. During the three decades prior to the American Civil War, the *Southern Literary Messenger* provided both a forum and a form for a southern literary regionalism that could be revised variously into a southern literary sectionalism, a southern literary separatism, and a southern literary nationalism, depending on the needs and desires of specific people in specific historical moments.

In assessing the legacy of pre-Confederate southern literary nationalism, I take a bit longer view than does Hubbell. Rather than look for immediate results, I am interested in the potential long-term influence of this pliable rhetoric. To return to an agrarian metaphor, these years represented the "critical preparation of the literary soil" that would later yield the bitter harvest of a Confederate literary culture (Spencer, *Quest* 273). Once again, it is crucial to note that such preparatory labors were far from coordinated; they were undertaken without a clear sense of either purpose or design. Put another way, no one knew when or even if harvest time would come. Such preparation was for an uncertain and inscrutable future.

This is wholly appropriate. All literary nationalists deal perforce in literary futurity; that is, they imagine, look to, and strive for a number of possible futures in which their literary labors might bear national fruits. As purveyors of a national literary culture in aspiration, southern littérateurs such as White, Heath, Minor, Thompson, Holmes, and even Poe marshaled the rhetoric of futurity ingeniously and recurrently. The pages of the *Southern Literary Messenger*—a periodical whose very title suggests presagement and preparation ("Messenger," def. 2a. and 2b.)—resound with such rhetoric. I conclude this chapter by examining briefly two further examples of the *Messenger*'s engagement with the future. Although both are, to some degree, extraliterary, the "probable" futures they imagine underscore the centrality of literary futurity to the pre-Confederate nationalist discourses of this period.

In June 1856 the *Messenger* published "The Country in 1950, or The Conservatism of Slavery," a think-piece by "L.C.B." of Westmoreland, Virginia, that ostensibly replies to the *London Times*'s query "what will be the condition of the slavery question in the year 1950?" The essay mounts a strongly "positive good" argument for slavery, noting that the South's agricultural interests "rest mainly upon the institution of slavery," which, in turn provides the "foundation" for both its economy and its culture (22: 437). L.C.B. credits the institution as providing white southerners with "leisure" and thus "mental culture" (434); a greater sense of Christian "morality" (435); remarkably, a "feeling of equality among all individuals of the same origin"; and a concomitant "*original* love for liberty, which, *a priori*, always makes them desirous of free government" (435).

As we might expect, the seemingly oxymoronic claim that slavery could engender a "feeling of equality" or "*original* love for liberty" is predicated on resolutely racialist thinking. L.C.B. holds that "the South has a great advantage over the slaveholding republics of antiquity, from the fact of her slaves being of another and inferior race to the masters, and thus of a greater natural chasm being placed between them, on the one side of which the *whole* white population finds itself, and not a mere minority" (435). Both racial difference ("another") and racial hierarchy ("inferior") are, the essay suggests, phenomenologically intelligible. As a result, white slaveholders can separate themselves psychically, if not physically, from their African slaves. This separation ("a greater natural chasm") in turn confirms filiation and encourages a sense of equality among the entire white population. Thus, L.C.B. opines, "the institution of African slavery, so far from being fatal to the development of the fundamental ideas of this republic, is highly favorable to those conditions in which they are most apt to flourish" (426).[42]

This carefully argued and utterly repugnant racialist reading sets the stage for the essay's prophesies about the year 1950. First and foremost, L.C.B. foresees a narrowly averted civil war followed by a period of begrudging sectional amity. The "probable future" L.C.B. describes includes a heavily industrialized North and a stubbornly agrarian South (428, 439). While his familiar King Cotton argument (that is, the North requires the South's raw materials and markets) does not mention slavery explicitly, L.C.B. assures his readers that in 1950 the peculiar institution will remain a cornerstone of southern civilization and republican government: "African slavery will in all probability, be found fulfilling its mission of supplying the constant newly arising wants of the State, and by its conservative influence, forming a strong support to the present edifice of Liberty" (438). In the North, where slavery will still be outlawed, the picture is painted in a less "roseate hue" (439). Without the benefit of slavery and its attendant "feeling of equality," the North will be "many degrees out of the course of true republicanism, as according to present usage, we understand that term" (433). Here L.C.B. renders the slaveholding South circa 1950 the habitat of liberty and true republicanism. In doing so, the essay imagines a future in which the South wins a civil war of sorts without ever having to fire a shot. In L.C.B.'s 1950, the South maintains its institutions and its independence; it also gains a sense of moral superiority over the North.

We might understand L.C.B.'s essay as a conflicted attempt to defend the institutions, interests, and purported rights of the South; rally readers to the cause; and, most urgently, further imagine the South as a community. Of course, in looking forward to 1950, this 1856 essay addresses a chaotic present, one in which secession and civil war were real possibilities, if not likelihoods, in the aftermath of Bleeding Kansas (Lawrence was sacked on 21 May 1856) and the caning of Charles Sumner on the floor of the U.S. Senate (22 May 1856). In appealing to the future, the essay suggests that time alone will be the judge of both the slavery question and southern society writ large. Given our knowledge of the history of the future that L.C.B. describes, this petition to posterity might seem both convenient and quixotic. However, such petitions were a prominent feature of the *Southern Literary Messenger* throughout its long tenure. Indeed, as early as 1837, with its review of Nathaniel Beverley Tucker's novel *The Partisan Leader* (1836), the *Messenger* had begun speculating openly on the sort of future—literary and otherwise—the South would engender.[43]

Tucker's novel is among the most confounding literary curios of the nineteenth century. The novel's deadly earnest pages offer an alternative history of a future, one in which Virginia struggles to free itself of the burden of federal occupation and oppression. The year is 1848, and the tyrannical Martin Van Buren has just secured a fourth term as president of the United States. In response to his draconian rule, the lower South states have seceded from the Union and formed a league of independent states—a hugely prosperous league of independent states due to a commercial treaty with England. Poor Virginia has been kept from joining its seceding "sister states" by Van Buren's "henchmen," and the Commonwealth is engaged in brutal guerrilla conflict with federal troops.

Against this backdrop, Tucker tells the tortured tale of the Trevor family, an august and noble clan of Virginians whose allegiances are spread thin among nation, region, and state. By the end of the bewildering narrative, the Trevor family is in fact a house divided, with one of its sons, Owen, fighting steadfastly for Van Buren's henchmen, and another, Douglas, fighting for Virginian independence. The latter is a disgraced U.S. Army officer who, emboldened by the encouragement of his uncle, Bernard Trevor, and the mysterious separatist leader "B——," becomes the titular hero of the novel, the partisan leader.

Along the way, the novel's "meager plot" provides a mere backdrop for Tucker's "frequent digressions" on a number of political issues: a national banking system, free trade, and states' rights constitutionalism, among others (Brugger 122). Tellingly, it is the tariff, not slavery, that leads to the secession of the southern states and the birth of a confederacy. This is not to say that Tucker avoids the issue of slavery; far from it. The novel makes a number of direct defenses of the institution, and, as one critic notes, even manages to "paint a very rosy picture of it" (B. D. Tucker 362). Among other things, the novel includes a scene in which loyal slaves aid and abet the southern cause by duping federal officers with exaggerated dialect and buffoonish behavior.[44]

Tucker intentionally left his novel unfinished, wanting to gauge public interest before continuing the story of Douglas Trevor. Because there was little to no public interest, additional volumes of this history were never published. I say "history" because Tucker insists that he is offering a historical account of 1848–49. He even violates convention and postdates the novel by some twenty years: *The Partisan Leader*'s title page lists 1856, not 1836, as the year of publication. In doing so, Tucker further emphasizes the novel's status as speculative fiction. More than anything else, Tucker's novel seems aimed at influencing contemporary opinion and events in order to avert the future he projects. The novel was rushed to print in the summer of 1836 in the dim hopes of influencing the outcome of the presidential election. It appeared as a two-volume edition that September. A few weeks later, Martin Van Buren won the presidency with the help of Virginia's electoral votes.

Much like "The Country in 1950, or The Conservatism of Slavery," *The Partisan Leader* appeals to posterity as the only able judge of the whirligig moments Tucker both addresses (that is, 1836) and imagines (that is, 1848–49 and 1856). Time alone can tell what fruits sectional strife will bear. And yet, just like L.C.B., Tucker cannot help but speculate on what time's tale will be. In narrating the secession of Virginia from the Union and attesting to its success as a "sovereign and independent" entity circa 1856, Tucker offers a prospective glimpse of a new southern nation that is "pure, agricultural, and nondemocratic" (McCardell 162). As John McCardell notes, for Tucker the "ideal society lay in the not-too-distant future, when the South, led by a reinvigorated Virginia, would restore its lost grandeur in a Southern nation" (175).

This bizarre novel and the future(s) it imagines may be read most fruitfully not in terms of its accuracy as a prophecy or presagement of the American Civil War but instead in relation to the nullification crises of the early to mid-1830s and in the shadow of the 1831 Nat Turner rebellion, which, as Carl Bridenbaugh reminds us, would have been very much on Tucker's mind in the early 1830s (N. B. Tucker, *The Partisan Leader* [1933], xxv–xxvii). At least one contemporary reviewer, Judge Abel Parker Upshur, recognized the novel's deep relationship to that context. In the January 1837 issue of the *Messenger*—the final issue of Poe's tenure and the one that included his review of Tucker's other novel, *George Balcombe*—Upshur published an impassioned, fourteen-page essay on *The Partisan Leader*.

Upshur, who would later become U.S. Secretary of the Navy and eventually Secretary of State, was in 1837 Judge of the General Court of Virginia, and his political sympathies are everywhere on display in the essay. Less a review than a series of long digressions on legal and social issues of the day, the essay recurrently loses sight of the novel altogether as Upshur holds forth on the U.S. Constitution, federalism, nullification, the Alien and Sedition Acts, the tariff, political nepotism, the "fraud, violence and usurpation" of the Jackson administration, abolitionism and domestic slavery, and the cultural differences between "the Roundhead and the Cavalier" (3: 79–80). In doing so he makes only cursory gestures toward the novel; for instance, "Many a man, like Mr. High Trevor in the book before us, yet supports the government from an undefined fear of worse evils from opposing it" (81).[45]

Yet, however brief, Upshur's commentary on the novel renders intelligible *The Partisan Leader*'s relationship to both its own vanishing present and pre-Confederate southern literary culture more broadly. First and foremost, Upshur locates Tucker's speculative fiction in its immediate historical context. He suggests that the anonymous author has "thought profoundly and with deep interest on the remarkable public events of the last few years; has understood their true character and tendencies, and has formed his own conclusions in regard to their probable effects on our future destiny. What these conclusions are he plainly tells us; but whether they are right or wrong, the future alone can determine" (73). Because he understands the "true character and tendencies" of his moment, Tucker is able, Upshur suggests, to project a "probable" future to which contemporary readers can and should respond.

The rhetoric of probability pervades the essay, and Upshur uses it to great effect to rally his readers to action:

> The reader rises from the perusal of the book with solemn impressions of the probable truth of all the writer's speculations; and he naturally asks himself, by what means the evils he has seen depicted may be prevented. His patriotic emotions are not suffered to waste themselves, in witnessing the triumph of liberty, nor to sink in despondency under the thought that the despot's power is confirmed, and that freedom struggles against it in vain. (73)[46]

To Upshur's mind, the novel has the potential to kindle readers' patriotism and thus stir them to anti-Jacksonian action. Later Upshur credits the sentimental power of the novel to its verisimilitude: "It is impossible to read his book, without imagining that the scenes he describes are actually passing before us. The incidents are all so probable, and follow each other so regularly and naturally, that we are forced to forget that we are not in the very career of the revolution which he imagines" (89). Brought fully into the novel's future tense, the sympathetic reader is paradoxically able to accept the fictionality of the future Tucker imagines because of the probability that these events will come to pass. Put another way, Upshur credits Tucker with a deft and complicated literary coup: The author encourages the reader to willfully suspend disbelief about the future he describes long enough to judge its likelihood. The result is a reading experience in which present and future come into dialectical play.

In keeping with such play, Upshur does not advocate outright secession from the Union nor treasonous actions against the federal government—at least not yet. While Upshur is at pains to voice his "sincer[e] hope" that "the future history of the country may falsify all these speculations," he also reserves the right for the South to do so at a later date, should such a "probable" future come: "If, however, a change in our institutions should take place, as there is too much reason to fear, we have in the book before us, a striking view of the course which events will probably take. The south, although the most patient people on earth, of the abuses of government, cannot bear everything" (81). This most thinly veiled threat returns readers to *of* the present of 1837, a year that would witness the onset of the Great Panic, secesia increasingly fiery debates about the annexation of Texas, and the murder of Elijah P. Lovejoy in Alton, Illinois. The year 1837 was also "in many respects the *annus mirabilis* of the literary nationalists" (Spencer, "National" 142). Upshur's incendiary essay on Tucker's troubling novel appeared the same year Emerson delivered his "The American Scholar" address and John L. Sullivan launched his *The United States Magazine and Democratic Review*. In 1837, the "future history of the country" was still very much up for grabs, and Nathaniel Beverley Tucker, Abel P. Upshur, and the *Southern Literary Messenger* were already marshaling literature and literary futurity in the service of an autonomous South.[47]

In closing this chapter, I want to return to the problem of literary harvests—to go back to the future one last time. One of Tucker's most astute critics was Vernon Parrington, who devoted a remarkable five-plus pages to Tucker and *The Partisan Leader* in the second volume of his *Main Currents in American Thought* (1927). It is in terms of literary harvest that Parrington concludes his discussion of Tucker:

> It was not granted to Beverley Tucker to know what harvests were to be gathered from his sowings. He did not live to see the fields of his beloved commonwealth drenched in the blood that he had done more than his share to let. . . . He had sown to the wind, and he would have welcomed the whirlwind. But the outcome must have broken his proud heart, and it is well that he was not spared to see his hopes turn to ashes in his mouth. (40)

This rhapsodic passage captures elegantly some of the contingency and provisionality with which Tucker—and indeed all pre-Confederate southern literary nationalists—struggled. Writing about an uncertain and inscrutable future, and writing to a complex and conflicted present, Tucker and the other writers treated in this chapter sowed the seeds of a southern literary nationalism, for better or worse, with or without clear intention or design. The whirlwind into which they cast those seeds did not abate until well after Appomattox—and, some might argue, until nearly one hundred years after that.[48]

The history of southern literary nationalist discourse in the three decades prior to the American Civil War thus provides a history of the future—or, better, a history of possible futures. After all, the coming of the American Civil War was never inevitable; any number of alternative outcomes was possible at any number of points in time. It is too easy to allow the catastrophic and eventually redemptive future that was to come—secession, civil war, emancipation, reconstruction, Jim Crow, civil rights—to eclipse the other once possible futures that southern literary nationalists imagined. Because literary nationalism exists first and foremost as an aspirational state of being—intentions rather than results, struggles rather than successes—those once possible futures are all the more urgent. Such futures mark early and crucial moments in a process of cultural integration that helped give rise to both the Confederate States of America and a fervent Confederate literary culture.

CHAPTER TWO

A New Experiment in the Art of Book-Making

Engendering the Confederate National Novel

> For wars are not men's property. Rather, wars destroy and
> bring into being men *and* women as particular *identities*
> by canalizing energy and giving permission to narrate.
> —Jean Bethke Elshtain, *Women and War*

> We seem unable to entertain the possibility that
> traditions, or even individual texts, could be radical
> on some issues (market capitalism, for example) and
> reactionary on others (gender or race, for instance).
> Or that some discourses could be oppositional without
> being outright liberating. Or conservative without being
> outright enslaving.
> —Lora Romero, *Home Fronts*

In the scant criticism that attends Augusta Jane Evans's Confederate nation-alist novel *Macaria; or Altars of Sacrifice* (1864), there is an anecdote retold with almost absurd regularity: that Evans's immensely popular wartime novel was deemed "contraband and dangerous" by Union general G. H. Thomas, who, it is said, forbid his troops from reading it (Fidler, *Augusta Evans Wilson* 107). Here a self-congratulatory Evans writes to her editor, J. C. Derby: "Are you aware that 'Macaria' was seized and destroyed by some Federal general who commanded in Kentucky and Tennessee, and who burned all the copies—Confederate edition—which crossed from rebeldom?" (Derby 393). This perhaps apocryphal anecdote about the ideological threat Evans's red-blooded novel posed to Union "hearts and minds" is a seductive one for writers, editors, and literary critics because it affirms that, in times of war, literature does indeed matter.[1]

Whether or not General Thomas really suppressed Evans's dense, ferociously pro-Confederate novel is somewhat beside the point. *Macaria* was certainly a well-read novel in both the South and the North during and after the American Civil War. Following its April 1864 publication in Richmond, Virginia, *Macaria* became the "literary sensation of the last years of the Confederacy," entering an unprecedented second edition and selling some twenty thousand copies by the end of the year (Harwell and Crandall xiii; Fahs 143). Despite its "dangerous and contraband" status, it was also reprinted in both New York and London within months of its Confederate publication. However, in the nearly 150 years since its sensational publication, *Macaria* has fallen out of critical and popular favor. Perhaps because the southern Confederacy for which it advocated was short lived, or perhaps because it remains bewilderingly difficult to read, today *Macaria* is treated as a piece of wartime propaganda and largely ignored.

This challenging novel was written by an equally challenging historical agent, Augusta Jane Evans, who cuts a confounding and contradictory figure. Because her novels evince an unshakable belief in the "ambitions and capabilities of women," she is often read in progressive, quasi-feminist terms (Skaggs 227). Yet Evans was also a "proper southern woman" who throughout her long career promulgated a profoundly conservative social politics. To take but one example, while she saw the deleterious effects of slavery on southern womanhood, Evans was also a steadfast racialist who remained largely silent on the most pressing social and political issue of her day. Such contradictions notwithstanding, Evans was among the most popular novelists of the nineteenth century. Her 1867 novel, *St. Elmo*, is believed to be the century's third-best-selling American novel, behind only *Uncle Tom's Cabin* and *Ben-Hur* (McCandless, "Augusta Jane Evans Wilson" 151). An early advocate of international copyright law and a would-be Confederate historian, political theorist, and military strategist, Evans put herself in contact with such Civil War luminaries as General P. G. T. Beauregard and Confederate congressman J. L. M. Curry. Her wartime novel bears the mark of that contact; it also speaks resoundingly to her total investment in the Confederate cause. As Evans would later say, "The sole enthusiasm of my life was born, lived, and perished in the eventful four years of the Confederacy" (qtd. in McCandless, "Augusta Jane Evans Wilson" 152). And her "*very heart beat in* [Macaria's] *pages*" (Derby 393).

While such "enthusiasm" and "heart" are indeed everywhere in the pages of *Macaria*, my interest here is in charting the relationship between Evans's novel and its immediate historical context. As the cultural sociologist Pierre Bourdieu notes, one of the "major difficulties" in offering a social history of literature comes in reconstructing the "spaces of original possibles which, because they were part of the self-evident givens of the situation, remained unremarked" (31). I argue that because of its intimate and dynamic relation to the Confederate national moment, *Macaria* offers unique access to the "spaces of original possibles" that were foreclosed the moment Robert E. Lee surrendered at Appomattox Court House. That is, *Macaria* returns readers to an unsettled moment in which the outcome of the American Civil War was far from determined.

Macaria was one of a very small number of original novels published in the South during the war and certainly the most accomplished. While it had little real competition for the honorific "Confederate national novel"—*Macaria* entered a literary field more or less absent serious Confederate fiction—its achievement is nonetheless impressive. Exploiting a series of deft textual effects, the novel elegantly manages tensions between the local and the national by presenting a delocalized, resolutely nationalistic narrative with a decidedly international set of intertexts. In turn, with its precise timeliness, *Macaria* also captures the sacrifices demanded and the upheavals brought on by the war. This is particularly the case with Evans's representation of wartime "Womanly Usefulness," a phenomenon she thought essential to the hopes of Confederate independence. Finally, in both representing the "determined militancy of Confederate women during the Civil War" and making women's political discourse a central presence in the narrative, Evans essentially remakes the southern domestic novel—outfitting it, as it were, for war (Elshtain 96).

The Improbability of the Confederate National Novel

It was no mean feat that *Macaria* accomplished any of this. Indeed, it is somewhat surprising that the novel even found its way into print in the Confederate States. All of the publishing difficulties discussed in the introduction—a limited number of presses and publishers, a single type foundry in the whole South, little available paper, scant skilled labor—were particular problems for long-form Confederate fiction. Even though Evans had a "significant national reputation" before the secession of the southern states—her 1859 novel, *Beulah*, made her one of the most commercially viable of the "southern domestics"—the prospects of getting her manuscript published in the South, during the war, in a timely fashion, were not good (Faust, *Mothers* 168). By locating her novel within its field of cultural production, readers gain a much fuller sense of its accomplishment and its oddity.

The bibliographer Richard Harwell counted a mere fifty-nine pieces of fiction published in the Confederate States during the war (*Confederate Belles-Lettres*). According to the 1987 Parrish and Willingham bibliography, which revised and updated Harwell's many Confederate bibliographies, the figure is slightly smaller. Of these, only a handful can be considered original (that is, published for the first time during the war), and few have page counts that can be considered long form (that is, more than one hundred pages). By my count, there were only seven original, novel-length pieces of fiction published in the Confederacy between 1861 and 1865: *The Step-Sister* (Richmond: Ayres and Wade, 1863), which, despite its 260-page length, was marketed as a "Novelette"; Alexander St. Clair Abrams's *The Trials of the Soldier's Wife* (Atlanta: Intelligencer Steam Power Presses, 1864); Sallie Rochester Ford's *Raids and Romance of Morgan and His Men* (Mobile: S. H. Goetzel, 1863); James Dabney McCabe Jr.'s *The Aid-De-Camp; A Romance of the War* (Richmond: W. A. J. Smith, 1863); William Henry Peck's *The Conspirators of New Orleans* (Greenville: Peck and Wells, 1863); Ebenezer W. Warren's *Nellie Norton; or Southern Slavery and the Bible* (Macon: Burke, Boykin, 1864); and *Macaria*.[2]

In lieu of original novels, the field of Confederate fiction was dominated by a vibrant culture of reprinting, one that repackaged earlier American texts (both southern and northern) and brought European novels into southern homes. As Robert H. Woody notes, such reprints were "needed to fill the gulf between the dreams of an autonomous southern literature and the reality of wartime publishing industry" (preface to Harwell, *Confederate Belles-Lettres* 8). For instance, in 1863 Burke, Boykin, and Company reprinted Georgian Francis Robert Goulding's *Robert and Harold; or the Young Marooners on the Florida Coast*, a historical romance originally published in 1852. In 1864, the same firm brought out an edition of Augustus Baldwin Longstreet's first novel, *Master William Mitten: or, A Youth of Brilliant Talents, Who Was Ruined by Bad Luck*, which had been serialized in the *Southern Field and Fireside* in 1859. While neither of these were original Confederate novels, they did make available to Confederate readers a discernibly southern literature at a moment of intense nationalist feeling.

Similarly, in reprinting Mary Elizabeth Davis's novelette, *The British Partizan: A Tale of the Olden Time* (1864), Burke, Boykin, and Company marketed an older southern text as being relevant to the Confederate national moment. Originally published in the late 1830s in the short-lived *Augusta Mirror*, the novelette tells a romantic tale of Revolutionary-era Georgia and South Carolina. Lamenting how *The British Partizan* had "passed out of print, and in time out of the memory of the public," the editors believed that Confederate readers would find much of interest in its pages. As they argue, "it is a story peculiarly suited to the times in which we live," since it is "a tale of true love, wrought out amid the stirring scenes and harsh vicissitudes of partizan strife" (3).

Not surprisingly, Nathaniel Beverley Tucker's *The Partisan Leader* was also reprinted in the Confederacy as *The Partisan Leader: A Novel, and an Apocalypse of the Origin and Struggles of the Southern Confederacy* (Richmond: West and Johnston, 1862). As its subtitle suggests, this edition emphasizes Tucker's purported powers of prophecy (cf. "Apocalypse," def. 1). Tucker's latter-day editor, the Reverend Thomas A. Ware, goes so far as to call the novel a "great prophetic story, whose thrilling events have been essentially fulfilled" (vii). He also sees in the republication of the 1836 novel an opportunity "to illustrate the necessity of our position, to vindicate the justice of our cause, and to intensify Southern patriotism" (viii). In making Tucker's "Tale of the Future" available to the inhabitants of that future, Ware hopes to shore up nationalist feeling and allow Confederate readers to locate their struggles within a historical context. Thus, properly repackaged and marketed, an unoriginal novel can prove both utterly timely for, and of imminent use to, the Confederate cause.[3]

While Burke, Boykin, and Company focused on reprinting American fiction, other publishers looked abroad for their source texts. For instance, S. H. Goetzel's wartime publishing list was distinguished by a number of European titles, including reprints of Bulwer-Lytton's *A Strange Story*, Charles Dickens's *Great Expectations*, George Eliot's *Silas Marner*, Julian Fane and Bulwer-Lytton's poem *Tannhauser*, and the first two American editions of novels by Clara Mundt (Luise Mühlbach) as translated by Mrs. Adelaide de Vendel Chaudron. Goetzel, an Austrian emigrant to Mobile, Alabama, discovered a burgeoning market for these foreign works, and other Confederate publishers soon followed his lead (Harwell, *Confederate Belles-Lettres* 20; cf. Bell).

Confederate editions of Victorian novelists were a particular favorite in the South during the war, with Wilkie Collins (*No Name*), Dinah Maria Craik (*Mistress and Maid: A Household Story*), and William Makepeace Thackeray (*The Adventures of Philip on His Way through the World*) all finding their way onto the Confederate market. The hugely popular sensationalist M. E. Braddon was the most reprinted of foreign authors, with five of the prolific novelist's titles appearing during the war. In addition, the French novelists Paul Féval and Octave Feuillet each had novels reprinted in the Confederate States. Although the resulting editions of foreign works tended to be less than stellar productions, they gave a Eurocentric cast to Confederate literary culture.[4]

Richmond's West and Johnston was by far the most enterprising Confederate publisher of fiction. It was also by wide consensus the most important publishing firm in the Confederacy—the "Appletons and Harpers of the South" (*SLM* 34 [March 1862]: 208)—and the one with which Evans entrusted *Macaria*. In addition to its relatively robust resources, West and Johnston had, according to the February 1863 issue of the *Messenger*, contracts with a number of English firms "to receive and sell [in the Confederacy] their latest publications, and to remunerate English authors for their labors" (35: 118). Claiming that "[h]itherto foreign writers have been robbed, by Yankee swindlers, of the fruits of their genius" in "a system of legalized piracy," the *Messenger* touts the Confederacy's extension of international copyright protection to the authors of any country that acknowledged the C.S.A. (118). As a result, West and Johnston brought to the Confederate States novels by Braddon, Collins, Craik, and Feuillet, as well as *Brown and Arthur* (1861), a text advertised as an episode from Thomas Hughes's ubiquitous 1857 British novel *Tom Brown's School Days*, and two of Ellen (Price) Wood's wildly popular novels, *East Lynne* and *Mrs. Halliburton's Troubles.*[5]

Yet the apex of West and Johnston's international literary ambitions was its five-volume edition of Victor Hugo's *Les Misérables* (1863–64). Upon its publication in Paris in April and May 1862, Hugo's capacious novel became an immediate international popular success, with English, Greek, Italian, and Portuguese translations appearing within two years of publication. West and Johnston based its edition of the novel on the 1862 Charles Edwin Wilbour translation, which had been published in New York by Carleton on 7 June 1862. Although the Wilbour translation provided the basis for the reprint, the Confederate edition aimed to correct "numerous errors and misapprehensions of peculiar French idioms, some of them even of a ludicrous nature" (iv). To this end, West and Johnston retained the services of Alexander Dimitry, a prominent translator and former U.S. minister to Costa Rica and Nicaragua (1858–61), who, due to other commitments, was able to retranslate only portions of the first forty-nine pages of the first volume of the novel.[6] The Confederate edition also removed from *Les Misérables* several "rather rambling disquisitions on political and other matters of a purely local character . . . exclusively intended for the French readers of the book," abridging significantly the thousand-plus-page novel (iv). These cuts may also have made Hugo's depiction of republican revolt more universal and thus more relevant to Confederate readers, many of whom believed that the American Civil War would determine the future of "Republican Liberty." Most urgently, the Confederate editor confesses to having suppressed a "few scattered sentences, reflecting on slavery—which the author, with strange inconsistency, has thought fit to introduce into a work written mainly to denounce the European systems of labor as gigantic instruments of tyranny and oppression" (1: iv). The editor hopes that "the absence of a few antislavery paragraphs will hardly be complained of by Southern readers," many of whom wanted to studiously avoid any further discussion of slavery while the war raged on (iv).[7] With these expurgations in place, the first two volumes of the Confederate *Les Misérables, Fantine* and *Cosette*, appeared in summer 1863 and sold extremely well. The novel purportedly became a favorite among Confederate soldiers, leading to the famous *Les Misérables*/"Lee's Miserables" pun. Indeed, Harwell considers the Confederate *Les Misérables* one of "probably the two most popular books of the war" (*Confederate Belles-Lettres* 20)— the other being *Macaria*.[8]

The Confederate culture of reprinting I have outlined here begs us to look again at the fiction published and republished in the South during the American Civil War. While Confederate fiction did little to add to a distinctively southern literature per se, it was distinguished by its increasingly transatlantic interests. When we take a bit longer view of this culture of reprinting, we find not a fallow literary field but instead a cultivated one, replete with a diverse set of authors representing a number of national literary traditions. Again, while these diverse Confederate fiction lists were in no way coordinated, they do suggest both a literary culture and reading publics that were far more worldly than has been previously assumed.[9]

Returning to the novel at hand, when *Macaria* was finally published in April 1864, it entered a literary field crowded with slight, pro-Confederate novelettes and reprinted European novels. As an original, novel-length piece of fiction at least in part about the American Civil War, *Macaria* was unusual, if not quite sui generis. Like Ford's *Raids and Romance of Morgan and His Men* and McCabe's *The Aid-De-Camp*, Evans's novel aimed to document current events and bolster Confederate war efforts. Yet as a novel invested in European literary traditions and sporting a decidedly international set of intertexts, *Macaria* also sat comfortably beside a number of Confederate reprints (for example, the novels of Clara Mundt). Thus, a good deal of *Macaria*'s exceptionality comes from its ability to complement texts positioned throughout the Confederate literary field (Bourdieu 45–52). Understood in the context of its literary field, Evans's novel emerges as the Confederate national novel par excellence—an idiosyncratic representative of an improbable genre.

Location, Location, Location

In October and November 1859, before there was a Confederate nation, much less a Confederate national novel, the *Mobile (Ala.) Daily Advertiser* ran a series of articles on the differences between southern and northern literary cultures. The mid-twentieth-century literary critic and biographer William Perry Fidler has argued persuasively that the author of these pithy, anonymous articles was Augusta Jane Evans, whose immediate antebellum pronouncements provide something of prolegomenon for her bellum novel writing. Published at the height of the cold war discussed at length in the previous chapter, Evans's first two articles, "Northern Literature" (11 and 16 October 1859), advance an aggressive critique of the decadence of northern periodical literature. Decrying its "decided tendency to evil" and deeming it "a disgrace to its authors and insulting to the intelligence of the American people," Evans figures northern periodical literature as a vile, "contaminating" threat to "the rising generation" (11 October).

Such alarmist rhetoric, with its performative concern for "our children" and calls for caution, gives way to a subtle extended metaphor. Evans warns: "[W]e of the south are drifting unconsciously into the wake of a vessel which, if it continues its course, will soon dash to fragments and all on board will be involved in a common destruction. There is a way to stop this current of events and it is the press of the country not yet involved in the stream to utter its sentiments with that irresistible power, which, as a unit it possesses" (11 October). The duty is not merely to right the proverbial ship but also to get out of a path of "common destruction" and chart an alternative course for the South. Here, some twenty-five years after James Ewell Heath's opening editorial in the *Southern Literary Messenger*, the twenty-five-year-old Evans becomes part of the second generation of southern literary nationalists to urge the South to "utter its sentiments."[10]

In the issue for 16 October 1859—in an eerie bit of irony, the first day of John Brown's raid on Harpers Ferry—Evans was much more specific about the sort of evil that appeared in the pages of northern periodicals. Evans holds that the "most prolific source of the evils of society" is the "pernicious principle that *anything* may be said through a newspaper, regardless of its tendency." Her example of such evil is a telling one, offered with no small amount of pith and pathos:

> The low sensual African is dragged up from his normal position and violently thrust into an importance which the Creator had denied him by indications as strong as physical inferiority and mental incapacity could make them. The demons of pandemonium are actually prowling through the Northern States, making efforts to tear down fabrics which genius, guided by the wisdom and experience of past ages, have erected, and the echo of their dismal howlings finds as ready access to Southern ears as the wisdom of the great and good. All comes to us mingled over the same pages, and if we take the one we must have the other also.

Evans is clearly referencing abolitionist periodical literature. Casting the debate about African slavery in religious and Manichean terms, Evans effectively inverts standard abolitionist arguments about the moral and religious implications of the peculiar institution. To Evans's mind, the "Northern States"—and not, for instance, Simon Legree's plantation—is hell on earth. Furthermore, God is on the side of the southern states since, in Evans's racialist thinking, "the Creator" decreed for the African a "normal position" as "low sensual" and presumably subjugated. Here Evans laments that the "dismal howlings" of abolitionists and the "wisdom of the great and good" coexist on the same periodical pages, placing the southerner in a precarious readerly position.

Having specified the types of periodical literature that give her the gravest concern, Evans returns to what is "great and good" in the wicked northern press. After framing her articles as a discussion of regional literary cultures, Evans unexpectedly rejects the very idea of a local or localized literature, suggesting that what is "great and good" is in fact national in character: "American writers have contributed some of the most noble monuments to English literature. Many of these writers have been born and bred in the North, but because of this circumstance the South is not less proud of their productions than the North. Such literature is not local in its character; it is national, and should be treated as such" (16 October). Evans marshals as evidence the fact that "Our great Dictionaries are national. . . . Our great Histories are national." She goes on to suggest that "[o]ur great political essayists know no locality, they are the sons of the nation," and to celebrate the "conservative spirit" of her favorite sons: Daniel Webster (born in New Hampshire), John C. Calhoun (South Carolina), Henry Clay (Kentucky), George Washington (Virginia), Thomas Jefferson (Virginia), and James Madison (Virginia).

Given her lambasting of northern periodical literature, we might expect Evans's final two articles, "Southern Literature" (30 October and 6 November 1859), to champion the conservative virtues of southern periodical literature; however, they do much more than that. Among many other things, the articles offer a refreshingly clear-eyed assessment of antebellum southern literature, clarify and deepen the critique of local literature, and betray Evans's resolutely international aspirations for literature produced in the South.

Writing for the 30 October 1859 *Mobile Advertiser*, Evans bemoans a "rapidly growing tendency among Southern writers of the present day to extol with indiscriminate praise whatever proceeds from a Southern pen, and to berate, with unbecoming severity, whatever originates on the other side of the 'Mason and Dixon's line.'" Seeming to echo Poe, Evans rejects outright the "principle which would lead Southerners to praise and even glorify everything Southern, regardless of quality." Instead, she advocates a discerning national literary criticism, one willing to "las[h] with sharp reproof everything unsound in substance and objectionable in point of style," be it northern or southern in origin.[11]

Evans also returns to the problem of "a literature purely local," calling it one of the chief "cause of the complaints" against southern literature. To her mind, southern authors hold "no higher aspirations than to create what they choose to denominate a Southern literature." In a bravura criticism, Evans deems such regional ambitions limited:

This idea of *creating* a Southern literature is the incentive, it is true, of all our efforts, but it is one which crushes rather than expands our thoughts, and crushes all the more fetally as it carries with it the ordinary allurements of a deceiver. A writer is likely to reach the goal of his ambition just in proportion to his breadth of view. If an author writes for a particular section, if he appeals to the sympathies of that section, if he professes to have special regard for it, in short, if he localizes himself on any ground, ten chances to one he is pronounced a poor fellow by the very community for which he professes to feel so deeply, and left after a little time without a reader anywhere. On the contrary, let him rise above special pleading and write for the people who speak the English language, and he will have honor even in his own country. (30 October)

The southern author is, Evans posits, hemmed in by her or his sectional ambition and "breadth of view." Localization leads ineluctably to provincialism. In sharp contradistinction to calls for a distinctively southern literature, Evans calls for writing that would transcend rather than represent the South, its people, cultures, and traditions.

In urging southern authors to write not merely for other southerners but "for the people who speak the English language," Evans also hints at her international ambitions for southern literature. In the final of the four articles, she makes clear such ambitions: "We desire that what proceeds from Southern pens shall be read wherever the English language is spoken and read" (6 November). Southern authors should, Evans argues, eschew localism and write for an impossibly broad audience: the entire Anglophone world. She does not want southern literature merely to best or trump northern literature; she wants southern literature to make a contribution to, and become an essential part of, an international republic of letters. Thus, Evans has broadly imperial aspirations for southern literature. She campaigns not for intranational dominance but for international reading publics: again, "wherever the English language is spoken and read."

Latent in Evans's argument for southern literary distinction is a deeply Jeffersonian understanding of the relationship between agrarian industry and literary culture. Evans avers, "[T]here is no class of people in the United States from whom so much is to be expected as the Southern planter. There is no other class which at present can command time to attend properly to the interests of the country, and there is no class from which we have a clearer right to demand contributions which shall reflect credit upon our literature" (6 November 1859). She cites as examples of this class Washington, Jefferson, Madison, Calhoun, Clay, and Webster. Opposing the acquisition of wealth, with which "[a]ll other classes are earnestly engaged," with "intellectual culture," Evans call for a southern planter presence in national politics as well, and then posits a subtle sympathy between the British aristocracy and the southern planter class: "Next to the British aristocrat we know of no position in the world more desirable than that of the southern planter" (6 November 1859).[12]

In articulating this unconventional program for southern literature, Evans largely rejects the history of the "agitation of the literary question" treated in chapter 1. She notes flatly, "We read too much in our papers and reviews about the necessity of creating a Southern literature, a literature of our own" (6 November). She also snipes at the glut of periodicals in the South "whose object is distinctly avowed in the use of the word 'Southern' as an important part of their titles." Espying the literary field to the North, she notes ruefully, "We do not now call to mind a single newspaper or periodical of any kind in the North, which designates by its title, its objects to be peculiarly Northern. If there is such a paper, then the tendency of it is to make of the North a mere province and its literature provincial" (6 November).

With this line of argumentation, Evans quietly addresses what Richard Gray calls the "familiar series of oppositions" by which the South and southernness are defined against a national other. As Gray notes, such definition proceeds via a binaristic logic: "'southern' versus 'American'/'northern' (the slippage between these two terms is, in itself, a measure of the Southern sense of aberrance)" (499). Because such a slippage was extant in 1859, it should come as little surprise that northern periodicals would prefer to flaunt on their mastheads their nationness rather than their northernness (for example, the *North American Review*, the *United States Democratic Review*). In emphasizing the national over the regional, northern periodicals avoid the pitfalls of provincialism. Evans wants southern literature to follow suit, widening its purview both in name and in deed.[13]

Peculiarly, then, Evans couches her advocacy for a delocalized, cosmopolitan southern literature in terms of nationalism. She describes "our argument in favor of directing all our energies towards the building up of a *national* literature" (6 November). Such nationalist rhetoric is frustratingly vague, in no small part because Evans's use of it seems inconsistent. For instance, she closes her final article by calling for the founding of a southern review "conducted on the general principles adopted by corresponding publications in England" and representative of "the national mind" (6 November). Elsewhere in the same article, she urges the South to "keep up our end of the national literary reputation." The former implies the existence of a separate southern national mind; the latter suggests that Evans wants to build up the reputation of American literature more broadly. Such vagueness notwithstanding, it is clear that, circa 1859, Evans saw national literary cultures as the locus of "great and good" writing. Here Evans theorizes literary nationalism as a much needed antidote to unambitious and provincial literary cultures and as an entrée to international reading publics. Such theory became praxis just a few years later, with the emergences of the Confederate States of America and Evans's red-blooded nationalist novel, *Macaria*.[14]

Macaria's nationalist cultural work begins in earnest on its second recto page, with a sinewy and loquacious tribute to the "ARMY OF THE SOUTH-ERN CONFEDERACY":

TO THE

ARMY OF THE SOUTHERN CONFEDERACY,

WHO HAVE DELIVERED THE SOUTH FROM DESPOTISM, AND WHO HAVE WON FOR

GENERATIONS YET UNBORN THE PRECIOUS GUERDON OF

CONSTITUTIONAL REPUBLICAN LIBERTY:

TO THIS VAST LEGION OF HONOR,

WHETHER LIMPING ON CRUTCHES THROUGH

THE LAND THEY HAVE SAVED AND IMMORTALIZED,

OR SURVIVING UNINJURED TO SHARE THE BLESSINGS THEIR

UNEXAMPLED HEROISM BOUGHT, OR SLEEPING DREAMLESSLY IN NAMELESS

MARTYR-GRAVES ON HALLOWED BATTLE-FIELDS WHOSE

HISTORIC MEMORY SHALL PERISH ONLY WITH

THE REMNANTS OF OUR LANGUAGE,

THESE PAGES ARE

GRATEFULLY AND REVERENTLY DEDICATED

BY ONE WHO, ALTHOUGH DEBARRED FROM THE

DANGERS AND DEATHLESS GLORY OF THE "TENTED FIELD,"

WOULD FAIN OFFER A WOMAN'S INADEQUATE TRIBUTE TO THE NOBLE

PATRIOTISM AND SUBLIME SELF-ABNEGATION OF HER

DEAR AND DEVOTED COUNTRYMEN. (3)[15]

This "much admired" dedication collects and consolidates a series of commonplace Confederate nationalist sentiments into an affective, and perhaps affecting, encomium (*Richmond Age* January 1865: 393). Present here is the hue and cry of northern "DESPOTISM," invocations of the Confederacy's defense of "CONSTITUTIONAL REPUBLICAN LIBERTY," and the charged rhetorics of "HONOR," "HEROISM," "MARTYR[DOM]," "PATRIOTISM," and "GLORY." Predictably, specters of maimed bodies ("LIMPING ON CRUTCHES") and dead soldiers ("SLEEPING DREAMLESSLY") haunt the margins of this text. If the dedication remains cagey about the actual outcome of the war—see, for instance, its deft conjunction "THE LAND THEY HAVE SAVED AND IMMORTALIZED" and the strange shifts in verb tense throughout—it is also insistently prophetic about the "GENERATIONS YET UNBORN" who will inherit the victories the army has won.

Among the many things that Evans's garrulous dedication accomplishes is the reification of a Confederate national community. Through a series of more or less performative utterances, the dedication does not simply celebrate the Confederacy and its "vast legion of honor"; it renders that Confederacy worthy of a vast legion of honor. Even in advance of its actual defeat, the South is figured in this elegiac dedication as the sort of "spiritual nation" or "redemptive community" that both Lewis P. Simpson and Benedict Anderson place at the heart of any nationalism (Simpson 203; Anderson passim). In emphasizing the nascent nation's sacrifices—the novel is, after all, subtitled "The Altars of Sacrifice"—Evans marshals loss in the service of nation building.

This is in many ways a predictable move, since death often helps to embody the nation and the national. Speaking of the necessary "fatality" of the imagined community, Anderson evinces a recurrent, perhaps perseverative interest in how and why "people are ready to die for these inventions" of their imaginations (141). "Why," Anderson asks, do nations "command such profound emotional legitimacy?" (4). Haunted by the violent deaths of "citizen soldiers," *Imagined Communities* concludes that there is in such sacrifice "something fundamentally pure," a sort of "moral grandeur," "an idea of purity, through fatality" (144). As Evans's dedication makes clear, death for one's country is not merely grand; it is in fact necessary in order for that country to become a viable nation, for nationality to be, as Walt Whitman would have it, "lastingly condense[d]."[16]

To say that these are commonplace sentiments is not to denigrate the presence of this dedication in *Macaria*'s front matter. This is, after all, an uncharacteristically lengthy and detailed dedication. As Gerard Genette reminds us, by the nineteenth century the dedicatory epistle had fallen out of favor, replaced most often by what he calls a "motivated" dedication, "a brief characterization of the dedicatee and/or of the work being dedicated" (125). We might think here (as Genette does) of Melville's dedication of *Moby-Dick* to Nathaniel Hawthorne: "In token / of my admiration for his genius, / this book is inscribed / to / Nathaniel Hawthorne" (v). However, *Macaria*'s dedication goes into almost painful detail about both the dedicatee and dedicator. Of particular note is the subtle introduction of female agency and authorship in the dedication's last half. The phrase "A WOMAN'S INADEQUATE TRIBUTE" both conjures and negates what Evans called wartime "Womanly Usefulness." (After all, this "INADEQUATE" tribute will soon be deemed "dangerous and contraband.") Although "DEBARRED" from "THE DANGERS AND DEATHLESS GLORY" of actual battle, the "WOMAN" in question wages war—for women's rights, cultural memory, and "CONSTITUTIONAL REPUBLICAN LIBERTY"—on the pages of her novel. This dedication becomes, then, her opening salvo.[17]

In lavishing such attention on the front matter of this book, I have perhaps made too much of too little. After all, one can't judge a book by its dedication page—unless one is a wartime editor of the *Southern Literary Messen-*

ger. In a "Literary Notice" for *Macaria* in its penultimate issue, the latter-day editor of the *Messenger* declares:

> We are satisfied that "Macaria" will fully realize in power, interest and general attractiveness the justly fastidious requirements which public taste will exact from it in view of its having the same authorship with Beulah. The hasty perusal which we have been compelled to give it, just as we are placing our last page in the hands of the printer, while it has assured us of the superior merit of "Macaria" has by no means satisfied our desire for a more familiar acquaintance with its beauties of style and manner.
>
> We are convinced of its great superiority to any similar production of Southern writers during the war, and are pleased to note its appearance as the most promising indication that we have yet seen of a future elevated standard of Fiction among Southern authors. (38 [May 1864]: 317)[18]

Given such a "hasty perusal," we cannot help but wonder what elements of the book would have led the reviewer to so quickly conclude *Macaria*'s "great superiority" as a "most promising indication" of the "future elevated standard of Fiction among Southern authors." What about *Macaria*'s "appearance" was so striking? Such heavy-handed literary nationalism must have taken root somewhere in that "hasty perusal."

I want to suggest that to both the hasty and the careful reader this extraordinary dedication may have provided just such a rooting. In celebrating the "NOBLE PATRIOTISM AND SUBLIME SELF ABNEGATION OF HER DEAR AND DEVOTED COUNTRYMEN," Evans leaves little doubt as to her political sympathies and steadfast belief in the cause of southern independence. By laying bare the novel's politics, Evans's dedication works to ensure *Macaria*'s reception as a nationalist novel. This is a particularly important textual effect since, as we will see, Evans remains relatively silent on political issues until nearly halfway through the novel. Thus, the dedication assumes what Genette calls a "prefacing function," offering readers a statement of the novel's subject and purpose (125).[19]

While Evans's dedication goes a long way to nationalizing *Macaria*, the narrative's relentless geographical indeterminacy also works to delocalize the novel, ensuring that it will not become, in Evans's words, "a literature purely local." The majority of *Macaria*'s action takes place in the town of "W——." Over the course of nearly two hundred two-column pages, we never learn in which state W—— is located, simply that it is in a secession state (see esp. 133). More to the point, W—— is not described in any detail until chapter 15, nearly halfway through the novel:

> The society of W—— was considered remarkably fine. There was quite an aggregation of wealth and refinement; gentlemen, whose plantations were situated

in adjacent counties, resided here, with their families; some, who spent their winters on the seaboard, resorted here for the summer; its bar was said to possess more talent than any other in the state; its schools claimed to be unsurpassed; it boasted of a concert-hall, a lyceum, a handsome court-house, a commodious, well-built jail, and half-a-dozen as fine churches as any country-town could desire. I would fain avoid the term, if possible, but no synonym exists—W—— was, indisputably, an "aristocratic" place. (73)

W—— is, in short, the very ideal of a refined, plantation-based municipality. In addition to its ample wealth, the town offers culture, learning, religion, and the rule of law; even its jails are "commodious, [and] well-built."[20]

Given the "fine" people who live there—the men of W—— tend to be gallant and courageous, the women "queenly" and self-sacrificing, the "servants" (read: slaves) loyal and contented—we might think of this as a Confederate utopia of sorts. As the narrator assures us, W—— has what "any country-town could desire." To describe W—— as a utopia is also to acknowledge its undisclosed location. The use of what Roland Barthes called an emancipated signifier (that is, "W——") to denote the setting of *Macaria* opens numerous interpretative possibilities for the reader. *W* evokes not only every southern town beginning with the letter *W* but also the very foundations of indeterminacy: who, what, when, and where. Unlike John W. De Forest's "New Boston" in *Miss Ravenel's Conversion from Secession to Loyalty* (1867), W—— is not a fictitious town in a fictitious state, merely an indeterminate town in an indeterminate state. This is indeed a place of no-place, a land nowhere (cf. "Utopia," esp. etymology).[21]

Thus *Macaria*, so ardent in its Confederate nationalist rhetoric and so clearly southern in its manners, never places itself; per Evans, it never "localizes [it]self on any ground." As Jan Bakker notes, *Macaria*'s characters "live in indeterminate geographical locations whose middle-class cottages are quaint and often vaguely English, and whose planter mansions are palatial and often vaguely Italian" (141). Bakker suggests that such "vagueness" of scene setting is "typical of the romances written by the female authors of the Old South" (134), and thus an unremarkable feature of *Macaria*. However, a zealously literary nationalistic review of Evans's previous novel, *Beulah* (1859), disagrees. The anonymous review, which appeared in the October 1860 issue of the *Southern Literary Messenger*, declares that *Beulah*'s "want of geographical location" was that novel's "most fatal error with regard [to] its interest" (31: 244). Arguing for the "necessity for definite location," the review contends, "the reader always loses interest when there is no place to locate the sympathies" (244). While such indeterminacy may indeed be "typical" of antebellum southern domestic fiction, the *Messenger*'s rhetoric of "fatal error," "necessity," and "interest" suggests that location and geographical determinacy were crucial elements of any contribution to the "dawning [of] a literature in the South" (243)—particularly at a moment of heightened sectional tension and protonationalistic feeling.[22]

Fatal error or no, *Macaria*'s indeterminate location elegantly manages the tensions between local and national affiliation. Evans deftly locates the novel in the South, in a seceding, slaveholding state, without specifying which southern, seceding, slaveholding state. Ingeniously, W—— is located at once in all Confederate states and in no Confederate state. As a result, the novel remains national without ever becoming localized. The resulting emphasis on W——'s relation to the nation, not to a specific state, helps to universalize the novel's prosouthern sentiments, removing any specific local content so that Confederate nationalism can signify above all else. This placement avoids in turn the problems of dissent and disunion that by 1864 plagued the Confederate States of America.[23]

Thus, in its insistence on a geographically indeterminate setting, *Macaria* transcends local interests in favor of national ones, gracefully sidestepping any number of vexed relationships: between the part and the whole, the state and the confederacy, and the local and the global. In choosing not to choose a definite location, *Macaria* makes its strongest claim to the title "national novel." While it would be difficult to conclude that *Macaria* rises above "special pleading"—again, this is a doggedly partisan wartime novel—it does seem to follow through on the literary program Evans outlined in her antebellum articles for the *Mobile Daily Advertiser*.

"O tempora! O mores!"

While Evans may not localize her narrative on any ground, she does temporalize it at every turn. That is, *Macaria* is an utterly timely novel; many of its battle scenes and wartime incidents are ripped from the headlines, as it were. In composing *Macaria*, Evans labored to keep the narrative both up to date and upbeat about the prospects for Confederate victory. The resulting balancing act finds Evans writing both for and about a vanishing present—no mean feat in a nearly 170,000-word piece of fiction produced at least partially during wartime. Throughout the novel, Evans marshals a number of textual effects to engender a sense of timeliness. Among the most effective of these is the sudden emergence of the threat of civil war and the novel's concomitant politics.

Macaria begins in the antebellum United States of America—not, importantly, in the Confederate States. Scant mention of mounting sectional tension appears until more than halfway through the novel. When sectionalism and the threat of war do arrive, it is as if by deus ex machina. As Evans's biographer acknowledges, "A reader who is unaware of the propagandistic motive of the author may find few materials in the early pages which distinguish this book from other novels of domestic sentimentalism" (Fidler, *Augusta Evans Wilson* 107).[24]

Indeed, without the novel's explicit dedication page, the "unaware reader" might remain oblivious to the novel's political interests until the following conversation takes place between Electra Grey and Russell Aubrey while both are visiting New York City:

> "Where are you going, Russell? Can't you spend the evening with me at Aunt Ruth's?"
>
> "No, thank you; I must go. There is to be a great political meeting at Tammany Hall tonight and I am particularly anxious to attend."
>
> "What! are you, too, engaged in watching the fermentation of the political vat?"
>
> "Yes; I am most deeply interested; no true lover of his country can fail to be so at this juncture." (96)

Up to this point in the novel, there has been no mention of a "political vat" and no description of Russell as a "true lover of his country." Through twenty chapters, neither slavery nor states' rights have warranted mention, and the relations between the South and North seem more or less peaceable. The narrative focus has been entirely on the personal ambitions of, and the complicated love triangle among, Irene Huntingdon (a wealthy and idealized plantation daughter), Electra Grey (a poor, aspiring artist, and Irene's close friend), and Russell Aubrey (the hard-working and virtuous young man both women love). Indeed, the first half of the novel seems to take place outside of time; its depiction of temporality is as slippery and as vague as its description of locality. Then, with Russell's "anxious" attendance at the political meeting, the possibility of secession and civil war explode into the novel's narrative consciousness. *Macaria*'s remaining eighty-seven two-column pages are dominated by the war and its effects.[25]

One heretofore unarticulated explanation for the sudden emergence of the Civil War in *Macaria* might be that Evans did not initially set out to write a Civil War novel but instead rewrote or reconceived a "domestic sentimenta[l]" novel-in-progress in order to incorporate the war. Fidler dates the composition of *Macaria* to between June 1862 and March 1863, suggesting that Evans "devoted every spare moment" to the novel during this period and perpetuating the romantic image of the author composing the novel by candlelight while nursing wounded Confederate soldiers (*Augusta Evans Wilson* 105). Yet, during these months Evans had very few moments to spare since she was already working tirelessly to support the Confederate cause. In addition to her work as a volunteer nurse, Evans organized sewing brigades, founded an army hospital, visited the war front, and corresponded with key figures in the

Confederate government and military (Fidler, *Augusta Evans Wilson* 90–98). As Evans herself conceded in a 20 August 1861 letter to her close friend Rachel Lyons, during the early part of the war her "thoughts ran more on rifled cannon, Confederate cotton loan, and winter uniforms for our noble soldiery, than pen, and letter" (Sexton 35; cf. 39).

In the same letter Evans writes exuberantly, "I received a letter from the Mr D a few days ago, acknowledging the receipt of my precious *MS*; and expressing himself as much pleased with it!" (35). The editor of Evans's correspondence, Rebecca Grant Sexton, speculates that "Mr D" is probably J. C. Derby, Evans's publisher and a friend of Lyons, and that the manuscript "is probably an early draft of *Macaria*" (36). If Sexton is correct about the identity of the mystery manuscript, as I believe she is, then it is possible that some version of the first half of *Macaria*—again, the half in which the Civil War is a present absence—was in hand as the war began. Between 1859 and 1869, Evans published a remarkable four novels: *Beulah* (1859), *Macaria* (1864), *St. Elmo* (1866), and *Vashti* (1869). Given that Evans was writing at such a clip, it seems perfectly reasonable to think that she would have been able to complete a novel-length manuscript in the two years between the publication of *Beulah* and the summer of 1861. This, in turn, would have left Evans a little less than two years—from late summer 1861 to 1 June 1863, the date Evans delivered the *Macaria* manuscript to West and Johnston (Sexton 88)—to revise and complete the war-centric second half. While the composition history I offer here is speculative, it would help to explain the novel's dramatic mid-narrative shift from so-called domestic to so-called political themes—impoverished critical terms to which I return at the end of the chapter.

No matter how or when Evans composed the novel, such a shift proves an effective way to document and recapitulate the upheavals caused by the American Civil War. First, because Evans is able to develop her central cast of characters for some twenty chapters before the war arrives, readers are given additional opportunities to feel invested in, and to sympathize with, those characters, especially as they face remarkable privations and make stark sacrifices in the novel's second half. The war brings widespread death and destruction to W—— and beyond. For instance, Irene's controlling but beloved father, Leonard Huntingdon, dies at the First Battle of Bull Run/Manassas, and near the end of the narrative, *Macaria*'s hero, Russell Aubrey, dies at Malvern Hill. The losses of these chief characters are clearly intended to be both the novel's affective apex and a direct appeal on behalf of the Confederate cause. Contemporary readers responded with particular force to Russell's death, a testament to Evans's meticulous character development and command of pathos.[26]

In narrating the tumultuous transition from the antebellum to the bellum period, Evans also produced a wartime novel with a broader purview than many of its peers. Unlike Sallie Rochester Ford's *Raids and Romance of Morgan and His Men*, which exclusively narrates the wartime exploits of John Hunt Morgan in Kentucky, *Macaria* is able to capture not merely the "world the war made" but also the unmaking of the old world. For instance, increasing sectional tensions during the mid- to late 1850s occasion a number of debates among the novel's characters about the fate of the Union and the southern states. In chapter 21, just a page after the sudden emergence of Russell Aubrey's deep interest in the "political vat," he and Eric Mitchell, Irene's doting uncle, discuss federalism, universal suffrage, and northern "demogogism" for nearly two full pages. At the end of his heady discussion with Eric, Russell opines, "The surging waves of Northern faction and fanaticism already break ominously against our time-honored constitutional dykes, and if the South would strengthen her bulwarks there is no time to be slept or wrangled away" (98). Without a properly developed narrative context for this debate, the resulting political discourse feels both pedantic and out of place. While many of Evans's characters are distinguished by their learning and broad knowledge, such undigested political oratory falls flat.

Elsewhere the political discourse seems more of piece with the novel's themes and plot, particularly when Evans is able to directly tie such rhetoric to character development. For instance, Russell Aubrey's rise from lowly clerk to eminent politician coincides with debates about increasing sectional strife. Sometime before Buchanan's election, Russell is nominated for the state legislature as an ardent states' rights candidate. In a predictable but crucial plot twist, he runs against Irene's father, Leonard Huntingdon, who holds a deep grudge against the Aubrey family because Russell's deceased mother, Amy, had rejected his marriage proposal years earlier. During a public debate, Russell rises above Leonard Huntingdon's vituperative personal attacks to make a case for both his candidacy and the importance of a "solid south":

> He was, he averred, no alarmist, but he proclaimed that the people slept upon the thin heaving crust of a volcano which would inevitably soon burst forth; and the period was rapidly approaching when the Southern states, unless united and on the alert, would lie bound at the feet of an insolent and rapacious Northern faction. . . . With his elegant, graceful delivery, and polished, sparkling diction, he stood, as it were, on some lofty cool pedestal, and pointed unerringly to coming events, whose shadows had not yet reached them, of which they had not dreamed before, and it was not wonderful that the handsome young speaker became an idol to be worshipped afar off. (102)

The transformation of Russell into "an idol to be worshipped afar off" is one of the novel's dominant narrative arcs. *Macaria* opens with a description of a determined sixteen-year-old Russell burning the midnight oil in order to secure money for his impoverished family. Russell later vows to his mother

that he will "trample out the stigma" attached to the family name following the public shaming and subsequent suicide of his father: "I will plant my
feet upon the necks of those that now strive to grind me to the dust. I swore
it over my father's coffin!" (7). Here, with his victory over the wealthy Huntingdon, Russell's rise to respectability is complete. In many ways that rise is
concomitant with, and predicated on, the rise of a southern confederacy. In
staging such coincidence, Evans deftly merges the novel's domestic and political interests in advance of the secession of the southern states and the bewildering bloodshed it would bring.

Remarkably, Evans does not shy away from the resulting carnage. Indeed,
her description of the First Battle of Bull Run/Manassas is among the most
graphic contemporaneous accounts of the war: "Hideous was the spectacle
presented—dead and dying, friend and foe, huddled in indiscriminate ruin,
weltering in blood and shivering in the agonies of dissolution; blackened head-
less trunks and fragments of limbs—ghastly sights and sounds of woe, filling
the scene of combat" (148). As per usual, Evans's rhetoric aims to shape readers' understanding of the conflict between South and North. This gory description underscores the high costs of a war brought on, Evans avers, by the
"avarice and hate" of the North (147). Lest the reader miss the point, Evans
adds the following, didactic reap-what-you-sow metaphor: "Such were the first
fruits of the bigotry and fanatical hate of New England, aided by the unprin-
cipled demagogism of the West; such were the wages of Abolitionism, guided
by Lincoln and Seward—the latter-day Sejanus; such the results of 'higher-
law,' canting, puritanical hypocrisy" (148–49)."

That Evans would use the First Battle of Bull Run/Manassas as a major
scene in the novel should come as little surprise. First Bull Run/Manassas was
a shocking Confederate victory, one that portended a much bloodier, much
longer war to come. As James M. McPherson observes, this was "a small
battle by later Civil War standards but one that would have important psy-
chological consequences in both the North and the South" (*Battle Cry* 338).
The battle also provided no small amount of intrigue and drama, something
to which Evans's keen, novelistic eye was no doubt drawn. Evans seems to
have found particularly compelling the role of two female Confederate spies
in the battle. Rose O'Neal Greenhow, a Confederate sympathizer based in
Washington, D.C., wanted to provide General Pierre Gustave Toutant Beauregard with the information that Federal troops were planning to advance
on the Confederate Army of the Potomac, then encamped near Manassas,
Virginia. Greenhow enlisted the assistance of an attractive sixteen-year-old
courier, Bettie Duvall, in whose hair she stowed the ciphered intelligence. As
the historian William C. Davis rightly notes, "The whole scene so reeked of
penny romance that it bordered on the ludicrous. A beautiful heroine . . .
unfolds her raven tresses before the chivalrous general of the Confederacy to

deliver a message of vital importance to the infant Southern nation. It was all really happening, but more like fiction come to life, a Waverley novel gone mad" (xviii).

On 17 March 1863, Evans, who was in the final stages of copying the manuscript for *Macaria*, wrote to General Beauregard himself to corroborate several facts she hoped to include in chapter 30. After apologizing at some length for disturbing the general during the ongoing siege on Charleston, Evans cuts to the chase: "I am extremely desirous to know that I am *entirely accurate* in all my statements relative to the Battle" (Sexton 56). Evans, who had held a previous, in-person discussion with Beauregard about the battle, was eager to know: if indeed Duvall's smuggled intelligence provided the first warning of a Federal attack; how long it took Beauregard to act on the intelligence; at what time Beauregard learned of the failure of one of his troop movements; and had Beauregard led a second, successful charge on Henry House Hill (Sexton 55–58). Such a concern for accuracy and detail—not to mention the ability to employ a military luminary as her fact-checker—says a great deal about Evans's dynamic attempts to keep her novel "nineteenth-century up-to-date with a vengeance."[28]

Having confirmed Duvall's role in preparations for the battle, Evans opens her chapter with a tribute to an earlier, young southern female spy, Emily Geiger, the American Revolutionary War heroine who purportedly ran intelligence across enemy lines during the spring 1781 Siege of Ninety-Six in South Carolina. Evans asks rhetorically, "Was not Emily Geiger's slender womanly hand instrumental in preparing for that battle, the results of which freed the Carolinas?" (147). Such a provocative question attempts to establish an unbroken chain of southern "Womanly Usefulness" extending from the "first Revolution" (147) to what Evans and many members of the Confederate intelligentsia considered to be the second American revolution. Noting in turn that the "Promethean spark of patriotic devotion burned in the hearts of Secession women," Evans celebrates the courage and resourcefulness of women like Duvall who were perfectly willing to "dare all things in a cause so holy" (147).[29]

Evans insists on the importance of patriotically devoted women to the Confederate nation, even daring to set Duvall's bold act of espionage prospectively alongside the battlefield efforts of Beauregard and Albert Sidney Johnston. Appealing to futurity, Evans asks: "When our national jewels are made up, will not a grateful and admiring country set her name between those of Beauregard and Johnston in the revolutionary diadem, and let the three blaze through coming ages, baffling the mists of time—the Constellation of Manassas?" (147). Thus, Evans not only renders a "slender womanly hand instrumental" in the Confederate war effort but also forcefully inserts women into a heavily masculinized space. Such an emphasis on wartime

"Womanly Usefulness" was consistent with both the historical context of, and Evans's broader ambitions for, *Macaria*.

Evans's attempts to keep her novel both up-to-date and upbeat about the prospects of Confederate victory were not limited to what she included in *Macaria*. She was also cunning in what she left out. As a number of critics have pointed out, the peculiar institution is peculiarly absent in the pages of this wartime novel. The words "slave" or "slavery" appear only three times in the novel. In the first two instances, slavery is used a metaphor (46, 97). In the third, slavery is discussed briefly—by two women, Irene and Electra, no less—and in the conditional: "If our existence as a Republic depends upon the perpetuity of the institution of slavery, then, it seems to me, that the aim of our legislators should be to render us *par excellence* an agricultural people—and, with the exception of great national arsenals and workshops, to discourage home manufactories" (162). This is the extent of the novel's direct engagement with the issue that was both at the heart of the sectional crisis and a point of fierce contention during the war. By the time Evans gave the manuscript of *Macaria* to West and Johnston, Lincoln had signed the Emancipation Proclamation and debates were raging in the Confederacy about both the use of slaves in the war effort and the future of slavery in the new nation. In a novel that engages the politics of its moment so ardently, such a studied avoidance of the issue of slavery is conspicuous.[30]

We can see at work in such representation—or in such lack of representation—the lineaments of what would become a central part of Lost Cause ideology: the avowal that slavery was not the issue that caused the war. Both during and after the American Civil War, many Confederates denied vehemently that slavery "had anything to do with the Confederate cause, thus decontaminating it and turning it into something they could cherish" (Stampp 268). But, as Kenneth Stampp notes, "[t]he speed with which white Southerners dissociated themselves from the cause of slavery is striking evidence of how great a burden it had been to them" (268). Evans's decision to sidestep the issue of slavery in *Macaria* constitutes a similar act of dissociation. As a novelist with at best ambivalent feelings about slavery and yet a firm belief in the inferiority of people of African descent, Evans essentially evacuates slavery per se from the novel. She mounts no ardent defense of it as either a Christian duty or a southern social institution. Instead, she quietly celebrates the devotion of the novel's "servants" and underscores their masters' benevolent affection.[31]

For instance, the Huntingdon family is primarily attended to by Aunt Nellie, Irene's "devoted nurse" (29; cf. 75), and Andrew, the "faithful negro," who on the occasion of his master's death at First Bull Run/Manassas, "could no longer repress his grief and sobbed convulsively, unable to reply" (152). Together these "devoted two" had "petted [Irene] from her childhood" (152).

As a result, Irene trusts them implicitly. When Leonard Huntingdon volunteers for the war, he worries about leaving Irene alone with the "servants." Irene assures him, "They will take better care of me than anybody else. Nellie and Andrew and John are the only guardians I want in your absence. They have watched over me all my life, and they will do it to the end. Give yourself no trouble, sir, on my account" (134). Other prominent "servants" in the novel include Cyrus, Dr. Hiram Arnold's slave, and Willis, Eric Mitchell's slave. Willis is described as being particularly "invaluable" to his master, as Mitchell himself confesses: "He is eyes, ears, crutches, everything to me, and never forgets anything or anybody. He has travelled over half the world with me—could desert me, and be free at any moment he felt inclined to do so—but is as faithful now as the day on which I first left home with him" (154). Evans hopes that Willis's self-abnegating commitment to his master—we are told that he repeatedly chooses slavery over freedom—will speak volumes about "servants'" *true* feelings about their masters and about the peculiar institution more broadly.

In W——, such slave devotion is not lost on the masters. William, the Huntingdons' cook, goes to war as Leonard Huntingdon's valet, vowing to Irene that he will "take good care of Master" (136). After William is killed in battle, Leonard Huntingdon is deeply moved: "'Poor William! he followed me so closely that he was shot through the head. He is lying three hundred yards to the left, yonder. Poor fellow! he was faithful to the last.' A tear dimmed the master's eagle eye as he muttered, rather than spoke, these words" (149). Here is the "faithful" slave who will sacrifice all for his master. And here, in return, is honest and open affection from said master. The resulting representations of "servant"-master relations are as sentimental and flat as they are troubling.

In lieu of a direct and forthright engagement with ongoing debates about slavery, Evans describes a "servant" utopia in which master and slave live together harmoniously and productively. Thus, twelve years after the publication of *Uncle Tom's Cabin*, *Macaria* offers a quiet anti-Tom response to Stowe's representation of the horrors of slavery. In replacing Simon Legree with Leonard Huntingdon and George Harris with "Poor William," Evans upholds another central tenet of what would become Lost Cause ideology: that slaves were contented with their status as chattel (Nolan 16). In *Macaria*, the faithfulness of "servants" such as Willis or Aunt Nettie is a function of their contentment. In emphasizing such devotion, Evans uses literary representation rather than political rhetoric to make the case for her slaveholding nation. Largely eschewing the most divisive issue of the period, Evans also finds a way to remain both timely and on message.

Evans was clearly writing a long-form fiction during and for a chaotic moment. Above all else, *Macaria* figures "the connection of the individual to a political immediacy" (Deleuze and Guattari 18). In the "cramped space" between the novel and its historical moment, Evans forces "each individual intrigue to connect immediately to politics" (Deleuze and Guattari 17). And the novelist seems to have been keenly aware of the pressures of that cramped space. Among other things, Evans was particularly eager to get the book out in the world. Unfortunately for her, the novel's production was much delayed. Walker, Evans, and Cogswell, the firm with which West and Johnston had contracted for the printing of *Macaria*, had to relocate their operations to Columbia, South Carolina, following the bombardment of Charleston in fall 1863. This delayed publication significantly, as did West and Johnston's preoccupation with the *Les Misérables* edition, their top priority during 1863 (Homestead, "Publishing" 673). On 21 November 1863 an exasperated Evans wrote to her friend Rachel Lyons: "The delay is very provoking, for the *MS* has been in the hands of the publishers, ever since the *first of June*" (Sexton 88). Evans's concern for a speedy production of her book speaks to both its potential impact as a wartime cultural object and its potential obsolescence once the war was over. Much to Evans's chagrin, the novel did not appear in print until April 1864.[32]

Because *Macaria* was an utterly timely novel, Evans had to make predictions about the outcome of the American Civil War. Of course, the majority of those predictions proved dead wrong. For instance, in chapter 28 Irene praises the people of the Confederacy in glowing and liberal terms: "A nation of laboring, nimble-fingered, prayerful-hearted, brave-spirited women, and chivalric, high-souled, heroic men, who had never learned that Americans could live and not be free" (137). Irene then pleads, "Grant us our reward, oh God! the independence of the land we hold so dear." During the war, the "reward" of Confederate independence may have seemed possible. In 1896, the year Augusta Jane Evans Wilson published a revised edition of *Macaria*, it did not. In the 1896 edition this breathless celebration of the Confederate people is retained, but the appeal to God is omitted (A. J. E. Wilson 351).

Such a revision calls to mind Evans's deft use of the conditional throughout *Macaria*. For instance, Irene, grieving the death of a young Confederate soldier she had nursed, says to the Reverend Harvey Young, "A mother's pride and solace, a sister's joy, one of a Nation's treasured guardians, stricken down in his first battle—bathing his country's riddled banner in his warm young blood. How long—how long will Almighty God withhold his vengeance from wolfish hordes who are battening upon the blood of freemen?" (172). In the 1864 edition, Irene declares boldly, "Harvey, if there be not a long and awful retribution for that Cain-cursed race of New England, there is neither justice nor truth in high heaven" (172). Not surprisingly, this conditional statement along with its fiercely antinorthern sentiment and quasi-blasphemous implications are excised in the 1896 edition of the novel

(A. J. E. Wilson 436). Save the loss of hundreds of thousands of lives and tens of millions of dollars, the Union did not in fact face "a long and awful retribution." As a result, the lingering suggestion that there is "neither justice nor truth in high heaven" would likely have made a large portion of *Macaria*'s postwar, post-Reconstruction audience uncomfortable.

"Womanly Usefulness"

While obsolescence and historical myopia are two risks of writing for and about a vanishing present, there are also remarkable opportunities in doing so. First among these is the chance to capture and consolidate evanescent phenomena. Because *Macaria*'s present comprised a civil war, such phenomena included violent and unprecedented shifts in gender roles and social expectations for women—what one literary historian describes as the "disquieting liberation from previously rigid roles" (Samuels 82). Speaking broadly about the literature of civil wars, the comparatist Margaret Higonnet has argued that "civil wars, which take place on 'home' territory, have more potential than other wars to transform women's expectations" (80). *Macaria* documents exhaustively such transformations and political choices. Thus, one crucial aspect of the novel's timeliness is its representation of wartime "Womanly Usefulness," something Evans thought essential to the prospect of an independent Confederate nation (168).[33]

Even before the war comes to W——, the novel's main female characters, Irene and Electra, exhibit remarkable independence and self-sufficiency. Readers are told that from an early age Irene had followed her own lead, exceeding and defying a number of proscribed gender roles. In addition to her rigorous equestrian style, Irene is distinguished by an abiding interest in mathematics and science. She is described as being an accomplished astronomer, even publishing an essay on "Laplace's Nebular Theory" in a scientific journal under the name "Sabæan" (110). In one of many narratorial digressions, Evans places Irene in a storied tradition of woman astronomers, including Caroline Herschel, Mary Sommerville, Maria Mitchell, and Emma Willard. Irene is, Evans avers, a "glorious attestation of the truth of female capacity to grapple with some of the most recondite problems of science" (78). Likewise, Electra is characterized by her preternatural artistic ability and placed in a "glorious sisterhood of artists" (66). Well before laying their lives on the "altars of sacrifice," Irene and Electra are portrayed as extraordinary female characters.

A good deal of the novel's antebellum domestic drama is due to Irene's steadfast refusal to marry her rakish cousin Hugh, to whom she was promised on the deathbed of Hugh's mother. Irene, a character Evans described as being her "ideal of *perfect womanhood*," rejects Hugh several times, both to his face and through his ardent advocate, her father (Sexton 104). When Hugh lays claim to Irene early in the novel—"Irene, you belong to me, and you know it."—Irene's response is unequivocal: "No! I belong to God and myself" (13). Later, she is more explicit about both her desires and her sense of self-possession: "No, I can't love you other than as my cousin; I would not, if I could. I do not think it would be right, and I won't promise to try. Father has no right to give me to you, or to anybody else. I tell you now I belong to myself, and only I can give myself away. Hugh, I don't consider this settled at all. You might as well know the truth at once; I have some voice in the matter" (53). When Irene staunchly stands her ground, her father sends her to New York for boarding school, and when that does little to change her mind, Leonard Huntingdon promises to disown his only daughter and heir. To this very real threat, Irene responds, "[P]overty does not frighten me half so much as a loveless marriage" (90).[34]

Irene's repeated rejections of Hugh's entreaties and her father's rule constitute a series of declarations of independence. Through her bold resistance Irene becomes a subtle figure for southern independence—womanly and otherwise. Evans's rhetoric draws attention to the similarities between the respective plights of Irene and the southern states. As her father pushes his case, Irene couches her resistance in specifically nationalistic terms:

> I do not hold myself bound by the oaths of another, though he were twice my father. I am responsible for no acts but my own. No one has the right to lay his hand on an unconscious infant, slumbering in her cradle, and coolly determine, for all time, her destiny. You have the right to guide me, to say what I shall not do without your consent, but I am a free-born American, thank God! I did not draw my breath in Circassia, to be bartered for gold by my father. I, only, can give myself away. (89–90)

By invoking Irene's status as a "free-born American," Evans echoes a dominant rhetoric of southern secessionists, who often cited encroachments on personal liberty as a rationale for secession. Fortunately for Irene, Hugh is killed during an ill-advised, late-night pleasure ride on the eve of the Civil War, thus drawing the curtain on one domestic drama at the moment the novel's political dramas take center stage.[35]

As we might expect, this movement from the antebellum to the bellum radically affects Irene and Electra's day-to-day lives. The sudden emergence of sectional strife in the novel gives Irene in particular a renewed sense of purpose. In one of the novel's first scenes, Irene confesses to Amy Aubrey that she is frustrated by the pampered life of a plantation daughter, one in which she "will never be obliged to do anything": "Everybody ought to be of some use in this world, but I feel like a bunch of mistletoe growing on somebody else, and doing nothing. I don't intend to sit down and hold my hands all my life, but what can I do? Tell me how to begin" (25). Although Electra's poverty does not allow her the leisure and opportunities afforded to Irene, she, too, refuses to sit idly by: "I want my name carved, not on monumental marble only, but upon the living, throbbing heart of my age! stamped indelibly on the generation in which my lot is cast" (95). The lead-up to the Civil War provides an apt starting place for both women.[36]

As debates rage about the future of the Union, Irene focuses her attention on needs of W——'s poor, something she worries the men of W—— have lost sight of. She remarks to Hiram Arnold, "It is very apparent that this fierceness of party spirit, this bitter political animosity, is driving the ship of State on the rock of Ruin. The foamy lips of the breakers are just ahead, but you men will not open your eyes to the danger" (122). When Dr. Arnold replies sarcastically, "Better get some of you wise women to pilot us, I dare say!," Irene calmly and deftly softens her critique, calling the doctrine of separate spheres a "judicious arrangement," one both "wise and happy." "Practically, women should have as little to do with politics as men with darning stockings or making puff-paste," she concedes, "but we should be unworthy of the high social *status* which your chivalry accords us were we indifferent to the conduct of public affairs" (122). With this forceful objection, Irene stakes claim to a place for (white) southern womanhood within the bounds of the political sphere.

And it does not take long for Irene to venture into that sphere. Having assured Dr. Arnold of her conservative gender politics, Irene then informs the good doctor that she wants him to aid her in "getting a bill passed by the legislature appropriating a school-fund for this county" (123). When an exasperated Dr. Arnold refuses her request and asks why she needs his help, Irene replies, "I do not wish to be known at all in the affair. It is not a woman's business to put forward legislative bills" (123). While this statement is in keeping with her "practical" understanding of a gendered division of labor, the very fact that Irene works behind the scenes to enact such legislation belies her legislative modesty. Here is a southern woman using her ample charm to influence the determination of public policy and the making of laws—something Augusta Jane Evans herself did throughout the American Civil War. While she might not be piloting the "ship of State," Irene is at the very least on deck.[37]

The mounting secession crisis allows Irene to engage in political discourse much more fully. Following the election of Lincoln, Irene and her father end up on opposite ends of the cooperation debate, with Irene coming out vocally in favor of secession: "For the first time in her life Irene openly confronted her father's wrath on political grounds. She realized the imminence of the danger, dreaded the siren song of co-operation, and dauntlessly discussed the matter without hesitation" (133). Prior to this moment of crisis, Irene had little compunction disagreeing with her forbidding father on domestic issues.

But here—again, "For the first time in her life"—Irene engages him on political issues. The timing of this newfound willingness to argue with her father is key. It is only in the service of secession and under the pressures of civil war that Irene can "dauntlessly" and "without hesitation" insert herself into a political debate with one of W——'s most eminent politicians. Per Higonnet, with civil war a near certainty, Irene is faced with and makes "explicit political choices" (80).[38]

Following the fall of Fort Sumter, which Mr. Huntingdon prophetically calls "Act 1, of a long and bloody civil war," Irene states her remarkable desire to follow her father into battle: "Oh, Father! if I were only a man, that I might go with you—stand by you under all circumstances. Could n't you take me anyhow? Surely a daughter may follow her father, even on the battlefield?" (134). As expected, Mr. Huntingdon responds with derision to Irene's proposition: "A pretty figure you would cut in the midst of my battery!" (134). However, upon reflection, he concedes that she would make a fine soldier: "Really, though, Irene, I do not believe that you would flinch before all the cannon of Borodino. My blood beats at your heart, and it has never yet shown a cowardly drop. If you were a boy, I swear you would not disgrace my name in any conflict" (134). At this point in the narrative, Leonard Huntingdon is still mourning the loss of his beloved nephew, Hugh, who for years stood in for the son Huntingdon never had. (Irene's mother died giving birth to her.) Thus the gender-bending fantasy of Irene as a gallant soldier was surely a compelling one to the proud old man. More to the point, with civil war imminent Huntingdon now seems to find valuable in Irene the very traits that had earlier driven him to distraction.

Irene next identifies a quandary facing both sides of the Mason-Dixon line: how to balance the demands of family and country. Irene's rhetoric elegantly captures the give and take of such intimate debates: "I should be unworthy of my country if I were selfish enough to want to keep you from its defence; and yet I were unworthy of my father if I could see you leave home, under such circumstances, without great grief. Oh! if I could only go with you! But to have to stay here, useless and inactive!" (135). We see in the passage Irene's clear affection for both her country and her father. More urgently, we witness Irene's fierce determination to be useful to, and active in, the Confederate war effort—both within and without proscribed gender roles.

Following the death of her father, Irene moves to the front to nurse wounded soldiers. Drawing on her experiences tending to W——'s poor, Irene becomes a favorite among the stricken and dying Confederates, often standing in for mother, lover, sister, and friend. Characteristically, Irene gives her all to her nursing duties, working long hours and compromising her delicate health. When her uncle warns her, "You will kill yourself," Irene responds without hesitation, "I could not die in a better cause" (166). This willingness to sacrifice is central to Evans's doctrine of wartime "Womanly Usefulness." This is, after all, a novel subtitled "Altars of Sacrifice," and the narrative returns again and again to scenes of female "self-abnegation." For instance, in describing the mobilization of Confederate troops the narrator draws a comparison between Confederate and "Spartan" women, noting that "all the stern resolution and self-abnegation of Rome and Lacedæmon had entered the souls of Southern women" (137). The narrator continues: "Mothers closed their lips firmly to repress a wail of sorrow as they buckled on the swords of their first-born, and sent them forth with a 'Godspeed!' to battle for the right; fond wives silently packed their husbands' knapsacks, with hands that knew no faltering; and sisters, with tearless eyes, bent by the light of midnight-lamps over canteens which their thoughtful care covered for brothers who were to start to the scene of action on the morrow" (137). This unpruned prose presents an idealized picture of the steely determination of southern women. According to Evans's hugely unreliable narrator, not some but *all* Confederate women act accordingly.[39]

While such blanket characterizations inevitably fall flat, Evans is a bit more effective in presenting Irene's Spartan womanhood. In addition to her service to her community and country, Irene is willing to sacrifice her loved ones for the cause. Speaking to Russell before he departs for war, Irene invokes the source of the novel's title:

> Of old, when Eurystheus threatened Athens, Macaria, in order to save the city and the land from invasion and subjugation, willingly devoted herself a sacrifice upon the altar of the gods. Ah, Russell! that were an easy task, in comparison with the offering I am called upon to make. I can not, like Macaria, by self-immolation, redeem my country; from that great privilege I am debarred; but I yield up more than she ever possessed. I give my all on earth—my father and yourself—to our beloved and suffering country. My God! accept the sacrifice, and crown the South a sovereign, independent nation! (146)

Once again, Irene laments the sacrifices she is unable to make, namely that of her own life in battle. However, in the same breath, she suggests that a Confederate woman can give more than her life: She can give the lives of those she loves.

At first glance this torrent of exclamations seems like boilerplate wartime rhetoric; however, the context of this speech and its tense suggest its underlying importance to the novel's twinned domestic and political themes. First, this is to be Irene and Russell's final meeting before she sees him on his deathbed. In the conversation that precedes this speech, Irene and Russell have at long last confessed their love for each other. As a result, Irene's rhetoric of sacrifice has a particular resonance and pathos here. It also has an eerie prescience. In a powerful apostrophe that brings together pagan and Christian traditions, Irene asks God to compensate the sacrifice of her father and Russell with a Confederate victory. The tense of this and the subsequent passage, in which Irene urges Russell to "win deathless glory on the battle-field in defence of our sacred cause" (146), renders those sacrifices fait accompli. However, at this point in the narrative (which is dated sometime in early summer 1861), neither Leonard Huntingdon nor Russell Aubrey has died. In fact, they have not even left for battle yet. But Irene's strangely fatalistic appeal seems to suggest that their deaths and her resulting "desolation" are inevitable. Thus, Irene sends her beloved Russell off to war not simply "without faltering hand" but with full knowledge that he will not be coming home. Less than thirty pages later, the novel confirms Irene's forecast when Russell suffers a grim death after taking a musket shot to the chest.

By 1864 women in the North and the South knew all too well the "infinitely more bitter fate" Irene describes. As Drew Gilpin Faust documents, the American Civil War touched nearly every person living in the United and Confederate States of America: "Loss became commonplace; death was no longer encountered individually; death's threat, its proximity, and its actuality became the most widely shared of the war's experiences. . . . for those Americans who lived in and through the Civil War, the texture of the experience, its warp and woof, was the presence of death" (*This Republic* xiii). This was particularly true in the South. Historians believe that at least one out of every five white southern men of military age died during the war. Thus, Irene's circa 1861 resignation to her father and Russell's death would likely have been both familiar to and comforting for readers in 1864. Put another way, this speech further locates *Macaria* in time, making it available and intelligible to reading publics in the war-ravaged South and beyond.[40]

Irene's reaction to the actual deaths of her father and Russell further bears out her prophecy. At the end of the novel, as she clutches Russell's body, Irene exemplifies the "stern resolution and self-abnegation" of both Macaria and Spartan women: "No burst of grief escaped her, to tell of agony and despair. . . . she sat, mute and resigned, at the foot of the Red Dripping Altar of Patriotism, where lay, in hallowed Sacrifice, her noble, darling Dead" (179). Evans's heavy capitalization suggests a near-Platonic ideal of patriotism and sacrifice. Tellingly, the narrative's interest seems to be in Irene (the living) rather than Russell (the dead). This is not surprising, since Irene's anticipation of, and reaction to, the deaths of her father and lover are figured as a crucial part of the war effort. If only Confederate women could approach the likely deaths of loved ones with the same sense of grace, resolution, and commitment to the Confederate nationalist cause as does Irene. Then, Evans seems to suggest, God would repay their sacrifices with victory and independence. Thus, one major vector of "Womanly Usefulness" in the novel is a "Spartan" understanding of the sacrifices every Confederate woman must make.

Near the end of the novel, Irene and Electra engage in a lengthy political dialogue that touches on an extraordinarily diverse set of topics. In addition to Spartan sacrifice, they discuss the purported justness and constitutionality of secession; the implications of the war for "anarchical pseudo-republics, like those of South America and Mexico" (162); suffrage and contemporary republican forms of government; sustainable agriculture; the stakes and status of "free-trade" and agrarian economies; and mimetic art and Poe's aesthetics, among other topics. The discussion fills more than five two-column pages, runs to well over 3,500 words, and includes quotations from Robert Walpole and John Montagu; references to Greek, Roman, and Spartan polities; allusions to Norse myth; and invocations of Cincinnatus and Aratus.

During this colloquy Electra broaches the issue of "Womanly Usefulness." While both characters agree that "the women of the South must exercise an important influence in determining our national destiny," they disagree about the forms and degree of that influence (161). Electra rightly notes that outside of war, southern white women of this period were afforded scant opportunities to wield such influence and few explicit political choices: "Ah! but their hands are tied; and they walk but a short, narrow path, from hearthstone to threshold, and back again. They have, I know, every inclination to exert a restraining influence, but no power to utilize it" (163). Such a limited sphere—"from hearthstone to threshold," as Electra notes—offers women only rigid, circumscribed roles.

Informed no doubt by her class privilege, Irene sees much more power in even that "short, narrow path." Once again, Irene is careful to note that southern women "have no desire to usurp legislative reins"; instead, she avers, "their appropriate work consists in moulding the manners and morals of the nation" (163). After a deeply conservative tirade about the "wild excesses of fashionable life, and the dangerous spirit of extravagance," Irene raises a familiar argument about statesmen being "trained up around the mother's armchair." A mother can, Irene opines, "imbue the boy with lofty sentiments, and inspire him with aims which, years hence, shall lead him in congressional halls to adhere to principles, to advance the Truth" (163). As in her earlier solicitation of Dr. Arnold's legislative assistance, Irene advocates that women quietly and indirectly exercise legislative power via their relationships with men (or men-to-be). Through these relationships the "conscientious, devoted, and patriotic Christian women of a nation" assume an essential role as the "safeguards of its liberties and purity" (163). In having Irene voice a conflicted if not contradictory stance—women should not "usurp legislative reins" but should steady and guide those reins—Evans manages to be both socially conservative and quasi-feminist more or less at the same time.

This passage represents one of the most articulate and sustained political commentaries made by a female character in nineteenth-century American fiction. It proffers a learned and provocative set of queries and captures in remarkable detail the sorts of political questions the Confederate national moment raised. And yet, for all its erudition, urgency, and conflicted gender politics, the majority of this several-page conversation was unceremoniously cut in the 1896 edition of the novel. That is, more than 2,200 words of this dialogue—all the text on pages 162 and 163, and nearly half of the text on page 164—are dropped from the 1896 edition (161–65; cf. A. J. E. Wilson 412–16). In the 1864 edition, Electra and Irene's heated political discussion ends: "They went upstairs together" (164). The 1896 Dillingham edition revises this cleverly: "An hour later they went upstairs together" (A. J. E. Wilson 414).

I suggested earlier some of the ways Evans and her editors may have revised this timely, wartime novel for a postwar, post-Reconstruction moment. Yet, a simple narrative of "road to reunion" revisionism cannot account for the bewildering silence this cut imposes upon Irene and Electra's nascent political subjectivities. If *Macaria* was revised in relation to widespread efforts to unify a fractured union, how might gender function in the excision of these passages? With regard to revisionary practices and cultural memory, "what difference does it make who is speaking" these lines (Foucault, "What Is an Author?" 222)? By way of comparison, the Reverend Harvey Young's equally verbose and vitriolic pro-Confederate speech near the end of the novel is left unaltered in the 1896 edition (171; cf. A. J. E. Wilson 436–37). Such a comparison raises the specter of gendered revision. What can a male character say that a female character cannot? More to the point, what can a female character say in an 1864 novel that she cannot say in an 1896 one?

The excision of Irene and Electra's political discourse bespeaks the "crisis in gender" that the Civil War incited. As Margaret Higonnet, Drew Gilpin Faust, Shirley Samuels, Nina Silber, LeeAnn Whites, and others suggest, the coming of the American Civil War offered both Union and Confederate women unprecedented political and social legibility. However, in most cases, the subsequent cessation of hostilities and the return home of patriarchal power forced those women to cede those political and social positions. Similarly, the 1896 excision of this conversation seems to return Irene and Electra to their "proper place," away from the public-political sphere in which the war had enabled them—however briefly and provisionally—to participate. In so doing, this excision also marks a return to the familiar confines and "normal" dictates of domestic fiction: to quote Electra, "from hearthstone to threshold."[41]

But that is the 1896 edition of the novel. The wartime edition remains very much focused on women's newfound opportunities, expectations, and usefulness. As we might expect with a novel that is so resolutely of its moment, *Macaria* ends with Irene and Electra peering into the future at a postwar world that promises yet more "disquieting liberation from previously rigid roles." Irene observes, "Our Revolution has beggard thousands and deprived many of their natural providers; numbers of women in the Confederacy will be thrown entirely upon their own resources for maintenance. All can not be mantua-makers, milliners, or school-teachers" (181). As a result, Irene commits to opening in W—— a "School of Design" for women, which she hopes Electra will superintend. More urgently, Irene and Electra also consider what postwar southern womanhood will look like. Electra worries in particular about the fate of the unmarried and widowed women who will, come victory or defeat, dominate the postwar South. Once again, Irene takes comfort in her doctrine of "Womanly Usefulness": "Electra, it is very true that single women have trials for which a thoughtless, happy world has little sympathy. But lonely lives are not necessarily joyless; they should be, of all others, most useful" (182). First and foremost, these single women will have work to do for their nascent nation.

Although *Macaria* ends with a quotation from Elizabeth Barrett Browning's *A Drama of Exile*, Irene gives the novel's final speech, a characteristically impassioned jeremiad about the work of Confederate women:

> You and I have much to do during these days of gloom and national trial—for upon the purity, the devotion, and the patriotism of the women of our land, not less than upon the heroism of our armies, depends our national salvation. To jealously guard our homes and social circles from the inroads of corruption, to keep the fires of patriotism burning upon the altars of the South, to sustain and encourage those who are wrestling along the border for our birthright of freedom, is the consecrated work to which we are called; and beyond this bloody baptism open vistas of lifelong usefulness. (183)

Looking past the devastation and privations that engulf them, Irene and Electra spy a distant, messianic world filled with "vistas of lifelong usefulness." Even and especially if that war-torn world proves largely absent fathers or husbands or brothers, these women may have the opportunity to play a "critical role in the public life of the new nation" (Faust, *Mothers* 173)—to enjoy lifelong, not merely wartime, "Womanly Usefulness."

Coda: "Noble Patriotism and Sublime Self-Abnegation"

In January 1865, while the Siege of Petersburg raged just twenty-five miles to the south, the short-lived "Southern Monthly Eclectic Magazine," *The Age*, of Richmond, Virginia, published a substantial fifteen-page review of *Macaria*. The occasionally caustic review, which praises Evans as "unquestionably a lady of fine intellect,—an intellect which has been trained and expanded by a course of masculine studies" and as possessing "courage," "skill, judgment, and reverence for lofty principle" (384), betrays a great deal of anxiety about the unprecedented gender and genre troubles *Macaria* posed. It also speaks directly to *Macaria*'s unusual position within both its literary field and its historical context.

The review endorses a rigid rubric for the contemporary novel: "The grand result of the novel . . . is marriage" (387) and the "highest evidence of artistic skill" is the "successful removal of the embarrassments which interrupt and thwart the course of true love between the hero and the heroine" (388). Given that *Macaria* pointedly and repeatedly rejects a marriage plot, the reviewer complains, "[W]e think the fair novelist has done no inconsiderable violence to our just expectations": "when she makes lovers her leading characters, we expect marriage to follow, as a sequence, as well by the laws of art as of nature" (388). Indeed, the reviewer is so flummoxed by Evans's conclusion that he feels obliged to reimagine significantly the final chapters of the novel, fantasizing that had Russell returned alive to Irene with only "one arm left to protect her" he would not have been "any the less acceptable as a lover" (392).

Equally scandalous for the reviewer are the implications of Irene's decision to "give up her lover, abandon her dearest prospects in life, and go into a hospital in order to evidence her patriotism, upon the first sounding of a war trumpet" (390). "[I]f Miss Huntingdon was determined on making some sacrifice," the review admonishes, "she should have offered up her heart on the altar of connubial affection, and devoted her life to Russell Aubrey" (392). Lest Irene become an icon of unruly, "Spartan" Confederate womanhood, the review scolds, "But the amiable and accomplished mothers of the land should never forget that the main theatre of their operations is the family, at the head of which they are placed, and their most queenly prerogatives, the solacing of their husbands, and the training of their children to become useful men and noble women in this life, and angels in heaven hereafter" (391).

Wartime "Womanly Usefulness" is one of the key targets of the reviewer, who seems particularly interested in redrawing and policing the lines of gender that the war had blurred. The reviewer seethes: "[Evans] too often places her heroine in the observatory, conning over the mysteries of the starry heavens, or tracing out the explorations of Newton, Kepler and Laplace, when she should be entertaining her visitors in her father's drawing-room. The political speculations towards the close of the book are such as would draw down rounds of applause at the hustings, but are out of place in a work of female art" (393). While the reviewer acknowledges Irene's and Electra's "unusual degree of political precocity for young ladies in the early bloom of womanhood" (396), he is not willing to allow any of the women in question—Irene Huntingdon, Electra Grey, or Augusta Jane Evans—to own their political views. Such political sentiments may be admirable ("rounds of applause"), but they are, like the women who speak them, "out of place" in the novel. Thus, as with the revisions discussed above, and as with the southern responses to Stowe discussed in the previous chapter, this review desperately wants to return women to their "proper" place.[42]

Indeed, the novel's break from "the laws of art as of nature" is so stark that the reviewer, "D.K.W.," refuses to acknowledge *Macaria* as a novel per se: "It may be urged, in reply to such criticisms, that the work before us is not a novel, but only a *quasi* novel, —a new experiment in the art of book-making called forth by the times through which we, the citizens of the Southern Confederacy, are now passing, and adapted to them" (390). This rejection of *Macaria* as novel is as damning as it is ambivalent. While the review withholds from *Macaria* the generic title "novel," "throwing it out of the pale of legitimate novels," it also affirms *Macaria*'s "experiment[al]" nature and its intimate relationship to "passing and fearfully interesting events" (390). *Macaria* is not merely a timely book; it is "a work of a peculiar type, having special adaptation" to the historical moment it both addresses and represents (390). Understood in relation to the chaotic, war-torn world it narrates, the review admits, "[W]e, as countrymen of the author, are proud" of *Macaria* (390), and concludes, somewhat begrudgingly, that it is "a noble contribution to the literature of the South" (398).[43]   ɔ ∧ ₹

The anxieties that pervade this remarkable review—anxieties about the proper place of Confederate women, the proper ends of the novel, and the proper relations between literature and history—grant access to at least one contemporaneous reader's response to this troubling and complex Confederate national novel. In the nearly 150 years since the publication of this review, subsequent critics have betrayed their own anxieties when describing the cultural work *Macaria* undertook. For instance, twentieth- and twenty-first-century criticism of the novel returns again and again to the term "propaganda." Betina Entzminger dismisses *Macaria* as "a piece of wartime propaganda" (66). Elizabeth Moss describes an "overtly propagandistic" novel, written by "one of the South's foremost female literary propagandists" (11, 154). Even Evans's biographer, William Perry Fidler, reduces the novel to mere propaganda. In a 1949 *Alabama Review* essay, "Augusta Jane Evans as Confederate Propagandist," Fidler describes "Miss Evans's *career* as a propagandist reach[ing] its height" with *Macaria* ("Augusta Evans Wilson as Confederate Propagandist" 33; emphasis mine). Such approaches to the novel resolutely prioritize *Macaria*'s political agendas over its aesthetic aims, denying at every turn any interpenetration between the two.[44]

Contemporary criticism tends to deem the overtly political fictions of northern, pro-Union writers "political novels" and to denigrate the overtly political fictions of southern, pro-Confederate writers as mere "propaganda" (Sizer 5). Such definitions betray a starkly binaristic logic that significantly obscures the complexities of literary history and perpetuates the "cultural history of winners" that Fliegelman identifies. Put simply, critics may persist in describing *Macaria* as propaganda because of the unsavory nature of the politics that suffuse the novel. Let me be clear: *Macaria* voices a strident defense of the Confederacy, at nearly every turn promulgating the profoundly conservative social politics that Evans espoused throughout her long life and career. A "southern nationalist to her core," Evans was a stalwart defender of southern values as "the embodiment of a healthy social conservatism that alone could contain the dangers of modern skepticism and materialism" (Evans, *Beulah* x; see also E. Moss 154). As we have seen, the novel is resolute in its attacks on northern "political duplicity, despotism, and the utter abrogation of all that had once been constituted American freedom" (136). In moments such as this, *Macaria* clearly has a political agenda and "designs" on its readers. But such moments are part and parcel of a lengthy novel that narrates more than a decade in the lives of more than a dozen characters. To deem it propaganda is, I suggest, to ignore the novelistic whole in view of its propagandistic parts.

Macaria evinces an interpenetration of the partisan and the aesthetic and a concatenation of domestic, political, and literary discourses that continue to defy and elude our critical vocabularies. Indeed, the merge between the political and the domestic that *Macaria* enacts was unprecedented in southern domestic fiction, as Moss herself concedes (186). But this merge was also entirely apt, since it reflected well the society and the moment of which Evans wrote. As Nina Silber has recently argued, one recurrent Confederate habit of mind was "to meld the personal and political, indeed to make the private obligation stand in for a larger ideological motive" (*Gender* 12). We witness such melding throughout this dense novel.[45]

Understood in these terms, *Macaria* seems very much a "new experiment" in southern bookmaking, one that calls into question the binarism that would set at odds the domestic and the political, the private and the public, fiction and nonfiction, progressive and conservative. Critics do indeed seem, as Lora Romero notes, "unable to entertain the possibility that traditions, or even individual texts, could be radical on some issues . . . and reactionary on others." The challenge of reading and responding to *Macaria* is in contending with the complexity of the cultural work it undertook—work both radical and reactionary. When we locate the novel within its literary field and historical context, *Macaria* allows us to delineate carefully the "spaces of original possibles" that the American Civil War enabled and necessitated. One such "possible" was not only a Confederate nation but also a Confederate national novel.[46]

CHAPTER THREE

Southern Amaranths

Popularity, Occasion, and Media in a Confederate Poetics of Place

> But poetry must be judged by its effects—by the way
> in which it stirs the blood, by the reception accorded
> to it among those for whom it was written,—not by its
> strict observance of artistic rule, not by the approval
> which a critic of cultivated mind and delicate taste
> alone will give it.
> —*The Index*, 21 May 1863

> Poetry that is commercially successful in its time has
> always been *public* poetry—that is, poetry that is keyed
> to the culture, the sophistication, and the language of
> contemporary readers. Public poetry has sometimes been
> written by poets of private power, but it was popular *in its
> time* for its public rather than its private qualities.
> Whether poetry of *any* quality is popular at all in
> a given society depends on the status of poetry in that
> society, and upon the media available for it distribution.
> —William Charvat, *The Profession of
> Authorship in America*

Published in the first days of the Civil War centennial, Edmund Wilson's *Patriotic Gore* offered what was for decades the final word on the poetry of the "war between brothers": "The period of the Civil War was not at all a favorable one for poetry. An immense amount of verse was written in connection with the war itself, but today it makes barren reading" (466). This dismissive pronouncement is as elitist as it is presentist. Invoking an unarticulated rubric of literary value, Wilson more or less excuses subsequent critics from having to read the extraordinary surfeit of poems produced during the war. Since none of it is very good, Wilson assures us, we need not tarry with the stuff. Given *Patriotic Gore*'s iconic status—the 816-page study of the literature of the American Civil War remains in print fifty years on—it is not surprising that two generations of literary critics have echoed this uncritical platitude.[1] Even those critics who have taken exception with Wilson's broad-strokes assessment of the period seem beholden to his critical terms. For instance, recent work on Civil War poetry has focused almost exclusively on individual and well-known poets, most of whom were sympathetic to the Union rather than the Confederacy. These studies of Walt Whitman, Herman Melville, Emily Dickinson, and even Henry Timrod emphasize the fertility of select poets while taking for granted the purportedly barren literary field in which they thrived.[2]

Bracketing the question of what constitutes barren or fertile reading, I begin with Wilson's acknowledgment of quantity: Might the mere existence of an "immense amount of verse" command literary-historical interest? That is, what is to be made of the fact that there was *so much* poetry produced during the war, especially in the resource-strapped Confederacy? Dismissing its quality misapprehends Civil War poetry in general, and Confederate poetry in particular. Confederate poetry was largely popular in orientation, occasional in character, and multimedial in circulation. A reading of the "immense amount" of Confederate poetry as a popular, occasional, and multimedia phenomenon reveals a robust poetic culture, one that represented well both local southern communities and tensions among the "sovereign and independent" Confederate states.

Poetry was a ubiquitous and at times tiresome part of cultural life in the Confederacy. As one beleaguered editor of the *Southern Literary Messenger* lamented in July 1863, "We are receiving too much trash in rhyme. What is called 'poetry,' by its authors, is not wanted. Fires are not accessible at this time of year, and it is too much trouble to tear up poetry. If it is thrown out of the window, the vexatious wind always blows it back" (37: 447). At first blush this statement seems to buoy Wilson's claims. This Confederate editor (likely George William Bagby) found little worth publishing in a glut of submitted poems. However, upon closer examination, this oft-quoted quip suggests that the poetry produced in the Confederate States of America was overwhelmingly popular in orientation: to reiterate, "Intended for or suited to the understanding or taste of ordinary people, esp. as opposed to specialists in a field; *spec.* (of literature, etc.) intended for and directed at a general readership" ("Popular," def. 4a.).[3]

The editor of the premier southern literary journal is clearly a specialist; in refusing to call this "trash in rhyme" poetry, he asserts his literary authority, expresses a preference for "polite" literature, and flouts the "understanding or taste of ordinary people." (As discussed in chapter 1, the *Messenger* was never "intended for and directed at a general readership.") And yet, those "ordinary people" responded rapturously to such "trash in verse." During the war, poetry achieved a widespread popularity in the South that was "probably unprecedented and almost certainly never to be equaled thereafter" (W. Moss 5). This brings to mind William Charvat's somewhat tautological definition of popular poetry: "poetry that communicates, *in its time*, to a large portion of the reading population" (105). Trashy or not, a great deal of Confederate verse met these conditions. Thus, in intention, direction, and reception, a great deal of Confederate poetry was popular in orientation.[4]

Charvat's italicized clause, "*in its time*," underscores a second signal characteristic of Confederate poetry: it was occasional in character. By "occasional" I do not mean merely "produced on, or intended for, a special occasion" ("Occasional," def. 4b.), although a great deal of this poetry did commemorate special occasions. Instead, I invoke a more capacious sense of "occasional verse." Arthur Marotti describes the "occasional character of Renaissance lyric verse" in the following terms:

> Their authors professed a literary amateurism and claimed to care little about the textual stability or historical durability of their socially contingent productions. Though modern scholars treat such works as autonomous pieces of literature separable from the circumstances in which they were created, such poems are best viewed first within the social context that shaped them and the system through which they were originally produced, circulated, altered, collected, and preserved. (2)

This redaction applies neatly to Confederate poetry, which was in fact heavily influenced by Renaissance literary culture. As a recent critic notes, when reading Confederate poetry, one "often feels as though transported back in time to the England of Richard Lovelace" (R. D. Watson 207). And, like their English predecessors, many Confederate poets show little interest in literary professionalism: Many published their poems anonymously or pseudonymously, and the majority were "amateurs in every sense of the word" (W. Moss 15). More to the point, their poems were very much "socially contingent productions," nonautonomous works largely inseparable from the circumstances in which they were created—especially those of privation, civil war, and emergent nationalism. In turn, a great deal of this poetry was written quickly and rushed to print; not surprisingly, it bears the marks of such hasty composition. To return to *Patriotic Gore*, if Wilson was looking for timeless verse—his invocation of "today" suggests as much—then the poetry of the Confederacy was bound to disappoint, since it was perforce a timely literature, one very much of and for its specific historical moment.[5]

Finally, that specific historical moment came as methods for the dissemination and circulation of poetry were converging. As I have argued elsewhere, between the beginning of the American Civil War and the end of World War I, popular print poetry in the United States was a multimedia phenomenon. That is, during these sixty years there were a number of media available for the distribution of poetry, and poems often circulated across media, reappearing multiple times in multiple settings. While we often privilege in our criticism and pedagogy single-author volumes of verse (for example, John Greenleaf Whittier's *Snow-Bound* [1866] and Edgar Lee Masters's *Spoon River Anthology* [1915]), popular poetry also—and primarily—circulated in periodicals, newspapers, advertisements, broadsides, annuals, and anthologies. This is particularly the case with Confederate poetry. Because of the various shortages and scarcities described in the introduction, single-author volumes of verse were the exception rather than the rule. Confederate verse also appeared as broadsides, on the pages of newspapers, and in anthologies. Thus, a comprehensive assessment of Confederate poetry must be pursued across multiple media.[6]

In the following pages, I do precisely that. Unlike in the previous chapter, in which a close reading of a single novel granted access to the broader field of Confederate fiction, my focus here remains relatively broad: on the fertile, even overgrown field of Confederate poetry. In tending this somewhat ruined garden of verse, I work systematically, medium by medium, through volumes of verse, broadsides, newspapers, and anthologies. This allows the contours of a vigorous poetic culture to come into view. That culture had as its sine qua non a "profoundly localized and particularized" poetics of place, one that both affirms the fervency of Confederate literary nationalism and betrays the provisional nature of a Confederacy made up of seceding states.[7]

Epic Ambitions

To describe the poets of the Confederacy as largely "amateur" is not to deny their poetic ambition, which often ran wild. This is particularly the case with single-author volumes of verse, defined here as any printed poem or collection of poems composed of more than a single sheet. Although such collections were few in number, they were often outsize in ambition. This is unsurprising given the financial and logistical difficulties of getting a book or pamphlet published in the Confederate States during the war; the very desire to publish a verse volume betrays ambition. And there was no more ambitious volume than John Hill Hewitt's *War: A Poem with Copious Notes, Founded on the Revolution of 1861–62*. Published in 1862 by West and Johnston, this eighty-five-page poem records exhaustively the first sixteen months of the war in an elevated tone and via epic conventions.[8]

Throughout the poem Hewitt alternates between heroic couplets, rhymed quatrains or octaves, and songs (for example, "Song of the Mounted Rangers" [19]), with shifts in rhyme scheme underscoring shifts in subject matter. Although *War*'s primary focus is on battlefield heroics, the poem also makes a number of apostrophes and digressions, incorporating, for example, scenes of camp life and a romance between a "Southern maid" and a "youth." To mediate such dilation, *War* uses running heads that usefully indicate the subject of the action being described: "Surrender of Fort Sumter," "War Feeling at the North," "The Martyr Jackson," and so forth. The result is a strong, quasi-teleological narrative, a textual effect that helps to counteract the "Copious Notes" that dominate the poem. Hewitt cannot seem to help himself: He peppers nearly every page with extensive and often pedantic notes that offer casualty statistics, popular press descriptions, quotations, and trivia. For instance, page 24 includes a mere six lines of verse; page 25 only four. This is not a poem including history but instead a poem overwhelmed by history.

Hewitt is clearly working in an epic mode here, trying desperately both to chronicle passing events and to imbue the Confederate war effort with a transcendent grandeur. Following a brief prose introduction, which narrates the "election of a sectional President" (5) and reads a bit like an epic argument, the poem begins in medias res:

> A sullen murmur, like the moan of waves
> That circle round old Ocean's hidden caves,
> Comes on the feverish air; now louder still
> The sound swells out o'er valley and o'er hill,
> Until it falls, like thunder on the ear—
> Stirs the proud soul and strikes the churl with fear.
> On, in his barb'd and fiery-steeded car,
> With Death and Rapine, rushes angry War,
> Flaunting his blood-red banner in the wind,
> And laughing at the crush'd hearts left behind. (7)

Although *War* does not open with an epic invocation per se, the poet-speaker appeals to the muse throughout the poem, most forcefully when it comes time to narrate an important Confederate victory, the First Battle of Bull Run/Manassas:

> Record, O Muse! that wild, that fearful strife,
> Where clashing hosts with bayonet and knife
> Prey'd on each other—spurred the fiery steed,
> And laugh'd to see their dying *kinsmen* bleed.
> Tell of the havoc of Confederate guns—
> The shameful flight of Northern myrmidons;
> Tell of the flash of bayonet and sword,
> Tell of the brave, the peerless Beauregard! (30)

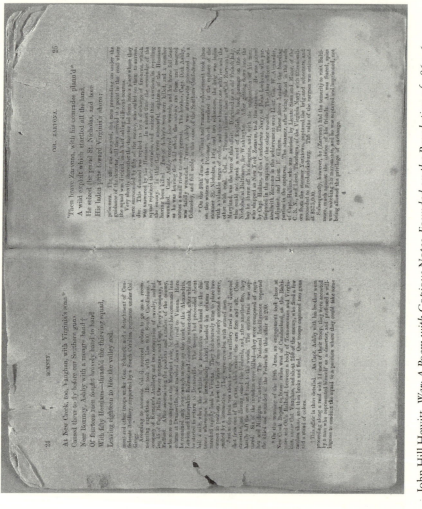

John Hill Hewitt, *War: A Poem with Copious Notes, Founded on the Revolution of 1861–62* (Richmond: West and Johnston, 1862), 24–25. Courtesy of the Boston Atheneaum.

Following a very detailed account of the Confederate victory, the poet-speaker then excuses the muse, commanding, "Muffle the harp strings, let the requiem swell, / Wreathe the laurel round the tombs of those who fell" (33).

Yet, unlike other epic poets, Hewitt wrote quickly and without the benefit of hindsight. The resulting poetry is, not surprisingly, quite pedestrian—a fact Hewitt readily concedes. In a dedicatory epistle to fellow poet James Barron Hope, Hewitt addresses the tension between the epic and the amateur, between historic and merely historical poetry: "Please excuse the liberty I take in dedicating to you the following hastily written poem, which I dare not dignify with the title of epic. . . . You will find, on perusal, much to condemn as bordering on the doggerel—but you must be aware that when a poet is bound down to *facts*, he is compelled to throw the *ideal* aside; at least, I have found it so in attempting to chronicle the events of the war in rhyme" (3). Hewitt's extensive use of epic conventions and grand plans for his poem belie the disingenuous refusal of the title "epic." Hewitt envisioned these 85 pages as but the first "Canto" of his poem-in-progress. The final lines of *War* read, "Now, rest thee, muse—but half thy task is done, / War's barbed chariot still rolls madly on; / His cry is heard all o'er the groaning land, / And armies melt beneath his blazing wand" (85). An accompanying note promises, "The 2d Canto of the poem of 'War' is in course of completion, and will be issued as soon as circumstances will permit" (85). While circumstances never permitted that publication, such a statement reveals a great deal about the ambition that produced *War*.[9]

While Confederate poets might claim (à la Hewitt) to have cast aside poetic ideals, their poetry often remains stubbornly ambitious—sometimes epically so—and clearly tied to broader literary traditions. Moreover, many Confederate poets frankly confessed the poor quality of their verse and then went right on writing and publishing said verse. For instance, Margie P. Swain's seventy-six-page poem *Mara; or, A Romance of the War* (1864) acknowledges immediately the inferior quality of its versification: "The Authoress is perfectly aware that there are many, and, perhaps, to the practiced eye, glaring errors, in this little poem" (5). Begging the indulgence of "our generous Southern critics," Swain forthrightly apologizes for her "childish production," but not before artfully noting that the poem is written entirely in "old English, heroic, or pentameter verse, by some considered difficult, yet in every way suited to epic narration" (5). Once again, a Confederate poet assumes (or feigns) a position of poetic abjection, and then immediately aspires to poetic mastery. Of course, litotes, the rhetorical term for deliberate understatement, especially as a means of expressing modesty, is itself a longstanding poetic convention. Confederates made such rhetoric a central part of their poetic programs.

Published in Selma, Alabama, by the Mississippian Steam Book and Job Office, *Mara*, like Hewitt's *War*, recasts the first several months of the American Civil War as an epic. And, like *War*, *Mara* is divided into cantos, punctuated by copious notes, and well acquainted with epic conventions (see esp. 35–36). Drawing on Edward A. Pollard's history *The First Year of the War* (Richmond: West and Johnston, 1862), the poem uses the Battles of Oak Grove/Wilson's Creek and Lexington as a backdrop for a story of star-crossed lovers, Mara and Eula; an evil Yankee, Lampier; and a mysterious "foreign" beauty, Ena. Not surprisingly, the hero and heroine are gallant and self-sacrificing; in the end, both give their lives for the Confederate cause.

Such gallantry and self-sacrifice are central features of another Confederate poem with epic ambitions, Margaret Junkin Preston's sixty-four-page *Beechenbrook* (Richmond: J. W. Randolph, 1865). Like so many Confederate poems, *Beechenbrook* is written in rhyming couplets; yet unlike many Confederate poets, Preston need not apologize for her versification. Preston, who was Thomas Jonathan "Stonewall" Jackson's sister-in-law, had made her reputation as a poet before the war, and *Beechenbrook* suggests a clear formal command. For instance, the poem concludes with the image of its stoic heroine, Alice Dunbar, who, despite the loss of her home and death of her husband, remains wholly committed to the Confederacy. The poem asks rhetorically, "Does she stand, self-absorbed, on the wreck she has braved, / Nor care if her Country be lost or be saved?" The answer comes in the form of an anaphora:

> By her pride in the soil that has granted her birth—
> By her tenderest memories garnered on earth—
> By the boon she would leave to her children, alone,—
> Right to live and breathe free, in a land of their own;
>
> . . . .
>
> By the blood of the heart that she worshipped,—the life
> That enfolded her own; by her love, as his wife;
> By his death on the battle-field, gallantly brave,
> By the shadow that ever enwraps her—his grave—
> By the faith she reposes, Oh! Father, in Thee,
> She claims that her glorious South MUST BE FREE! (64)

Despite its length, this desolate domestic poem enjoyed a remarkable popularity after the war, in both the South and the North (Fahs 145–46; Klein 60–62).

Even shorter Confederate poems betray epic ambitions. The anonymous thirty-two-page *Adventures of the Marion Hornets, Co. H, 7th Regt. Fla. Vols* (Knoxville, 1863) opens with a winking epic invocation: "Ye muses nine descend and give / My feeble powers your aid, / While I rehearse in simple verse / The tour the 'Hornets' made" (1). It seems that even "simple" Confederate verse requires divine intervention. Similarly, R. Lynden Cowper's sixteen-page poem *Confederate America* opens with an invocation that mixes the Christian and the classical:

> To God the Great Almighty King
> Let harps resound: attune and sing
> Of Jupiter, Mars, or Achilles,
> And gods of wars, and purpled seas
>
> . . . .
>
> Awake then Lyre, praise Father, Son,
> And Freedom's battles fought and won! (3)

To Cowper's mind, the birth of a southern confederacy is an occasion for divine exultation: "Rejoice! a new born Kingdom's here! / A Land of splendor, fresh and dear!" (3).

Published in Raleigh, North Carolina, in 1864 by the Book and Job Office Steam Power Press Print, *Confederate America* includes the sort of "doggerel" that drove Edmund Wilson to distraction. However, the poem is of keen literary-historical interest given the way it ties together epic ambition, poetic ineptitude, and quasi-imperial policy. For all its inelegant rhymes, forced meter, and trite imagery, *Confederate America* offers a resolutely international Confederate literary nationalism, one intimately connected to Confederate trade and commerce and bound by a rhetoric of maritime empire:

> Sphere of the brave, earth's richest clime,
> Onwards, upwards, move thro' time:
> May on thy seas grand Navies ride,
> May white-wing'd commerce and blue-tide,
> Bear off our cotton, corn and wheat,
> Bring products good from foreign State! (11–12)

The Confederacy's agricultural riches will supply the world. So, the poem urges, "Rise, millions, rise,—'tis glorious morn,— / Praise in thunders the Nation's dawn!" (12). Apparently it is morning in "Confederate America."

Immediately following this lusty chanticleer's call, the poem makes a de rigueur and performative plea for cultural distinction: "Let art and science unsurpass'd— / Let virtue, learning, rival,—yes / Reach far beyond the brightest mind / Of any other noted clime!" (12). While this is predictable nationalist rhetoric, what follows is an extraordinary twinning of commercial and literary interests:

> Here, sculptor, hew for self a name—
> Give thy genius deathless fame—
> Here poets write, and upwards fly—
> (With cripp'd wing, alas! we try)—

And tho' they mount to realms of bliss,
We are destined—*chain'd to this!*
My country fears no artist-hand
That shall exceed her genius-man;
Her merchants rich, they speak with pride;
Sound are their names, their honor wide;
Her tradesmen true; with honest heart
Extend their blessings and their art!
Her farmers till the fertile plain—
Feed foreign spheres with native grain—
They dwell in plenty; millions blest—
In this kingdom of the west!
Her docks shall throng with countless sail;
And from all lands of distance hail. (12)

In an otherwise humorless poem, the candor of the parenthetical clause, "Here poets write, and upwards fly— / (With crippl'd wing, alas! We try)," is sublimely comical. Once again here is a Confederate poet's forthcoming declaration of both amateur ambition and poetic ineptitude. But it is the shift from literary art to agricultural and commercial art that commands interest. The parallel structure of these lines and the repetitive claims of "pride" "honor," "honesty," and "plenty" suggest that the "genius" of Confederate America lies not with its "crippl'd wing[ed]" poets but with its "merchant rich," "tradesman true," and "farmers [who] till the fertile plain." While the literary art of the new nation may fail to reach Olympian heights, its terrestrial arts will "throng" the world.[10]

This represents another agro-literary appeal, but with a crucial difference: the addition of a nascent Confederate internationalism. Although the world the poem addresses seems at best Eurocentric—the "blest" "kingdom of the west"—*Confederate America* embraces a broader world still: "Feed foreign spheres with native grain"; "And from all lands of distance hail." Such internationalism is comforting to the poem's speaker, who, as a result, need not worry about the relative achievements of literary culture: "My country fears no artist-hand / That shall exceed her genius-man." In the closed economy of arts that the poem explores—a closed economy very much predicated on international trade—the poverty of literary art is compensated for by the "riches" of agricultural commerce. Bad poetry can be redeemed by good international trade.

Near the end of the poem, the speaker uses an elevated and anachronistic tone to reveal "Confederate America's" imperial ambitions: "Mighty nation of the brave, / E'er may thy banners wave; / Thine empire stretch from sea to sea, / Thine breath as lasting as eternity!" (14). Later, the Confederate States are described as "[t]his empire broad, *God's choicest gem*" (14). In point of fact, the Confederacy was far from a broad empire in 1864; we might say it stretched from sea to gulf, but certainly not from "sea to sea." While such rhetoric is not unexpected in a poem of patriotic bluster, it also captures well the ideology of national exceptionalism that undergirded the Confederate States' actually existing imperial designs. Suffice it to say that *Confederate America*—a poem whose very title insinuates that the Confederacy will one day creep beyond the borders of the seceding southern states—remains both epically and imperially ambitious.[11]

Other palpable, material indices of Confederate poetic ambition are collections of poems about the Confederacy rushed to print in the early days of the war. At least two such collections appeared in the first two years of the conflict, Claudian Bird Northrop's *Southern Odes* (1861) and William J. Shelton's *Confederate Poems* (1862). Credited to "The Outcast," a "Gentleman of South Carolina," the forty-page *Southern Odes* collects Northrop's occasional poems from a number of local South Carolina periodicals and newspapers: the *Charleston Courier, Charleston Mercury, Charleston Evening News, Charleston Catholic Miscellany*, and *Lancaster Ledger*. Like so many Confederate poems, Northrop's odes move fluidly across media and bespeak local affinities and allegiances. Indeed, the collection remains stubbornly South Carolina–centric; these are, in fact, South Carolinian rather than "Southern" odes. In addition to predictable plaudits for Fort Sumter and endless images of palmettos and crescents, poems such as "The South Carolina Hymn of Independence" and "The Single Star, and the Palmetto Banner" never miss an opportunity to remind the reader that South Carolina was the first southern state to secede from the Union: "All hail to our generous State!" one poems demands (7).

Northrop, a slaveholding attorney, politician, and sometime political essayist, was a late convert to Catholicism, and his odes bear clearly the mark of his faith and argue for the justness of a divinely sanctioned Confederate war effort: "Then, when, in war we fight, / For sacred Truth, and Right, / Our battle shout shall be, / Saint John, and Victory!" (32). The remainder of Northrop's poems celebrate battle flags and make urgent calls to arms.[12] In several of these poems of agitation, Northrop employs a powerful and contentious image: "our loyal slave," who "With prompt obedience, stands" with his or her master against the tyrannous North (23). Northrop avers that it is the loyal slave who will make it possible for South Carolinians to do their part for their state and country:

Come to war, from your homes,
   —Children and women secure—
Gather, where the ocean foams;
   Our slaves are faithful and sure—

Guarding the hearth,—tilling the field,—
While we'll force th' invaders to yield. (13)

This fantasy of fidelity, safety, and continued plantation productivity was no doubt comforting for Northrop, who at the time of the publication of *Southern Odes* owned more than two dozen slaves and helped to oversee several dozen more at Bishop Patrick Lynch's Malta Plantation (Heisser 248–49).

Shelton's *Confederate Poems* is a bit more tongue-in-cheek than Northrop's earnest collection, as witnessed by the collection's cartoonish woodblock illustrations and poems such as "The Yankee's Lament for His Whiskey, Lost in the Battle of Seven Pines." Nonetheless, Shelton, a former newspaper editor, shares Northrop's sanguinity about "our loyal slave." In the bewilderingly racist poem "The Yankee Prisoner in Richmond, and the Little Darkies," Shelton narrates a northern prisoner's realization that Virginia slaves do not want to be emancipated:

Well, "hoss," says the darkie,
Nobody didn't ax you;
Here you'll get no thankee—
The home we've got will do

. . . .

Old massa gim'me bread—
Plenty meat to grease it;
I's nussin 'tall to dread—
So, "hoss," you clear de grit. (24)

The poem's wince-inducing dialect stages the loyalty Northrop could only promise in his poems. Through ventriloquism—something Northrop's more polite, gentlemanly odes will not brook—this poem makes the case for a slaveholding republic. Shelton's nameless slave even offers a modest endorsement of Confederate treatment of "chattel": It "will do." The poem in turn suggests the veracity of that endorsement and the senselessness of the Union war effort. After witnessing the "glee" of the "darkies," the Yankee laments from his prison cell, "If we had only known / What now we plainly see" (24).

However, slaves and the peculiar institution are not the animating subjects of Shelton's poetry. The majority of *Confederate Poems* is spent lampooning prominent northern political and military figures: Alfred Ely, the New York congressman captured by Confederates following the First Battle of Bull Run/Manassas; Major Generals George B. McClellan and Benjamin Franklin Butler, "The Beast of New Orleans"; William H. Seward, the Secretary of State; Salmon P. Chase, the Secretary of the Treasury; and Simon Cameron, the Secretary of War. But Shelton reserves his greatest satiric venom for President Lincoln, whose imminent "doom" is predicted in several poems (9).

"Lincoln's March" concludes ominously, "O Abram! O Abram you cannot escape, / For stern justice demands the skin of an Ape" (30).

Anti-Lincoln sentiment was a mainstay of Confederate poetry across all of its media; the president functioned as something of an epic villain in Confederate poetry. Like Satan in Milton's *Paradise Lost*, Lincoln garnered more attention from Confederate poets than did Jefferson Davis, whose heroic qualities were rarely enumerated in verse. Because poets often exaggerated or fabricated his characteristics and actions, the Lincoln that emerges from Confederate poetry would be unrecognizable to most twenty-first-century readers. These representations also prove eerily prescient, since in Confederate poetry the Great Emancipator is often tragically doomed. Again and again, Confederate poems imagine a bloody end for the sixteenth president of the United States. One hundred and fifty years later, the violence of such poems makes for chilling reading.[13]

Reverend Edmund Pendleton Birch's eight-page poem *The Devil's Visit to "Old Abe"* features a drunk, frightened Lincoln welcoming the devil to the White House. In Birch's telling, "Old Abe" is well acquainted with "Old Nick," who, we are lead to believe, made a deal with the Republican party that ensured Lincoln's electoral victory in 1860: "I invented your platform, and gave it *éclat*, / About 'niggers,' and 'freedom,' and the great 'higher law'" (5). But Satan himself is taken back by the evils President Lincoln has perpetuated: "But it stirs up my soul with grief and vexation / To see your abominable Yankee nation / Outstripping me far in the depths of its shame, / And heaping reproach on my kingdom and name" (7–8). The devil goes on to warn that "The avenger is coming. O'er your dark future path, / Is brooding a storm of terrible wrath" (8). Having "ruined [his] nation—degraded its name— / And hurled on its people a heritage of shame," Lincoln has a place reserved for him in hell (8).

William Russell Smith's gossipy, eighty-five-page closet drama *The Royal Ape: A Dramatic Poem* (1863) concurs with the devil's assessment in Birch's poem. Written largely in heroic couplets and deeply indebted to Shakespeare, *The Royal Ape* imagines in intimate detail Lincoln's public and private lives, focusing on the inner workings of his cabinet and the domestic dramas of the First Family. Indeed, the poem is remarkable for its willingness to satirize not only the president but also his wife, Mary, and son, Robert. Throughout the poem, Mary Todd Lincoln gives a number of soliloquies, one comparing her disgrace to that of Eve, another lamenting her choice of husband: "I might have known when first I married thee / That all our hopes would end in misery" (65). Similarly, Robert Lincoln is characterized as a rakish and feminized "prince," who, at the end of the poem, flees Washington in women's clothing. Not surprisingly, the Abraham Lincoln of this poem is cerebral and cowardly; he is even described as having once been a honey-tongued poet. He is also tragically aware of his legacy and political ineptitude. At one point the "Royal Ape" confesses that as president he is "out of place . . . not himself," "As Cicero in war, / And grand Demosthenes, in errant spheres" (74).[14]

The president is once again caricatured as an ape in the quasi-epic *Abram, a Military Poem* (Richmond: Macfarlane and Fergusson, 1863). Credited to "A. Young Rebbelle, Esq. of the Army," *Abram* is written as a series of tightly rhymed "Cantos" (each set in the common ballad scheme abcbdefe), which tell a meandering, martial tale. The poem concludes with a bloody dream:

> One night last week I had a dream
> 　I may as well now give it,
> I dream'd I saw old Abraham,
> 　A swinging on a gibbet;
> And who do you think, boys, held the rope,
> 　'Twas Mr. Jefferson Davis,
> And as he pulled, old Abram cried,
> 　For writ of Corpus Habeas. (47)

After Lincoln is executed by Davis the phrase "*Hic Jacet, Illinois Ape*" is emblazoned on his tombstone (52).

Another closet drama, Stephen Franks Miller's *Ahab Lincoln: A Tragedy on the Potomac* (Milledgeville, 1861), offers an even bloodier Confederate revenge plot. The blank verse of this poem depicts an honorable if "weak and shallow" (17) Lincoln, who, like the "Royal Ape," sees clearly the error of his ways: "I am the guilty cause of all the blood / Spilt on either side in this unnatural war, / And terrible shall be my expiation" (15). Predictably, that expiation is quick in coming. Lincoln confesses his sins and asks that the public be told "How, that having my country ruined, / I yielded up my life in honest retribution, / Hoping that my sins will be forgiven, / As all men freely I forgive—Farewell!" (16). Lincoln then stabs himself and dies. In response, General Winfield Scott, who is horrified to see "Lincoln dead and his office cast to Hamlin, / Who with negro blood is said to be defiled" (16), kills himself: "[*With an energetic thrust he drives his sword into his heart . . .*]" (16). The final scene of this tragedy looks not unlike that of *Hamlet*: The sight is dismal and shows much amiss.[15]

Confederate poets were obsessed with Abraham Lincoln. Imagining the president's inner life was as irresistible as forecasting his death—a consummation devoutly to be wished, it seems. In at least one instance, fantasies of expiation or execution give way to open advocacy for Lincoln's assassination. One of the earliest collections of Confederate verse, Robert Blackwell's lavishly illustrated *Original Acrostics on All the States and Presidents of the United States, and Various Other Subjects, Religious, Political, and*

Personal (Nashville, 1861), is explicit about what should be done to the "Rail Splitter":

Abe Lincoln.

ELECTED PRESIDENT BY THE BLACK REPUBLICANS, NOVEMBER 6, 1860.

ABHORRED by all,
Both great and small,
Existing on this Southern soil.
Lean, hungry,
Insidious,
Nefarious man,
Cunning, and trying
Our ruin to plan;
Let Northerners bow to him,
No Southerner can.

Following a "Moral Lesson" about an eagle and a fox's cub, Blackwell urges the assassination of Lincoln in "The Application": "The most powerful tyrants can not prevent a resolved assassination; there are a thousand different ways for any private man to do the business, who is heartily disposed to do it, and willing to satisfy his appetite for revenge at the expense of his life" (45). This poem was published for the first time in 1861, four years before a very public man, John Wilkes Booth, shot the "villainous" Lincoln in the back of the head.[16]

Thus, in addressing a seemingly compulsive desire to "chronicle the events of the war in rhyme" (Hewitt 3), Confederate poets used their amateur verse ambitiously. Painfully aware of literary convention, their own poetic limitations, and the vicissitudes of the ongoing conflict, these poets crafted verse volumes that would grant the Confederate war effort a sense of epic splendor. Such splendor had, in turn, real political consequences, since it encouraged readers to see the Confederate struggle for independence in relation to a *longue durée* history and as a part of a broad literary tradition. However, verse volumes, with their longer duration and greater material capacity, were by no means the only media available to ambitious Confederates.

Ephemeral Arts

A more ubiquitous and ephemeral medium for Confederate verse was the broadside poem, defined here as any poem or collection of poems printed on a single sheet. Often produced by obscure job printers in small batches with and on whatever materials were at hand, broadsides were a central part of a Confederate print culture that lacked a centralized publishing industry. The broadside could be produced not merely on the cheap or on the fly but also anywhere one could find a simple printing press. As William Moss argues in his descriptive bibliography of Confederate broadside poems, the various scarcities and privations that characterized life in the Confederacy made broadsides the favored medium for popular poetry (36). This leads Moss to conclude that "During the Civil War, we can be fairly certain, the poetry-reading people of the South were reading broadside poems" (viii).[17]

The remaining material evidence bears out Moss's speculation. Despite the ephemerality of these highly portable single-sheet productions, hundreds of Confederate broadside poems survived this most "destructive war" and its aftermath (Royster). Taken together, these "cheap print" artifacts underscore the diversity of Confederate poetic culture. These broadside poems represent various topics and themes, a number of verse forms and genres, and local communities from across the whole of the Confederacy. Such diversity makes it difficult to characterize Confederate broadsides in broad stokes. Indeed, the most consistent characteristics of this verse are its "literary amateurism" and dynamic relationship to its social context. This was, in short, a resolutely occasional poetry.[18]

But let us begin with a familiar topic and theme: Abraham Lincoln, who was a favorite target of Confederate broadside satire. Although the material constraints of the broadside may have limited the length of these anti-Lincoln diatribes, it did little to dampen their noxious spirit. As with volumes of verse, broadside critiques of Lincoln shuttle between the political and the personal. In "Oh! Abraham, Resign!" (n.p., [1861–65]) a "New Contributor" cites increasing political strife in the North and makes a direct appeal to the president: "You've killed the Constitution, / Framed by patriots, 'lang syne;' / You've gagged the mouths of freemen; / Oh! Abraham, resign!" Other poems prove a bit less earnest in their addresses. "To Mr. Linkhorn's" final stanza devolves into simple name-calling: "So good-by Abe, you are a babe, / In military glory; / An arrant fool, a party tool, / A traitor and a tory" (P&W 6578). Similarly, "The Last Race of the Rail-Splitter" ridicules Lincoln's absence from the battlefield and characterizes him as a resolute coward. The poem's refrain also describes Lincoln, a noted teetotaller, as "Soak'd with whiskey, or with rum," and assures its reader that "[w]hen southern troops shall press him hard," Lincoln will flee Washington at the earliest opportunity. Intriguingly, one broadside version of the poem includes a woodcut portrait not of Lincoln but of an escaped slave. This widely used stock image was likely on hand because the unnamed print shop had previously printed advertisements for runaway "chattel." Nonetheless, the juxtaposition of a slave fleeing to freedom and "Old Black Abe" fleeing Washington powerfully conflates policy and politician.[19]

Confederate broadsides did much more than merely caricature Lincoln and his cabinet and generals. A good deal of the surviving verse comments exten-

128

THE LAST RACE OF THE RAIL-SPLITTER.

When Zerxes and when Cyrus led;
  When Bonaparte and Washington,
They took the *field*, as it is said,
  Not so King Lincoln, finds his fun.
    Says Old Abram, as is he,
      Soak'd with whiskey or with rum,
    In the city safe I'll be,
    And the bullets, I will shun.

When dying soldiers strew the plain,
  In Washington he keeps his guard,
Far from the peril and the pain,
  Prepar'd to run from Beauregard.
    Says Old Abram, as is he,
      Soak'd with whiskey, or with rum,
    In the city safe I'll be,
    And the bullets, I will shun

But there's a race he'll likely take,
  When Southern troops shall press him hard,
Some morning, when he early wakes,
  And hears the guns of Beauregard.
    Says Old Abram, at his tea,
      Soak'd with whiskey, or with rum,
    "In the city safe I'll be,"
    In the morning, HE WILL RUN.

In that great race, he'll be the first,
  And Northward streak his hurried way;
When Baltimore he cannot trust,
  And Washington's too hot to stay.
    Says Old Abram, as is he,
      Soak'd with whiskey, or with rum,
    Seward, we had better flee,
    Take a drink and let us run.

Quick—out of bed—no time for pants ;
  Says he, from bullets we must run ;
The shirts they fly—the linen flaunts—
  The little dog laughs at the fun.
    Says Old Abram, we will be,
      Soak'd with whiskey, or with rum,
    Seward, let's the bullets flee,
    Take a drink and let us run.

As frightened rats, when houses burn,
  Escape before the ruin falls,
So honest Abe, his tail will turn,
  To save his skin from rifle balls.
    Says Old Abram, as is he,
      Soak'd with whiskey, or with rum,
    Seward, we had better flee,
    Take a drink, and let us run.

He was so scar'd that dreary night, *
  When hidden like a cask or bail,
In railroad cars, from ev'ry sight,
  He pass'd this city on the rail.
    Said Old Abram, as is he,
      Soak'd with whiskey, or with rum,
    These city boys, are death to me,
    'Tis safer hide and from them run.

The night he hid, and sent his wife,
  Where dead next day she might be found,
And lose, on Central Road, her life,
  Whilst hidden, he went dodging round.
    Said Old Abram, as was he,
      Soak'd with whiskey, or with rum,
    My wife is very good, you see,
    To die for me and let me run.

———— * It will not be forgotten that Lincoln, after his election, on his way to Washington, heard at Harrisburg, that a plan was laid to run the cars off, and kill him on the Northern Central Road, or in Baltimore; (a mere invention, when not a soul thought of hurting a hair on his head,) and to avoid the imaginary danger to himself, he slipped around in the night, in disguise, by the Philadelphia Road, and sent his wife and son by the cars, which were to be smashed up, to be killed in his place.

"The Last Race of the Rail-splitter" [n.p., 1862?]. Courtesy of the Confederate Broadside Poetry Collection, Special Collections and Archives, Z. Smith Reynolds Library, Wake Forest University, Winston-Salem, North Carolina.

sively and tartly on the policies of the U.S. government, with nearly every U.S. action and proclamation subject to Confederate poetic critique. This suggests that poetry was a not-insignificant weapon in the Confederate ideological arsenal. For instance, "Lines on the Proclamation Issued by the Tyrant Lincoln, April First, 1863" lambasts Lincoln for issuing a seemingly innocuous "Proclamation Appointing a National Fast Day" (P&W 6492). Lincoln's 30 March 1863 statement called for a day of "National prayer and humiliation," which the president hoped might result in "no less than the pardon of our national sins, and the restoration of our now divided and suffering Country, to its former happy condition of unity and peace" (Lincoln, vi, 155–56). This deeply religious poem takes great exception to such a divine appeal, deeming it blasphemous for Lincoln "To ask the pure and holy God / To bless his guilty plans, / And with approval sanctify / The tyrant's blood-washed hands." After six twelve-line stanzas of stormy rhetoric, the poem closes with its own Confederate national prayer—"the wail of the oppressed," we are told—which entreats a vengeful God to smite Lincoln: "Thy lightning-dagger thrust / Into that shameless tyrant's heart."

The broadside poem "A Southern Scene" (n.p., [1861–65]) offers an equally pointed response to another, much more famous proclamation, Lincoln's 1 January 1863 Emancipation Proclamation. Staged as a dialogue between a plantation owner's young daughter and her seemingly illiterate "Mammy," the poem opens with a dispatch from the northern states: "'Oh! mammy have you heard the news?'" Quoting the "Yankee President, / Whose ugly picture once we saw," the child announces:

"Well he is going to free you all,
  And make you rich, and grand
And you'll be dressed in silk and gold,
  Like the proudest in the land!

"A gilded coach shall carry you,
  Where'er you wish to ride;
And mammy all your work shall be,
  Forever laid aside!"

Mammy's response to this news is immediate and definitive. While she may not be lettered, Mammy is exceedingly wise, since she is able to see through Lincoln's duplicitous rhetoric. Mammy corrects the child's misplaced and naïve faith in Lincoln's proclamation by ventriloquizing—in dialect, no less—two common defenses of slavery. First, she has the child compare her own "soft and fine" skin to Mammy's "black as any coal" skin, her "yeller ringlets" to Mammy's "heaps of knotty wool." Rehearsing a familiar racialist logic, the elderly slave woman asks, "'My chile who made dis difference /

'Twixt mammy and 'twixt you? / You reads de dear Lord's blessed book, / And you can tell me true.'"

Having assured her charge that "[d]e dear Lord said it mus' be so," Mammy then explains that only God has the authority to set her free. The final eight stanzas of the poem find Mammy renouncing all earthly possessions while pledging continued fidelity to her slave-masters. "And when at las de times's done come, / And poor ole mammy dies, / Your own dear mother's soft white hand / Shall close dese tired ole eyes." To Mammy's mind, the slave system is divinely sanctioned and just; she is in her proper place. The poem's final stanza dismisses the Emancipation Proclamation outright, consigning its author to hell: "'So honey let Abe Linkum be, / For here he cannot come, / But he mus stay in Washington, / Till de debil calls him home!'"[20]

As these examples suggest, broadside poetry seems to have fulfilled an important "news-in-verse function" for Confederate readers, keeping them abreast of current events while also modeling appropriate responses to said events. To read Confederate verse—be it satire or elegy, humorous lyric or fiery war song—is more often than not to witness direct engagement with the politics of the day. Because they were often anonymous and rarely attributed to a printer or publisher, broadside poems also allowed a certain freedom of expression that occasionally exceeded the limits of nineteenth-century mores. Thus, perhaps better than any other media, these ephemeral artifacts provide a record of complex and at times contradictory public feeling during a cataclysmic war in progress.[21]

Confederate broadsides were not singularly focused on news and politics from the North. Confederate victories (and defeats) and heroes (and villains) were also ubiquitous topics. While Jefferson Davis may not have engendered as strong a set of public feelings as his "tyrannous" counterpart, a number of broadside encomiums to the Confederate president survive. The majority of these lyrics remain somewhat abstract in their praise. "Jeff Davis Forever" spends most of its poetic energies in an extended metaphor about the ship of state. Guiding the helm and charting "A free navigation, commerce and trade" is "Davis! the man of our choice" (n.p., [1861–65]). This vaguely internationalist poem avoids making any specific claims about Davis's greatness or exemplarity, emphasizing instead—and somewhat tautologically— that he is the leader that the Confederacy has chosen. Similarly, "Jeff Davis in the White House" (n.p., [1861–65]), a poem directed at "Ye Northern Men in Washington," cannot seem to stay focused on its titular subject. Even as the poem imagines a monumental victory in which Davis assumes the presidency of the United States, its attention wanders back to Lincoln: "Jeff Davis in the White House, / What glorious news it will be; / Abe Lincoln in an inglorious flight / In a baggage car we will see." Although the poem states flatly that "JEFF DAVIS is a brave man," little else is offered about the qualities that distinguish his wartime leadership.

Confederate broadside poets seem to hit their stride as they turn from the abstract "ship of state" to the very concrete theater of war. Not surprisingly, the earliest of Confederate victories, the First Battle of Bull Run/Manassas, engendered broadside ballad after broadside ballad. As they spread the good word of Confederate victory, these poems made outlandish characterizations of battlefield heroics, particularly those of General Pierre Gustave Toutant Beauregard, the Confederacy's first bona fide hero. One heavily reproduced poem, "Beauregard at Manassas," emphasizes the signal importance of gallant leadership to wartime victory:

> But once our spirits faltered Bee and Bartow, were down,
> And our gallant colonel Hampton, lay wounded on the grond;
> But Beauregard, God bless him! led the Legion in his stead,
> And Johnson raised the colors, and waved them o'er head.
> E'en a coward must have followed, when such heroes led the way,
> And not a drop of dastard blood, flowed in Southern veins that day.
> (P&W 6269)

Here Beauregard and the misnamed Joseph E. Johnston are celebrated as paragons of wartime masculinity, able to inspire gallantry and valor from even the most yellow of cowards. With its long line and muddled meter, the poem, credited to "Mrs. Colonel Clark, 14th N.C. Regt.," suggests a heavily hierarchical, top-down understanding of combat-politik. It is the dauntless generals rather than the dumb grunts who embody Confederate courage.[22]

Susan Archer Talley's oft-reprinted ballad "The Battle of Manassas" betrays a similar investment in the differences between "our gallant officers" and "our eager men" (P&W 6570). Early in the poem the speaker seems to identify with rank and file Confederates, assuming a first-person collective perspective: "*We* stood as stony statues stand" (emphasis mine). However, at the end of the sixth stanza, the narrative focus shifts suddenly: "We gripped our sheathen sabres, / We reigned our chargers hard— / And looked to where brave Johnston stood, / And gallant Beauregard." The remainder of the poem renders that "we" as "serried ranks"; through an extended simile in stanza eight, said ranks even become "Gibraltar's living rock" against the "Northern Horde." The representation of tens of thousands of Confederate soldiers as a unified and monumental entity renders the many one. This, in turn, allows Talley to turn her full attention to the heroics of individual officers, such as General Beauregard and Colonel Arnold Elzey (who led a successful brigade charge), as well as to President Davis (who made a late appearance on the battlefield). Once again it is the presence of heroic leadership that steels the common soldier against both cowardly retreat and fast-approaching death:

On, on! ye gallant victors,
    And press your charges hard;
For yonder leads our President,
    And noble Beauregard!
"Hurra! for gallant Davis!"
    The dying strain their eyes,
And feebly join the mighty shout
    That rends the very skies.

As these lines suggest, the seventeen tightly rhymed stanzas of "The Battle of Manassas" are obsessed with ocularity and spectacle. Here the mere proximity of the president and his general—the fact that both are within sight—provides a crucial x-factor for Confederate victory.[23]

This emphasis on the "big bugs"—Private Sam R. Watkins's appellation for important Confederate officers—is to be expected. Since at least Homer, war poetry has tended to privilege battle leaders and officers over "humble privates" (Watkins 11). This is not to dismiss the important cultural work performed by poems about individual Confederate officers. Particularly in the context of an emergent nationalism, the Confederate cultural imaginary needed heroes—and quick. Thomas Jonathan Jackson, who earned the nickname "Stonewall" at the First Battle of Bull Run/Manassas, became one of the Confederacy's earliest heroes and a favorite topic of broadside poems. For instance, the six brisk, hagiographic stanzas of "Stonewall Jackson's Way" affirm the utter confidence that "Old Blue Lights" elicited from his men (P&W 6566). Dated "Martinsburg, Sept. 13th, 1862," the poem claims to have been "(Found on a Rebel Sergeant of the old Stonewall Brigade, taken at Winchester, Va.)." Such an attribution suggests that even in death enlisted soldiers (among others) carried with them an abiding faith in Stonewall Jackson's "Way."

Poems and accounts like this lead Aaron Sheehan-Dean, a historian of the experiences of Confederate soldiers, to conclude that Jackson was a "mythic figure even before his death" at the Battle of Chancellorsville in May 1863 (119). After his death, Jackson moved from the mythic to the legendary, as witnessed by poems like "Lines on the Death of Lieut. Gen. T. J. Jackson C.S.A." (P&W 6407). This elegy opens with an epigraph adapted from a common Scottish epitaph, "He was—but words are wanting to say what, / As what a man *should* be—and he was that." With its very first words the poem tells us that Jackson is a masculine ideal that the speaker of the poem is loath to relinquish. Indeed, the speaker does not seem to have accepted, much less assimilated, the death these "Lines" describe. One macabre stanza even asks a personified death for appeasement: "Dread king of the grave, Oh! return us dear 'Stonewall,' / Unfetter his heart from the cold chains of death! / Monarch of terrors, so gloomy, so silent, / Loose the adamant clasp of the cold icy wreath!" Such a direct, postmortem appeal is highly unusual in broadside elegies, which often thematize acceptance and supernatural comfort. Yet this is in keeping with the resolutely dour tone of the poem. These lines document the utter abjection brought on by Jackson's death, an event that occasioned an extraordinary outpouring of public feeling throughout the Confederacy. Crucially, "Lines on the Death of Lieut. Gen. T. J. Jackson C.S.A." is voiced in the first-person plural—"Oh! return us dear 'Stonewall'"—suggesting the sort of shared intimacy that is at the heart of any act of national mourning.[24]

As Max Cavitch has argued powerfully, elegies in general "seek to extend the lives of individuals and of groups, augmenting personal remembrance and collective heritage" (32). This was particularly the case during the Confederate national moment, and such extensions and augmentations were dominant modes for the Confederate broadside elegy. For instance, a little-read elegy for an obscure Confederate officer, Henry Clay Gorrell, artfully blurs the lines between the individual and the group, between the personal and the collective. Credited to "A Friend of the Cause," the poem is a reflexive and performative affair, one that moves quickly from interment to memorialization:

> They laid him away in the cold damp ground,
>   On the banks of a Southern stream;
> Not far from his home in his own native land
>   Where the rays of a tropic sun gleam.
> No coffin to enclose his mangled remains
>   No shroud save his uniform coat,
> But his name is entwined with the laurels of fame,
>   And on memory's tablet 'tis wrote. (P&W 6410)

By the end of stanza one, Gorrell's meager and unceremonious burial has been redressed; we are told that these "Lines" grant him the immortality his actions demand.

As with so many Confederate poems, this elegy is animated by a tension between universality and specificity. Here the indeterminacy of the poem's referents chafes against the strict literalness of its title. Gorrell's remains are placed next to a nameless "Southern stream," and his family awaits his return in a nondescript "little white cottage in the land of the South." (One might think of *Macaria*'s relentless geographical indeterminacy.) Yet the title reads in full "LINES Sacred to the Memory of Capt. Henry C. Gorrell of Greensboro', N.C., Of the Second North Carolina Regiment, *Who fell in an attack which he led against the Federal Batteries at the battle of Fair Oaks, June 14, 1862.* MAY HE REST IN PEACE." The play here between text and paratext, between the seemingly universal rhetoric of the verse and the highly specific language of the title, allows readers to identify with the poem in a range of ways, from the abstract to the concrete and back again. This tension could be, then, a deft poetic effect. Given the strange ways of Confederate poetic circulation, we can imagine this elegy engendering a range of readers both in and well beyond the regiment in which Gorrell served.

The somewhat familiar imagery of the poem leaves open the possibility of readerly identification with the loss being described—even if the reader had never known Gorrell, or, for that matter, anyone else from the Second North Carolina. In its second stanza, the poem rather awkwardly martyrs Gorrell, using common rhetoric to imbue his death with a sense of nationalist purpose and pride: "For his 'home' he fought, for his 'rights' he died, / He's a martyr to a 'Glorious Cause'; / The Confederacy he loved, and to see her prevail / He died while defending her laws." Yet by placing Gorrell in a specific regiment, locality, and moment, the poem's prolix title also encourages local audiences to identify with this son of "Greensboro'." Regardless of audience, such details grant the poem a sense of intimacy, suggesting that the "Friend of the Cause" is offering a personal remembrance in these otherwise formulaic "Lines." As a result, this at times abstract tribute has the potential to be affecting for any number of Confederate readers, both near and far.

Such incongruous desires for both specification and generalization are a hallmark of Confederate poetry, which rarely struck an easy balance between the two extremes. For every poem like the Gorrell elegy, there are dozens more that hew to either the specific or the general. We might understand such bifurcation in relation to the precarious political position established by a Confederacy made up of seceding states. The second dependent clause of the preamble to the Confederate Constitution of 1861 puts the problem succinctly: "We, the people of the Confederate States, each State acting in its sovereign and independent character." As with the U.S. Constitution, it is no mean feat to square the collectivity imagined by "We, the people" with the varied interests of individual states, especially if one acknowledges immediately and explicitly the "sovereign and independent character" of said individual states. By way of closing this consideration of Confederate broadside verse, I turn to the stark differences between poems written in celebration of the Confederate States of America and those written in celebration of individual states thereof.[25]

The secession of the southern states and formation of a provisional Confederate government in early 1861 occasioned a spate of commemorative broadside poems, many of which celebrate the new nation and call its citizens to arms. "The Spirit of 1861" represents neatly these poems of agitation. With the large-font letters "C.S.A." breaking up its middle stanza, this cocksure poem predicts that "The Confederate States will claim a brilliant fame, / From her arise a nation proud and free, / We'll raise her flag, and vindicate her name, / Land of the free—the home of Liberty!" (P&W 6561). Couching the plight of the Confederates in the rhetoric of oppression, the poem seems to miss the tragic irony of its refrain, "The yoke of slaves we'll never, never bear!" Again and again, early nationalist broadsides imagine the Confeder- ate States of America as a nation to be reckoned with. Eager for international recognition and approbation, poems like "Song! Hail to the South" call out loudly to other nations: "Another star arisen, another flag unfurled, / Another name inscribed among the nations of the world!" (n.p., [1861–65]). While such recognition proved frustratingly elusive (as discussed in chapter 5), the declaration of recognizability was a leitmotif of Confederate poetry.

As these examples suggest, a good deal of Confederate broadside verse re- mains stubbornly abstract, extolling the virtues of southern courage, southern climate, and southern agricultural plenty without going into great detail. As shorthands, nationalist mottos and emblems come to dominate these poems, which often have little concrete to say about the emblem being venerated. A representative moment comes in the opening lines of "The Confederate Flag": "Bright banner of freedom, with pride I unfold thee. / Fair flag of my country with love I behold thee" (n.p., [1861–65]). In jingoistic couplet after jingo- istic couplet, these poems, which were commonplace in both the South and the North during the early years of the war, ripple with patriotic bluster.

While it is easy to dismiss these poems as being so much hot air, they were in fact important to an emergent Confederate cultural imaginary. Among many other things, these nationalist broadsides helped prepare Confederate citizens for war and the privations it would bring. Many of these poems pull no punches, suggesting that a bloody war with the North was inevitable. In one astonishing poem, "It Is I!," no less than the "great Jehovah" concedes this fact and yet urges "southern freemen" to the battlefield: "Unsheath your swords—be bold—be brave! / . . . In Federal blood your broadswords lave" (P&W 6374). Yet God the Father was not the only authority urging Confed- erate men to pick up their swords. "The Confederate Soldier's Wife Parting from Her Husband!" opens with the titular wife literally pushing her hus- band out the door: "Here is thy trusty blade! / Take it, and wield it in a glori- ous cause," she urges (P&W 6278). Showing some of the "Spartan woman- hood" discussed in the previous chapter, this Confederate wife acknowledges the dangers her husband will face: "What if thou fallest? my heart will throb to know / He died, O South, for thee!" With both God and their wives on their side, newly constituted Confederates could begin fighting for what re- mained a somewhat inchoate national cause.[26]

One way that Confederate broadside verse managed the problem of a still nascent nationalism was by emphasizing the subsumption of local and state allegiances under a broader, national allegiance. This led to the marshaling of an ingenious poetic form, the roll call poem. Calling out to each state in the Confederacy, as well as to border states, such as Maryland and Missouri, these broadside poems canvassed the new geography of the South in an attempt to shore up membership and encourage a sense of national belonging. One of the most reproduced of these poems was "The Southern Wagon," which, through an extended metaphor, urges individual states such as Missouri, North Carolina, and Arkansas to join the Confederacy: "Come all ye sons of Freedom and join our Southern band, / We're going to fight the enemy and drive them from our land; / Justice is our motto and Providence our guide. / So jump into the wagon and we'll all take a ride" (P&W 6552). While poems like "The Southern Wagon" may not offer much in the way of specifics—one couplet reads, "Our cause is just and holy, our men are brave and true— / To fight for our Confederate flag is all we'll have to do"—they do name names, adding a pointed specificity to their appeal for southern accord.

Roll call poems continued to circulate well after the formation of the Confederacy and the onset of Civil War hostilities. "Song. Sunny South!" seems to date from sometime after the formation of the C.S.A., since it sings the praises of all eleven seceding states and spends a good deal of time lamenting the fates of fettered Maryland, occupied Kentucky, "Unhappy Missouri," and "poor lost Delaware." This roll call opens with a couplet that flaunts the fruits of secession, "To arms, to arms, and old Abe shall see / That we have a Southern Confederacy" (P&W 6568). Another roll call poem, V. E. W. (McCord) Vernon's "The Battle Call," is a rara avis: an attributed, copyrighted, and dated broadside produced by a major publisher, West and Johnston. Over twenty eight-line, rhyming stanzas, the 20 February 1862 poem calls out to all eleven Confederate states, plus Kentucky, Missouri, Maryland, and the territory of Arizona. The poem's first and final stanzas open with great hope, "Rise Southmen! the day of your glory, / The hour of your destiny's near— / The fame of your chivalrous story / All nations are eager to hear" (P&W 6592). As with actual military roll calls, these poetic lists both affirm presence and perform unity; the implied responses to these calls signify collectivity and cohesion during a moment of crisis and creation in the tenuous Confederacy.

What is most remarkable about the Confederate broadside poetry that survived the war is how far-flung its geographies prove, how errant its itineraries seem. Despite wide discrepancies in available resources, remaining broadsides represent *every* state in the Confederacy. For example, "North Carolina. A Call to Arms!!!" upbraids its audience with emphatic exclamations and rousing rhetoric: "Ye sons of Carolina! awake from your dreaming! / The minions of Lincoln upon us are streaming!" (P&W 6443). "Tennessee! Fire Away!" opens with a similar tone and tenor: "Black Republican Bandits / Have crossed to our shore, / Our soil has been dyed / With Tennessee's gore" (P&W 6571). A bit more thoughtfully, "The Georgia Volunteer" stages a soldier's explanation to his wife of the reasons he needs to leave his home state and fight for the new nation: "Our rights have been usurped, dear, / By

Northmen of our land, / Fanatics raised the cry, dear, / Politicians fired the brand" (P&W 6329).[27]

These state-based battle hymns and patriotic odes effectively localize the broader conflict and its nationalistic context, resulting in what we might call a nested nationalism. By grounding the new Confederacy in a set of older, local affinities and allegiances, these poems work to naturalize and concretize a constructed and abstract nationalism. In the majority of these poems, the state at hand maintains its "sovereign and independent character," despite its pledge of allegiance to the Confederacy. As a result, several surviving broadside poems beam with state pride. "Texan Rangers," a poem published in Galveston, Texas, in early 1861, makes a swaggering claim about the signal contribution Texans will make to the Confederate war effort: "But their souls feel no tremor, they smile in their pain / They know that the South will have freedom again; / Be hallow'd such suffering, and bless'd every sigh, / They are Texans, who know how to triumph and die!" (P&W 6572). Here allegiance to one's state is not at odds with allegiance to one's nation. When the one is nested within the other, the state and the nation, Texas and the Confederacy, are easily reconcilable.

However, Confederate broadside verse also went well beneath the level of the state. Surviving poems also represent specific communities, bear the marks of locality, and take up obscurely local topics and tropes. This was not merely a poetics of state but also a poetics of place. For instance, poems representing individual Confederate regiments seem to have found their way into print with surprising regularity. To take a few wide-ranging examples, one group of guerrilla fighters in Missouri, "Kelly's Irish Brigade," circulated a broadside bragging about their victory over a group of "cowardly Lincolnites" (P&W 6386). Similarly, a "Captain Alexander" of the "Baltimore Light Artillery, CSA" published a broadside that sang the praises of his "Maryland Boys" (P&W 6214). Perhaps the most local of these regimental poems is a re-working of the lyrics to the popular song "Happy Land of Canaan" by one "Yendis Nilknarf" (Sidney Franklin?). Each of the poem's ten stanzas pay homage to a different company of the Fifth Regiment of Texas Volunteers, including the "Bayou City Guards," "Polk County Rifles," and "Waverley Confederates," to whom the poem is dedicated. One broadside version of the poem even includes a "Muster Roll" of the members of the Waverley Confederates, suggesting the coterie circulation and commemorative potential of these ephemeral documents (P&W 6320).[28]

Another apt example of this localism is "Rebel Gunpowder," a scatological poem that reflects well the sacrifices and shortages that characterized the final two years of the Civil War in central Alabama. "Rebel Gunpowder" purports to respond to an October 1863 advertisement published in the *Selma Sentinel* by a "John Harrolson," who asked the "Ladies of Selma" to save the

contents of their chamber pots so that it could be turned into saltpeter. One
key stanza reads,

> John Harrolson! John Harrolson!
>   How could you get the notion
> To send your barrels 'round the town
>   To gather up the lotion.
> We think the girls do work enough
>   In making love and kissing.
> But you'll now put the pretty dears
>   To patriotic pissing! (n.p., [1861–65])

An intimately local poem if ever there was one, "Rebel Gunpowder" makes
light of the various personal sacrifices made by civilians to support the war
effort. Perhaps because of its ribald rhymes, the poem was widely reprinted
in both the South and the North during the war; it also became a popular
song, one that is still performed a century and a half later.

Like "Rebel Gunpowder" the broadside poem "Ladies of Richmond" also
catalogs local sacrifices made for a national cause but in a very different
mode and mood. Given its title we might expect the poem to be a celebration
of Virginian beauty or social grace. Instead "Ladies of Richmond" speaks directly to the elite women of the Confederate capital, imploring them to:

> Fold away all your bright tinted dresses,
>   Turn the key on your jewels to-day,
> And the wealth of your tendril-like tresses
>   Braid back in a serious way;
> No more delicate gloves, no more laces,
>   No more trifling in boudoir or bower,
> But come with your souls in your faces,
>   To meet the stern wants of the hour. (P&W 6395)

This emotive poem identifies the nursing of wounded soldiers as the most
urgent of said "wants." After six evocative and gory stanzas, the ladies' mission is laid out in stark, forbidding terms: "You must balsam the wounds of
a nation, / Nor falter nor shrink from your part." It is for this somber cause
that the upper-class women of Richmond should eschew common comforts
and luxuries.

Because of the broadside's fundamental dynamism—its ability to be produced and reproduced in a number of settings—the preceding discussion offers a view of Confederate poetic culture at the margins. Poems such as the
ones considered above stress the at-times fraught coexistence of local and national belonging. At the center of this poetic culture lies a more static medium,
the national periodical, which further suggests how an emphasis on locality
can both produce and threaten the coherence of Confederate community.

Everyday Appositions

The periodical is the medium through which the majority of Confederate poetry circulated at some point in time. Poetry was a ubiquitous presence in southern periodicals during the war; periodicals were, in turn, a mainstay of Confederate literary culture. For evidence of this, we need only return to *Southern Odes*, Claudian Bird Northrop's 1861 volume of verse. The litany of local, South Carolina publications in which Northrop's poems initially appeared underscores the signal importance of periodicals to the distribution of Confederate poetry. The relationship between broadside and newspaper verse was particularly intimate, since printing forms used for one could easily be reused for the other. As William Moss notes, "Few Southern towns of any size were without a local paper, and few of those papers were without their 'Poets' Corners.' Many of the popular poems later printed as broadsides began their public careers in that humble but wholly respectable feature of nineteenth-century journalism" (30). Although we need not accede to his unidirectionalism—in truth, poems moved fluidly among the various poetic media; absent attribution, it is difficult to determine if a poem's public career began as a broadside or in a newspaper—Moss's comments about the omnipresence of local newspaper poetry are spot-on.

Confederate newspaper verse offers an uncommon opportunity to read southern poetry in material and cultural context. Because these poems appeared alongside a number of other social forms, they force us to confront directly nineteenth-century reading practices. Juxtaposed with journalism, fiction, humor, essays, editorials, advertisements, cartoons, and illustrations, newspaper poems allow us to see Confederate poetry as it was: a commonplace part of everyday life. Newspapers are also a collaborative and edited affair; their pages are the result of social agents working in tandem to select content and layout. As a result, newspaper verse is curated in ways that the volumes of verse and broadside poems discussed above are not. Such curation yields a complex interplay among authorship, intention, ideology, and reception. In turn, the larger print runs of newspapers brought Confederate poems into a wide range of hands and homes, thus producing a number of different reading publics. In all, newspaper verse might be considered the most sociable form of Confederate poetry.[29]

Such sociability is on full display in the pages of the fiercely nationalistic *Southern Illustrated News*. Printed in Richmond, Virginia, by Ayres and Wade, an important publisher of Confederate textbooks and children's literature, the family-oriented *News* appeared weekly from 13 September 1862 to 25 March 1865. This was an impressive run for a Confederate periodical, even excepting a number of suspensions and production delays. Indeed, the *News* was one of the few publishing successes of the Confederacy, increasing its circulation despite rising subscription prices and readers' diminishing disposable incomes.[30]

From its first issue, the *News* was clear about its aims: to be "an unexceptionable and elegant *parlor journal*" (26 December 1863). Although recent historians have described the *Southern Illustrated News* as a Confederate answer to northern weeklies such as *Harper's Weekly* and *Frank Leslie's Illustrated Newspaper*, in fact its editors claimed to look a bit farther afield for inspiration. The first issue of the second volume claimed, "We shall not be quite content with our work until we have established, in connection with a Southern publishing house of the first class, a weekly equal in all respects to the 'Illustrated News' of London, or 'L'Illustration" of Paris'" (2 [4 July 1863]: 5).[31] While *Harper's* and *Frank Leslie's* may have been more familiar to the *News*'s readers, these European weeklies provided the editorial lodestar. Indeed, as a journal "devoted to polite literature and the fine arts," the *News* often brought Confederate and European literature into close conversation. Such international commerce was a stated editorial principle of the journal: "In literature it is *chiefly* original, comprising the productions of the *novelist*, the *poet*, and the *critic*. It encourages native genius and industry. . . . *It does not, however, ignore exotic productions*, but culls from time to time, with studious care, the *roses* and *laurels* that have sprung on a foreign soil" (26 December 1863: 196). Once again, foreign flowers provide a context for Confederate literary aspiration.[32]

Produced in the capital city, the *Southern Illustrated News* was the Confederacy's only self-consciously national newspaper. Not surprisingly, intellectual and cultural historians have stressed the importance of its eight-page issues to our understanding of Confederate nationalism. Linda Frost goes so far as to argue that the periodical "contains within its pages the ideological, philosophical, and literary seeds of the Confederacy" (87). Yet, despite such critical attention, no one has acknowledged fully the central role that poetry played in the *Southern Illustrated News*. This periodical was exceedingly poetic—lousy with lyric, even. Any given issue might include as many as six poems scattered among the second, third, sixth, and eighth pages. By its third volume, poems had begun to appear as the first item in the first column of the paper's first page. Suffice it to say, the *Southern Illustrated News* had several "poet's corners" in each issue.[33]

These poems appeared on the same pages and in the same columns as an impossibly diverse set of features. A lover of poetry would have to navigate her or his way through dispatches from the warfront, biographical sketches of generals and war heroes, and discussions of pressing political issues. In looking for poems, she or he might stumble on literary criticism and extensive coverage of "The Drama," as well as short fiction and excerpts from novels and novelettes. Perhaps a more exotic piece might catch her or his eye.

The *News* offered excerpts from Carlyle's *French Revolution* (21 February 1863); a collection of "Turkish Proverbs" (6 June 1863); descriptions of Japanese women (3 October 1863); recipes for "hot weather drinks" (2 [24 July 1863]: 18); even a pseudoscientific dissertation on the rapidity of thought in dreaming. Toward the end of a given issue, she or he might find one final poem tucked among advertisements, notices to correspondents, aphorisms, enigmas, and cartoons.

Perhaps because of its extensive roster of regular contributors, the *News* largely eschewed the newspaper exchange system, which encouraged the attributed reprinting of material from other newspapers. Instead the paper published original poems, many of which were proudly advertised as having been "Written for the Illustrated News." In doing so, the periodical showcased both obscure and established poets. The latter group included a who's who of southern letters, including Paul Hamilton Hayne, James Barron Hope, William Gilmore Simms, Susan Archer Talley, John R. Thompson, and Henry Timrod. Alongside these luminaries appeared such lesser-known poets as Mary A. McCrimmon and Margaret Stilling (a nom de plume for Mary Evans), both of whom were regular contributors. Finally, the *News* did not hesitate to publish anonymous and pseudonymous poems as well. The result of this diversity was a compelling mixture of low and high, of various verse forms and topics. This was poetry for all kinds of readers.[34]

The topics of the poems that appeared in the *Southern Illustrated News* resemble closely those that appeared in broadsides. A good number of poems commemorated specific battles and battlefield heroics. For example, "Tenella" was responsible for a set of poems focused on the contributions of local regiments and minor battles such as "The Charge of the 24th North Carolina Reg't at the Battle of Sharpsburg" (10 January 1863: 3) and "The Battle of St. Paul's: Fought in New Orleans, on Sunday, October 12th, 1862" (14 February 1863: 5). Many other poems were political in nature, commenting on military and public policy in the Confederacy and beyond. John R. Thompson's unattributed "England's Neutrality" was a clever poetic satire of a parliamentary debate about recognition of the Confederate States (2 [8 August 1863]: 38). "The Rebel Sock," described as "A True Episode in Seward's Raids on the Old Ladies of Maryland," offered a withering critique of Federal efforts to confiscate Confederate provisions (20 December 1862: 7). The *News* even reprinted "Lines on the Proclamation Issued by the Tyrant Lincoln, April First, 1863," the broadside poem that critiqued Lincoln's "Proclamation Appointing a National Fast Day" (2 [31 October 1863]: 133).

Thomas Jonathan Jackson proved a pliable muse for the *Southern Illustrated News*, which devoted its inaugural illustration to "Stonewall."[35] In addition to reprinting "Stonewall Jackson's Way" (13 December 1862: 7), the *News* spent the summer of 1863 publishing original elegy after original elegy for the hero of Manassas, including "Jackson's Funeral" (20 June 1863: 6), "Stonewall Jackson" (2 [11 July 1863]: 10), and "Over the River" (2 [24 July 1863]: 18). In all, the elegiac was a dominant mode for the poetry of the *Southern Illustrated News*—and with good reason. The first issue of the second volume of the *News* hit the streets just as the Battle of Gettysburg began—a conflict that would alone produce an estimated 28,000 Confederate casualties. The summer of 1863 was to be the summer in which Robert E. Lee hoped to "conquer a peace"; however, cataclysmic losses at Gettysburg and Vicksburg ensured that the bloody war would continue for the foreseeable future, providing innumerable occasions for deathly poems (McPherson, *Battle Cry* 664–65).[36]

Several issues of the *News* are dominated by poems of death, dismemberment, and disease. The issue for 13 December 1862 offers poems about both limb loss ("The Empty Sleeve") and a painful demise ("Dead") (5–6). Similarly, the issue for 14 March 1863 pairs the repetitive lament "Fallen!" (3) with C. C. Cole's "The Departed" (4), emphasizing the experience of loss from afar. Finally, the issue for 7 May 1864 is bookended by Cuba's "The Dying Soldier" ("I am dying, comrades, dying") and George Walter Sites's "The Soldier's Farewell" (3: 137, 144), suggesting a prolonged, eight-page goodbye for the nameless soldier. Although not all of these poems are explicitly about battlefield casualties—the lachrymose lyric "The Dying Children" (1 November 1862: 4) laments all premature deaths; "I Loved Her," by "Louise, of New Orleans," is a devastating lament for a dead daughter (17 May 1863: 3)—such lyrics capture well the "culture of death" that Mark S. Schantz argues was a precondition for the "unprecedented destructiveness" of the American Civil War (3).

Such a forthright engagement with the horrors of war distinguishes the poetry of the *Southern Illustrated News*, which did not blanch in the face of widespread death. At the same time, the *News*'s editors seem to have been aware of the relentlessness of such dour poems; occasionally they offered their readers respite. Unlike broadsides, which are almost universally centered on wartime topics, the newspaper also ran light, everyday verse, poems that had little to do with the conflict between the United and Confederate States of America. Although much of the poetry in the *News* remained stubbornly occasional, not every occasion being marked was political or martial in nature. The *News* regularly published poems about the current season (for example, "Autumn Signs" 3 [26 November 1864]: 247) and upcoming holidays (for example, Vivian's Valentine's Day poem "To ***" 7 February 1863: 7). The presence of these nonwar poems could lead to jarring juxtapositions. For instance, Mary A. McCrimmon's lighthearted verse about Santa Claus appeared on the same page opening as James D. McCabe's red-blooded battle cry "Mississippians Never Surrender" (27 December 1862: 6–7).

Of course, it is possible to root out subtle or veiled references to the ongoing conflict in some of these everyday poems. This is particularly easy with the number of poems that express nostalgia for simpler times or hope for better days. The poem "Dreams," which opened the issue for 30 April 1864, begins with a wistful dream of "my childhood's home"; includes a vision of the future, "I dream of a happy future spread / Enchanting to my view. / That honor and prosperity / Fall like refreshing dew"; and ends with the speaker confessing that "I feel in sleep I'm happier / Than in the busy day" (3: 130). Although the poem makes no direct reference to the war, we can imagine the *News*'s war-weary readers identifying with its longing for a happier state of affairs. Similarly, we can readily read Grace Millwood's elusive poem "Divided," which narrates the dissolution of a transatlantic friendship, in terms of British refusal to recognize the Confederacy: "Minnie, I sever all ties—tis o'er— / Our friendship, faith and trust of yore" (25 October 1862: 4). However, much of the *News*'s everyday verse proves more recalcitrant. It would be difficult to find evidence of the war in "The First Gray Hairs" (2 [12 September 1863]: 77) or "The Tooth Ache" (3 [6 February 1864]: 35). Sometimes a toothache is just a toothache; these are merely poems about quotidian events.

Other poems seek out moments of peace, quiet, and pleasure in wartime. At least two poems apostrophize songbirds that have found their way into camp. E. T. W.'s "To a Mocking Bird, on Being Waked by Its Song, near the Camp, in the Dusk of Morning" discovers both the pastoral and a promise of peace in an unexpected setting:

> But if thou com'st to cheer my soul
> With hints of what shall be—
> A prophet with the dusky stole,
> And pipe of jubilee—
> Let not, amid these glooms of war,
> Thy holy matins ceases,
> 'Till thou shalt *prove* the morning star
> That leads the dawn of peace. (18 April 1863: 5)

"Reminiscences of a Breakfast," which affectionately sends up a soldier's epistolary tribute to a meal he had while on furlough, finds pleasure in a more familiar place: "'As winds the ivy 'round the tree,' / As to the morn its misty fogs, / So Fancy ever clings to thee, / Ye *linked essences* of Hogs" (3 [23 April 1864]: 127).

If all is fair in love and war, then it should come as little surprise that the pages of the *News* brim with lyrics of love. Although a handful of these love poems are addressed to specific personages (for example, G. C. W.'s "Lines to Miss Mattie W. Goodwin, of Louisa County, Va.," 17 January 1863: 8), the majority aim for a broader audience. Poems like "Trust Me, and Be Mine" (18 October 1862: 3), "Oh! Meet Me." (17 January 1863: 7), "Affection" (2 [24 October 1863]: 125), and "That Sweet Old Love" (2 [24 October 1863]: 126) could have appeared in any nineteenth-century "poet's corner." This is not to say that this is timeless verse, in terms of either quality or context. Again, we can read this glut of love poems as a function of the fact that the American Civil War separated innumerable lovers and shattered countless families in both the South and the North. However, these lyrics leave such interpretive work to the reader.[37]

More than anything else, these poems of love and sausage links, of toothaches and childhood homes, remind us that, even as casualties mounted and privations multiplied, life went on in the Confederate States of America. Perhaps these lyrics offered comfort or distraction for the readers of the *News*. In any case, they grant us a fuller sense of the diversity of Confederate poetry and its central role in the intellectual life of the new nation.

One final, recurrent topic of the poems in the *Southern Illustrated News* is poetry itself. Consider, for instance, a 12 December 1863 poem entitled "Battle Hymns." This metapoetic verse, which appeared directly under an amateurish illustration of "Louisianians, of Hays's Brigade, Burying the Dead at 'Malvern Hill,'" calls for the abandonment of "languid lays" in favor of lyrics that show the "heat of strong desire" that lies "Cankering in a Nation's heart" (2: 184). But the *News* published no more reflexive poem than Paul Hamilton Hayne's "The Southern Lyre." Hayne was among the *News*'s most prolific contributors. Over the course of the war, he published more than a dozen poems in the *News*, including numerous sonnets and songs, as well as several "Paraphrases of Oriental Poetry" (6 June 1863: 6; 2 [12 September 1863]: 74). The *News* even granted Hayne a recurring feature, "Poems of the War," in which he published a range of war-related poems, including "Stuart!" (6 December 1862: 7), "Our Martyrs" (10 January 1863: 7), "The Substitute" (31 January 1863: 7), and "Scene in a Country Hospital" (30 May 1863: 4).

For the first issue of its second volume—dated 4 July 1863, no less—the editors of the *News* pulled out all stops, allowing Hayne some two full columns to breathlessly "sin[g] the praises of his brother minstrels" (2: 5). In all, "The Southern Lyre" comprises a staggering five dozen tercets. This was clearly a major publication for the *Southern Illustrated News*, and not simply because of its length. The editors considered the poem so important that they offered it a laudatory introduction immediately following some celebratory comments marking the *News*'s second volume. Among other things, the editors concur with Hayne's assessment that, save for Poe's "The Raven," Philip Pendleton Cooke's "Florence Vane," and Richard Henry Wilde's "My Life Is like the Summer Rose," "all Southern effusions" had been systematically excluded from prewar anthologies of American literature. But, "The Southern Lyre" promises, never again (5).[38]

Hayne's "Procession of Poets" opens emphatically:

No longer shall the darksome cloud
Of Northern Hate and Envy shroud
The radiance of our Poets proud.

They come, a glorious Band to claim
The guerdon of their poet-fame—
Their brows with heavenly light aflame! (6)

Beginning predictably with Poe, "Whose genius lives in realms of Blight," Hayne works systematically through some of the best-known male poets of the South, going as far back as the early national period and Washington Allston. However, a great deal of the poem is spent celebrating more contemporary verse: that of John Esten Cooke, James Barron Hope, Albert Pike, James Randall, William Gilmore Simms, Henry Timrod, and John R. Thompson. What do these poets have in common? They were all published in the pages of the *Southern Illustrated News*. And where in this procession is Hayne himself? Rest assured, in their introduction to "The Southern Lyre" the editors offer three tercets that celebrate the purportedly modest poet.

"The Southern Lyre" is what Poe might have called a piece of self-puffery. But, as discussed in chapter 1, puffery performs real cultural work, particularly in a literary nationalistic context. In addition to not so subtly affirming the quality of the *News*'s poetry selections, the poem and its editorial frame proffer a canon of southern-cum-Confederate poetry. If, as Gregory Jusdanis argues, canons "instill in people the values of nationalism," then this lengthy poem functions as something of a crash course in Confederate poetic nationalism (*Belated* 49). Here are the poets that a Confederate reader needs to know.[39]

Hayne draws particular attention to poetry's nation-building promise in the final stanzas of "The Southern Lyre," which forgo individual tributes and urge Confederates to continue to write and champion southern poetry: "Still must we make our music heard: / These genuine numbers, long deferred / Full audience, shall not leave unstirred." The result of ongoing poesis will be a new day for the Confederate States of America:

Then, with the war-clouds rolled afar,
And all undimmed our natal star,
Mankind SHALL know us—AS WE ARE!—

A People, liberal, noble, brave,
And courteous to the feeblest slave
Trembling at fourscore o'er his grave;

Unmoved 'mid Battle's wild alarms—
Supreme in will—sublime in arms—
Yet cultured, open to the charms

Of Beauty! from whose genial Lyre
Hath poured full oft a strain of fire,
To rise in future Ages higher!

Unshackled by the Northman's rule,
Freed from the Bigot's canting school,
The maxims of the knave and fool,

The Genius of this youthful Land,
Like some rare blossom, will expand,
Upflowering to the Fair and Grand!

Then, Art will build her stately Fane,
And Song resound from Height to Plain,
Re-echoing to the Heights again!

Till, in the ripened time, shall rise,
With deep, divinely-thoughtful eyes,
And brow whereon the Destinies

Placed, even at birth, a shadowy crown,
The Poet whose august renown
Will smite the haughtiest natures down

To homage!—from whose "golden mouth,"
(Fit well-spring for a World in drouth,)
Outspeaks the Shakspeare of the South!

At stake in Confederate poetry is southern identity itself: "AS WE ARE!"
Southerners have been misrepresented or ignored for too long, the poem
opines; now is the time to acknowledge what has come before and set to work
creating more. But national perfection is yet to come. The tense of these stanzas is simple future—"will expand," "will build," "shall rise," "will smite"—
reminding readers that Confederate nationalism remains an ongoing project,
at best an aspirational state of being. In advance of "the ripened time" when
the Confederate States will have a national literature that rivals England's—
the reference to Shakespeare neatly encapsulates the *News*'s Anglophilia—
Paul Hamilton Hayne offers his fellow Confederates a canon, "the experience
of an idealized tradition," on which to build (Jusdanis, *Belated* 52).

Likewise, a poetry-loving reader of the *Southern Illustrated News* would
not have been disappointed by the newspaper's prose. Poetry was also a frequent topic of commentary in essays and editorials. An early essay, "What Is
Poetry?" (24 January 1863: 2–3), defines the gay science via Wordsworth's

famous "spontaneous overflow of powerful feeling . . . emotion re-collected in tranquility" before working through several examples of (British) poetic excellence: Shakespeare, Pope, Moore, Burns, Scott, and Milton. Subsequent essays include a history of the position of Poet Laureate (11 April 1863: 3); a dissertation on poetic genius and poetic temperament as witnessed by the lives of Dante, Milton, Shelley, Byron, and Felicia Hemans (3 [23 April 1864]: 124); and a lengthy, three-column review of Tennyson's *Enoch Arden* (2 [20 August 1864]: 193). One gossipy piece even considered a number of poems purportedly written by Abraham Lincoln. After reprinting a letter from the *London Times* attributing the authorship—which Lincoln had already disclaimed—to the Scottish poet William Knox, the *News* mocks the very idea of Lincoln as poet: "We can hardly fancy the lantern-jawed, lank, gaunt, jocular rail-splitter wooing the coy and reluctant muse, either on a Mississippi flat-boat, or in the clearings of Illinois, or yet in the sumptuous parlors of the White House. The pensiveness, the quiet meditation, the dreamy moods of the poet, belong not to the reciter of questionable anecdotes, the paragon of buffoons" (14 February 1863: 2). It seems that poetry is a Rebel rather than a Yankee pastime.[40]

As the Lincoln piece suggests, the editors of the *Southern Illustrated News* took seriously their role as arbiters of poetic taste. They were not above criticizing vehemently what they took to be mediocre Confederate verse. Over its three-and-a-half-year run, the *News* became one of the most outspoken critics of the "Rebel muse," arguing that the army of popular poets who had volunteered their services for the Confederacy "for the most part have proven most stale, flat and unprofitable" (29 November 1862). And the editors of the *News* would have known. Their criticisms of Confederate poetry were almost always accompanied by grousing about the flood of unsolicited submissions they had lately received.[41]

In all, the *News* seems to have taken little exception to fervent patriotic feeling; feeble prosody, on the other hand, was unforgivable: "The 'rebel' muse, we grieve to say, is so disobedient and wayward a child, so slip-shod a Sibyl, that she rebels against all the laws of rhyme, and cares less than nothing about her *feet* . . . the rebellion of the Southern poets against authority is bold and reckless indeed" (1 November 1862: 3). We see in this statement a clear discomfort with some of the amateurism endemic to Confederate poetry. Such concerns notwithstanding, the periodical continued to publish popular songs, anonymous lyrics, and light verse throughout the war, perhaps as a concession to its diverse readership. The editors' tack with regard to popular taste seems to have been to instruct readers on how best to appreciate "proper" poetry. For instance, a "semi-occasiona[l]" series called "Our Selected Poem" reprinted obscure poems for both the delight and the edification of readers. Drawn mainly from British sources, these "lost diamonds" were accompanied by brief explications, poet biographies, and publication histories—"such commentary as shall conduce to the reader's enjoyment of it" (15 November 1862: 2).[42]

Taken together, these poems, essays, and editorial principles reveal the importance of poetry to the nationalistic mission of the *Southern Illustrated News*. For the editors of the *News*, poetry was an essential part of a national culture in aspiration. Again and again they marshaled historical precedent to make the case for poetic nation building. In early 1863 the *News* placed the Confederate States of America in a long line of poetic nations, essentially normalizing the versification of patriotic feeling: "from the days of heroic Greece down to the last issue of the 'News,' in every nation, rude or civilized, there are evidences of effort to embalm in poetry the deeds of glory and pride of patriotism" (28 February 1863: 3).[43] A few weeks later, in an occasional series called "Southern Poetry," the editors state flatly the need for a national poetry: "we never can be truly independent, until we have a literature of our own, both periodical and permanent, of which we may be justly proud, because it will be equal to any, and leave no room for temptation to seek elsewhere for intellectual ailment" (28 March 1863: 3). This rhetoric should be familiar by now, bringing to mind the literary nationalist debates of the 1830s. However, it is notable that the editors specify poetry as a privileged part of such nationalism.

In closing this discussion of the *Southern Illustrated News*'s poetics of nationalism, I return to the vexed relationship between local and national belonging evidenced by Confederate broadside poetry. A similar tension between the local and the national was on full but subtle display in the pages of the *News*, which made a practice of including place and date names at the end of an original poem. For every poem like "The Young Dragoon" (2 [17 October 1863]: 120), which is identified with "Atlanta, Ga.," there is another like "To a Faithless One," which is placed in the much more obscure "Citronelle, Ala." (18 April 1863: 4). To be sure, such credits were an unremarkable characteristic of Confederate poetry; they appeared not only in newspapers but also in volumes of verse, broadsides, and anthologies. But rather than read these credits as a transparent part of print and periodical culture during the period—a mere indication of where a given poem was written—we might consider the poetic effect of these paratextual features, especially in the context of a nationalist newspaper.

The appearance of a place-name in or around a poem has a locality effect: It essentially places a poem. Even if a given poem is not about the locality named in its credit, the poem nonetheless becomes associated with that locality. Readers of the *Southern Illustrated News* were confronted with a series of localities—for example, Atlanta, Georgia; Citronelle, Alabama; Lancaster, South Carolina; New Orleans, Louisiana; Galveston, Texas—which they could then constellate into the outline of a nation. Thus, regardless of intention, these credits may well have helped Confederates to rationalize other states and other citizens within a new national framework. This, in turn, likely encouraged "that remarkable confidence of community in anonymity which is the hallmark of modern nations" (Anderson 36). Of course, the imposition of a place-name at the beginning or conclusion of a poem was a commonplace feature of nineteenth-century American and British poetry, especially occasional verse. But in the context of the Confederate national moment—and perhaps in *any* national moment—such place-names rise above mere poetic convention to take on additional resonance or importance.[44]

The poem "Our Dead" from the 4 October 1862 issue of the *News* opens with the dedication, "*Written in commemmoration of the 'Battle of Secessionville,' fought near Charleston, June 16th, 1862.*" It concludes by noting the presumed location and date of its composition, "*Charleston, September 9th, 1862.*" The juxtaposition of the place-names and dates suggests not merely the passage of time—something crucial to an elegiac, commemorative poem—but also intimate access to the events being narrated. The poet, "M.L.G.," doubly places her- or himself in Charleston, near the site of conflict (that is, Tower Battery/Fort Lamar). Yet, despite this insistence on locality and proximity to the battle scene, the poem initially thematizes a more mediated and distant relationship to the conflict. One stanza reads, "Alas! sad tidings from afar, / With anxious hearts we read, / Of those who for sweet liberty, / Are numbered with the dead." Thus, it is the reading of mediated news ("from afar") rather than immediate, proximate experience that confirms "Our Dead." The passive voice of this stanza underscores the sense of distance from the scene and events being described; this, in turn, allows for a more abstract and eventually nationalistic mourning. Later, the poem says of the titular dead, "O'er thy graves *a nation* mourns" (emphasis mine).

Were the poem to end here, "Our Dead" would seem a striking example of the mass-mediated experience of "homogenous, empty time" that Benedict Anderson believes to be so crucial for the imagining of a national community (33). Put simply, "deep horizontal comradeship" is possible when "we read" "Sad tidings from afar" of "Our Dead" (Anderson 7). But the poem's final stanza beats a hasty retreat from the national, returning readers jarringly to the local: "Carolina, thy sons are victors, / Of a bloody and hard-fought field, / Champions of a holy cause, / With Liberty their shield" (2). Taken with the echoed "Charleston" of the poem's dedication and attribution, these final lines raise the question that the poem has been begging all along: *whose* dead? The Confederacy's? South Carolina's? The Carolinas' in general? Are these, finally, mutually exclusive?[45]

Thus, this poem produces yet another violent back and forth between the local and the national. Such poetic shuttling was, as we have seen, a distinguishing feature of Confederate poetry, particularly in the glut of poems that celebrate the specific actions of specific regiments in specific battles or encampments. Although such poems often muse on nationalist themes or invoke Confederate causes, more often than not their interests and subjects are overwhelmingly local in character. This fudging of the line between locality and nation was a commonplace practice in a Confederate poetics of place. Local poems often flew under the flag of an emergent Confederate nationalism, celebrating the Confederacy in name but going on to commemorate an individual state or locality in deed.

For example, a poem from the 22 August 1863 issue of the *News* entitled "Gettysburg" remains deeply bound up in locality—and not the "hallowed ground" of that famous Pennsylvania battlefield. Credited to "A North Carolinian," the poem is dated and located "*Raleigh, N.C., August 3, 1863.*" Perhaps unsurprisingly, the poem's narrative of the horrors of 1–3 July 1863 focuses almost exclusively on North Carolinians at Gettysburg, emphasizing the one (that is, regiments from North Carolina) in the many (for example, regiments from Alabama, Georgia, Louisiana, Mississippi, Virginia, and so forth). The poem proclaims, "For Carolina's brave sons—the pride of the South— / Lie cover'd with glory at the dread cannon's mouth" (2 [22 August 1863]: 50). Making deft use of the dash, this couplet asserts the favored status of "Carolina's brave sons." That is, in the aftermath of a crucial military defeat, the poem flaunts the local on the pages of an ostensibly national newspaper.

Occasionally the nationalist frame of a Confederate poem is obscured or confused by the attribution of its place of composition. For instance, a poem by Mary A. McCrimmon celebrates the "Land of the South" in invitingly vague terms:

Land of beauty—blooming ever
　In the golden summer sun;
Land of perfume—blighted never
　By the borean blast; where one
Unfading, dreamy, spring-time still,
Lies like a veil on plain and hill. (29 November 1862: 6)

In remaining cagey about the specific locality of this sunny South, the poem seems to celebrate the whole of the Confederacy. Yet the appearance of the place-name "Forsyth, Ga." at the poem's conclusion has the potential to localize and thus limit its possible meanings and power. Elsewhere, the introduction of place-names in a poem also has the potential to establish or imagine relations among localities. For instance, Hayne's sonnet "Addressed to the Muse of the Graceful Virginia Poet, John R. Thompson" is dated and placed "Greenville, S.C., March, 1864" (3 [19 March 1864]: 84). The paratextual features of this poem suggests amity and affiliation not simply between two major Confederate poets, Hayne and Thompson, but also between South Carolina and Virginia.

Per Anderson, I do not underestimate the power of these locality effects to encourage readers to imagine other readers and other communities, especially on the pages of a national newspaper. However, I also read locality as a persistent and more vexing presence in the poems of the Confederacy. Locality can both produce and threaten the coherence of national community. I say "both produce and threaten" because the course of nationalism rarely did run smooth. The local and the national never sit in static, binaristic relation to one another. Instead, the play between the two defines any national moment. It is, to return to Shakespeare, a "customary cross."

This is in keeping with Arjun Appadurai's sense that localism can and often does exceed its immediate referent or intention. Appadurai argues that "as local subjects engage in the social activities of production, representation, and reproduction . . . they contribute, generally unwittingly, to the creation of contexts that might exceed the existing material and conceptual boundaries of the neighborhood" (185). Thus, local poems are not anathema to national literary culture; indeed, they can be unwitting participants in such culture. To be sure, such nested cultural work can lead to no small amount of tension and conflict among contexts. Moreover, as Appadurai notes, locality can be a "potentially treacherous" phenomenon in national settings, since localities "represent anxieties for the nation-state, as they usually contain large or residual spaces where the techniques of nationhood . . . are likely to be either weak or contested" (190).

To be clear, I do not read these local poems as registering either the failures or nonexistence of Confederate nationalism. Nationalism is never a zero-sum prospect; it is instead a structure of feeling characterized by uneven construction and conflicting sentiments. Thus, it is for good reason that Appadurai couches his discussion of locality in affective terms: again, "anxieties for the nation-state." Anxious is a very fine way to describe the balance that Confederate poetry struck between emergent national pride and entrenched local affiliation. As Edward Ayers and Peter Onuf cautioned several years ago, "[n]ationalists do not work on blank slates: they must reconcile, reorient, or replace preexisting loyalties" (Ayers et al. 9). We see clearly in Confederate poetry the difficulty of such reconciliation, reorientation, and replacement.

In its opening issue, the *Southern Illustrated News* adapted a Latin phrase, "*Inter arma silent litera*," to express a concern that "[t]he minds of men are too much pre-occupied by the stirring events of the hour to be amused with the situations of the novelist or beguiled by the fancies of the poet." Despite this fear, the *News* set forth to "present more vividly to the reader the grand and imposing events that are happening around us" (13 September 1862: 2).

Such "fancies of the poet" became, I argue, an essential means through which the *News* both documented and helped to imagine an emergent national culture.

Coda: Anthologizing the Situation of Confederate Literature

Edmund Wilson was right: The Confederacy did indeed produce an "immense amount of verse" between 1861 and 1865. Popular in orientation, occasional in character, and multimedial in circulation, the poetry of the Confederate States of America bespeaks a fervent literary nationalism. Read in and across its original, material contexts, this poetry also represents well local southern communities. One final medium for Confederate verse deserves examination here, the poetry anthology, which helped to shape how subsequent generations read (or did not read) that "immense amount of verse."

Because poetry anthologies almost always serve a retrospective function— a backward glance o'er roads traveled, as Walt Whitman might have it—they have the ability to collect, preserve, and make available exuberant and diverse poetic cultures. Anthologies are, as the Australian poet and critic Jennifer Strauss suggests, "essential to the transmission of poetry from the relative ephemerality of periodicals and slim volumes into a more mainstream communication with readers" (87). Thus, to read the pages of a popular poetry anthology is to encounter in a single setting poems that likely appeared in a number of other venues and media. This is particularly the case with anthologies of Confederate poetry, which began to appear as early as 1862 and continued to be published well into the twentieth century. Indeed, the cessation of Civil War hostilities resulted in a minor publishing boom, as anthologists in the South, North, and England used their collections to commemorate and make sense of the atrocities they had just endured.[46]

The majority of these anthologies argue for the historical importance of Confederate poetry. For instance, William G. Shepperson, the editor of the first anthology of Confederate verse, *War Songs of the South* (1862), is keenly aware of the need to collect war poetry as the war progresses: "In every age, martial songs have wrought wonders in struggles for national independence" (5). Noting that many of the popular poems and songs of the American Revolutionary War had been lost to history, Shepperson asks, "Shall we not try to insure against so deplorable a fate the songs of our own revolution?" (3). After all, bellum anthologists claim, Confederate verse can help to contextualize the "cause" for which Confederates are fighting. A northern wartime publication, Frank Moore's *Rebel Rhymes and Rhapsodies* (1864), emphasizes the explanatory power of Confederate poetry, which, Moore hopes, "will illustrate the spirit which actuates [Confederates] in their Rebellion against the Government and Laws of the United States" (v). Similarly, the anonymous editor of a war-time anthology published in Liverpool, England, *Lays of the South: Verses Relative to the War between the Two Sections of the American States* (1864), believes that Confederate poetry can speak to international audiences as well: "[These poems] manifest the nature and force of the feelings engendered by the unhappy strife, which has deluged a continent in blood and impaired the prosperity and happiness of distant nations" (1). Thus, to read Confederate poetry—in the South, the North, or even England—is to better understand what brought about a conflict with wide-ranging and catastrophic effects.[47]

But many anthologists were not content merely to preserve poems; they also aimed to influence how the war would be interpreted après coup. Shepperson, for instance, argues that the poems he collects "give the lie to the assertion of our enemy that this revolution is the work of politicians and party leaders alone" (4). These pages represent, the anthologist asserts, authentic, popular nationalist feeling. William Gilmore Simms concurs in his important postwar anthology, *War Poetry of the South* (1867). Writing ostensibly to a northern audience (the anthology was initially published in New York), Simms argues that the "emotional literature" he collects is "essential to the reputation of the Southern people, as illustrating their feelings, sentiments, ideas, and opinions—the motives which influenced their actions, and the objects which they had in contemplation, and which seemed to them to justify the struggle in which they were engaged" (v). Perhaps quietly echoing John Adams ("The Revolution was in the minds and hearts of the people"), Simms plays the disinterested intellectual historian here, urging readers to be sympathetic as they peruse his nearly five-hundred-page anthology. Stifling his strongly southern nationalist sentiments, Simms does not offer an apologia for the Confederacy; instead, he hedges a bit. Note the passive construction and use of the past tense here: These motives and objects "*seemed* to *them* to justify" the southern war effort (emphasis mine).[48]

The deftness of Simms's rhetoric betrays the delicate political position in which a postwar anthologist of Confederate poetry worked. How could she or he present aggressively nationalistic verse—poems that risk being "too 'fierce' and 'bitter' to suit the taste and temper of the present" (Mason 7)—to a newly re-United States? Abram Joseph Ryan, the author of the hugely popular Lost Cause anthem "The Conquered Banner," worried that his incendiary anthology of Confederate verse, *War Lyrics and Songs of the South* (1866), would be censored in the North. As a result, he had the collection printed in London (iii). Thomas Cooper De Leon, a Confederate veteran and older brother of Confederate diplomat Edwin De Leon, instead begged his (northern) readers' indulgence and made a familiar appeal to the historical record: "If poems, born of revolution, bore no marks of the bitter need that crushed them from the hearts of their authors, they would have no value whatever, intrinsic or historical" (vii).

But it is Simms who makes the most original argument for how to square wartime invective with postwar imperatives to reconciliation. One need only subsume Confederate literary nationalism under a broader American literary nationalism:

> Several considerations have prompted the editor of this volume in the compilation of its pages. It constitutes a contribution to the national literature which is assumed to be not unworthy of it, and which is otherwise valuable as illustrating the degree of mental and art development which has been made, in a large section of the country, under circumstances greatly calculated to stimulate talent and provoke expression, through the higher utterances of passion and imagination. Though sectional in its character, and indicative of a temper and a feeling which were in conflict with nationality, yet, now that the States of the Union have been resolved into one nation, this collection is essentially as much the property of the whole as are the captured cannon which were employed against it during the progress of the late war. It belongs to the national literature, and will hereafter be regarded as constituting a proper part of it, just as legitimately to be recognized by the nation as are the rival ballads of the cavaliers and roundheads, by the English, in the great civil conflict of their country. (v)

It is as though the American Civil War never happened. Despite having strongly advocated for secession and steadfastly supported the Confederacy, Simms reverts to his antebellum agitations for a national literature. Once again, the South is in the subordinate position, making contributions to a national literature that is not entirely its own. Looking to England for a model or precedent, Simms argues that nationalist poetry is a fungible good. The canon of Confederate poetry is just like the cannon of the Confederate army: a strategic asset that will benefit the newly re-United States.

Such contortions of logic were not unusual in postwar anthologies, many of which sought to reset not only the terms of Confederate literary nationalism but also the very definition of Confederate poetry. In presenting their anthologies to a number of publics, editors openly acknowledge the multimedial circulation and localism of Confederate poetry.[49] At the same time, at least one editor felt ill at ease with its popular orientation and occasional character. To Thomas Cooper De Leon's mind, the work of the postbellum anthologist is to protect his or her readers from the "rhymster of low degree," to select out only those rare blooms of poetic beauty: "The garland is to be gathered from a field extensive and teeming with a rank luxuriance of growth, that it must often puzzle the analyst to separate from the really valuable" (v). Calling the popular poetry of the Confederacy "ephemera that have lived out the day for which they were born," De Leon highlights "the quality, and not the quantity, of Southern poetry" (vi). As a result, he includes "few even of the most popular" poems in his *South Songs*, privileging instead "polite" poems by established poets (vi). For De Leon (whose rhetoric sounds strikingly similar to that of Edmund Wilson), poetic quality and poetic popularity are irreconcilable.

Although postwar anthologies reprint several of the anonymous and pseudonymous poems discussed in this chapter, De Leon and his contemporaries tend to favor the verse of established poets (Mason 9–16; Simms 1–6). De Leon even tried to get each of his selected poems "carefully corrected by its author" (vi). These attempts to fix authorship and texts render professional what had been chiefly amateur. This, in turn, shifts the register of Confederate poetry from the popular and the occasional to the specialized and the timeless, from the messiness of multimedial circulation to the neatness of anthologization. In re-presenting Confederate poetry in such a light, these anthologies begin to consolidate a critical consensus that would find voice in later critics like Edmund Wilson and crown "polite" poets like Henry Timrod, Paul Hamilton Hayne, and (anachronistically) Sidney Lanier the poets laureate of the Confederacy.

Because anthologies are, in the words of Anne Ferry, both "where many readers of poetry first and perhaps most of the time meet poems" and "an effective instrument in shaping the direction of criticism," it seems likely that these anthologies have played an outsize role in determining our literary-historical understanding of Confederate poetry (1, 6). To take but one example, Wilson cites anthologies in his very brief discussion of Confederate poetry (466–72). When we return to the multiple media through which this verse originally circulated, we gain, I hold, a much fuller sense for a dynamic poetic culture and an important part of intellectual life in the Confederacy. With all due respect to Edmund Wilson, such poetry makes for very fertile reading indeed.

CHAPTER FOUR

The Music of Mars

Confederate Song, North and South

The world of print is an imperfect mirror of
intellectual experience, a partial reflection of all
that is thought and believed.
—David Hall, *Cultures of Print*

A nation does not choose its songs on the ground of
poetical merit. In fact, it does not choose them at all.
It is impossible to trace where a song begins its career
of popularity, and its diffusion throughout a nation
depends upon some fortunate conjunction of time, mood,
association, and circumstance.
—Henry Timrod, 24 January 1864

In *Behind the Scenes, or, Thirty Years a Slave and Four Years in the White House* (1868), Elizabeth Keckley, former slave and modiste to Mary Todd Lincoln, shares a provocative anecdote about President Lincoln and the Confederate anthem "Dixie." Writing of Robert E. Lee's imminent surrender, Keckley records an exhausted Lincoln's speech from early April 1865: "'And now, by way of parting from the brave soldiers of our gallant army, I call upon the band to play Dixie. It has always been a favorite of mine, and since we have captured it, we have a perfect right to enjoy it.' On taking his seat the band at once struck up with Dixie, that sweet, inspiring air" (172). Here "Dixie" denotes both a musical interlude and the Confederate South as a whole. In a scene to be repeated with absurd regularity, Dixie-as-locution comes to signify Dixie-as-location. Latent in such a confusion of Dixies is the commodification of both: "Dixie" is an object ("it") that can be physically taken and occupied ("captured"). Like all commodities, "Dixie" demands an almost juridical discourse to tie up its ownership and possession ("a perfect right").

And, as with any "favorite," "Dixie" elicits great feeling from both Abraham Lincoln ("a favorite of mine") and his interlocutor, Elizabeth Keckley ("that sweet and inspiring air"). Given the various "manifestations of applause" the song provokes, these reactions betray how the strains of a purportedly southern song can elicit emotion from a northern audience.[1]

Keckley's anecdote raises a number of perplexing questions: What cultural and nationalistic work is "Dixie" doing here? What boundaries are being crossed in this capture and through such a cathexis of northern feeling? What is at stake in the appropriation of popular song during a time of war? In pursuing these questions, this chapter argues that the play between these two Dixies—between the anthem and the nation, the local and the global, and, crucially, the northern and the southern—reveals not simply the multiplicity of "Dixie" as cultural artifact but also the crucial role that music played in the imagining of both the United and Confederate States of America during the war.

The American Civil War both partook of and helped to produce a robust culture of musical performance. These were, after all, the "Singing Sixties" (Heaps and Heaps). In mid-nineteenth-century America, music was integral to the practices of everyday life in ways that may seem curious or obscure to our contemporary critical moment. Nonetheless, as Caroline Moseley contends, during this period "more people, regardless of sex and social station, sang out loud in front of other people than is customary today, and more in wartime than in time of peace" (48).[2]

In the Confederacy, popular song had a particular purchase on the hearts, minds, lips, and ears of new southern nationals. This is because song was able to infiltrate parts of Confederate life that more traditional forms of literature could not: Unlike novels or short fiction, the circulation of Confederate song was by no means limited to a print public sphere. Indeed, song's oral component gave it a marked advantage over even popular poetry, its close cousin. As Richard Harwell suggests in *Confederate Music*, "with its tune to carry it, [song] could invade areas not reached by the printed page" (5).[3]

More to the point, song's circulation in oral and nonprint forms also helped to circumvent the Confederacy's relatively low literacy rates and rampant resource scarcities. As a result, popular song represents one of the few instances where the great expectations of Confederate literary nationalism were, in some ways, met. The Confederate States of America produced hundreds of pieces of sheet music and song sheets; this is to say nothing of the countless versions of songs that never found their way into print (Parrish and Willingham 573–630). In fact, in the realm of popular song, Confederate production actually rivaled that of the Union. As Keckley's anecdote intimates and as this chapter makes clear, such a rivalry produced no small amount of anxiety in the North. As a result, popular song became a constitutive part of Confederate nationalism in general and Confederate literary nationalism in particular.[4]

This chapter tells the story of song in the Confederacy through its de facto national anthem, "Dixie." To be clear, "Dixie" was but one among many songs wildly popular in the Confederate States. However, its complex revisionary history provides an uncommon account of the international nature of this so-called war between brothers. In the following pages I argue that "Dixie" was not only an extraordinarily effective vehicle for Confederate literary nationalism but also the subject and site of intense conflict. From the moment of its composition, "Dixie" was constantly crossing boundaries of nation, allegiance, politics, race, and class. Neither a strictly southern nor a strictly northern cultural property, "Dixie" was given to various local appropriations and rewritings and engendered a series of hotly contested proprietary claims. By exploring "Dixie" as a malleable, even promiscuous cultural object, this chapter underscores the instability of the song's circulation in and beyond the Confederacy and identifies a process of revision that enabled this "sweet and inspiring air" to fit local, regional, and national agendas. In so doing, this chapter shows how the people of both the United and Confederate States of America used "Dixie" to manage the existence of competing nationalisms.

Locating Dixie

"Dixie" was a both ubiquitous and urgent presence in the mid-nineteenth-century cultural imaginary. Particularly during the war years, "Dixie" enjoyed a fervid, even unparalleled popularity in both the South and the North. However, years of revisionist history and the omnipresence of Lost Cause ideology have tended to obscure the northern roots and routes of the song. Surely the most ironic aspect of the song's *official* compositional history is its birthplace: New York City. Often credited to Ohio native Daniel D. Emmett and first heard on Broadway on 4 April 1859, "Dixie" emerged as a set piece for Bryant's Minstrels in 1859 and 1860. Originally performed in blackface and published in "Negro dialect," the song was a product of secession-era anxieties that expressed a bewildering racial politics all its own.[5]

In its earliest performances, "Dixie" offered a complex image of African American longing for the plantation South. In lyrics such as these, identification, desire, and affect transgress the increasingly contested Mason-Dixon line:

I wish I was in de land ob cotton,
Old times dar am not forgotten,
Look away! Look away! Look away! Dixie Land.

In Dixie Land whar I was born in,
Early on one frosty mornin,
Look away! Look away! Look away! Dixie Land.

Den I wish I was in Dixie, Hoo-ray! Hoo-ray!
In Dixie land, I'll took my stand to lib an die in Dixie;
Away, away, away down south in Dixie,
Away, away, away down south in Dixie. (Emmett, *I Wish*)

Here, the "black" speaker—or the specter of white fantasy embodied in black-face—is betwixt two places. The site of longing is, presumably, the North; the site longed for is, presumably, the South, or Dixie, whose precise location is obscure, somewhere "away, away, away down south." This undifferentiated and indeterminate longing is rooted in the past: The "land ob cotton" is narrated in past tense, as if the speaker is separated from Dixie not simply by space but also by time.

Given this dynamic, the vexed status of North-South circulation in 1859–60, and the increasingly binaristic logic of the period (for example, abolition-proslavery, North-South, us-them), we might ask where the speaker's allegiance lies. Is this a song of the South or a song of the North? Because the verses remain stubbornly ambivalent, textual evidence for either reading is scarce. Without textual determinacy, we are left only with nineteenth-century responses to the song, a history of reception that aptly registers how "Dixie" defies or exceeds the logic of a single and simple national allegiance.

Emmett, the purported author of "Dixie," pithily redacts its reception: "It made a hit at once, and before the end of the week everybody in New York was whistling it. Then the South took it up and claimed it for its own" (qtd. in Spaeth 138). Contemporaneous accounts of the song's emergence support Emmett's self-congratulatory remark. In the weeks that followed its first performance, Dixie achieved immediate renown. As the *New York Commercial Advertiser* proclaimed, "whenever 'Dixie' is produced, the pen drops from the fingers of the plodding clerk, spectacles from the nose and the paper from the hands of the merchant, the needle from the nimble digits of the maid or matron, and all hands go hobbling, bobbling in time with the magical music of 'Dixie'" (qtd. in Nathan 271; see also Muzzy 4). In response to this "magical" popularity, sheet music for "I Wish I Was in Dixie's Land" appeared in June 1860, produced by New York's Firth, Pond, and Company. But even before this publication, the song's popularity had moved beyond the confines of New York. By July 1860, the song was playing in theaters across the North, including those in Boston, Chicago, and St. Louis.

Contrary to Emmett's redaction, the South's "claiming" of "Dixie" was more or less synchronous with the North's "whistling" of the song. A hugely popular version of "Dixie" found its way onto the southern stage on 6 March

1860 in New Orleans; a printed version of the song was distributed soon after by New Orleans publisher P. P. Werlein, without any reference to Daniel D. Emmett: "Words by J. Newcomb. Music by J. C. Viereck." However, the first southern printing of "Dixie" was as a broadside song sheet issued by New Orleans printer John Hopkins in late 1859, some six months before Firth, Pond, and Company's publication of "I Wish I Was in Dixie's Land" (Spaeth 138–39). The fact that Hopkins's "Dixie" was a song sheet—that is, a set of lyrics without musical notation—suggests just how widely the song had circulated by early 1860.[6]

During the first few months of the American Civil War, Henry Hotze, the journalist, propagandist, and editor of the London-based, pro-Confederate newspaper *The Index*, described the immediate ubiquity of "Dixie" in the South. Writing that the song spread with a "wild-fire rapidity," Hotze proved prophetic: "Considered as an intolerable nuisance when first the streets re-echoed it from the repertoire of wandering minstrels, ['Dixie'] now bids fair to become the musical symbol of a new nationality, and we shall be fortunate if it does not impose its very name on our country" (1: 140). By late 1860, the southern "Dixie" achieved a circulation comparable to, and concomitant with, that of its northern counterpart (Harwell, *Confederate Music* 42).

The song's initial emergence in both New York and New Orleans belies a strictly southern association. It would take until at least 18 February 1861 before "Dixie" achieved its "southernness." On that date, in Montgomery, Alabama, bandleader Hermann Arnold changed the tempo of "Dixie" from a marching tune to a military quickstep in honor of Jefferson Davis's inauguration as President of the Provisional Government of the Confederate States of America. As several music critics and historians note, this was the moment at which "Dixie" became associated with Confederate nationalism. Although never formally declared the Confederate national anthem, "Dixie" emerged as the de facto battle hymn of the Confederacy through simple force of apposition: The moment of Confederate nationalism became the moment of "Dixie." As James Hill Hewitt noted in a footnote to his 1862 poem *War*, the song "became spontaneously the *national* tune" (11). This relatively late date is crucial given the histories it elides or overshadows. "Dixie" existed in both the southern and northern cultural imaginaries well before Arnold and Davis claimed the song for the southern nation, well before such a coexistence would have proved politically troublesome.[7]

The profound indeterminacy that attends the song's inscrutable and charismatic subject, Dixie, exacerbates such confused and confusing claims. What, or better, where is this longed-for Dixie? While scholars have speculated endlessly on the etymology of the word *Dixie*, many concur that Emmett's version of the song founded a U.S. South–Dixie metonym.[8] Compellingly, the *Oxford English Dictionary* suggests Emmett's "Dixie" as the first use of the word to denote "the southern United States; the South" ("Dixie," def. 1). Given the subsequent outpouring of tracts, broadsides, poems, novels, cartoons, newspapers, spellers, songsters, and plays that bore the sign "Dixie," the song's wide dissemination in the context of the Confederate national moment heralded the ascendancy of this metonym. Thus, despite both its geographical indeterminacy and its northern roots, "Dixie" came very quickly to signify the southern portion of the United States. In the wake of both Davis's inauguration and the state secessions that occasioned it, the song's further dissemination proved bizarre. Though understood to be the de facto Confederate national anthem, "Dixie" continued to be played throughout the North during the Civil War—even at Abraham Lincoln's 4 March 1861 inauguration. Thus, despite a southern-cum-Confederate claim to the song, "Dixie" traveled transgressive and transnational paths throughout the war.[9]

It Growed

The doubled emergence of "Dixie" in New York and New Orleans proves portentous since multiple, competing versions of the song circulated before, during, and after the American Civil War. At least thirty-nine versions appeared in print between 1860 and 1866 alone—or so music historians tell us. Given the ephemeral nature of nineteenth-century sheet music, broadsides, and songsters, this figure is no doubt conservative. Censuses such as these beg a number of questions: What constitutes a version of "Dixie"? How much lyrical or musical variation is necessary to distinguish one "Dixie" from another? What is it about this song that gave rise to so much revision and reproduction?[10]

Any reliance on printed material to reconstruct the revisionary history of "Dixie" belies the fact that the song circulated in oral and nonprint settings as well. Since Civil War songs were sung by dynamic groups of singers in various settings—parlor sing-alongs, slave work sites, military encampments, church gatherings, abolitionist meetings, political rallies, and other publics—there is no material record of the countless versions of "Dixie" that never found their way into print. In these settings, "Dixie" achieved a free-flowing circulation in and of revision. These unrecorded, errant versions— versions with their tunes modulated and harmonized, their lyrics forgotten, misremembered, and improvised—surely number more than thirty-nine.

Of course "Dixie" was but one of many Civil War songs subject to such wide circulation and revision, as Brander Matthews's 1887 essay "The Songs of the War" suggests: "The taking of the air of a jovial college song to use as the setting of a fiery war-lyric may seem strange and curious, but only to those who are not familiar with the adventures and transformations a tune is often made to undergo" (622). In Matthews's account, revision, in the guise of alteration to "fiery war-lyric," is unsurprising, even predictable. For instance, Matthews writes enthusiastically of "John Brown's Body," a song he dubs "the song of the hour":

["John Brown's Body"] has been called a spontaneous generation of the uprising of the North—a self-made song, which sang itself into being of its own accord. Some have treated it as a sudden evolution from the inner consciousness of the early soldiers all aglow with free-soil enthusiasm; and these speak of it as springing, like Minerva from the head of Jove, full-armed and mature. Others have more happily likened it to Topsy, in that it never was born, it growed; and this latter theory has the support of the facts as far as they can be disentangled from a maze of fiction and legend. (622)

The provocative opposition of these metaphors—the compositional history of "John Brown's Body" as either Minerva or Topsy—has a hermeneutic density and an ideological depth worth sounding. Whether the song emerged fully formed from the head of its progenitor or was without one entirely, its birth seems less important than its subsequent growth. Intriguingly, Matthews contrasts an icon of classical wisdom with a precocious and unruly slave child from *Uncle Tom's Cabin*. Although the former is a more elegant description, the latter is somehow more evocative, and, Matthews concedes, a much more accurate account of "John Brown's Body." While neither of these fictive figures experienced a normal gestation period—Minerva is, after all, birthed mature from her father's forehead—Topsy's nonbirth and growth is, in Matthews's terms, particularly "strange and curious."

Topsy first appears in chapter 20 of Stowe's *Uncle Tom's Cabin*. Interrogated by Miss Ophelia, Topsy describes her origins, "'Never was born,' reiterated the creature, more emphatically, "'never had no father nor mother, nor nothin'" (282). Without father, mother, or author, Topsy is a pitch-perfect metaphor for the circuits of variation that produced Civil War songs. Like Topsy, Civil War songs in revision deny their origins and histories by asserting their immanent qualities (for example, their current lyrics and melody), as well as their propensity for growth. Moreover, Topsy comes to us through a genre (reform literature) that is adamant about progress. Since the latter chapters of the novel chart a series of forward movements—political progress toward abolition, Topsy's progress toward gentility, Miss Ophelia's progress toward sympathy—such a disregard for origin seems apt for the "songs of war" Matthews treats. Like Topsy, these songs obtain in the moment of their performance; they signify only in the present or future tense, never in the past. Matthews's complex metaphor is urgent for the purposes of this chapter, particularly given this admission: "Curiously enough, the history of 'Dixie' is not at all unlike the history of 'John Brown's Body'" (623). His invocation of *Uncle Tom's Cabin* also subtly reminds us of the specters of slavery and race that make a phrase like "songs of the Civil War" signify in the first place. In the case of both "John Brown's Body" and "Dixie," slavery is clearly in negotiation through, and at stake in, their revisions. Therefore, Matthews's choice of Topsy to allegorize the strange ways of Civil War song circulation seems entirely appropriate.

The Topsy-like growth of a song like "Dixie" cannot be easily reconstructed. It may be asked after, speculated on, theorized, but not recreated. It is possible, however, to reconstruct contemporary accounts of the song's circulation and variation. For instance, Henry Hotze spent the first months of the Civil War embedded with the Third Regiment of Alabama Volunteers. Recounting his experiences with the Third Alabama in a 26 June 1862 issue of *The Index* (a periodical I discuss at length in chapter 5), Hotze describes his regiment rewriting "Dixie" "commemorative of the recent accession of Virginia and Tennessee to the Confederacy, and especially complimentary to the former" (140). Hotze goes on to note that the Third Alabama sang this revised "Dixie"

> on every appropriate occasion, with marked effect upon the hearts of the Virginian beauties. Such was the popularity of the song at Norfolk, where it originated, that some considerate persons bethought themselves of having it printed on little slips of paper, as "The Song of Dixie, sung by the 3rd Regiment of Alabama Volunteers, on their passage through Virginia." These slips have been plentifully distributed on the road, and, I doubt not, will be preserved as historical relics, when the pretty girls who welcomed us shall have become grandmothers, and relate to the wondering little ones about the times when the first troops of Confederate volunteers came from the far South to fight the Yankees on Virginian soil. (140)

Hotze's anecdote documents the timely, occasional nature of this revision, as well as the circulation of "The Song of Dixie sung by the 3rd Regiment of Alabama Volunteers" in oral performance, manuscript, and printed forms. This "Dixie" was revised by a specific group of singers; in turn, its performance and circulation in all three forms constituted a series of publics. Although Hotze takes pains to note the importance to posterity of the printed version of this song, he does not indicate competition among those forms. Print functions in the service of cultural memory here, preserving this "Dixie" as a "historical relic." Yet it is the oral performance version—not, importantly, the printed version—that has a "marked effect upon the hearts of the Virginian beauties." As a result, we might take seriously Hotze's rhetoric of the "relic," which the *Oxford English Dictionary* defines as "something kept as a remembrance or souvenir of a person, thing, or place; a memento" ("Relic," def. 1d.) but also as "a surviving trace of some practice, fact, idea, quality, etc.; the remains or remaining fragments (of a thing); the remnant, residue (of a nation or people)" ("Relic," def. 4a.). Here, print offers not an authoritative or definitive version of "The Song of Dixie sung by the 3rd Regiment of Alabama Volunteers" but instead the "residue" and "surviving trace" of the practice or performance of that song.

Thus, print was not the only medium through which nineteenth-century songs circulated; it was merely the least ephemeral. For instance, there is no known extant copy of the "Dixie" Hotze was so confident would be preserved as a historical relic. Yet despite the lack of a surviving trace of the Third Regiment's "Dixie," we have strong anecdotal evidence that such a version did in fact exist. Rather than accede to the purported authority of printed songs, we might think of these versions as merely standing in for the often-elusive manuscript and oral performance forms of "Dixie."[11]

So what was it about "Dixie," finally, that caused such a proliferation of verses and versions? Speculation on the causes of cultural reception often proves slippery; however, we can easily grasp the structures of signification, ambivalence, and reiterability that allowed "Dixie" to be revised multiply. Writing on what he calls the "repeatable materiality" of statement, Michel Foucault traces the ways such structures enable repetition. For Foucault, the presence of "a number of constants—grammatical, semantic, logical—" within the structure of a statement allows that statement to remain recognizable through various reiterations: "The time and place of the enunciation, and the material support that it uses, then become, very largely at least, indifferent: and what stands out is a form that is endlessly repeatable, and which may give rise to the most dispersed enunciations" (*Archaeology* 101–2). Foucault sees the statement as "a specific and paradoxical object," one that "enters various fields of use, is subjected to transferences or modifications." The statement "circulates, is used, disappears, allows or prevents the realization of a desire, serves or resists various interests, participates in challenge and struggle, and becomes a theme of appropriation or rivalry" (105). "Dixie" might be conceptualized as just such a "statement": specific yet paradoxical. It entered various fields and was modified multiply. It circulated widely, served and resisted various interests, and participated actively in the challenges and struggles of its period. "Dixie" became a theme of appropriation and rivalry before, during, and after the American Civil War, as Elizabeth Keckley reminds us.[12]

Considering the grammatical, semantic, and logical "constants" of the song at the level of melody, not lyric, the song's "repeatable materiality" seems to lie in the structures of its tune. Indeed, for one contemporary writer, "Dixie" was very much about tune: "'Dixie' bears its charms in its music rather than its words. It would seem to be impossible to wed serious poetry to the plantation jingle of its insouciant melody" (Elson 245). While it may not have been "serious poetry," "Dixie" was "the favorite model for soldier parodies and various propaganda efforts" (Silber and Silverman 50). Thus it was the dynamic, infectious melody of "Dixie" and not its specific lyrical content that propelled its popularity and ubiquity.[13]

Again, this is not unique to the case of "Dixie." A number of songs attest to the rapport between well-known tunes and eminently revisable lyrics. For instance, songsters and broadsides from this period rarely if ever offer musical accompaniment for their lyrics; instead they quietly indicate, for example, "Air—Dixie." Thus, these printed texts assume the knowledge of a common repertoire of tunes. That is, these printed versions of songs assumed that their readers/singers would be so familiar with a certain set of melodies that they would not require additional musical notation to perform these songs.[14]

As the Hotze example affirms, the culture of lyrical revisionism that a common repertoire of tunes enabled found not only northerners and southerners singing different words to the "same" song but different groups of northerners and different groups of southerners singing different words to the "same" song. As a result of the complementary relationships among print, manuscript, and oral performance, each individual group of singers—whether a regiment of Confederate soldiers sitting around a campfire, a group of abolitionists in a planning meeting, or a Lincoln reelection club—might well have had its very own version of "Dixie." In some cases, the lyrics to these individualistic or local "Dixies" would have been the lyrics printed in songsters, on broadsides, or as sheet music; in other cases, the lyrics would have been circulated in manuscript (perhaps someone might have copied in longhand the lyrics to a song that celebrated a recent Union victory); in still other cases, such lyrics would have been impromptu, even improvised on the spot. Such adventurous lyrical revisionism is not difficult when a group has a particularly catchy tune to work with.[15]

Thus, what "stands out" about "Dixie" is a melody "that is endlessly repeatable," one that seems to have "give[n] rise to the most dispersed enunciations." Yet its lyrics also mark the site of the most politically troublesome aspects of the song: issues of place, region, nation, race, class, gender, and sexuality. In turn, it is at the level of lyric that the cultural work of revision is most intelligible. To suggest then that the form of "Dixie" trumped its content, that its global structures overshadowed its local meanings, and that its melody proved more compelling than its various lyrics is not to claim that the lyrics were in any way unimportant or disposable. Instead, it is to acknowledge the ways in which the formal structures of melody enabled—even encouraged—singers, musicians, and poets to rewrite its lyrics to fit their specific ideological, political, and personal agendas. While the melody of the song seems to have been quite "charming" indeed, the mere fact that the lyrics were revised so thoroughly, ardently, and frequently bespeaks a profound and complex cultural investment in what words would be sung over the melody of "Dixie."[16]

To return to the song's restless wartime movement, a January 1862 *Harper's Weekly* political cartoon subtly sends up the proliferating versions of "Dixie" already in circulation during the first few months of the war. Of particular note is the cartoon's final pseudo stage direction: "[*They part, singing, mournfully*, Dixie, *without the Variations.*].". The image is of longing for the presumably warmer climes of Dixie. The implication that Confederate soldiers, miserable and cold in western Virginia, would long for the comforts of home is unremarkable. The cartoonist's distinction between competing versions of "Dixie" is, however, extraordinary: There is "Dixie," and there are its variations. In turn, the cartoonist's assumption that the audience would get the joke, that they would be familiar enough with revisions made to "Dixie," is compelling evidence for the wide dissemination of proliferating versions of the song. In fact, there seems to be no "Dixie" "without the Variations." Amid the acute culture of revisionism that characterized the United and Confederate States of America between 1861 and 1865, there was no single, no authoritative, no definitive "Dixie"—only variations. In manuscript, print, or oral performance forms, the presence of competing versions of "Dixie" challenges the authority of any claim to the song. When one evoked "Dixie" during the Civil War, one meant many, multiple, legion.

Not Forgotten

These proliferating versions of "Dixie" pose a daunting methodological challenge. Which "Dixie" provides the copy-text? The "first" printed version? If so, which "first" version: the Hopkins broadside or the Firth, Pond, and Company sheet music? While the differences among these are important, and while the 1860 Firth, Pond, and Company's "I Wish I Was in Dixie's Land" provides the copy-text for this discussion, these two texts have one crucial element in common: Both render their lyrics in "Negro dialect"—"I wish I was in de land ob cotton, / Old times dar am not forgotten." While the song opens emphatically in the first person, the peculiar substitutions ("de" for *the*, "ob" for *of*, "dar" for *there*, "am" for *are*, "whar" for *where*, "mornin" for *morning*, "lib" for *live*) frustrate readerly expectations of clarity and coherence. Who is speaking here? The substitutions in this first verse and chorus are so subtle that the reader may make it to the second verse before realizing that she or he is supposed to be reading—or singing—in dialect. There, with the introduction of "Old Missus" and "Willium," and the clever rhyme of "Will-de-weaber" with "a gay deceaber," the vernacular quality of the speaker's voice is unmistakable.

Such a voice led many members of the southern literati to denounce the song's "low," "doggerel" lyrics. For instance, Hotze lamented the song's "rude, incoherent words, which lend themselves to so many parodies, of which

HARD TIMES IN OLE VARGINNY, AN' WORSE A CUMIN'!

Scene.—Rebel Pickets in Western Virginia.

FIRST PICKET. "Awful Cold, ain't it?"

SECOND PICKET. "Co-o-ld! yes, an' I'm jist gitting another Shake of that Ager, and no Quinine in the 'Federacy!"

FIRST PICKET. "Worser still! Got them Blue Devils after me, an' nary drop o' Whiskey." (*With much feeling.*)

SECOND PICKET. "I wish I was Ho-o-me."

[*They part, singing, mournfully,* DIXIE, *without the Variations.*]

Harper's Weekly, 11 January 1862: 16.

the poorest is an improvement on the original" (*The Index* 1: 140). He goes on to suggest that any lyrics would be better than the "original" ones; through revision, Hotze intimates, "improvement" is possible. Hotze also draws his readers' attention to the proliferating "parodies" of the song already in circulation in 1861. Yet what proved so "rude" to Hotze and his contemporaries? What about the lyrics so offended a specifically southern audience? The first major southern revision of "Dixie" suggests that the original dialect may have been to blame.

In 1860, New Orleans's P. P. Werlein published "I Wish I Was in Dixie," credited to "J. C. Viereck," as sung by "W. H. Peters, Esq." (Nathan 268). One of many versions of "Dixie" published before Emmett/Firth, Pond, and Company secured copyright for the song in 1861, this edition is noteworthy for the revisions made to the voice of the speaker. Replacing the song's dialect with more "standard" vernacular—"I wish I was in de land ob cotton," becomes "I wish I was in the land of cotton"—Werlein/Viereck's "Dixie" "anglicized" Emmett's lyrics (Abel 32). Emmett "authored" dozens of minstrel songs and was revered for his ability to capture the purported sounds and rhythms of black vernacular speech. As one account enthused, Emmett's "understanding and rendering of the negro dialect were perfect" (Sheerin 958). Given such "perfect[ion]," Werlein/Viereck's decision to "anglicize" the song demands careful consideration.

It is impossible to reconstruct the intentions that led to any set of revisions; however, we can labor to reconstruct the social worlds in which revisions occurred. And dialect was a particularly vexed phenomenon in the many social worlds "Dixie" inhabited. In his searching study *Strange Talk: The Politics of Dialect Literature in Gilded Age America* (1999), Gavin Jones underscores the potentially subversive power that dialect wielded. Arguing broadly that the "distinctiveness of late-nineteenth-century American literature lay largely in the generative role of dialect within it" (3), Jones contends that dialect sets into play a more ambiguous set of significations and enacts a more heterogeneous set of political realities than has previously been acknowledged. For Jones, dialect is a purposefully ambivalent textual effect that encodes both dominance and subversion, both constraint and resistance. The resulting dialectic of dialect has great pertinence to the blackface speaker of "Dixie," since, quoting Jones, "misrepresentation of African-American dialect . . . was a popular means of encoding racist beliefs in black intellectual inferiority. Yet black languages also encompassed the power of cultural contamination. African-American dialect was a sign of black-white intermixture; it was a hybrid form with the force to infiltrate and adulterate the dominant language" (10–11).

Did audiences and readers recognize such power and hybridity in "Dixie"? Two aspects of the song's reception and revisionary history suggest that they might have. The hue and cry of critics such as Hotze who lamented the song's "low pretensions" reveals something at stake in Emmett's lyrics. While there is no smoking gun, no anxious contemporaneous expression by Hotze or others that confirms that that something was the song's dialect, there are several accounts of southerners who especially disliked the original lyrics. More persuasively, these dialect lyrics were short lived: The 1860 Firth, Pond, and Company edition of the song is the last major sheet music publication to appear entirely in dialect. After that 1860 edition, both northern and southern versions overwhelmingly offer anglicized lyrics. While neither of these characteristics fully corroborates Jones's narrative of cultural agency and anxiety, they do intimate the importance of dialect to the song's initial reception and immediate revision.[17]

Perhaps the dialect of "Dixie" was unwritten because, per Jones, audiences felt uncomfortable with the powers of subversion and significations of intermixture that its dialect enacted—especially while trying to imagine new political communities and traditions. Motivation aside, vanquishing dialect from "Dixie" obscured the important racialized setting and locution of the song. Gone with the dialect were the traces of blackface performance, Broadway, and "festive dance." Gone too were the complex semiotics of white bodies performing black caricature and the concomitant dialectics of spectatorial knowingness and implication. This racial revision also rewrote many of the song's specifics, shifting its significations from the local to the universal, from the particular to the general. The first and most profound of such shifts occurs at the level of voice. In "anglicized" versions, the speaker need not be of African descent. If, in turn, the song's speaker is no longer a slave or former slave, then a desire to be back "in the land of cotton" is not so troubling. That is, given the lyrical indeterminacy outlined above—where is Dixie again?— this racial revision enables a much less ambivalent longing for place.

It might be too easy to suggest that this revision conspired with proto–Lost Cause ideology to exorcise the specters of race and slavery from what was to become the South's new nationalist anthem; however, we can say that this revision attempted to whitewash "Dixie," to blot out the traces of a pervasive culture of racist and racialized performance. No matter how successful such whitewashing proved—the residue of the song's blackface minstrel origins was acknowledged periodically during and after the Civil War—the fantasy of perfect "angelic" whiteness replacing burnt cork and exaggerated vernacular would have been a powerful one for the nascent Confederate nation and its many revisers.[18]

This racial revision was radical both in how it broke from previous versions of the song and in what it enabled in subsequent versions. Since the removal of dialect made the song eminently revisable, Werlein/Viereck's attempts to whitewash "Dixie" informed nearly every revision—southern and northern—that would follow. First, the revision unmoored the already free-floating second, third, fourth, and fifth verses from the mast of the chorus and first verse, making it possible for subsequent editions to jettison these verses entirely. Because it obviated the song's "doggerel" lyrics, this revision rendered the verses of "Dixie" a nearly blank slate onto which subsequent revisers could write and rewrite their own lyrics, agendas, and ideologies. Second, this revision helped unburden the song's weighty baggage of "northern origin." The disappearance of dialect seems to have allowed (white) southerners to claim the song as their own. Finally, in attempting to erase the racialized context and personae of the song, this revision allowed (white) audiences to make a much broader set of identifications with the first verse and chorus's sense of longing: "*I* wish *I* was in the land of Dixie . . . To live and die in Dixie's land" (see Nathan 260). In this articulation, one need not be either a minstrel or of African descent to participate in such a sense of place. Through the voice of its now presumably white speaker, "Dixie" became a song of explicit rather than ambivalent longing for the South. As we will see, it did not take long for this sense of pride in place to become pride in nation.

"Dixie Land's a Nation Now"

In the wake of Jefferson Davis's inauguration, Hermann Arnold's instrumental "Dixie" became a hugely popular backdrop for revised Confederate nationalistic lyrics. To reiterate, Arnold rearranged "Dixie" as an instrumental quickstep, with new accents and a quicker tempo that forever left behind its original, "heavy, nonchalant, inelegant strut." "Dixie" became instead something of "a military statement," an up-tempo song that was well suited to Confederate martial and nationalist ceremony (Nathan 247).

Confederate Army brigadier general Albert Pike, particularly dissatisfied with the "low" pretensions of the song's lyrics, wrote eight verses of red-blooded, patriotic bombast to accompany Arnold's quickstep:

> Southrons, hear your country call you
> Up! lest worse than death befall you,
>   To arms! to arms! to arms! in Dixie!
> Lo! all the beacon fires are lighted,
> Lo! all hearts be now united!
>   To arms! to arms! to arms! in Dixie!
>
> . . . .
> Swear upon your Country's altar,
> Never to submit or falter,
>   To arms! etc.
> 'Til the spoilers are defeated,
> 'Til the Lord's work is completed!

To arms! etc.
Advance the flag of Dixie, etc. (Shepperson 17–18)

Lyrics to Pike's "Dixie" first appeared in the *Natchez (Miss.) Courier* on 30 May 1861; one month later, the New Orleans firm P. P. Werlein and Halsey published "The War Song of Dixie." With lyrics credited to Pike and music to J. C. Viereck, "The War Song of Dixie" became an immediate favorite in the new Confederacy, spreading quickly in the tumult that accompanied the fall of Fort Sumter on 13 April 1861. This "Dixie" opens with a full-throated and interpellative cry to the speaker's newfound countrymen: "Southrons, hear your country call you!" Throughout, the song is strident and agitated, as witnessed by its numerous exclamation points—twenty-two in the first verse and chorus alone!

Pike's most significant revision comes in the chorus.

I wish I was in Dixie,
    Hoo-ray! Hoo-ray!
In Dixie land, I'll take my stand
To live and die in Dixie;
    Away, away,
Away down south in Dixie
    Away, away,
Away down south in Dixie

becomes:

Advance the flag of Dixie!
    Hurrah! hurrah!
For Dixie's Land we'll take our stand,
And live or die for Dixie!
    To arms! to arms!
And conquer peace for Dixie!
    To arms! to arms!
And conquer peace for Dixie! (Shepperson 17)

The shift in pronoun use here is commanding: "I" becomes "we," "my" becomes "our." Given the nationalist ends this "Dixie" seeks, such proliferation of subjects is crucial. In the short space between the first verse and the chorus, the speaker's interpellation has proved successful: "our" indicates polyvocalism; a chorus of voices sings this chorus. Throughout, Pike's revisions are slight and yet absolute. For instance, the shift from "And live *and* die *in* Dixie" to "And live *or* die *for* Dixie" elevates Dixie from place to principle. Replacing a preposition of habitation ("in") with a preposition of allegiance ("for") and a conjunction of continuity ("and") with a conjunction of contingency ("or"), Pike's deft revision transforms Dixie into an ideal. Dixie is now not only a place to live in but also something to die for.[19]

This invocation of death should come as no surprise. As observed in chapter 2, death paradoxically helps to embody the nation and the national. Indeed, Pike's "Dixie" is suffused with the "moral grandeur" that, Benedict Anderson argues, attends death for one's country (144). And here, too, are the "battles, martyrs, agonies, blood, even assassination" that Walt Whitman thought could "only lastingly condense a Nationality" (1046). Such nationalistic necessity was not lost on Pike, whose verses, rendered in a strict tetrameter form, with feet generally made up of three trochees and a spondee, are jingoistic in the extreme. The first verse's ominous directive "Up! lest worse than death befall you" is an apt example. Although the lyrics remain silent about the specifics of those fates worse than death, such indeterminacy imbues the song with a sense of inception and urgency. Likewise, the refrain "To arms! to arms! to arms! in Dixie!" deftly redirects any accompanying anxiety about these fates. By replacing the earlier, inchoate "Look away!" refrain with the more proscriptive "To arms!" this revision offers its audience a decisive and clear plan of action.

Once Emmett's passive, spectacular "Look away!" becomes Pike's active, martial "To arms!"—that is, once the song's audience is duly armed—this war song next appeals to the audience's heart: "Lo! all hearts be now united!" A speech act of sorts, this affective appeal aims to consolidate and then reify a quasi-spiritual community of southerners, as does the chorus's evocation of "the flag of Dixie" (Abel 36). Through both subtle turns such as these and explicit ideological declarations—in one late verse the justification for war is made explicit: "For faith betrayed and pledges broken, / Wrongs inflicted, insults spoken" (Shepperson 18)—Pike's "Dixie" emerges as the first truly nationalistic anthem of the Confederate States of America.[20]

It was by no means the Confederacy's only nationalistic "Dixie." Henry S. Stanton's similarly titled "Dixie War Song" offers an equally bold and programmatic imagining of the southern nation. "Dixie War Song" opens by posing a series of rhetorical questions:

Hear ye not the sounds of battle?
Sabres clash and muskets rattle?
To arms! to arms! to arms in Dixie!
Hostile footsteps on our border,
Hostile columns tread in order,
To arms! to arms! to arms in Dixie!

No doubt following Pike's lead, "Dixie War Song" also exhorts its audience to act and "fly to arms in Dixie! to arms! to arms!" Stanton's lyrics prove a bit more apocalyptic than Pike's (for example, "See the red smoke hanging o'er us!"), and he does not stint in confronting the costs of war. One late couplet asks, "What though every hearth be saddened? / What though all the land be reddened?" In posing these questions, the song addresses directly the fears of many southerners—and many northerners. However, in a move characteristic of nationalist cultural objects, these concerns are conjured only to be negated by the repetitive call "to arms" and the evocation of a fight for "Freedom's labor." Saddened hearths and reddened lands are not, Stanton avers, too high a price to pay if "Dixie's Land's a nation now."[21]

The striking similarities between these versions of "Dixie" register both ideological harmony and the song's fundamental adaptability. The latter materializes not just in sheet music but also on the many Confederate song sheets that offer lyrics to be sung to the tune of "Dixie." As with much Confederate popular poetry, these broadsides prove occasional in character. A "Dixie" like the "Battle Song of the 'Black Horsemen'" (P&W 6258) celebrates the bravery of an individual regiment of soldiers at the First Battle of Bull Run/Manassas: "On the 21st, 'twixt sun and sun, / We made the boasting Yankees run. / Hurrah! hurrah! hurrah in Dixie's land!" This "Battle Song" nests its nationalism in a local setting, even changing the sacrosanct chorus of "Dixie" to "Then hurrah for old Virginia! / We'll fight for old Virginia boys! / We'll die for old Virginia boys! / Hurrah for old Virginia!" In relocating "Dixie" in the "Old Dominion," these lyrics make clear the reasons the "Black Horsemen" are fighting:

> We've come from the snow clad-mountains,
> And the land of the purest fountains,
> > Hurrah! hurrah! hurrah in Dixie's land!
> Our sweethearts and our wives conjure us,
> Not to leave a foe before us!
> > Then hurrah for old Virginia, &c.

This regiment claims to fight primarily for hearth and home. Although the lyrics are steadfast and impassioned, they make no direct reference to the Confederacy per se. The alternation between a "Dixie's land" refrain and an "old Virginia" chorus seems telling. These men are willing to die for their long-standing state, if not for their newly founded country. Here again are those tensions between local and national belonging.

Other "Dixie" broadsides seem aimed at bolstering flagging morale in the Confederacy writ large. "Southern War Song" (P&W 6554) begins as a variation on Pike's "Dixie":

> Ye patriots, hear your country's call;
> Your South's invaded—leave your all,
> > And go, repel the invading band.

Their leaders swear destruction dire;
They come with rifle, sword, and fire,
  To desolate and waste your land.

These lyrics are remarkable for their direct—we might even say manipula-tive—affective appeals. In making the case for why Confederates should con-tinue to fight an increasingly hopeless war, the lyrics go well beyond the tired rhetoric of an invaded South. This didactic "Dixie" asks its auditors to con-sider: the fact that "Your wives and mothers bid you go"; the bravery of "your sires"; the eyes of the world ("Convince the world by actions now / That free-men dwell in all our coasts"); even the judgment of the Almighty ("Remem-ber that you're in the right, / And trust in God, and bravely fight"). Punctu-ating these heart-tugging pleas is a chorus that urges soldiers to "March on, brave boys, and meet the foe, / March on! March on!"

And march on many did. Not surprisingly, "Dixie" was often used to commemorate and celebrate specific battles. For instance, "Great Big Bethel Fight. Awful Calamity" (P&W 6339) offers a decidedly tongue-in-cheek, pro-Confederate take on one of the earliest battles of the war:

I'll tell you of a tale that lately befel,
And the place where it happened was big Bethel,
Keep away, keep away, keep away you crop eared knaves,
Magruder peppered away like the devil,
'Till Pierce began home to travel.

Even the death of Union lieutenant John T. Greble, one of only eighteen Fed-erals to lose his life in the battle, is played for laughs: "But very soon a can-non ball / Upon his head quite soft did fall."

As "Great Big Bethel Fight" suggests, "Dixie" accompanied many sets of comical lyrics. Although the work of Confederate nationalism was deadly serious—after all, it helped to produce more than 620,000 deaths during the American Civil War—not all of its texts were. Yet even failed attempts at wit reveal a great deal about Confederate ambitions, literary and otherwise. "The Song of the Exile" (P&W 6224) devotes most of its stanzas to extract-ing a pound of flesh from Abraham Lincoln. At the same time, it also offers an admirably clear-eyed assessment of the Confederate machine of war: "We have no ships, we have no navies, / But mighty faith in the great Jeff Davis." Dated "Martinsburg, Va., *Dec.* 10, 1861," such an acknowledgment is re-freshing in the context of so much saber rattling. Then again, "The Song of Exile" also has great faith in a Confederate secret weapon of sorts, "Dixie" itself: "We hear the words of this same ditty, / To the right and left of the Mis-sissippi [. . .] In the land of flowers hot and sandy, / From Delaware Bay to the Rio Grande." The Confederate States may not have a navy, but it does have an endlessly pliable anthem that is available throughout the new nation.

Versions of "Dixie" appeared in Confederate newspapers and anthologies as well. For instance, Shepperson's *War Songs of the South*—which, to reiterate, was published in the first full year of the war—includes no fewer than three versions of "Dixie," two of which had been culled from local newspapers. In addition to versions of Pike's "Dixie" (17–19) and "The Battle at Bethel" (106–7), Shepperson also reprints E. Young's "Song. *Written for the 'Gilmer Blues' of Lexington, Ge.*" (156–57). Like "The Song of Exile," Young's lyrics tout "Dixie" as a central part of the Confederate war effort:

> Comrades, come and join the chorus,
> Sing for the land whose flag waves o'er us,
>   Hurrah! hurrah! hurrah! Dixie's Land.
> Bright as the sun that shines upon her
> Is th' escutcheon of her honor.
>   Hurrah! hurrah! hurrah! Dixie's Land.
>   God bless the Land of Dixie!
>   Hurrah! hurrah!
>   By Dixie's land we take our stand
>   To live and die for Dixie.
>   Hurrah! hurrah!
> We'll live and die for Dixie. (Shepperson 156)

While other Confederate versions of "Dixie" open with a call to arms, this one calls its comrades to song. Of course Young's extended metaphor is a familiar one. Abraham Lincoln closed his first inaugural address predicting that the "mystic chords of memory . . . will yet swell the chorus of the Union" (Lincoln 4: 271). Here, the chorus of the Confederacy is "Dixie," and it is through the communal performance of the song that the new nation will be realized. Such reflexivity is only possible in a social world in which "Dixie" is not merely well loved but also ubiquitous.[22]

In outfitting "Dixie" with such occasional and local lyrics, Confederates confirmed the elasticity of this "magical" tune. "Dixie" lyrics benefitted, in turn, from multimedial circulation: as sheet music, on broadsides, and in newspapers and anthologies. Again, this is to say nothing of manuscript and oral-performance versions of the song that never have found their way into print. Although these manifold versions of "Dixie" share a great deal in common, they, like the nation they helped to imagine, also represent disparate and even divergent interests. After all, what had once been a regional abstraction—a place "I wish I was in"—was now a national reality, one replete with local affinities and allegiances. "Dixie," too, embodies the "profoundly localized and particularized" poetics of place described in the previous chapter.

A boom in Confederate versions of "Dixie" speaks resoundingly to the centrality of music in the creation of Confederate nationalism. However, music was also of great importance to the Union culture of war. As the war progressed, popular songs like "Dixie" became sites of international contestation; the "music of mars" was, then, a cultural front in the conflict between the United and Confederate States of America. How else can we explain General Benjamin Franklin Butler's order to destroy the entire stock of the South's largest music publishing firm, A. E. Blackmar and Brothers, when Butler's troops took New Orleans in 1862 (Heaps and Heaps 8)?[23]

Dixie Unionized

North using "Dixie" too

By late 1861, as "Dixie" war songs began populating the South, there seemed to be a growing sense in the North that the song's musical charms could be redeemed if only its new Confederate nationalist significations could be vanquished. As one northern writer lamented: "Won't somebody localize 'Dixie,' give it a habitation, a place where it may be hailed from? Set words of Union sentiment to its 'ta la, ta la' and 'rum di di di do' etc." (qtd. in Nathan 271). In answer to this call for localization, several fascinating versions emerged in late 1861: "Dixie for the Union," "Dixie for Our Union," "Dixie Unionized," and "Union Dixie," among them. In all these versions, Emmett's popular melody was retained but with new, pro-Union lyrics set to the by-then familiar tune. Taken together, these Union "Dixies" speak to the profoundly nationalistic ends of music during the period and to the urgency of Civil War–era literary nationalism in a comparative context.[24]

The first of these Union "Dixies," "Dixie for the Union," appeared in 1861 as sheet music published by New York's Firth, Pond, and Company and credited as "Words by Frances J. Crosby . . . Melody by Dan. D. Emmett." Printed in vibrant color, the sheet music's cover shows two rippling U.S. flags with their staffs twined together. The accompanying lyrics prove remarkable if only for their specificity. Rather than speak in broad, universal rhetorics, the song deploys topical and timely allusions to actual events, places, and people:

> On! ye patriots to the battle,
> Hear Fort Moultrie's cannon rattle;
> Then away, then away, then away to the fight!
> Go meet those Southern Traitors with iron will.
> And should your courage falter, boys.
> Remember Bunker Hill.
> Hurrah! Hurrah! Hurrah!
> The Stars and Stripes forever!
> Hurrah! Hurrah! Our Union shall not sever!

Specific references to Fort Moultrie's cannon or, in the second verse, a quatrain such as "Though Beauregard and Wigfall / Their swords may whet, /

WORDS BY

FRANCES J. CROSBY.

MELODY BY	QUARTET ARRANGED BY
DAN. D. EMMETT.	S. LASAR.

New-York:

PUBLISHED BY FIRTH, POND & CO., 547 BROADWAY.

Entered, according to Act of Congress, in the year 1861, by FIRTH, POND & CO., in the Clerk's Office of the District Court of the United States for the Southern District of New-York.

"Dixie for the Union" cover image. Courtesy of the Historic American Sheet Music Collection, Rare Book, Manuscript, and Special Collections Library, Duke University, Durham, North Carolina.

Just tell them Major Anderson / Has not surrendered yet," work to root this "Dixie" in time. These topical references suggest a desire to facilitate both readerly recognition and a sense of spectatorial knowingness. While the resulting song may sacrifice some of its universality and permanence, such timeliness likely proved attractive to consumers who desired mementos of the times in which they lived.[25]

"Dixie for the Union" is similarly invested in lyrics that tie this trial of Union to the trials of revolution that preceded—or, some argue, occasioned—it. Particularly through its evocations of the paternal (for example, "Your sires, who fought before you, / Have led the way. / Then follow in their footsteps / And be as brave as they" or "As our fathers crushed oppression / Deal with those who breathe Secession"), the song labors to imagine a community with a long tradition of liberty and sacrifice. George Washington, that most paternal and national of figures, is deployed in the third verse as a reminder of the sacred cause of union: "Is Virginia, too, seceding? / Washington's remains unheeding?" Spurred by the presence of Washington, the song closes with a typically jingoistic invocation of divine order and right: "The star that lights our Union / Shall never set! / Though fierce may be the conflict, / We'll gain the victory yet." The rhetorical hedge of that third line is itself timely; by late 1861, the war had already proved to be a much bloodier, much more arduous affair than many unionists had anticipated. Nevertheless, these final lyrics evince an unwavering, cocksure assurance that the Union would indeed prevail, that the heavens would continue to shine on the United States indefinitely.

"Dixie for the Union" was widely admired during the period, with its lyrics reprinted again and again on song sheets (Silber and Silverman 63–64). However, as witnessed by the extraordinary number of variants and revisions that followed it, one Union "Dixie" simply would not do. An alternative "Dixie for the Union" replaces Crosby's timely and topical allusions with more universal ones:

Away down South in the land of traitors,
Rattlesnakes and alligators,
Right away, come away, right away, come away.
Where cotton's king and men are chattels,
Union boys will win the battles,
Right away, come away, right away, come away.

Then we'll all go down to Dixie,
Away, away,
Each Dixie boy must understand
That he must mind his Uncle Sam,
Away, away,
And we'll all go down to Dixie.

Away, away,
And we'll all go down to Dixie. (Silber and Silverman 63–64)

This is one of the earliest versions of "Dixie" to address directly the peculiar institution. "Where cotton's king and men are chattels" draws together two of the most cited causes of the American Civil War: a distinctly agrarian economic system ("cotton's king") driven by African slavery ("men are chattels"). This line also quietly bestows on slaves the status of manhood, granting them both agency and a protopolitical subjectivity. This was no small gesture during the period, even for the most ardent of abolitionists. Also of note here is the paternalistic relationship between "Each Dixie boy" and "his Uncle Sam." This "Dixie" figures the North as a disciplinarian sent to right the wrongs of disobedient "Dixie boys." The deployment of a familial rhetoric also anticipates the need for, and inevitability of, reunion. After all, "Dixie boy" and "Uncle Sam" are still family; even the prodigal Dixie son shall return home. But, in the meantime, as one late verse demands, "And let our motto ever be— / 'For Union and for Liberty!'"[26]

"The Traitors' Land," another Union "Dixie," uses familial rhetoric to very different ends. One of the most aggressive versions of "Dixie," "The Traitors' Land" pulls no punches, declaring: "We'll hush these ranting, hot seceders, / Rout their troops and hang their leaders. . . . We'll make them give up to our forces, / E'en though we march o'er brothers' corpse's." In promising widespread bloodshed, this "Dixie" offers Confederates dual roles in the drama of civil conflict: brother and traitor. The implication is that southerners must choose between the two. If one fights against the Union, his status as a brother is forfeit. Similarly, "Dixie's Land, No. 5" (published in New York by J. Wrigley) is characterized by violent and menacing images. One couplet prophesies that "Massa Jeff Davis soon shall vanish, / Traitors all must quick walk spanish"; another line pledges that "We'll swing their Leaders high as Haman, / As should be done to such highwayman." Needless to say, this is a long way from the intersectional affection of the first issue of the *Southern Literary Messenger*.[27]

"Dixie's Land, No. 6," another New York song sheet, is a bit more measured in its depiction of Confederates: "They want to have a revolution, / But we'll fight for the Constitution." This relatively generous couplet cogently redacts how unionists and secessionists saw their respective causes. Another upbeat song sheet is "The Dixie of Our Union," which went through several editions during the war. This "Dixie" celebrates the Union in downright joyous terms:

Let all good Union men about,
Come, join us in a glorious shout,
Hurrah, hurrah, hurrah, hurrah!

For Union and our Country dear,
We'll raise aloft a hearty cheer,
   Hurrah, hurrah, hurrah, hurrah!

Chorus.—Then for our Union we will stand,
      Hurrah, hurrah!
And all, throughout this happy land,
   Will join together heart and hand;
Hurrah, hurrah! Then hurrah for our Union!
Hurrah, hurrah! Then hurrah for our Union![28]

Such generosity and joy were not, however, the norm. For instance, "Dis-Union Dixie Land" is utterly dismissive of southern efforts at statehood: "Away, away, away down South in Dixie, / Away, away, away down South in Dixie, / Big folks in a solemn convention, / Declared themselves a separate nation." The reintroduction of dialect seems to add to the song's mocking tone, characterizing these "Big folks" as uneducated. The clever opening stanza also betrays an intimate knowledge of Emmett's original lyrics:

I'm glad I'm not in de land ob cotton.
   Good times dar am now forgotten,
Look away, look away, look away, cotton land.
   In South Carolina dis fuss was born in,
   Dar Secession had its dawnin,
Look away, look away, look away, cotton land.

As with the "Dixie boy" above, the Confederacy is trivialized, if not infantilized, by these lyrics.

The Confederacy was not the only target of Union vitriol. The possibility of foreign intervention in this "war between brothers" was a recurrent theme of Union versions of "Dixie." For instance, "Freedom's Guide" by one P. Sharkey warns that "The freedom that our father's won, / Shall be defended by each son." Similarly, "Our Yankee Generals," another song sheet printed by H. De Marsan, promises that the United States will "show to all the world / Our banner still remains unfurled." This "Dixie" then makes a not-quite-veiled threat to the British: "Let England do her blowing she has before, / We'll show her, if she wants to, / That we can now defend our shores." However, no Union "Dixie" is as emphatic about British involvement in the war as "We're Marching Down to Dixie's Land." Published in Philadelphia by "Johnson," its prolix lyrics reference the Trent Affair and then conclude:

John Bull is in a growling mood,
   For Dixie's land, for Dixie's land,
He'd help the rebels if he could,
   Lest treason should go down,

We've whipped him twice, if he'll call again,
    On sea or land, on sea or land,
He'll find us stocked with pluck and men,
    And treason shall go down;
John Bull we'll meet as friend or foe,
    On sea or land, on sea or land,
We love his smiles, we dare his blow,
    But treason shall go down!

Flaunting victories in the Revolutionary War and War of 1812, this "Dixie" voices a swaggering willingness to engage multiple enemies in order to suppress treason. As chapter 5 suggests, such a broader conflict was very much a possibility in 1861.

The proliferation of northern, nationalist versions of the song reflects a strong desire for the Union to "unionize" "Dixie"—and in so doing, to unionize itself. This call and response for a Union "Dixie" was likely rooted in anxieties about the lack of a proper U.S. national anthem. As Wilbur Zelinsky notes, "the nonexistence of a national anthem was acutely embarrassing for loyal unionists at the outbreak of the Civil War" (172). Intensifying this embarrassment was the fact that, despite its brief tenure, the Union's southern other possessed a wildly popular de facto national anthem, "Dixie." Such anxiety and embarrassment led to the formation of an 1861 Union "Committee upon a National Hymn," which sought to solicit from the masses an appropriate national anthem. The committee, made up of several eminent politicians, writers, critics, and artists, was chaired by the sometime editor and Shakespeare scholar Richard Grant White, who would publish an account of the committee's work entitled *National Hymns: How They Are Written and How They Are Not Written: A Lyric and National Study for the Times* (1861).[29]

In this charismatic text, White articulates his committee's criteria for selecting a national hymn. He does so in terms that suggest a deep understanding of the ways in which communities imagine themselves:

> As to a hymn for Americans, it must of all things proclaim, assert, and exult in the freedom of those who are to sing it. Let this be the expression; let it be brimful of loyalty to the flag, which is our only national symbol, and for that all the dearer; let its allusions be to our fathers' struggle for national existence, and its spirit be that of our nationality; let it have a strong, steady, rhythmical flow; and these points secured as to the words, the air is the most important matter. If that be such a one as all who sing can sing, and as the majority will like, association and habit will accomplish the rest. . . . A song which fulfilled these conditions . . . would pervade and penetrate, and cheer the land like sunlight. (75)

Such a criteria elegantly summarizes the various "Dixies"—both southern and northern—encountered thus far. These "Dixies" are overrun with allusions to the "founding fathers" and their "struggle for national existence." Through all its revisions, "Dixie" maintained "a strong, steady, rhythmical flow." As several contemporary critics note, the song's "air" was clearly "the most important matter," perhaps because it allowed "all who sing [to] sing." By 1861, "Dixie" had very much pervaded and penetrated and cheered both the South and the North "like sunlight." This is not to suggest that the hymn the committee sought was in fact "Dixie." It is, however, to underscore how this "Lyric and National Study for the Times" affirms the nationalistic resonances of all these versions of "Dixie"—and to emphasize the sometimes anxious and always provisional nature of American literary nationalism during this vexed period of international conflict.

After vetting nearly 1,200 manuscripts, the committee, and the nation, still lacked a national hymn. A 16 November 1861 *Harper's Weekly* review of White's book argued that national hymns cannot be contrived and that "some chance-born melody, like Dixie or Yankee Doodle," is more likely to become "in a manner national" (723). Or in a manner binational.

Coda: Silent through the Verses

In his oft-cited *Imagined Communities*, Benedict Anderson writes evocatively of national anthems:

> No matter how banal the words and mediocre the tunes, there is in this singing an experience of simultaneity. At precisely such moments, people wholly unknown to each other utter the same verses to the same melody. The image: unisonance. Singing the Marseillaise, Waltzing Matilda, and Indonesia Raya provide occasions for unisonality, for the echoed physical realization of the imagined community. . . . How selfless this unisonance feels! If we are aware that others are singing these songs precisely when and as we are, we have no idea who they may be, or even where, out of earshot, they are singing. Nothing connects us all but imagined sound. (145)

Anderson's sense of unisonance is significantly complicated in the case of the promiscuous anthem "Dixie," which was always and already evoking at least two unisonances and imagining at least two communities at the same time. If "Dixie" is to be read as a national anthem, to which nation is it anthemic, and in which of its many forms? What might be said of the song's *poly*sonance? In answering these questions, one must contend with the song's status as a transnational cultural phenomenon, a cultural object engaged with, and revised by, not one but two nations: the United and Confederate States of America.[30]

In a probing essay on nineteenth-century literary transnationalism, Paul Giles reminds us "how unstable the [U.S.] boundaries were in the earlier part of the nineteenth century and how the conflicts with Britain and Mexico raised the distinct possibility of United States geography being mapped differently from the subsequent sea-to-shining-sea model" ("Transnationalism" 66). Giles's emphasis on alternative mappings of U.S. geography is perceptive and much needed, rendering curious his reluctance to consider the conflict between the United and Confederate States of America in terms of transnationalism. Following Philip Fisher, Giles laments that American cultural criticism of the past thirty-plus years has privileged the American Civil War over all other "international confrontation[s]." For Giles, such a fixation on the Civil War "works implicitly to shore up the nation-building agendas of the United States, since the political and geographical divisions of that internecine struggle always anticipate as their corollary a parallel state of unity and indivisible liberty" (74). "Returning so obsessively to the trauma of the Civil War," Giles suggests, "indirectly asserts the primacy of traditional American ideals of federal unity and freedom" (74).

The opportunity Giles misses here to acknowledge the profound geographical and sociopolitical remapping that the Confederate national moment threatened is significant. Understood in transnational terms, the Civil War emerges as a quite serious challenge to the ideals of "indivisible liberty" and "federal unity and freedom." After all, to describe the conflict between the United and Confederate States as transnational in nature is to acknowledge that the Confederacy was in fact a nation, one with complex circuits of national feeling and an entire repertoire of nationalist cultural objects— "Dixie" being but one among many. As several of the "Dixies" discussed here suggest—to say nothing of the literary criticism, novels, and poems discussed in previous chapters—southern nationalism was a sinewy and multifarious phenomenon, one not easily dismissed. Similarly, acknowledging the brief political sovereignty of the Confederate States of America betrays the provisional nature of U.S. federalism during this period. It also resets the very terms of Giles's critique. Conceptualized as a sovereign nation at war for its independence, the Confederate States of America emerges as one of many "alternative nationalisms" that competed with, and proved a threat to, U.S. imperial nationalism during the nineteenth century.[31]

This conceptualization, in turn, allows the phrase "international confrontation" to signify in its fullest sense: "Existing, constituted, or carried on between different nations; pertaining to the relations between nations" ("International," def. 1a.). The American Civil War was an "international confrontation" inasmuch as it was a war between "different nations." While "internecine struggle[s]" such as the American Civil War may well "anticipate" "parallel state[s]" of federal unity, they also threaten a total dissolution of that unity. Such anticipation and threat are dialectically engaged; neither the achievement nor the failure of such states of unity is an assured outcome of these struggles. If civil wars "shore up" nation-building agendas, it is only under the often oppressive threat of the breaking apart of a nation. To understand this bewildering and bloody conflict as a war between sovereign nation-states—not as one between "brothers"—is to travel roads not taken in American literary historiography.[32]

The contentious circulation of "Dixie" during and after the American Civil War remains unintelligible without an understanding of the song's transnationalism. Given its legion revisions, the song's status as both intellectual and national property proves deeply vexed. "Dixie" was the express property of neither the South nor the North, neither the Confederacy nor the Union. Instead, "Dixie" is an ethereal and dynamic cultural object, one embedded not in the static forms of the nation-state but in the free-flowing circulation of a transnational public domain. Despite the increasingly contested lines of allegiance it traversed, "Dixie" found commerce in and of revision. As a "common property," the song moved fluidly across several orders of social boundaries, particularly those of nation, region, race, and class—the very boundaries that Keckley's anecdote acknowledges. It is this fluidity—the seemingly endless ability of "Dixie" to negotiate difference as it crisscrossed heavily contested boundaries—that distinguishes the song's movement during and immediately after the American Civil War.[33]

We see in the conflicts over "Dixie" an instance—perhaps the single instance—in which the cultural dominance of the Union was in any real way tested by the Confederacy. Of course nationalism is never a zero-sum game. To acknowledge Union cultural dominance is not to dismiss outright Confederate cultural production. Again, great expectations and outsize ambitions can be instructive in and of themselves. At the same time, the Confederate claim to or association with "Dixie" produced a great deal of anxiety in the North. If, as Jusdanis claims, "nationalism emerges out of comparisons people make regarding the relative standing of nations," then contested, transnational cultural forms provide particularly rich case studies of those comparisons in process. Put simply, "Dixie" allowed the people of the United and Confederate States of America to make sense of and manage the presence of competing nationalisms.

Returning to the Keckley anecdote that opened this chapter, we can now think of "that sweet and inspiring air" not as a "captured" property but as a fungible cultural form onto which various constituencies were cued to project their nationalist fantasies. The history of its restless, seemingly perpetual revision backlights the ways "Dixie" defied or exceeded the logic of a single and simple nationalism. Thus, "Dixie" emerges from the American Civil War as a transnational cultural object because its revisions bear the palimpsestic traces of two warring nations' attempts to imagine themselves, and one another, through song.

I close this chapter with a brief consideration of the problem of legibility posed by such traces. The popularity of "Dixie" did not stint following the

Civil War. The song has remained a stalwart part of American popular music and culture since its first performances in 1859 (or before). However, following the war, many musical enthusiasts were left to ask a deceptively simple question: Which "Dixie" shall we sing? In the South this seems to have been a particular problem given the extraordinary overproduction of Confederate versions of the song. Indeed, the question led the United Daughters of the Confederacy, United Confederate Veterans, and Sons of United Confederate Veterans to form a joint committee in 1904 to consider "an argument in favor of the adoption of [a single] version" of "Dixie."

The rationale for such an adoption is laid out clearly by the committee:

> since so many versions now exist and a different one is being used in every place, it is impossible for any assembly to sing "Dixie" when the words to be used are unfamiliar. As has been already demonstrated in our gatherings, the chorus will be sung with a vim, but all are silent through the verses. Let us unite in the selection of one "Dixie" and upon this be a solid South. (*Joint Committee* 2–3)

At the heart of this report are the difficulties posed by a multiplicity of "Dixies": multiplicity per se. Multiple versions of the song are tantamount to competing versions, with "a different one . . . being used in every place." Such diversity, the report suggests, actually inhibits the ability for the song to help imagine the postwar southern communities that the report represents: "but all are silent through the verses." Here, then, are the fruits of all those "adventures and transformations." The American Civil War helped to localize "Dixie" so effectively that subsequent singers had a difficult time performing it outside of strictly local settings.

The committee continues, "[O]nce our Confederate organizations have agreed upon rythmic words of patriotic fervor . . . it will be a question of a very short time when the song 'Dixie' will be used in our public schools, sung on all patriotic occasions, and known by heart, as the air is now known by every child. In such union of purpose nothing is impossible! Is not this our duty in making and preserving history?" (3). We see again in this remarkable, red-blooded passage an operative distinction between an air that is "known by heart" and a set of nonuniform, competing lyrics. The accompanying rhetoric of patriotism, "union of purpose," and possibility—above all, rhetoric of a "solid South"—speaks to the continued importance of popular song well after the cessation of Civil War hostilities. In turn, the committee's invocation of a "solid South" both imagines and attempts to realize a postwar southern community no longer riven by internal conflicts. That these veterans' groups would feel compelled to form a committee to adjudicate which words should be sung over "Dixie"—and then sung in Dixie—evinces just how high the stakes were, and sometimes continue to be, for the lyrical content of this oft-revised song.

CHAPTER FIVE

In Dreamland

The Confederate Memoir at Home and Abroad

> Most important, early memoirists believed that they wrote
> in a contest with time and with their former enemies'
> versions of the war. Many were ready for reconciliation,
> but they preferred it on the terms of their own choosing,
> and through narratives that they themselves told.
> —David Blight, *Race and Reunion*

> I wished that I was a man, such a man as Columbus or
> Captain Cook, and could discover new worlds, or explore
> unknown regions of the earth.
> —Loreta Janeta Velazquez, *The Woman in Battle*

In 1876 the Philadelphia publisher H. W. Kelley produced a broadside advertisement for a new Civil War narrative, *The Woman in Battle: A Narrative of the Exploits, Adventures, and Travels of Madame Loreta Janeta Velazquez*. The broadside claimed, with seeming hyperbole, that *The Woman in Battle* charts a "career of adventure which has never been paralleled on this continent"; as a result, the broadside puffed, the Velazquez narrative is "[t]he most intensely interesting war book ever published" (1). Yet, after reading the book, subscribers who had been seduced by the advertisement's over-the-top rhetoric might have felt that the broadside in fact undersold Velazquez's dizzying adventures, which were indeed unparalleled and by no means limited to "this continent."

For those not familiar with Velazquez's pulpy, six-hundred-plus-page book, here is a brief précis: *The Woman in Battle* narrates the chaotic life and times of a Cuban-born, cross-dressing Confederate sympathizer, soldier, and spy. Born in Havana in 1842 to a wealthy Spanish official and his French-American wife, Loreta Janeta Velazquez had a transient childhood in St. Lucia, Mexico,

Texas, and New Orleans. At fourteen, Velazquez eloped with an unidentified U.S. Army officer and moved to Kansas. With the onset of the American Civil War, Velazquez persuaded (or compelled) her not-long-for-this-world first husband to renounce his commission and fight for the Confederate States instead. Soon after, Velazquez, whose childhood dream had been "to see some real warfare, to engage in real battles, to do some real fighting" (95), "unsex[ed]" herself, donning men's clothing in order to fight for the "cause of Southern independence" (53).

Passing as Lieutenant Harry T. Buford, Velazquez recruited a company of 236 men, fought in the First Battle of Bull Run/Manassas, and at Fort Donelson and Shiloh, and she even proved to be quite the "ladies' man" (288).[1] After being wounded and having had her sex revealed numerous times, Velazquez "resume[d] the garments of [her] own sex" (292) and worked as a spy, blockade-runner, and Secret Service agent. Most impressively, late in the Civil War, Velazquez infiltrated Lafayette C. Baker's shadowy U.S. Secret Service as a double agent. After the defeat of the Confederacy, Velazquez fled the United States, traveled extensively, married two more times, and became involved with a Venezuelan emigration plan for Confederates as well as a number of money-making schemes in the western United States.

In all, Velazquez's "adventuresome career" (606) took her through nearly every state in the United and Confederate States of America, parts of Canada, England, France, Germany, Poland, Mexico, Cuba, St. Lucia, Puerto Rico, Venezuela, Demerara, Trinidad, Barbados, and St. Thomas. Along the way, Velazquez met numerous Civil War luminaries, including Presidents Davis and Lincoln, and assumed a daunting number of disguises and personae. In addition to Harry T. Buford, Velazquez passed as a Spanish officer, a white Northern woman, a Canadian woman, an English woman, a French Creole woman, and a Spanish woman.

Or so *The Woman in Battle* claims. Not surprisingly, the authenticity of Velazquez's spectacular narrative has been in question since the moment of its publication in Richmond, Virginia, and Hartford, Connecticut, in 1876. While recent scholarship has uncovered documentary evidence that substantiates several of Velazquez's narrative claims and personae, it seems unlikely that the authenticity of *The Woman in Battle* will ever be fully determined.[2] In the absence of full authentication, Velazquez's most recent and best editor, Jesse Alemán, concludes judiciously that "Velazquez's very existence, as with the narrative attributed to her, rests somewhere in between history and story, where even a seemingly inauthentic author can nonetheless produce an authentic cultural text that embodies and enacts the prevailing beliefs and anxieties of its historical context" (*Woman* xix). Then again, such is the case with many memoirs. From Benjamin Franklin's *Autobiography* (1793) to James Frey's *A Million Little Pieces* (2003), American autobiographical writing has tended to represent the prevailing beliefs and anxieties of a given historical context much more consistently than actual or authentic lives. As a result, I am not interested in Velazquez's memoir as the representation of the life of an uncommon woman; instead, I consider it an uncommon representation of the times in which that woman lived—or claimed to live.[3]

The following pages emphasize an understudied aspect of both the Velazquez narrative and its historical context. I argue that *The Woman in Battle* elegantly "embodies and enacts" the international dimensions of the American Civil War, and in so doing, continues the work of Confederate literary nationalism long after the fall of the Confederacy. Pursuing the internationalism broached in the previous chapter, I demonstrate that *The Woman in Battle* is a restless text, one that moves dexterously and recurrently across lines of region and nation. As Velazquez travels from state to state, nation to nation, and continent to continent, her narrative effectively remaps the American Civil War within a global system of immigration, foreign intervention, transnational capital, transatlantic slavery, and competing nationalisms.

In *The Woman in Battle*, the Civil War is played out not only on the battlefields of Shiloh and Manassas but also in a series of unexpected contexts: Europe, South America, and the Caribbean. Perhaps because of her cosmopolitan background, Velazquez as narrator has a particularly keen eye for the international aspects and implications of the war. Indeed, her narrative recapitulates and her rhetoric underscores such internationalism, forcing readers to acknowledge the ways that this harrowing conflict exceeded the provincial limits and logics of North versus South. In sum, Velazquez's awareness of a world outside of the United and Confederate States helps to disrupt the insularity of Civil War narrative convention. Moreover, because the narrative sets up a loose representational relationship between the Confederacy and its restless "Woman in Battle," Velazquez's "Exploits, Adventures, and Travels" become, to some degree, the Confederate States'. Thus *The Woman in Battle* tells the belated story of a Confederacy in and of the world.[4]

In tracking Velazquez's many movements, this chapter considers one final genre of Confederate literature: the postwar memoir. As the conflict shifted from the field of battle to the field of cultural memory, autobiographical texts like Velazquez's sought to memorialize the Confederate States of America in print. Having lost a physical struggle for independence, former Confederates sought to win a new, ideological struggle over the causes and costs of the war, its legacies and meanings for a newly re-United States. Yet, in a moment of national reconciliation and reunion, *The Woman in Battle* continues to pick fights, not merely with the "northern invaders" but also with Confederate political and military leaders; ungallant southern soldiers; and an international community that would not intervene on the Confederacy's behalf. In doing so, the narrative's formal features emphasize the contingent nature of the American Civil War, even going so far as to imagine alternative and counterfactual outcomes. In turn, Velazquez does not spend much time romanticizing the Confederacy, nor is she as dogmatic about the so-called Lost Cause as were many of her contemporary memoirists. Instead, *The Woman in Battle* offers a perceptive—which is not to say unbiased—account of the great expectations and stultifying disappointments wrought by the Confederate national moment. Here, then, is the bitter taste of all those apples turned to ashes in the mouths of southern nationalists.

These Memories Can't Wait

The Woman in Battle's historical context was particularly fraught. Published at the height of the U.S. Centennial and in the final days of Reconstruction, Velazquez's narrative emerged at an awkward moment of transition between Old and New Souths. It also entered a literary market already glutted with war-related material. During the late 1860s and early 1870s, volumes that commemorated the recently concluded war in narrative, verse, song, and image were ubiquitous, as writers and publishers looked to capitalize on a broad memorial impulse. However, by the mid- to late 1870s, readers and book buyers appear to have grown a bit weary of the war. As Alice Fahs notes, during these years, "interest in all aspects of the war waned dramatically" (313). It was not until the 1880s that such interest resurged, thanks in large part to the ascendance of a new genre: the book-length Civil War memoir.[5]

David W. Blight has suggested that the latency period between the cessation of hostilities and this boom in Civil War memoirs is to be expected: "As in other large-scale wars, most Civil War soldiers did not readily talk or write about their conflicted emotions in the immediate postwar period" (142). While this seems a plausible broad-strokes explanation for the delay, I am hesitant to conflate Union and Confederate soldiers. The postwar experiences of Confederate soldiers differed from those of Union soldiers in both degree and kind. Among other things, the Confederate soldier returned home to an utterly devastated South. In addition to taking the lives of over a quarter of a million Confederates—nearly one-fifth of all white southern men between the ages of eighteen and forty-five—the war had decimated livestock populations, farm machinery, and railroad lines throughout the South. The emancipation of slaves had also, in the words of James McPherson, "destroyed the principal labor system on which southern productivity had been based. . . . Two-thirds of assessed southern wealth vanished in the war" (*Battle Cry* 818). Thus, the Confederate soldier-cum-memoirist likely approached his—or, in the case of Madame Loretta, her—task with much more than "conflicted emotions."

In his rich comparative study of the "culture of defeat," Wolfgang Schivelbusch describes the "state of unreality—or dreamland" that sets in after a national defeat: "The deep and widespread depression caused by lost wars in the age of nationalism is as obvious as the joyous public celebrations of victorious ones" (10). Schivelbusch goes on to observe that the South experienced an "unusually long duration of the dreamland condition" following Lee's surrender at Appomattox (14). Thus, we might understand the belated emergence of the Confederate memoir as a function of both postwar devastation and this dreamland state. Faced with stultifying defeat and a gutted homeland, it is not surprising that the majority of Confederate memoirs did not appear in print until after the official conclusion of Reconstruction in 1877.[6]

Once Confederate memoirs did appear, they told a remarkably consistent story about the behavior and character of the people of the Confederate States of America; the reasons they fought for independence; and their steadfast moral superiority. Contemporary historians recognize this romantic cultural narrative as part and parcel of the Lost Cause ideology that would come to dominate how the American Civil War has been remembered, in both the South and the North, over the past 150 years. Alan T. Nolan offers a particularly cogent definition: "The Lost Cause is therefore an American legend, an American version of great sagas like *Beowulf* and the *Song of Roland*. Generally described, the legend tells us that the war was a mawkish and essentially heroic and romantic melodrama, an honorable sectional duel, a time of martial glory on both sides, and triumphant nationalism" (12). Described alternately as "a mood, or an attitude toward the past" (Blight 258) and "a rationalization, a cover-up . . . distinctly marked by Southern advocacy" (Nolan 14), the ideology flourished in the 1880s and 1890s but had its roots in the immediate postwar period.

Indeed, it likely drew its name from Edward A. Pollard's 752-page harangue, *The Lost Cause: A New Southern History of the War of the Confederates*. Published in 1866—hot on the heels of the third volume of Pollard's contemporaneous *Southern History of the War*—*The Lost Cause* closes with a careful call to intellectual arms: "All that is left the South is 'the war of ideas.' She has thrown down the sword to take up the weapons of argument, not indeed under any banner of fanaticism, or to enforce a dogma, but simply to make the honorable conquest of reason and justice" (750). Pollard is quick to qualify this war imagery as being just a "harmless figure of rhetoric," but his purpose seems deadly serious: "It is to be feared that in the present condition of the Southern States, losses will be experienced greater than the immediate inflictions of fire and sword. The danger is that they will lose their literature, their former habits of thought, their intellectual self-assertion, while they are too intent upon recovering the mere *material* prosperity, ravaged and impaired by the war" (751).

Although Pollard's long-winded history has been much discussed in the historiography of the Lost Cause, few critics have noted his explicit concern with the future state of southern literature. Emphasizing the point, Pollard reiterates his fear of literary extinction, this time citing the example of Greece "under the Roman yoke" (751): "States reduced by war are apt to experience the extinction of their literature, the decay of mind, and the loss of their distinctive forms of thought" (750–51). Postwar southerners must, Pollard avers, turn swords to pens, not ploughshares, in order to avoid the fate of the Greeks. It bears repeating: Pollard was writing in 1866, following a period of intense nationalist cultural production. The literature that he worries will be lost was Confederate in nature. The literature that will make an "honorable conquest of reason and justice"—that is, the literature that is to come—will be a Lost Cause literature.[7]

It is in an interstitial context, betwixt and between Confederate and Lost Cause literatures, that we can best understand Velazquez's eccentric memoir. Published ten years after the war and a few years before the most concentrated period of Lost Cause ideological production, *The Woman in Battle* occupies an exceptional position within its literary field. First, *The Woman in Battle* appeared in print earlier than most canonical Confederate memoirs of the war: Jubal Early, *A Memoir of the Last Year of the War for Independence, in the Confederate States of America* (Lynchburg: Charles W. Button, 1867); Ralph Semmes, *Memoirs of Service Afloat* (Baltimore: Kelly, Piet, 1868); Joseph E. Johnston, *Narrative of Military Operations, Directed, during the Late War between the States* (New York: Appleton, 1874); George Cary Eggleston, *A Rebel's Recollections* (Cambridge: Riverside, 1875); John Bell Hood, *Advance and Retreat* (1880); Richard Taylor, *Destruction and Reconstruction* (New York: D. Appleton, 1879); Sam R. Watkins, *1861 vs. 1882. "Co. Aytch"* (1882); John Singleton Mosby, *Mosby's War Reminiscences, and Stuart's Calvary Campaigns* (New York: Dodd, Mead, 1887); and James Longstreet, *From Manassas to Appomattox* (Philadelphia: J. B. Lippincott, 1896).

Second, *The Woman in Battle*'s relationship to an emergent Lost Cause ideology is at best vexed. The Velazquez narrative never commits fully to an idealization of the Confederacy, and its memory of the war is hardly sentimental. To be sure, the narrative's dedication resounds with the "losers in battle, winners in spirit" ethos of the Lost Cause: "To My Comrades of the Confederate Armies, who, although they fought in a losing cause, succeeded by their valor in winning the admiration of the world" (Schivelbusch 19; Velazquez 3). Yet, the narrative that follows is anything but dogmatic about the war having been "an honorable sectional duel, a time of martial glory on both sides, and triumphant nationalism." Indeed, as we will see, Velazquez goes out of her way to question the valor of individual "Comrades."

A willingness to break ranks with other, more romantic memoirs is not the only distinguishing feature of the narrative. Equally extraordinary are its formal elements, which Velazquez herself significantly undervalues. For instance, at the midway point of her grueling tale, the peripatetic narrator urges her reader to keep up the pace. She claims, somewhat disingenuously, that she is merely "giving in plain language an unadorned narrative of the personal experiences of a single adherent of the Confederacy—experiences which gain their chief interest from the fact that they were different in a marked degree from those of any other participant in the war on either side" (275). While her experiences may seem sui generis to twenty-first-century readers, Velazquez's was not the first narrative of a cross-dressing Civil War solider and spy. That distinction belongs to Sarah Emma Edmonds's *Nurse and Spy in the Union Army* (1864). And at least two memoirs of female Confederate spies predate *The Woman in Battle*: Rose O'Neal Greenhow's *My Imprisonment and the First Year of Abolitionist Rule at Washington* (1863) and Belle Boyd's *Belle Boyd in Camp and Prison* (1867). These women in and around battle shared at least some of Velazquez's experiences.

However, the cross-dressing soldier and spy memoir are but two of several genres to which the Velazquez narrative nods. *The Woman in Battle* also incorporates elements of the picaresque novel, the travel narrative, and the bildungsroman, among others. Indeed, it is its genre bending as much as its gender bending that makes the Velazquez narrative "different in a marked degree" from its peers. As a result of such generic promiscuity, this slippery text moves fluidly among a number of positions in its literary field. Thus, *The Woman in Battle*'s adherence to and departures from emergent conventions reveal the narrative possibilities available to postwar Confederate memoirists. More to the point, the narrative's illumination of a murky aspect of war—its internationalism—renders intelligible several key features of a Confederate literary culture that had a decidedly international purview.[8]

The Urge for Going, the Wings to Go

Before moving to consider the ways the narrative frames the internationalism of the American Civil War, it is important to understand Velazquez's decision to devote herself to the Confederacy—a decision that would literally take her around the world. Although the steadfastness of Velazquez's commitment to the Confederate cause is never in doubt, the motivation behind that commitment is a bit surprising. Velazquez states again and again that she was motivated to fight for the Confederacy because she desired fame and excitement; more to the point, she wanted earnestly to become part of an unbroken and cosmopolitan chain of women in battle. The narrative opens with a breathless and learned history of "the woman in battle": Deborah, Semiramis, Boadicea, Bona Lombardi ("the Italian peasant girl"), Catalina de Eranso (the Spanish "nun-lieutenant"), Molly Pitcher, Agostina Domenech ("the maid of Saragossa"), and Apollonia Jagiello (33–36).

As she compasses the globe in search of women in battle—the Middle East, Africa, England, Italy, Spain, the United States, Hungary, Poland, and France—Velazquez reserves her strongest praise for "the greatest and noblest of them all":

> From my early childhood Joan of Arc was my favorite heroine; and many a time has my soul burned with an overwhelming desire to emulate her deeds of valor, and to make for myself a name which, like hers, would be enrolled in letters of gold among the women who had the courage to fight like men—ay, better than most men—for a great cause, for friends, and for father-land. (37)[9]

Joan of Arc is a recurring, even patronal presence in Velazquez's lengthy narrative. Yet her veneration of the Maid of Orleans is idiosyncratic; Velazquez emulates the French heroine in order that her own name can be "enrolled in letters of gold" as well. As Elizabeth Young notes, Velazquez "admires Joan of Arc for her fame, not her patriotism" (162). Refreshingly, Velazquez pulls no punches: She states flatly, "[M]y heart was fixed on achieving fame, and of accomplishing even more than the great heroines of history had been able to do" (62). This frank declaration makes clear why Velazquez wants to fight in a war, but it raises two questions: why this war, and why fight for the Confederacy?

Unlike nearly every woman in battle before her, Velazquez's cause involves a community she cannot claim as her own. Velazquez is, after all, a southern sympathizer, not a southerner per se, and she is careful throughout the text to refer to southerners as "my *adopted* country people" (6; emphasis mine). Without a default patriotic raison d'être—"I am fighting for my land and my people"—Velazquez's relationship to the Confederate cause remains obscure, especially given her Cuban (or Spanish colonial) background and transient childhood. To this end, one of the most peculiar aspects of the Velazquez narrative is the absence of any sustained discussion of states' rights, northern despotism, slavery, cultural difference, or Old South gentility—the standard reasons offered by southerners and southern sympathizers to justify their support of the Confederacy. Although Velazquez deploys the phrase the "cause of Southern independence" repeatedly (70, 95, 127, 159, 161, 177, 218), she does not account for why such independence is necessary or advantageous. Velazquez's reiteration of the rhetoric of cause without a concomitant discussion of the specific merits of that cause is conspicuous, especially given her tenuous connection to the southern states.

From its first pages, the narrative deploys a starkly mercenary rhetoric to explain Velazquez's decision to go to war: The American Civil War offers her "an opportunity" to "carry-out my long-cherished ideas" (37). Again, those ideas involve celebrity rather than patriotism, political ideology, or sense of duty. Given this bald confession, it seems fair to conclude that the Civil War was a convenient and timely occasion for Velazquez to fulfill her dreams: "to see some real warfare, to engage in real battles, to do some real fighting, and, as I fondly hoped, to have some opportunities of distinguishing myself in a signal manner" (95). Later in the narrative, Velazquez notes that she is, "by instinct and by education," a partisan—someone who *must* choose sides in any given conflict: "It is an impossibility for me to limit or divide my affections and predilections" (161). This may go a long way to explaining her fierce devotion to, and optimism about, the Confederate cause. In selecting the side to which she would be a partisan, Velazquez confesses a certain impulsivity: "I trusted to my impulses, perhaps, more than to my reason; but every strong partisan must do this, in a greater or less degree" (161–62). And yet, motivation aside, Velazquez did in fact "see the thing through" with remarkable dedication and initiative, despite a series of major obstacles (37).[10]

Velazquez's commitment to the Confederate States was significantly complicated by the fact that she did not have an officer's commission, and she "had no fancy" to lead the life of a private soldier (182). (The Confederate States of America did not as a matter of course give commissions to foreign-born women.) As a result, almost all of Velazquez's actions during the war were "undertaken entirely on [her] own account, without authority from anybody" (139). This afforded Velazquez-cum-Buford a great deal of both autonomy and frustration. The lack of an official commission meant that Velazquez could go where she pleased, but it also meant that she could not count on steady employment as either a soldier or a spy. Velazquez notes: "By entering the army as an independent, I secured a freedom of action and opportunities for participating in a great variety of adventures that I otherwise would not have had, but I also cut myself off from opportunities of regular promotion" (346). As a result, Velazquez's independence forced her into itinerancy throughout the war. Indeed, had she been able to secure a long-term, official commission as either a soldier or a spy, it seems unlikely that *The Woman in Battle* would have been as restless or international a text.[11]

In any case, Velazquez seems well suited to an independent life, one in which she did not have to "depen[d] upon the authority of another" ("Independent," def. 1a.). Logistically, her ability to come and go as she pleased proved essential because camp life, with its repetitive drilling and long periods of boredom, was maddening for Lieutenant Harry T. Buford. As Velazquez confesses, "It was an absolute necessity for me to be in motion, to be doing something, and the slow and inconclusive progress of the military movements annoyed me beyond expression" (126). Though she "determined to be as patient as [her] impatient disposition would let [her]" (147), Velazquez nonetheless "chafed under the *ennui* of the camp, and felt irresistibly impelled to be moving about and doing something" (129). But as an independent, Velazquez stayed in constant motion, flitting from place to place, company to company, and intrigue to intrigue with alarming frequency. That motion allowed her to witness the American Civil War played out on an international stage. Moreover, through such motion Velazquez becomes a figure for an independent and eventually cosmopolitan Confederacy. Against constructions of the South as provincial backwater, Velazquez's movements suggest a worldly Confederacy, one with international connections and imperial aspirations.[12]

Independent States

Yet there is more at stake in Velazquez's independence than mere freedom of movement. Throughout the narrative Velazquez celebrates causes of independence, both personal and political. For instance, her championing of Confederate, Cuban, and Polish independence can be read as an index of her steadfast belief in the virtues of self-government, in every sense of that phrase (248; cf. 527). At the same time, the narrative voice of *The Woman in Battle* is independent in another sense: "Not depending on others for the formation of opinions or guidance of conduct; not influenced or biased by the opinions of others; thinking or acting, or disposed to think or act, for oneself" ("Independent," def. 5a.). Velazquez's willingness to speak frankly about the shortcomings of Confederate politicians, military leaders, and soldiers departs dramatically from both a nascent Lost Cause ideology and many of her fellow memoirists. This is not to say that Velazquez is without bias—far from it—but her book reads as one of the more independently minded of Confederate memoirs.

We can understand the narrative trajectory of *The Woman in Battle* as moving, in Velazquez's own words, from "Romance" to "Reality" over the course of the war and its immediate aftermath (127). As a result, the character that emerges from these six-hundred-plus pages is dynamic, and the narrator takes pains to ensure that her readers can chart her development in and over time. In one of *The Woman in Battle*'s many metanarrative moments, Velazquez belatedly reveals her methodology:

> In writing this narrative, it has seemed to me that the only proper method is to represent events as they actually occurred, and to record the impressions they made upon me at the time of occurrence, and not as they were colored by subsequent developments. My ideas and feelings under particular circumstances are as much a part of my story as the narrative of actual events, for my proceedings were guided and influenced by them. (347)[13]

Although such historicism is difficult to achieve in a retrospective autobiography, Velazquez for the most part maintains this narrative mode throughout the text. Her reluctance to "break the thread of [her] story" (401) and her stated concern for narration in "due order" (461) amplifies Velazquez's independent voice. In claiming to reject hindsight, Velazquez promises reality over romance and tries to grant this highly partisan narrative an air of objectivity. Such reality effects work to bring readers into Velazquez's experiences of frustration, disillusionment, and defeat. Because of her careful manipulation of narrative sequence, it is as though Velazquez and her readers are together in time.

What Velazquez confesses to her readers would have turned the heads of many a Confederate and Confederate sympathizer. First and foremost, on several occasions Velazquez slays that most sacred of Confederate cows, the gallant southern soldier. Her critiques begin mildly: Having infiltrated the purportedly male-only space of the military camp, Velazquez is disgusted by the "vulgarity of language and profanity" of her colleagues, as well as the "blackguardism which many men are so fond of indulging in." Yet it is the "manner in which too many men are in the habit of referring to the other sex" that she finds most despicable. Indeed, she wishes that women "could only listen to some such conversations as I have been compelled to listen to, and learn how little respect or real regard of any kind men have for them" (59). The crass and sexist antics of soldiers in camp may seem like a trivial topic for Velazquez to address; however, she sees such ungentlemanly behavior as being of a piece with more important deficiencies in Confederate character.

Like many Confederates, Velazquez began the war holding "the most exalted opinion of the invincibility of our Southern soldiers, and of the skill of our generals" (162). However, having faced the "rough experiences of actual warfare," she revises her opinion quickly (145). By the midpoint of the narrative, Velazquez has lost her "old-time faith in the irresistible valor of Southern soldiers or the masterly generalship of Southern commanders" (245). She remarks tartly: "The old boast which I was accustomed to hear so often at the outbreak of the war, that one Southerner could whip five Yankees, had turned out to be mere boasting, and nothing more" (245).[14]

It is remarkable how early in the war Velazquez's "school-girl romance" gives way to dour reality:

> I had learned much concerning some of the very weak points of human nature; that all men are not heroes who wish to be considered as such; that self-seeking was more common than patriotism; that mere courage sufficient to face the enemy in battle is not a very rare quality, and is frequently associated with meanness of spirit; that it is easier to meet the enemy bravely in battle, than it is to exercise one's brains so as to meet him most effectively; that great names are not always worthily borne by great men, and that a spirit of petty jealousy is even more prevalent in a camp than it is in a girl's boarding-school. (145–46)[15]

Needless to say, critiques of southern wartime masculinity were not the norm in Confederate memoirs. Although Velazquez is careful to note that many of her brothers-in-arms acquitted themselves admirably, this catalog of human frailty in a time of war runs counter to a number of postwar and Lost Cause cultural imperatives: to reconcile, to memorialize, to sentimentalize. In a scene like this, *The Woman in Battle* seems to anticipate the ironic realism of Ambrose Bierce and Stephen Crane, not the mawkish melodrama of Thomas Nelson Page or Margaret Mitchell. David Blight has observed that the Civil War "remains very difficult to shuck from its shell of sentimentalism" (4). And yet here is a text from 1876 doing precisely that.

Velazquez's final comparison of military camps to girls' boarding schools rehearses one of her central arguments: that this "Woman in Battle" out-manned many of her fellow fellows. She claims, with no small amount of swagger, that there was "not a man in the Confederacy who was more will-ing to fight to the last than I was, or who was willing to venture into greater peril for the sake of the cause; and, perhaps, if all the men had been as eager to find the last ditch as myself, before giving up, the war might have had a different termination" (144). If only the Confederacy had had more men like Madame Loreta Janeta Velazquez.[16]

The woman in battle is not the only person in the narrative who compares favorably with Confederate soldiers. Early in the narrative, Velazquez tells an unflattering story about a Confederate lieutenant who steals away from a battle. When he returns to camp, the lieutenant tells a dubious Velazquez-cum-Buford that he had been captured by, and then escaped from, federal troops. Velazquez suggests that such cowardly duplicity was far from rare in the Confederate officer corps: "I have seen a good many officers like this one, who were brave enough when strutting about in the streets of cities and vil-lages . . . but who were the most arrant cowards under fire, and who ought to have been court-marshalled and shot, instead of being permitted to disgrace their uniforms, and to demoralize their men, by their dastardly behavior when in the face of the enemy" (121). In a stunning bit of bluster, Velazquez then declares, "My colored boy Bob was a better soldier than some of the white men who thought themselves immensely his superiors" (121–22). She even feels a sense of pride in "the darkey's pluck and enthusiasm" (122).

Taken together, these comparisons to schoolgirls and slaves not only de-bunk the myth of the "irresistible valor of Southern soldiers" but also signifi-cantly overturn social hierarchies of gender and race. By Velazquez's account, some Confederate men were no better than women or slaves, despite their sense of superiority over both groups. Such an unflattering depiction of Con-federate wartime masculinity was extremely uncommon during this period, when a great deal of energy was being spent reconstructing white masculin-ity in both the South and the North. Much more representative is the purple prose of Lieutenant-General Jubal Early. Writing from exile in Canada, Early celebrated the Confederate soldier in unequivocal terms: "I believe that the world has never produced a body of men superior, in courage, patriotism, and endurance, to the private soldiers of the Confederate armies." He continues: "I have seen, with my own eyes, ragged, barefooted, and hungry Confederate soldiers perform deeds, which, if performed in days of yore by mailed warriours in glittering armour, would have inspired the harp of the minstrel and the pen of the poet" (v). These at-odds depictions may help to explain why Early condemned *The Woman in Battle* with great verve and pith.[17]

One final feature of the narrative that both adheres to and departs from Confederate memoir convention is the measured tone Velazquez assumes when discussing the Union war effort. While there was a great deal of pressure circa 1876 to reconcile the North and South, her memoir appeared in print at the end of a very contentious period of legislative and social upheaval. The fact that *The Woman in Battle* was published in separate editions in both the North and the South further complicated Velazquez's task as memoirist. Yet, the narrative is at times downright generous to northerners—even to that most hated of Yankees, Abraham Lincoln. Following a purported meeting with President Lincoln, Velazquez expresses profound sympathy for the Great Emancipator: "[M]y interview, brief as it was, induced me to believe, not only that he was not a bad man, but that he was an honest and well-meaning one, who thought that he was only doing his duty in attempting to conquer the South" (141–42). By 1876 Abraham Lincoln had been fast-tracked for sainthood in the North; however, he remained an extremely divisive figure in the South (Schwartz 79–82). As a result, Velazquez's suggestion that Lincoln was "well-meaning" would have been quite controversial in the states of the former Confederacy.[18]

Near the end of the war, Velazquez's sympathy for the Union cause grows exponentially, along the same axis as her sympathy for Lincoln:

> I loved the South and its people with a greater intensity than ever, while at the same time many of my prejudices against the North had been beaten down by my intercourse with its people during the past eighteen months. There were good and bad in both sections, and I believed that if the good men and women, both North and South, would now earnestly and patriotically unite in an endeavor to carry out the ideas of the founders of the government, they would, ere many years, be able to raise the nation to a pitch of greatness such as had yet been scarcely imagined. (517–18)

This sounds very much like the Lost Cause and "road to reunion" narratives that dominated the last quarter of the nineteenth century. Here is the triumphant nationalism and latent imperialism produced by a "war between brothers." Such rhetoric is surprising in a narrative that spends so much time and energy challenging the provincialism of Civil War history and memory.[19]

Throughout *The Woman in Battle*, Velazquez seems to have a preternatural awareness of the global importance of the events that are unfolding around her. Midway through the narrative, she discusses the "irresistible fascination in being an active participant in the great events upon which the destinies of a continent were hanging" (318). Although she confesses that her fascination is a function of her desire to be "immortalized," her sense that the American Civil War was a conflict that had implications for the whole continent, not just the United and Confederate States of America, testifies to Velazquez's wide-angle view. Such a perspective is unusual in the popular literature of the war, and it has gone all-but-unnoticed in the small body of scholarship that treats the Velazquez narrative.[20]

The American Civil War involved the destinies of several continents, a fact that *The Woman in Battle* underscores through its incessant movements north, south, east, and west. For instance, the possibility of foreign intervention is a recurrent concern in the narrative. Early in the war, Lieutenant Buford is asked his opinion on foreign intervention: "This was something I had never given even a thought to; but I answered very boldly, and in a style that I thought would be appreciated by my auditors, 'We don't want any foreign help in a war like this. I reckon we can manage to do our own fighting'" (67–68). Buford's performative response gains the approbation of his audience, but the question haunts Velazquez for the remainder of the narrative.

France and England's potential involvement in the American Civil War was a source of great international prognostication, debate, and anxiety during the war years. As Confederate historian Emory Thomas notes, "if Europe intervened, the distribution of world power would be at stake" (170). The so-called American question (that is, whether or not to recognize the nascent Confederate nation) proved particularly precarious for England, whose largest industry in 1860 was based on cotton. While both countries could "imagine benefits accruing from a permanently disunited states," both worried about being drawn into an international war (Thomas, *Confederate Nation* 170). As a result, Confederate agents abroad worked tirelessly for their respective national causes, laboring to win official recognition from Europe in general and from France and England in particular.[21]

Perhaps because in the end France and England stayed out of the war, few Civil War battle narratives spill much ink over the issue of foreign intervention. Relegated to the realm of the counterfactual, the promise of France's and England's involvement in the war only exists as a spectral presence in most Civil War narratives.[22] Yet Velazquez is constantly thinking about the Old World and the ways it could aid and abet the Old South—despite the fact that she is composing her narrative in 1876, more than a decade after the Confederacy's diplomatic efforts had failed. For instance, after the fall of New Orleans, Velazquez finds herself trapped in a Federal-occupied city and imprisoned under suspicion of spying for the Confederacy. With no way to flee the city and desperate to continue her espionage, Velazquez uses a set of papers she had bought from a British woman sympathetic to the Confederacy. The ruse of "invoking the protection of some foreign power" works wonders (240). Armed with her British papers, Velazquez claims the "protection of the British flag" and enlists the assistance of acting British Consul George Coppell. Much to the chagrin of General Benjamin Franklin Butler, she successfully passes as an Englishwoman, escaping both prison and the city of New Orleans (262).

As she leaves prison, Velazquez trades barbs with several Federal troops who brag about "how they were going to thrash Johnny Bull" (264). Characteristically, Velazquez refuses to hold her tongue: "I could not resist the temptation of turning to Mr. Coppell, who must also have heard the remark and saying, 'That fellow must be crazy. He and his friends had better wipe out secession first, before they talk about whipping Johnny Bull'" (264). This pointed exchange reveals the fault lines in U.S.-British relations during the period, reminding readers that the "war between the states" could easily have extended beyond North America. Moreover, Velazquez's British cross-dressing escapade insinuates a cultural kinship between the Confederacy and England. This scene suggests that, with little effort, the Confederate "Woman in Battle" can become "Johnny Bull."

As the war progresses, and as the Confederate future begins to look bleak, the Velazquez narrative represents growing impatience with the noncommittal British and French governments. Velazquez recalls:

> Great expectations were also built upon foreign intervention, which every one felt had been delayed longer than there was any just reason for, but which it was thought could not but take place shortly. Every little while exciting rumors were set afloat, no one knew how or by whom, that either France or England had recognized the Confederacy, and many bitter disappointments were caused when their falsity was proved. (342)

As desperate Confederates found fewer and fewer bellwethers of foreign intervention, impatience turned to bitterness and resentment. Late in the war Velazquez herself consented to take part in a complicated counterfeiting and securities fraud that had as its victim "Britishers," whom Velazquez and her coconspirators considered "fair game" (474). Velazquez seethes: "[W]e regarded their conduct as treacherous to both parties in the great contest, and thought that they might as well be made to pay some of the expenses of conducting it. From first to last the British government had deluded the people of the Confederacy with false hopes of recognition and interference" (474).

Apparently the irony of a double agent using the rhetoric of delusion is lost on Velazquez.

This withering assessment of the British government is remarkable for its focus on transnational capital. Taking advantage of "gross immoralities" in the U.S. Treasury, Velazquez's complicated scheme involved exchanging counterfeit Confederate and Union securities and currency for British securities and gold, which were then converted into U.S. greenbacks (477). The decision to "go for Johnny Bull's pocket" (475) meant flooding the international market with bogus notes. Thus, Velazquez's scheme entangled countries and economies outside those of North America, a fact that suggests the range of contexts in which the American Civil War signified.

As one of the chief architects of the scheme, Velazquez had to follow the trail of those bogus notes. In the final weeks of the war, she traveled to London and Paris to oversee the execution of her swindle. Indeed, Velazquez learned of Lee's surrender to Grant while she was en route to New York via a British steamer. Velazquez spends her first postwar hours on Wall Street trying to settle her transatlantic accounts amid a chaotic mass of agitated bankers and brokers. What she witnesses on Wall Street is, to her mind, unprecedented: "It was a spectacle to be remembered; nothing that I had ever beheld—and I had certainly participated in many exciting scenes—at all resembled it" (506). Given the hundreds of pages of spectacle that precede this sentence, Velazquez's claim is startling. She continues, "[S]ome momentous event had occurred which had seriously affected innumerable important financial operations, and that in a moment great fortunes had been lost and won" (506). The Velazquez narrative captures with remarkable clarity the tumult and uncertainty that attended the conclusion of the American Civil War. Yet it does so by focusing on an unexpected topic: the postwar fate of international financial markets, here embodied by Wall Street, an emerging economic hub. In the final days of the war, Loreta Janeta Velazquez is the woman in financial, not martial, battle.

England and France are, of course, not the only nations involved in these markets and intrigues. Canada and several Latin American and Caribbean countries also play important roles in the Velazquez narrative. As a result, *The Woman in Battle* becomes something of a hemispheric text, one that locates the American Civil War on a map that extends beyond both the Tropic of Cancer and the 49th parallel north. For instance, in the summer of 1864, Velazquez became involved with a group of Confederates in Canada who were planning what came to be called the Lake Erie Conspiracy. Until 1867, Canada comprised a loose set of British colonies, not yet a federated nation. As a collection of British North American colonies, Canada was officially neutral in the war. Yet despite close economic and cultural ties with the North and strong antislavery sentiment in the colonies, Confederates found Canadians who were sympathetic to the cause of "Southern independence"—and especially to the possibility of having a significantly smaller and diminished United States as its neighbor to the south.[23]

It is in this vexed political context that Velazquez claims to have made a bold run to Canada in 1864. Passing once again as an Englishwoman, but this time employing an Irish brogue, she smuggled correspondence, packages, and $82,000 in U.S. currency (413–15). The monies and documents Velazquez carried were to be used for an ambitious raid on Johnson's Island, a large prison camp on Lake Erie near Sandusky, Ohio. Once freed, the Confederate prisoners planned to join with southern sympathizers, incite Native Americans to hostility, and begin a border war with the United States. The conspirators hoped that such a conflict would pull Federal troops away from the southern front and cause sufficient panic in England to draw that nation into the war at last. As Velazquez notes, "We also placed great reliance on the effects of the panic which, it was hoped, would be created, and also on British intervention, which it was expected would be brought about by a border war, in which it would be impossible to prevent trespass upon British territory" (441).[24]

Needless to say, none of this came to pass. A Confederate turned traitor and revealed the details of the plot to Federal troops days before the raid. The U.S. gunboat *Michigan* was waiting for the conspirators in Sandusky Bay, and the mission was aborted. Velazquez's narration of these riveting events backlights again the fragility of U.S.-British relations during the war. Moreover, it reveals the political and imaginative importance of the U.S.-Canadian border—one of the lesser-known "fronts" in Civil War lore. Not least, this section of *The Woman in Battle* invites counterfactual questions. What if a border war had broken out? Would the American Civil War have escalated into a world war? As Velazquez notes, with no small amount of pride, the excitement generated by the failed raid suggests just "how great *would have been* the panic that the successful execution of the scheme *would have caused*" (443; emphasis mine).

After the unsuccessful raid on Johnson's Island, a furious Velazquez turned her full attention to blockade-running, an activity she had engaged in periodically throughout the war. Although her discussion of blockade-running is sparse, it too reveals the centrality of transnational capital and international markets to the progress of the American Civil War. By her own account, Velazquez's pithy description of blockade-running constitutes a "secret history of the war" in which bodies, goods, and money snaked their way across borders of region, nation, and continent, as well as lines of allegiance and ideology (459). The blockade-running that Velazquez describes finds commodities moving variously among Lewes, Delaware; New York, New York; and Philadelphia, Pennsylvania; Liverpool, England; La Havre, France; Antwerp, Belgium; and Watling's Island (San Salvador); St. Thomas; Havana, Cuba; Nassau, Bahamas; and Barbados, among other West Indian ports; and various southern states (411, 461). Velazquez's narration of this international circuit once again places the Confederacy in the world, revealing the Confederate States' ambitions to be a player in a world economy.

Despite her implication in such trade, Velazquez is irritated throughout the text by the "purely pecuniary light" in which blockade-runners view their "very paying business" (462). She reserves particular venom for those runners who show a "total indifference to the fate of the Confederacy" (462). But if the bad business of blockade-running reveals to Velazquez the "unveiled depths of human depravity" (458), it reveals to her readers a dense, global web of fungible capital. And Velazquez's partisan anger reminds readers that the American Civil War had an immense effect on the global economy. As Velazquez observes immediately after the cessation of hostilities, "great fortunes had been lost and won" because of the American Civil War. In fact, great fortunes had been lost and won all over the world.[25]

While involved in this lucrative transnational and transatlantic trade, Velazquez also became enmeshed in substitute-brokering and bounty-jumping schemes, with which she hoped to reduce "the strength of the Federal armies in the field, by preventing the re-enforcements demanded by the government from reaching the front" (464). Through these complicated machinations, Velazquez realized that commodities are not the only things moving fluidly across those borders of region, nation, and continent during the war. In one of its most affecting scenes, *The Woman in Battle* narrates schemes that enlisted emigrants under false pretenses:

> They were surrounded [at Castle Garden] by crowds of shouting and yelling brokers until they were fairly bewildered, and found themselves enlisted before they well knew what was the matter with them. To those who hesitated, the most lavish promises were made; their wives and children were to be cared for; they were to receive one hundred and sixty acres of land; money in larger sums then they had ever beheld before was flaunted in their faces. (491)

She goes on to describe these duped foreigners as "poor devils," "who came over here to better their fortunes, had but little chance to become anything but food for Confederate bullets" (492). Velazquez recalls one particular enlistment conspiracy involving Irish emigrants. The "poor foreigners" were promised that once the Confederacy was defeated, the Federal government intended to declare war with England in retribution for the Trent Affair. Such a war would lead of course to "the liberation of Ireland"—especially if a sufficient number of Irishmen enlisted in the U.S. Army to fight against the Confederacy first (493).

Velazquez discloses that such schemes were themselves transnational in nature, with emigrants having been "picked up in Europe by agents, under all kinds of pretexts and promises, and shipped for this side of the ocean just like so many cattle" (492). The specter of slavery and race makes a sudden appearance in the narrative as Velazquez laments a transatlantic traffic in German emigrants: "Captain P. considered himself as their owner, and he sold them to the government exactly as he would have sold cattle, if that sort of traffic had been as profitable as dealing in white human beings" (492).

In accordance with an emerging Lost Cause ideology, *The Woman in Battle* makes little mention of black slavery up to this point, despite the fact that throughout the war Velazquez is "attended" by a slave, Bob, whom she forces under the threat of death to fight for the Confederacy. (Velazquez does not mention this fact when she celebrates his "pluck and enthusiasm" above.) Her quotidian descriptions of Bob's service to her and to the Confederate States have the force of normalizing her exploitation of him. Yet, even in a postwar, postemancipation context, Velazquez has little to say about slavery as a social institution—unless, as in the case of emigrant enlistment schemes, it involves white slavery. Velazquez's image of cattle and her horror at the prospect of white chattel suggest that slavery is intelligible in the narrative only through a lens of whiteness. Slavery is unremarkable when it involves black bodies, but an act of "villany" when white bodies are being trafficked (458). Such sub-rosa racial politics are on full display in the narrative's final pages as Velazquez searches in vain for a new homeland in the post–Civil War world.[26]

An Index of Internationalism

But before following Velazquez into that postwar world, I want to take a brief detour and discuss another foreign-born and cosmopolitan Confederate, Henry Hotze, who served the Confederate States as a commercial agent to England during the American Civil War. Again, because the fate of the Confederacy rested in part on how other nations answered the American question, England was the target of tireless Confederate diplomatic efforts, as well as an "animated and well coordinated" propaganda program, which was largely orchestrated by Henry Hotze (Cullop 135). Hotze's strange career as a "literary soldier of fortune" can be usefully illuminated, I argue, by the Velazquez narrative, and vice versa (Bigelow 121).

Henry Hotze was born in Zurich, Switzerland, in 1834 and immigrated to the United States as a child. In 1856 he became a naturalized citizen in Mobile, Alabama, where he rose quickly through the ranks of the elite class on the basis of his manners, grace, intelligence, and white supremacist views (Dufour 269; Burnett 2–3). Hotze was responsible for the first English-language translation of Joseph Arthur Comte de Gobineau's *Essai sur l'inégalité des races humaines* (1853–55), a founding document of scientific racism. Commissioned by Josiah Nott and published in 1856 by J. B. Lippincott and Company, Hotze's edition, retitled *The Moral and Intellectual Diversity of the Races*, was heavily edited. It included an "Analytic Introduction and Copious Historical Notes" that recast Gobineau's arguments as an endorsement of the institution of slavery in the U.S. South.[27]

After a failed appointment as secretary of the U.S. Legation at Brussels, Hotze was named associate editor of John Forsyth's *Mobile Register*, a position he held until the outbreak of the American Civil War, when he volunteered for the Mobile Cadets, a corps that, as discussed in chapter 4, became part of the Third Alabama Infantry. Hotze never saw action, but his dispatches to the *Register* proved popular back home in Mobile. Not satisfied with the contribution he was making to the war effort, Hotze left the cadets after three months and was commissioned as a commercial agent to England.

The language with which Hotze was commissioned for this position is revealing. Here is a selection from Secretary of State Robert M. T. Hunter's 14 November 1861 letter:

> You will be diligent and earnest in your efforts to impress upon the public mind abroad the ability of the Confederate States to maintain their independence, and to this end you will publish whatever information you possess calculated to convey a just idea of their ample resources and vast military strength and to raise their character and Government in general estimation. (United States Naval War Office 293)

Put simply, the tactful and urbane Henry Hotze was to be a propagandist for the Confederate States. Initially granted a measly $1,500 salary and a $750 contingent fund (both of which were paid out of Jefferson Davis's secret service account), Hotze would have to win British hearts and minds through subtle means. Arriving in England in early 1862, Hotze used his "European manner and tastes"—as well as a cache of Cuban cigars and American whiskey—to help place pro-Confederate "leaders" (or editorials) in several major London papers and gain access to the House of Lords (Oates 133, 139).

Hotze's propaganda efforts reached their apex with his decision to "establish a newspaper wholly devoted to [Confederate] interests" (United States War Department 400). In May 1862, on a shoestring budget, Hotze published the first issue of *The Index*, a sixteen-page, ten-by-thirteen-inch, three-column weekly that stressed economic sympathy between the two countries and underscored the similarities between English and Confederate "culture, tradition, and character" (Oates 142). Modeled on the *London Index*, Hotze's weekly journal had an impressive run. Over nearly four years, *The Index* published 172 issues and boasted of correspondents in Dublin, Frankfort, Berlin,

Versailles, Paris, Turin, New Orleans, New York, and Hartford, Connecticut, as well as a perhaps-apocryphal correspondent in a "unnamed city" in Australia (Oates 143). The circulation of the paper never exceeded 2,250 issues (400 of which were earmarked for the United States and 150 for France), but that circulation infiltrated London's polite society. Indeed, *The Index*'s primary aim was to influence public opinion from the top down, beginning with those writers, parliamentarians, and cabinet members who helped to shape public opinion in England.[28]

With recognition of the Confederate States as the "do-all and be-all" of his mission, Hotze took a cautious approach with his propaganda (Dufour 280). The tone of the journal remained, for the most part, measured, with Hotze appealing to "the spirit of fair play upon which every Englishman prides himself" and differentiating *The Index* at every turn from "the flippancy and indecorum of American Journalism" (19 June 1862: 127). Late in the war, Hotze would claim that the object of *The Index* had been to be "the representative, in English journalism, of a gallant and struggling people appealing to the world not only for political but still more for moral recognition . . . to enlarge and extend the common ground upon which two nations may cordially meet, which need only to understand each other in order to cherish the warmest mutual appreciation and lasting friendship" (20 April 1865: 248).[29]

Despite an expanding diplomatic portfolio, which came to include France and Germany, Hotze maintained exclusive editorial control over the weekly throughout the war, taking pains to ensure that his connection with it be "known only to a few initiated and . . . not be suspected by the public at large" (United States War Department 400). This is to say that Henry Hotze worked covertly, disguising his official state commission, and, at times, passing in print as an Englishman, Frenchman, American, and so forth. Hotze also wrote countless pieces for *The Index*, making the anonymous argument again and again that this was a war for independence—one the Confederacy could and should win.[30]

A typical issue of *The Index* might include "Notes of Events of the Week," the "Cotton and Dry Goods Market," and the "Latest Direct Intelligence from the South." Recurrent themes included: free trade, the federal blockade, military successes of the Confederacy, the purported legality of secession, and racial anthropology as proof of the inequality of the races and naturalness of slavery (Burnett 21–22). *The Index*'s coverage of news had an international profile, with events from Russia, France, Mexico, and the Papal States also receiving coverage. As this suggests, Hotze had high literary ambitions for *The Index*, which he saw as being more than a mere tool of the Confederate state. In a letter to an editorial assistant, Hotze declared that the "cherished ambition of my life is to make the Index a worthy representation in journalism of the highest ideal of that Southern civilization which is as yet only in its infancy." He urged his staff to try "to make the Index more & more a news-paper, an epitome of the world" (qtd. in Harwell, *Creed* 4–5).[31]

While *The Index* has garnered attention from historians of Civil War diplomacy, literary critics have all but ignored this remarkable text. This is despite the fact that *The Index* repeatedly and ingeniously deployed literature as a way to win British hearts and minds. Indeed, *The Index* was a profoundly literary endeavor—and not merely because it was subtitled *A Weekly Journal of Politics, Literature, and News*. Hotze labored to create a sense of "cultural kinship" between the two nations, arguing for their shared heredity; extolling the virtues and refinement of southern schooling; even observing that southerners enunciated their vowels quite like the English (Cullop 57–58). Literature remained an essential ground for this kinship. In addition to numerous reviews of novels, plays, poems, and songs, *The Index* offered a several-column response to Trollope's *North America* (1862); an essay on sensation fiction and *Lady Audley's Secret*; features about the "Literature of the Masses" and freedom of the press in the Confederacy; a wholesale dismissal of Lowell's Second Series of *Biglow Papers*; and, perhaps inevitably, a comparison of Fanny Kemble's *Journal of a Residence on a Georgian Plantation* (1863) and Stowe's *Uncle Tom's Cabin*.

The plight of Confederate literature was a theme of commentary on the pages of *The Index* as well. A 24 September 1863 essay (previously quoted in the introduction) concedes the difficulties faced by Confederate littérateurs during wartime—and then characteristically looks past the current conflict to a moment when said littérateurs could fulfill their promise: "What is now written, though necessarily hurried and imperfect, gives promise of a brilliant future, when the people of the Confederate States will have a literature worthy of their glory in arms and of their descent" (347). That final phrase, "worthy . . . of their descent," is classic Hotze: a subtle reminder that British literature is the model for, and the progenitor of, Confederate literature.

The Index treated both the hurried and the imperfect, addressing several pieces of Confederate literature discussed in previous chapters. For instance, the issue for 1 December 1864 reviewed *Macaria*, concluding, "Altogether the story is not satisfactory" (764). The 24 September 1863 issue discussed several other West and Johnston publications, including *The Royal Ape* and *War: A Poem with Copious Notes*. The former is lambasted for casting a "slur upon the domestic life of Mr. Lincoln"; the reviewer considers it "indecorous to drag his private life into a public controversy." The reviewer is much more complimentary to the latter, even defending John Hill Hewitt against his own claim that the verse borders on doggerel (347). A few months earlier, an unnamed correspondent from Mobile provided *The Index* with a nine-column, nearly three-page selection of "The War Songs of the South" (21 May 1863: 60–63). As the correspondent notes dryly, "We have an abundance of it, good (*meo judicio*), bad, and indifferent" (60). Finally, *The Index* also made several references to the de facto Confederate national anthem. For instance, a 27 November 1862 announcement heralded the publication in London of sheet music for the "*Southern National Song. 'War Song of Dixie*,'" noting that "there has been numerous versions, and the melody has been for many years sung by the negroes employed on the Southern rivers" (79).

A particularly deft example of Hotze's attempts to imagine a literary kinship between England and the Confederate States comes in a 5 June 1862 article titled "The South as a Literary Market." This anonymous article observes that the shared interests "of commerce and capital" between the two nations are "sufficiently explained. . . . But the interests of literature, scarcely less in magnitude, no one has ever taken the pains to consider" (89). The piece goes on to offer a brief discussion of a Confederate States' resolution to extend reciprocal international copyright to foreign authors. Decrying "to what heavy losses British authors and publishers have been subject by the wholesale and systematized piracy" of the United States, the article figures copyright as a morality play, with the United States cast in the role of the unscrupulous villain and the Confederate States as the honorable hero (89).

Given this dramatic tension, the piece urges England not to underestimate the South's ability to consume—that is, to pay for—literary property. Comparing the opening of the South as a market to "the discovery of another India" (89), the article trumpets Confederates as "a reading people" (90) who can help to buoy the English book trade: "The independence of the Confederate States enlarges the appreciative and remunerative audience of every man who lives by his pen . . . by some six or seven millions of his own race and language, eager to receive intellectual instruction from the parent source of their language and literature" (89). And what, pray tell, is an "appreciative and remunerative audience"? An audience more than happy to listen to the courtly muses of Europe—and even willing to pay for the privilege of doing so.

Once again, Confederate literature plays the role of devoted offspring, a scion of English literature yet in its infancy. The piece then makes an ingenious side-step, assuring those Europeans who live by the pen of the stability of the South as a literary market: "[I]t is fair to say that the Confederate States, in the career of independence which they have so heroically commenced, will not for many years be able to supply their own literary wants, or to give an equivalent for what they must necessarily receive from Europe" (90). The Confederate market for literature offers much more than a short-term boon for British authors and publishers. Until the Confederate States can develop a proper (read: properly Anglophilic) literature of its own, this "reading people" will continue to buy British books.

Here is the process of national differentiation that Corse and Jusdanis cue us to look for played out on an international stage. And here is a prime example of the triangulation of Confederate literary nationalism. *The Index* presents the Confederacy's international copyright resolution as both an act of literary independence from the United States and an expression of a cultural kinship between the Confederate States and England. Propaganda or no, this discussion recapitulates central features of a Confederate literary culture in aspiration.[32]

Velazquez's retrospective narrative helps render intelligible Hotze's activities in Europe on behalf of the Confederate States. Those efforts, in turn, speak resoundingly to the international aspirations of Confederate literary nationalism and offer us a context for Velazquez's restless movements during the war. *The Index* and the Velazquez narrative are, finally, sympathetically international. For instance, at about the same time Velazquez was helping to plan the raid on Johnson's Island, *The Index* ran an essay on "The Position of Canada in the American War" (24 July 1864). Similarly, like Velazquez, *The Index* placed the Confederacy in the context of other, nascent independence movements. Following the January Uprising in Poland (1863), Hotze published an essay on the topic "What Constitutes a Nation." Explicitly comparing the cause of the Confederacy to that of Poland, the essay concludes: "But this much is certain, that whenever and from whatever cause the consciousness of national identity pervades a population, a nation is born" (26 February 1863: 282; cf. Velazquez 527). Finally, like Velazquez, Hotze fretted endlessly about the effects of German and Irish immigration on the Union war effort (Dufour 292).

In the first issue of *The Index*, Henry Hotze defined the journal's "Object" via a literary metaphor: the Confederate States as "a sealed book to the intelligence of England." *The Index* aimed to "awake the interest of an indifferent reader, and induce him to turn over the pages" (1 May 1862: 8). In this regard, *The Index* proved a remarkable success, attracting the support, readership, and services of many eminent Londoners. As a result, the historical consensus on Henry Hotze is that his tireless efforts on behalf of the Confederacy were wholly impressive—and futile. By summer 1863, the hopes for British recognition were all but dead in the cold Atlantic water, a fact that Hotze himself had to admit by September 1864 (Dufour 291–94). Yet he soldiered on, publishing *The Index* until late August 1865, long after Lee and the journal itself had conceded defeat.[33]

A New South and a New World Order

Following the collapse of the Confederacy, while Henry Hotze was trying to repurpose *The Index* as a Lost Cause organ, Velazquez beat a hasty retreat, fleeing the continent in order to travel through Europe with her brother. Although she felt a "pang of regret" at leaving North America, Europe promised both a safe refuge and some distraction from the cataclysmic destruction and unrest Velazquez left behind her (519). For Elizabeth Young, the final eight chapters of the narrative pass by in "carnivalesque flux" (156). Indeed, in its last hundred pages, as Velazquez wanders through Europe, Latin America, the Caribbean, and the U.S. West, *The Woman in Battle* becomes something of a travel narrative, with gracious recommendations about points of interest in various ports of call. Despite such shifts in narrative convention and tone, Velazquez's postwar travels need not be cordoned off from her wartime exploits and adventures. Instead, the restlessness of the narrative's final eight chapters continues the work of its first forty-four: to place the American Civil War in a global context. In doing so, these chapters also narrate the fate of a post-Confederate South via a new personification, "The Woman *after* Battle."[34]

As she travels aimlessly through Europe, the late war and the fate of her adopted country haunt Velazquez. In Paris, she cannot help but notice the "great contrast" between the "manifold pleasures of Parisian life" and her recent experiences "wearing a uniform of gray, and living the roughest kind of a life in camp and on the battle-field" (522–23). Likewise, a proposed visit to the catacombs draws out painful memories of wartime trauma and guilt. *Les carrières de Paris*, "filled with the mouldering remains of poor humanity," cause Velazquez to shrink back: "I feared not the dead; but to have gone among these skeletons would have revived memories of the past that were anything but pleasant ones. It made me shudder to think how many poor souls I had seen launched into eternity without a moment's warning, some of them, perhaps, by my hand" (524). Later Velazquez feels great sympathy for the Polish people, whom she hopes will soon "regain their independence. They are cruelly oppressed now, and their beautiful country is a waste and desolation" (527). Wherever Velazquez goes, she seems to find either the echoes or the ghosts of the Confederacy and its costly war.

After the political unrest of the immediate postwar period abates, Velazquez returns to the newly re-United States and embarks on a tour of the "late Confederacy" (531). While in the South, Velazquez also takes a fervent interest in local emigration schemes: "I longed to quit the scene of so much misery, and fully sympathized with those who preferred to fly from the country of their birth, and to seek homes in other lands, rather than to remain and be victimized, as they were being, by the wretches who had usurped all control of the affairs of the late rebel states" (536). Velazquez's strident account offers us insight into the motivations—or the stated motivations—of southerners who refused to confront Reconstruction and the realities of the world the war made.[35]

In the years following the cessation of hostilities, thousands of former

Confederates fled the South for destinations west and north; others sought an Old South life in the Old World of Europe; many more looked to Latin America for a fresh start. Gaines Foster has described this emigration movement as "the 'utopian dream' of Confederates who would not accept the results of the war" (16). Such dreams often turned into logistical and financial nightmares, as Velazquez learned firsthand when she traveled to Venezuela to "go and see what was to be seen" in one of the lesser-known Confederate emigrant colonies (537). Velazquez writes that from afar Venezuela seemed "like a second Garden of Eden, where all was peace, happiness, and prosperity, with no free negroes or carpet-baggers to intrude upon them" (539). Yet when she and her fellow colonists arrive in South America, they discover a less idyllic new world than they had hoped to find. Most troubling, they learn that there were in fact "free negroes" in their second Eden. After having had two successive "negro" pilots, the captain of the expedition asks:

> "Good Lord, are all the officials in this country niggers?" A good many of the emigrants were quite as much disgusted as the captain, and seemed to think that if the negroes were of as much importance as they seemed to be in Venezuela, it would have been just as well to have remained at home and fought the battle for supremacy with the free negroes and carpet-baggers on familiar ground. (543; cf. 552–54, 558)

Here the Confederate exiles are horrified to have their colonial fantasy of a white paradise disrupted by Venezuelan racial diversity. That these pilots are "officials"—people of color who are of some importance to the Venezuelan state—is all the more distasteful to those southerners who were fleeing Reconstruction and its promises of enfranchisement for "[a]ll persons born or naturalized in the United States."

After spending several months in and around Bolívar, Velazquez advises her "adopted country people" to "remain at home," citing as reasons the instability of the Venezuelan government, lack of a centralized credit system, and dearth of available building supplies. I sense that the colonists' "disgust" at the racial state of affairs also informed her recommendation. After returning to the United States, Velazquez is similarly appalled to find "the freedmen and carpet-baggers were having things completely their own way throughout the length and breadth of the late Confederacy" (570). Everywhere she turns, Velazquez is confronted by that which her narrative has largely repressed: the revolutionary promise of a new social order that might bring racial equality.[36]

This returns us to Pollard and *The Lost Cause*, which concludes by emphasizing the issues he believes the war did not settle: "But the war did not decide negro equality; it did not decide negro suffrage; it did not decide State Rights, although it might have exploded their abuse. . . . And these things which the war did not decide, the Southern people will still cling to, still claim, and still assert in them their rights and views" (753). Yet, rather than stay in the South and assert her "rights and views," Velazquez flees the states of the former Confederacy, embarking on a seemingly endless search for financial and social security. And so, appropriately enough, *The Woman in Battle* closes with Velazquez on the move again, this time through a number of sites associated with struggles for independence: Demerara, Trinidad, Barbados, St. Lucia, St. Thomas, and Cuba. Finally, Velazquez works her way "across the continent": Utah, Nevada, California, Colorado, New Mexico, and Texas.[37]

I want to end this feverish tour of Loreta Janeta Velazquez's Civil War world where it began: Cuba. It is a little-acknowledged fact that Velazquez's narrative does not spend much time in Cuba. She makes two brief trips to Havana during the war and one immediately after. In fact, Velazquez spent minimal time there as a child; her father's official duties seem to have kept the family on the move throughout the Spanish-speaking world. Of the six Velazquez children, Loreta was the only one born in Cuba, and she notes that she was "almost one year old" when her father "fell heir to a large estate in Texas" (40). Although the family returned to Cuba after the Mexican-American War (1846–48), young Loreta was sent to New Orleans shortly thereafter, sometime in 1849. Given all of this, it should come as little surprise that the words "Cuba" and "Cuban" appear only 24 times in this capacious 230,000-plus word text.[38]

Yet recent criticism of *The Woman in Battle* has focused almost entirely on its Cuban connections and has tended to overstate the imaginative importance of Velazquez's "native island" in the text (248). In so doing, critics have privileged a single location, when, as we have seen, Cuba is but one among many backdrops against which Velazquez's "Exploits, Adventures, and Travels" play out. In fact, when Velazquez finally goes "home" at the end of the narrative—to the "family burying ground" and "the old-fashioned stone house where [she] had lived with [her] father and mother, and brothers, and sisters, when a little girl"—it is not to Cuba but to St. Lucia, where she spent a significant part of her childhood (560–61). Predictably, her visit is brief:

> I was reluctant to leave the place, but felt impelled to go on and seek the destiny that awaited me in another land. . . . Before leaving the tomb I knelt down to pluck some ivy leaves, to carry away as remembrances, but as I stretched out my hand to gather them, something restrained me, and I went away empty-handed as I had come. (561)

Velazquez's inability to take away a bit of home provides a graceful figure for the estrangement and displacement that pervades the text—and an injunction against identifying her with any single location or nationality. We would do well, then, to keep the Velazquez narrative in transit, as it were. *The Woman in Battle* moves restlessly among a number of nations, regions, and continents. To privilege Velazquez's place of origin—or any other single stop on her never-ending tour of duty—is to deny the purposeful wayward-ness of her transnational movements and to place a limit on what I take to be a signal achievement of the narrative: to situate the American Civil War in a truly international context.[39]

When we take seriously its restlessness—when we track its various move-ments and chart its transnational routes—the Velazquez narrative allows us to revisit and revise the ways we conceptualize the American Civil War. Too often this bloody conflict is read in provincial terms, as either a war between brothers or a largely domestic dispute in a house divided. As I have argued here and in the previous chapters, the predominance of these familial meta-phors works to obscure the international nature of the conflict between the United and Confederate States of America. Even if we beg the question of Confederate States' sovereignty, we must acknowledge that at any number of moments the American Civil War threatened to become an international conflict, one into which Mexico, France, England, and others might well have been drawn. Yet, perhaps as a function of a critical tendency to over-state the "civil" aspects of the conflict, literary and cultural historians have to date been unable to tell a compelling story about the internationalism of the American Civil War. The book subtitled *A Narrative of the Exploits, Adven-tures, and Travels of Madame Loreta Janeta Velazquez* tells just such a story. As I have argued, the Civil War narrative offered by *The Woman in Battle* is resolutely international. As such, it offers a series of emergent fields and methodologies—New World, New South, Comparative American, Transna-tional American, and Hemispheric American Studies—an uncommon op-portunity to remap the American Civil War along new axes.

Coda: "Her voice would not cease, it would just vanish"

Each of the previous chapters has ended with a coda that looks forward to the future. With this final chapter, I look forward to another Confederate woman whose postwar narrative came under no small amount of scrutiny: Rosa Coldfield from William Faulkner's *Absalom, Absalom!* (1936). In par-ticular I want to ask after "Miss Rosa's" missing Confederate poetry. Readers of the novel are told early on that Rosa is a poet of Emily Dickinson–esque prolificacy who writes verse after verse about southern soldiers.

Quentin Compson initially assumes that he has been summoned to Rosa's close quarters *"because she wants it told . . . so that people whom she will never see and whose names she will never hear and who have never heard her name nor seen her face will read it and know at last why God let us lose the War"* (6). However, he soon realizes that "if she had merely wanted it told, written and even printed, she would not have needed to call in anybody."

As Joseph Boone points out, Rosa is the only *"published* writer" in the novel's panoply of narrators; publishing is fundamental for her (319). After the American Civil War, Rosa had become "the town's and the county's poetess laureate by issuing to the stern and meagre subscription list of the county newspaper poems, ode eulogy and epitaph, out of some bitter and implacable reserve of undefeat" (6). Like the memoirists discussed earlier in this chapter, Rosa seems to have taken up "the weapons of argument . . . to make the honorable conquest of reason and justice" (Pollard 750); that is, she had volunteered herself for duty as a Lost Cause warrior.

As the novel's diffuse narratives rise and converge, Rosa's career as a poet comes into sharper focus. At "the very time" her father, Goodhue Coldfield, was staging his grim protest in the attic, Rosa was "accumulating her first folio [of poetry] in which the lost cause's unregenerate vanquished were name by name embalmed" (6). Later we learn, through the rather untrustworthy narration of Quentin's father, that "the first of the odes to Southern soldiers in that portfolio which when [Quentin's] grandfather saw it in 1885 contained a thousand or more, was dated in the first year of her father's voluntary incarceration and dated at two oclock in the morning" (65). Thus, Rosa Coldfield's career as a "poetess" began in 1861. Although Quentin describes these early verses as tributes to "the lost cause's unregenerate vanquished," in fact they would have been tributes to the Confederacy's unregenerate not-quite-vanquished. In this narrative present, the cause had not yet been lost. Denied the opportunity to watch the Jefferson regiment march off to war, the sixteen-year-old Rosa had taken a keen, imaginative interest in the valor and sacrifices of Confederate soldiers fighting for their new nation.

Faulkner pointedly does not allow us access to any of Rosa's poetry—Confederate or Lost Cause. Although her narrative of the events surrounding Thomas Sutpen's rise and fall is essential to the novel, apparently her verse is irrelevant. The mock-heroic title "poetess laureate" says it all. She may have produced an immense amount of poetry—"a thousand or more" poems by 1885 alone—but, per Edmund Wilson, we needn't tarry with the stuff. Indeed, both Quentin and his father seem uninterested in the content of Rosa's poetry, as witnessed by Quentin's inability to mark the difference between its historical periods and Mr. Compson's phenomenological account of its production. What the poems actually say is beside the point.[40]

Perhaps predictably, I want to read Rosa's poetry as a synecdoche for the literature of the Civil War South. The absence of her poems on the pages of *Absalom, Absalom!*, as well as other characters' utter indifference to her writing, recapitulates the critical history of Confederate literature. While we seem eager to hear retrospective narratives of the South in the American Civil War—especially if they are as grand and tragic as those offered by Rosa, Mr. Compson, Quentin, and Shreve—we cannot be bothered to read the literature actually produced in the Confederacy. When faced with the Civil War South, both American and southern literary studies seem impatient to get to the postwar and post-Reconstruction periods—or, better yet, to Faulkner and the Southern Renaissance. Much more comfortable in those well-defined and well-trod literary-historical fields, scholars miss an uncommon opportunity to study the literature produced by a failed national movement.

Even those enterprising scholars who have paid attention to Confederate literature have tended to claim, per Antonio in *The Tempest*, that the Confederate past is mere prologue. For instance, Richard Harwell—whose extraordinary midcentury bibliographical work made a book like this possible—concluded that the Confederacy's "literary accomplishments were not in vain. They proved that the seeds of a regional, if not national, literature were among her people" (Harwell and Crandall xix). Returning once again to the poetics of literary harvest, Harwell intimates that those seeds would bear fruit in the early twentieth century.[41]

But "what's past" is also worthy of consideration in and on its own terms. As the preceding pages show, the Confederate national moment was, in its way, the first "cultural awakening" of the South, one that has profound implications for how we study not only what was to come but also what came before, in both the South and the North. By emphasizing Confederate literature's once great expectations—the apples not the ashes—we can see the specific mechanisms by which literary nationalism helped to engender the Confederate States of America. Here, then, is the development of a national literature both in process and in miniature.

This book has asked: What can we learn when we take the trouble to seek out and read texts that do not fit neatly into a literary history, texts that are inconvenient or politically troubling? When we do not let Confederate literature "just vanish" like Rosa's voice, we gain a better sense for the relationship between literature and nationalism; the international aspects of this harrowing conflict; and the provisional and contingent nature of the American experiment. In short, this literature helps us to tell the stories of the American Civil War in less exceptionalistic and romantic ways.

Absalom, Absalom! has been justly celebrated for its representation of the importance and incomprehensibility of the past.

> It's just incredible. It just does not explain. Or perhaps that's it: they dont explain and we are not supposed to know. We have a few old mouth-to-mouth tales; we exhume from old trunks and boxes and drawers letters without salutation or signature, in which men and women who once lived and breathed are now merely initials or nicknames out of some now incomprehensible affection which sound to us like Sanskrit or Chocktaw; we see dimly people, the people in whose living blood and seed we ourselves lay dormant and waiting, in this shadowy attenua-

tion of time possessing now heroic proportions, performing their acts of simple passion and simple violence, impervious to time and inexplicable. (80)

Confederate literature was, at base, a literature of simple passion and simple violence. But, as with any literature, it requires some explication; it does not explain itself, much less the actions and motivations of its characters and authors. Nonetheless, I do not think that Confederate literature is "inexplicable," in no small part because it amounts to much more than "a few old mouth-to-mouth tales" and letters written in stove polish. Instead we have an extensive and easily accessible archive of this literature. (Digitization means that the work of "exhuming" Confederate texts has never been easier.) By paying close attention to it, we can illumine a particularly "shadowy attenuation of time possessing now heroic proportions": the American Civil War.

Acknowledgments

Let me begin by acknowledging my teachers: at Lakeridge, Karen Hoppes; at Vanderbilt, Teresa Goddu, Roy Gottfried, Mark Schoenfield, Sheila Smith McKoy, and Cecelia Tichi; and at Northwestern, Brian T. Edwards, Betsy Erkkila, Wendy Griswold, Jay Grossman, Larry Lipking, Jeffrey Masten, Carl Smith, and Julia Stern. Teresa, Julia, and Betsy deserve special thanks. Teresa remains a model for how to be in this profession and a dear friend. Julia is the best "Jewish mother from hell" (her words, not mine) that a boy could have. And Betsy's support has been just extraordinary. I am immensely proud to be her student.

Since arriving in Austin, my colleagues at The University of Texas have been—to a person—warm and encouraging. They have also provided no end of feedback and conviviality. If I thought I could get away with it, I would name all of them here. Instead let me thank in particular Phil Barrish, Doug Bruster, Mia Carter, Oscar Casares, Matt Cohen, Jim Cox, Ann Cvetkovich, Brian Doherty, Barbara Harlow, Rich Heyman, Michael Johnson, Martin Kevorkian, Julia Lee, Wayne Lesser, Allen MacDuffie, Karl Miller, Gretchen Murphy, Domino Perez, Wayne Rebhorn (and the members of his grant-writing workshop), Liz Scala, Polly Strong (and my fellow fellows in the Humanities Institute), Frank Whigham, Jennifer Wilks, and Michael Winship. The support of my department chairpersons, Jim Garrison and Liz Cullingford, has been unstinting, as has that of my faculty mentors, Alan Friedman and Evan Carton.

I also owe a great debt to my colleagues beyond UT who have solicited and responded to my work: Michael Bibler, Martyn Bone, Chris Castiglia, Tommy Crocker, Austin Graham, Sharon Holland, Gordon Hutner, Benjy Kahan, Robert S. Levine, Dwight McBride, Annie McClanahan, Stephanie McCurry, Lloyd Pratt, Ben Railton, Elizabeth Renker, Scott Romine, and

Patricia Meyer Spacks. Several editors have had the perspicacity to send my work to Kathleen Diffley. This book is much better for Kathleen's superb suggestions and capacious knowledge of Civil War history and culture. Last but not least, I was fortunate to be part of an uncommon cohort of graduate students at Northwestern: Sarah Blackwood, Katy Chiles, Marcy Dinius, Ryan Friedman, Chris Hager, Peter Jaros, Terry McDonnell, Sarah Mesle, Doug O'Keefe, Guy Ortolano, and Glenn Sucich, among others. The mark of their intelligence and friendship is everywhere on these pages.

This book about the Confederacy began, appropriately enough, in the heart of abolitionist Boston. In 2005, I was a Caleb Loring Jr. Fellow at the Boston Athenaeum. It was during my residency there that I first realized that a literary history of the Confederate States was both possible and in order. I am very grateful to the Athenaeum's staff, especially Lisa Starzyk and Mary Warnement. I returned to Boston in 2010–11 as a Visiting Scholar at the American Academy of Arts and Sciences. Despite the distraction provided by my fellow "Scholar-Patriots," I finished this book during my time at 136 Irving Street. I am much obliged to the Academy and its Visiting Scholars Program. This project has also been buoyed by the generous support of The University of Texas at Austin College of Liberal Arts, The University of Texas at Austin Humanities Institute, the American Antiquarian Society, the Huntington Library, and the Bibliographical Society of America.

Apples and Ashes concludes by touting the accessibility of Confederate imprints. I must thank the staffs of several libraries for making that so. At UT, I've made extensive use of three libraries' collections: the Dolph Briscoe Center for American History, the Harry Ransom Humanities Research Center, and the Perry-Castañeda Library. I thank in particular Lindsey Schell and Molly Schwartzburg for their timely assistance and goodwill. Further from home, I am also grateful to the staffs of Duke University's Rare Book, Manuscript, and Special Collections Library, Harvard University's Houghton and Widener Libraries, the Library of Congress, the Newberry Library, the University of North Carolina's University Library, and Wake Forest University's Z. Smith Reynolds Library.

At the University of Georgia Press, it has been a sincere pleasure to work with Nancy Grayson, whose editorial generosity and advocacy have meant a great deal to me. I also thank Jon Smith, one of the series editors for the New Southern Studies, for seeing something new in this seemingly old-fashioned topic. On the production end, Monica Riese and Courtney Denney provided eagle-eyed edits, Jon Davies got the manuscript into shape, and Nicole Gray produced the terrific index. Earlier portions of chapter 4 appeared in *American Literary History* and the collection *Cultural Narratives: Textuality and Performance in American Culture before 1900* (Sandra Gustafson and Caroline Sloat, eds. Notre Dame, Ind.: University of Notre Dame Press, 2010); a portion of chapter 5 appeared in *Comparative American Studies*. I thank the editors for permission to publish revised versions of these pieces.

Finally, I must acknowledge my family—far-flung and extended, though it may be. My sister, Terry, and the Whitten clan have provided endless love and support. The same goes for my brother, Matthew, to whom I'll always look up. In addition to my siblings, I have the best best friends in the world. I thank Andy Goodman, Jeff Mercer, David Curtis, Jeffrey Max, Hunt Howell, Jenny Mann, Kasey Evans, Dan Birkholz, Neville Hoad, and Sarah Tillman for their abiding affection. With friends like these, is it any wonder how often I say things like "I love my life"? My parents, who passed away in the last few years, took great pleasure and pride in hearing me say that very phrase. This book is for Betty and Jim. I miss you both terribly, and I wish you were around to hear me say, again and again, "I love my life."

Notes

Abbreviations

P&W Parrish and Willingham, *Confederate Imprints*
SIN *Southern Illustrated News*
SLM *Southern Literary Messenger*

Introduction. Great Expectations

1. Aaron grants wartime southern publications only one full section (229–34) in *The Unwritten War* before turning to consider the "Unwritten Novel," George Washington Cable, "The Neo-Confederates," and, predictably, Faulkner. Tellingly, both critics spend significant time discussing Sidney Lanier, the poet and novelist, who did not publish before or during the American Civil War. For a cogent critique of Wilson's and Aaron's respective methodologies, see Richards, "U.S. Civil War."

2. There are any number of indices for such poor relations between Confederate and southern literature. For instance, there is no mention of the literature of the Confederacy in the "List of Topics Suggested for Further Study" in Louis D. Rubin and C. Hugh Holman's 1975 survey, *Southern Literary Study: Problems and Possibilities* (227–35). Similarly, in his *Nineteenth-Century Southern Literature* (1980), Joseph V. Ridgely focuses his chapter on "The Confederacy and the Martyred South" on the latter topic, suggesting once again how eager critics are to get to the postwar period and its literature. Finally, Jack Trammell's entry "Civil War in Literature" in the *New Encyclopedia of Southern Culture* (2008) echoes Aaron: "although much was written, less has remained cogent or significant over time" (Inge 56). See also Rayburn S. Moore's two-page entry on "Confederacy, Literature of" in Flora, MacKethan, and Taylor, 178–79.

3. On the "truly staggering" physical and logistical obstacles faced by Confederate publishers, see Bernath 89–93 and 250–57; Harwell, *Confederate Belles-Lettres* 25–27; and Faust, *Creation* 16. On the gross disparities between antebellum northern and southern publishing industries, see Fahs 21–23. On the Confederate printing industry, see Detlefsen, as well as Van Tuyll.

4. See Michael O'Brien 703; and Bernath passim. Examples of this doubt are legion. To take a well-cited example, in early 1864 the *Southern Punch* asked, "Are we a literary people?" Paraphrasing *Hamlet*, it concluded, "More in sorrow than in anger, we answer: it is to be feared we are not" (27 February 1864: 2).

5. On these nationalists' critique of northern culture, see Bernath, esp. 35–76. Earlier historians have made this same case, but not as cogently or as exhaustively as Bernath. See London 96; also Harwell and Crandall, xiii. In truth, quantity/quality is something of a false dichotomy. Contemporary literary historians tend to ask how a given literature might matter and mean, not "Is there enough of it?" or "Is it any good?"

6. Faust, Gallagher, and Bernath all acknowledge how difficult this has been for Civil War historians. See Faust, *Creation* 3–4; G. W. Gallagher, *Confederate War* 3; and Bernath 3.

7. See Fliegelman's epigraph. Both Gallagher and Drew Gilpin Faust cite the work of David M. Potter, who first described the promises and pitfalls of studying Confederate nationalism. See especially "The Historian's Use of Nationalism and Vice Versa" in *The South and the Sectional Conflict*, where Potter notes the difficulty "for the historian to attribute nationality to movements of which he morally disapproves, since the attribution itself would imply that the movement has a kind of validity" (63). See also Faust, *Creation* 3.

8. In 1988, Drew Gilpin Faust posed an urgent rhetorical question to her colleagues in southern history: "If southern nationalism is to be dismissed, how then explain the birth of the Confederacy and its willingness to fight four years of the bloodiest warfare then known to mankind?" (*Creation* 4). In recent years a number of historians—George C. Rable, Gary Gallagher, William Alan Blair, Anne Sarah Rubin, Robert Bonner, and Michael T. Bernath—have affirmed the surprising strength of Confederate national sentiment. Gallagher's thesis is representative: "Far from being a loosely knit collection of individuals whose primary allegiance lay with their states, a substantial portion of the Confederate people identified strongly with their southern republic" (*Confederate War* 7). On the relationship between Confederate and U.S. nationalisms, see Grant, esp. 153–72. On the othering of the South, see Goddu; Ladd, esp. 1–35; Duck; and Greeson.

9. For example, Deleuze and Guattari claim that "national consciousness uncertain or oppressed, necessarily exists by means of literature" (16). Similarly, Gregory Jusdanis argues that "[a]t its inception national culture is really literary in nature, for literature . . . is thought to mirror the nation as well as encourage the acquisition by the population of socially important values and norms" (*Belated* xi). Anderson's work has also had a wide-ranging influence in the social sciences. See, for example, Corse passim.

10. Following Faust's and Gallagher's leads, Anne Sarah Rubin has argued persuasively that "attachment to a symbolic or sentimental Confederacy, or at least to a separate Southern identity, existed independently of the political Confederacy, and thus was able to outlast the state" (2). She pursues that attachment into the postwar period, showing that "the end of their state did not signal an immediate end to their sense of themselves as a separate people" (7). This claim resonates with Jusdanis's ar-

gument that nationalism is "ultimately a cultural phenomenon," something that can emerge autonomously, in advance of state apparatuses (*Necessary* 10). It also brings to mind Žižek's discussion of the "tautological character" of the "nation Thing." See esp. 200–203. I am grateful to Jon Smith for bringing this discussion to my attention.

11. Twentieth-century critical interest in Timrod has tended to distort our understanding of the poetry of the wartime South. In the words of one latter-day critic, Timrod's poetry would come to embody "the heart of Southern nationalism" (Budd 437). Louis D. Rubin makes a similarly aggressive case for Timrod as the "Poet Laureate of the Confederacy" (see *Edge* 211). See also Aaron 234–41. While Timrod's wartime poems were indeed popular during the war (see chapter 3), he was part and parcel of a diverse Confederate poetic culture, one that literary historians have not reckoned fully.

12. The sense of urgency and inception present in Timrod's poem recurs throughout Confederate literary culture. For instance, the *Southern Literary Messenger* made the following emphatic declaration as the war commenced: "A subject people are to be rescued from the domination of fanatics; a new literature and new centres of trade are to be established. Until this is accomplished, perish all minor matters" (*SLM* 32 [April 1861]: 322).

13. Many nineteenth-century periodicals appeared a week before their issue dates. However, for clarity's sake, I will be referring to issue dates.

14. See also the issue of *The Index* for 8 May 1862, which once again assures European readers of the Confederacy's "brilliant future": "At present we must not look for any new or important books from the South; the pen is abandoned for the sword. But when the struggle is over . . . we are convinced the Confederacy will occupy a distinguished position in the Republic of Letters" (23). See also "The Intellectual Future of the South," *SLM* 34 (May 1862): 314–15. For a discussion of "practices of deferral" in the production of southern communities, see Romine. On the "hope for peace in the future" in "Ethnogenesis," see Budd 441.

15. Bernath is very good on the "forward looking, even millennial" (3) culture of the Confederacy, which he describes as promoting "a grand vision of the Confederate nation, not as it was, but as it was supposed to be" (287). See esp. 219–20 and 267–74. Paul de Man had something like this in mind when he discussed the relations among literary history and literary modernity. For de Man, modernity "exists in the form of a desire to wipe out whatever came earlier, in the hope of reaching at last a point that could be called a true present, a point of origin that marks a new departure" (148). Given that the "spread of nationalism" is often considered a signal feature of modernity, the imbrications of literature, modernity, and nationalism in southern discourse of this period should come as little surprise. See esp. Greenfeld 1–26; Gellner; Appadurai 1–25; and Jusdanis, *Necessary* 114–18.

16. As chapter 1 details, such agro-literary appeals also appear in pre-Confederate southern literary nationalist discourses, which often exhibit anxiety about whether a "purely agricultural people" can in fact produce a national literature. See William Gilmore Simms's "Literary Prospects of the South," *Russell's Magazine* 3.3 (June 1858), esp. 194. I draw the adjective "agro-literary" from Gellner.

17. In a later, much more explicitly antinorthern version of the poem, Timrod comes closer to acknowledging slavery with the couplet "On one side, creeds that dare to teach / What Christ and Paul refrained to preach." See Parks and Parks, 180–83. Timrod's reluctance to depict slaves or slavery in the poem brings to mind Toni Morrison's discussion of a "dark, abiding, signing Africanist presence" (5). An often too-real Africanist presence was indeed crucial to southerners' sense of Confederate Americanness. And it shows.

18. Credited to "The Wanderer," the sixteen-page poem appears to have been composed before the secession of the southern states. The authorial preface is dated "July 17th, 1859" (Turner 4). In this instance, I disagree with Anne Sarah Rubin, who claims that "private expressions of national identity, as well as public exhortations aimed at nation-building, all but ignored the question of racial slavery. . . . Confederates took slavery as a given, albeit a sometimes problematic one, subject to neither challenge nor conversation" (3). A closer examination of Confederate literature significantly complicates this claim. On the proslavery elements of Confederate nationalism, see Anne Sarah Rubin, 100–111; Bonner, *Mastering* 264–85; and Bernath 103–5.

19. See also Kolchin, who emphasizes "a shared ideological vision" rather than "a shared religion, language, or ethnicity" in the Confederacy (90).

20. See especially R. D. Watson. On the history of the title of Timrod's poem, see Parks and Parks, esp. 180.

21. On the repeated assertions that Confederate wartime literature was "essentially different from the literature of the North—despite all evidence to the contrary," see Fahs, esp. 9. She concludes that "one major reason why Southern literary culture should be seen as different from Northern literary culture is simply because so many Southerners insisted that this was so" (9). Fahs argues—largely on the basis of a handful of northern stories that appeared in southern periodicals—that the Confederacy was "unable to break free of the North's literary influence" (5). While I find much of her work convincing, I remain dubious about this claim, partly because it suggests a flat and unidirectional understanding of literary influence. It is certainly the case that the North and South had a "set of shared literary sensibilities" (5), but those sensibilities were also part of a much broader set of literary conversations and traditions. Bernath argues more persuasively that a critique of northern literature helped to construct "a foil against which the purity, originality, and distinctiveness of a future Confederate national literature could be judged" (75; cf. Fahs 26). On the high stakes of such cultural differentiation and independence, see Bernath, esp. 9. See also Kolchin, esp. 7–38.

22. Bernath casts the embrace of European models late in the war as a "radical turnabout" for Confederate cultural nationalists (275). However, as this quotation demonstrates, and as I argue throughout, the use of European models was a constitutive part of Confederate literary culture from the beginning. See Bernath 274–78.

23. Elisa Tamarkin's recent study of antebellum American deference toward England is relevant here. She argues that Anglophilia "allowed for an experience of belonging that was made possible because [Americans] had no one to belong to but themselves" (xxiv). I see a similar dynamic at work in Confederate literary culture.

Other recent sympathetic studies of U.S.-U.K. literary relations include Tennenhouse and Giles, *Transatlantic*.

24. See especially the *SLM* article "The Intellectual Future of the South" (34 [May 1862]: 313–14). On the prospect of "keeping up appearances before the rest of the world" see A. S. Rubin 27. See also Bernath 246. On southern periodicals' identification with "conservative European nationalism of the post-1848 period," see Faust, *Creation* 13. See also A. S. Rubin 3–4; and Bernath 101. McCurry's study admirably underscores the international aspects of the war. See also Kolchin, whose comparative frame helps to deprovincialize the conflict.

25. See Gellner, who describes nationalism as the "general imposition of a high culture" on "low cultures" (56). See also, Corse, esp. 4–7. As Fahs notes, "distinctions between 'high' and 'low' often obscure as much as they reveal within nineteenth-century literary culture" (3). She goes on to make a persuasive case for popular literature's "vitally important" role in "shaping a cultural politics of war" (1). Finally, this characterization brings to mind Deleuze and Guattari's rejection of literary mastery in a minor literature. See esp. 17.

26. In distinguishing between our methodologies, I do not mean to overstate the disciplinary differences between history and literary studies, especially since I hope that this book will be of use to intellectual and cultural historians. Like Wilson's and Aaron's, Fahs's work has been foundational for me. My sole complaint about her study is that Confederate literary culture gets less attention than U.S. literary culture. Bernath's fine study, which came from press after I had a first draft of this book, has also been immensely helpful in locating Confederate imaginative literature in broader intellectual context. In the end, Bernath's *Confederate Minds* is, as its title suggests, an intellectual history that focuses on the wartime agitations for, and production of, Confederate literature broadly conceived. Bernath goes out of his way to note that his is "not intended to be a literary history of the Confederacy" (8). This is borne out by the impressive range of texts he treats: not just imaginative and periodical literature but also sermons, fine arts, scientific papers, medical journals, religious tracts, and textbooks.

27. I use the adjective "imaginative" as per Bernath, who notes that "Confederate critics used the term 'literature' in its broadest possible sense" (60). On the question of what constitutes a Confederate imprint, see Heartman. Richard Harwell defines "*bona fide* Confederate imprints" as being published after "the secession of the state in which they were printed" and before "the fall of the Confederate government in April 1865" (*Confederate Belles-Lettres* 18). As Harwell notes, the dramatic output of the Confederacy was "negligible" (*Confederate Belles-Lettres* 23); elsewhere he quipped, "There are times when the play is not the thing" ("Brief Candle" 41). On Confederate drama, see Harwell, "Brief Candle"; Waal; C. S. Watson, *History* 74–84; and Bernath 205–9. On Confederate oratory, see Fritz.

Chapter One. A History of the Future

1. I take the ingenious, Janus-faced rhetoric of "campaign" from Benjamin T. Spencer, whose *The Quest for Nationality: An American Literary Campaign* re-

mains, decades after its publication, a singularly useful history of American literary nationalism.

2. Spencer rightly notes that "a persistent use of affective language" is often central to the literary nationalist projects (*Quest* ix).

3. See, for example, Hubbell, "Literary Nationalism"; Current-Garcia; and Craven. To his credit, McCardell largely eschews such a developmental model. See esp. 141–76. Robert S. Levine hopes that his nonteleological, episodic approach to literary nationalism will "restore a sense of contingency to the literary history of the United States consistent with the contingency of the nation itself" (5). See also Spencer, *Quest* viii.

4. Readers in search of exhaustive surveys of pre-Confederate southern literary nationalist rhetoric should see Hubbell, "Literary Nationalism"; Current-Garcia; and McCardell, esp. 141–76.

5. As Leon Jackson notes, the *SLM* "lasted not only longer than any other Southern magazine but also for longer than most Northern magazines too," and published an "incredibly prestigious" roster of authors (129). McCardell reads the *SLM* as both representative of, and hugely influential on, the intelligentsia of the South during this period. See 172. See also, Ridgely, *Nineteenth-Century*, esp. 17–31.

6. Spencer argues that by the early 1830s the force of the postrevolutionary movement for a national literature had "to an appreciable degree spent itself" but that the "Jacksonian triumph" and "democratic expansion" that followed helped to reinvigorate such movements ("National" 125, 158). For a dissenting opinion, see Frederick, who views the period 1825–1850 as one literary nationalistic definition.

7. To name but two very visible studies of time and nationality, see Benedict Anderson's familiar discussions of simultaneity (esp. 22–36) and memory and forgetting (esp. 192–99), as well as Bhabha's oft-cited essay "DissemiNation" in *The Location of Culture*.

8. Heath, a prominent Richmond lawyer and politician, was also an aspiring author. In 1828, he published a plantation novel, *Edge-Hill; or, The Family of the Fitzroyals* (Richmond: T. W. White); in 1838, a satirical play followed, *Whigs and Democrats; or, Love of No Politics* (Richmond: T. W. White). The editorial makes repeated reference to Virginia, the "Old Dominion," and "the state." To be sure, throughout its tenure the *SLM* was a very Commonwealth-centric periodical. However, given the broader discussion of "Southern Literature," I think we might understand Heath as drawing on a synecdochal relationship between Virginia and the South as a whole. If Heath is indeed doing so, he may well be following the example of Thomas Jefferson, whose *Notes on the State of Virginia* famously exploited such a synecdoche.

9. See Gellner, esp. 8–18.

10. It should be noted that Heath espoused the gradual abolition of slavery and in doing so was at odds with Tucker, among others. See especially his "Editorial Remarks" on Tucker's "Remarks on a Note to Blackstone's Commentaries" in the January 1835 issue (*SLM* 1: 254).

11. See, for instance, a lengthy review of Emerson's essays in the April 1852 issue of the *SLM* (18: 248). On the importance of sectionalism to the emergence of American literary nationalism, see R. S. Levine, esp. 1–16 and 67–118. For a compelling ac-

count of the broader movement from regionalism to nationalism, see Current-Garcia 335–36.

12. Both McCardell and Current-Garcia comment on Simms's ability to "reconcile the conflicting demands of section and nation" (McCardell 147; Current-Garcia 325). The subject of Simms's movement from "nationalism to secessionism," as Charles S. Watson describes it, has engendered an enormous body of criticism. See esp. C. S. Watson, *Nationalism* passim; Parks, *William Gilmore Simms* 89–109; and Wakelyn 158–87. John D. Kerkering's work on Simms, which emphasizes Simms's use of the genius loci trope, is particularly compelling. See esp. 68–110.

13. Some extant versions of the first issue end with a publisher insertion announcing the receipt of a prospectus for James Haig's *Southern Magazine*. After quoting from the prospectus, White exclaims, "The South is awakening!" (32). See Silverman 100. Even Cooper gets in on the rhetorical action: His letter of encouragement notes that the *SLM* might "arouse [southerners] from their lethargy" (1). Indeed, the trope reappeared throughout the *SLM*'s thirty-year career, particularly at moments of editorial crisis and flagging support. See esp. 1 [May 1835]: 532; 9 [August 1843]: 450; and 10 [March 1844]: 181. See also Jacobs 68.

14. Much of the best criticism of the *SLM* comes from Poe scholars, who have paid assiduous attention to the periodical. See esp. Dayan, "Poe" and "Amorous"; D. K. Jackson; Rosenthal; Rowe, "Poe"; Watts; and Whalen, *Edgar Allan Poe* esp. 58–75 and 122–30. For instance, Terence Whalen has recently dispelled two long-held "truths" about Poe's time at the *SLM*. First, that *SLM* circulation soared during Poe's tenure as editor. From the evidence of the first census of White's published circulation figures, Whalen concludes: "During the period of the magazine's greatest commercial success, Poe was essentially an irrelevant variable; he may have written interesting reviews, but he had no significant impact on the circulation of the *Messenger*" (*Edgar Allan Poe* 68). While Whalen's Dupinian detective work is impressive—in truth, the evidence really was, per "The Purloined Letter," "full in the view of every visitor"—the matter of those "interesting reviews" is, I hold, not to be dismissed. Whalen's second, more urgent refutation is of the attribution of the so-called Paulding-Drayton review to Poe. See below.

15. On the complicated editorial give and take between Poe and White, see D. K. Jackson 57. See also Pollin and Ridgely 45–46 and Mott 634.

16. This is all the more impressive given that *SLM* did not have many sister southern literary publications to help them wage this battle. See M. O'Brien 548.

17. For a thorough discussion of Poe's relation to both sectionalist and nationalist discourses, see Kennedy, whose compelling essay argues for the "radical, oppositional role" that Poe's "antinational nationalist" fiction and criticism of the 1840s played in debates about a national literature (27).

18. For an important revisionist account of White's stewardship of the journal, one that highlights his deft use of gift economies and direct solicitations to keep the journal afloat, see Leon Jackson, esp. 120–39. See also Whalen, who documents the strange ways of the *SLM*'s circulation (*Edgar Allan Poe*, esp. 122–23). In 1838 nearly 90 percent of the paid subscriptions were sent to slave states, and almost 49 percent of all paid subscriptions stayed in Virginia (*Edgar Allan Poe* 122).

19. As Sidney Moss notes, this withering criticism of Fay's first novel was a bold move for the young editor, especially given that Fay was an increasingly important figure in the New York literary circles in which Poe's own work would circulate for years to come (see 42). For more on the lengthy back and forth over Poe's editorship, see also the final "Critical Notice" of June 1836 (2: 445–60). On 2 September 1836, Poe also published in the *Richmond Compiler* a widely recirculated letter defending his "cutting and slashing" editorial style. Remarkably, Poe rehearses all of his *SLM* reviews to date, even estimating the percentages of "highly laudatory" reviews he had penned: by his count 79 of 94. See Pollin and Ridgely 273–77.

20. The July 1836 issue concluded with yet another supplement, this one including "*every* late criticism received," even negative ones (2: 517). For instance, the *Newbern (N.C.) Spectator* harshly criticizes Poe and expresses dubiousness about the prospects of a southern periodical with "great literary pretentions" (517). In contradistinction, the *New York Courier and Enquirer* is quoted as praising the "vigor and manliness" of the *SLM*'s reviews and as placing the journal "at the very head of the periodical literature of its class, in the United States" (518). The *New York Weekly Messenger* seemed to agree: "We really do think it is as good as any, if not the very best in these United States" (524).

21. See, for instance, Simms's contemporary notice of Poe's reviews in the July 1836 issue of the *Southern Literary Journal*. While Simms praises Poe's "very spirited and racy" reviews, he notes that Poe is not without bias: "He has favorites, it is true, but his bias seems rather the result of intimacy and habitual deference, than of any mean or mercenary disposition to conciliate" (qtd. in Thomas and Jackson 213).

22. Later Poe suggests that one of the novel's scenes is "told with a raciness and vigor which would do honor to the pages of Blackwood" (288). Similarly, he remarks that the sketch "The Fight" "would positively make the fortune of any British periodical" (289). On Poe's relationship to British periodical culture, see M. L. Allen.

23. Poe speaks favorably of Bird's rendering of the "Nigger Tom" character and the "very excellent chapters upon abolition and the exciting effects of incendiary pamphlets and pictures, among our slaves in the South" (666).

24. Even White found Poe's review of *George Balcombe* "eulogistic." See Thomas and Jackson 244. Despite Poe and the *SLM*'s better efforts, *George Balcombe* fell into more or less immediate obscurity; it has never been reissued or republished.

25. For instance, as Terence Whalen has demonstrated authoritatively, Poe edited but did not compose Tucker's infamous April 1836 "Slavery" notice—what Poe critics have for many years called the Paulding-Drayton review. That text—as Joseph V. Ridgely remarked, "less a book review than an excuse for a proslavery essay" ("Authorship" 1)—used J. K. Paulding's *Slavery in the United States* and William Drayton's *The South Vindicated* as an occasion to advance a strong "positive good" argument for domestic slavery. See Whalen, *Edgar Allan Poe*, esp. 113–21. On Tucker's interest in and advocacy for Poe, see Thomas and Jackson 189–90.

26. In the letter in which White informed Tucker that he planned to fire Poe, the publisher implored Tucker to assume some of the editorial duties: "You, my friend, are my helmsman. And I again beg you to stand by the rudder" (qtd. in D. K. Jackson 110).

27. By way of comparison, see also Poe's less favorable review of Ingraham's historical novel *Lafitte: The Pirate of the Gulf* in the August 1836 issue (2: 593–96). See also Poe's superficial July 1836 review of Anne Grant's *Memoirs of an American Lady* (2: 511). Over the past four decades, Poe studies have spent a great deal of time figuring and refiguring Poe's views on slavery. For exemplary studies, see esp. Dayan, "Poe" and "Amorous"; Erkkila; Goddu; M. Lee; Rowe, "Poe"; and Whalen, "Average."

28. Historians and literary critics have disagreed about the "injury" Poe did or did not inflict on the *SLM*. For generations, Poe criticism insisted that he rescued the *SLM* from obscurity and that White "did not appreciate Poe's talents" (D. K. Jackson 108). Recently, that *doxa* has begun to be overturned, as Poe critics have begun to look more closely at White's deft management of the *SLM*. See esp. Whalen, *Edgar Allan Poe* 58–75, and L. Jackson 126–39.

29. In announcing Poe's "retire[ment]" from the *SLM* in January 1837, White assured readers that "Mr. P. however, will continue to furnish its columns, from time to time, with the effusions of his vigorous and popular pen,—and my old contributors, among whom I am proud to number some of the best writers in our state and country, will doubtless continue to favor me with their valuable contributions" (3: 96). By the time Poe departed Richmond, some of best writers in Virginia and the United States were indeed contributing to the *SLM*. To take but one example, the August 1836 issue featured texts by Lydia H. Sigourney, William Gilmore Simms, James K. Paulding, Robert Montgomery Bird, Matthew Carey, and Sarah Josepha Hale (Pollin and Ridgely 247). To this end, Poe's much-admired "Autography" hoax can be read as an index of the *SLM*'s increasing visibility during this period, since Poe forged "the autographs of our principal literati" largely from correspondence they had had with the *SLM* (2: 205). In its peculiar way, "Autography," which appeared in the February and August 1836 issues, demonstrates that American literature was indeed coming to the South. See McGill, "Duplicity" and *American Literature*, esp. 180–86. See also Thomas and Jackson 191. Moreover, despite his difficult personal and professional relationship with White, Poe contributed to the *SLM* long after his dismissal. Over the course of his subsequent career, the periodical published his "Marginalia," a revised version of the "Rationale of Verse," and a number of reviews.

30. See also Minor's early editorial notice, "Ourselves" 9 (September 1843): 575. In December 1845 Minor bought the *Southern and Western Monthly Magazine* from William Gilmore Simms. The merger resulted in the awkwardly titled *Southern and Western Literary Messenger and Review*. As was his wont, Minor took the occasion to state again the editorial principles of the journal. See 7 (January 1846): 61.

31. For an exemplary history of proslavery rhetoric during the 1830s, see Roberts-Miller.

32. See the issues for January, March, June, and August 1844. See also October 1839.

33. For an insightful discussion of Lincoln's perhaps apocryphal greeting of Stowe, see Vollaro.

34. For a southern woman's response to Stowe, see Louisa S. McCord's review in the January 1853 issue of the *Southern Quarterly Review* (81–120).

35. This is not to suggest that the review is uninterested in more traditional forms of literary critical assessment. For instance, the review takes pains to critique Stowe's management of the dual Uncle Tom and George Harris plot lines. Similarly, it dismisses George Harris's "Spanish masquerade" escape as unbelievable and not even suited for a minstrel show: "[T]hey would not go down as part and parcel of the burnt-cork melodrama of the Bowery" (632). Later the reviewer concedes the affective power of the death of Little Eva but immediately notes that the scene seems derivative of Dickens's *The Old Curiosity Shop*. Finally, the reviewer describes the deus ex machina conclusion of the novel as a "string of unnatural incidents" (636).

36. Similarly, the review takes up the legality of the "sale of Cassy apart from Eliza," when Eliza was "eight or nine" years old. See 637.

37. See especially Nelson passim.

38. In the annual New Year's address for 1853, Thompson echoed this language (19: 57). Jacobs notes that Thompson, "reflecting his stand against uncritical literary nationalism," increased the space given to European literature (92). See also, Current-Garcia 336–37.

39. For an excellent survey of southern responses to *Uncle Tom's Cabin*—and Stowe's response to her southern critics—see C. Weinstein. See also, Jordan-Lake.

40. For instance, in the lead-up to the publication of Stowe's novel, Thompson returned to the trope "awakening from sleep" when describing a *DeBow's Review* piece, "The Cause of the South," as "endeavoring to arouse the Southern people from the comatose state in which they have been slumbering for years" (16 [August 1850]: 518). His "broken-hearted" puff goes on to suggest that the prospects for a distinct southern literary culture were in August 1850 quite grim (see 518).

41. Not surprisingly, W.R.A. also cites Stowe's novel and deploys the "awakening from sleep" trope, noting that a southern literature could "arouse the sleeping intellects of our section" (242).

42. Étienne Balibar has such logic and rhetoric in mind when he describes the constitutive role of "fictive ethnicity"—particularly vis-à-vis "the fiction of a common race" (Balibar and Wallerstein 99)—in imagining the "ideal nation." See esp. 96–100.

43. Jacobs suggests that while the periodical occasionally "laments for the past," the *SLM*'s policy was "to support Southern progress" (75).

44. On the reasons for southern secession, see 2: 16–25. Early in the second volume, Mr. B——, the heroic voice of resistance, suggests that northerners could never "comprehend the negro character" or that of southern "cavaliers" (7). See 2: 6–9. See also, Hubbell, *The South* 430.

45. Brugger suggests that Upshur and Tucker may have collaborated on the review. See 241n20. While Upshur is no literary critic, he does praise Tucker's characterization of the women of the novel, whose manners, he notes approvingly, "have not been learned in a boarding school" (74). He also underscores the novel's roman à clef elements and recommends "to all abolitionists" its depiction of domestic slavery (74).

46. In describing the novel's 1848–49 revolution, Upshur later deploys the "waking from sleep" trope, noting that Virginia has "shaken off her lethargy, and become sensible of the necessity of uniting herself with her sister states of the south" (73).

47. Upshur's "review" was so incendiary that White distanced himself and his periodical from it in a brief footnote on its first page. See 73. Nonetheless, the review seems to have caused quite a stir in the Commonwealth, if not beyond it. Tucker's own brother, Henry St. George Tucker, who may or may not have been the basis for the character Hugh Trevor, was so offended by Upshur's essay that he cancelled his subscription to the *SLM*. He did so without knowing that the novel under review was penned by his brother. See B. D. Tucker 375–82.

48. In underscoring the ways pre-Confederate southern literary nationalists went back to the future, I have in mind both Walter Benjamin's angel of history ("irresistibly propel[led] into the future to which his back is turned" [257–58]) and Robert Zemeckis's character Marty McFly (someone who wants earnestly and preposterously to return to the future).

Chapter Two. A New Experiment in the Art of Book-Making

1. Melissa Homestead's superb publication history of *Macaria* sheds new light on both this anecdote and Evans's role in northern publication of her novel. See "Publishing."

2. Many pieces of Confederate fiction were advertised as novelettes. See, for example, M. E. M. Davis 3. The relative brevity of the war may help to explain the dearth of long-form Confederate fiction. The novelette provided a more manageable form for both writers and publishers, since a short piece of fiction required less composition time from the former and fewer material resources from the latter. Like *Macaria*, Ford's novel saw a second edition and was published in the North during the war. Two other texts were written—if not in press—before the official start of the war. The anonymous author of the anti-Tom novel *Old Toney and His Master* (1861) dates his preface to 10 April 1860 (viii). Similarly, A. B. Seals's *Rockford: A Romance* (1861) makes no mention of the war.

3. West and Johnston's 1862 edition was not the first wartime reprinting of the novel. In 1861 Rudd and Carleton published a northern edition, which publically identified "Beverley Tucker of Virginia" as the novel's author (i). Retitled *A Key to the Disunion Conspiracy*, this edition frames the novel not as a prophesy or "Apocalypse" but as proof positive that the South had been long gunning for a civil war. See also the June 1861 issue of the *SLM* (32), esp. 481–83.

4. As Harwell notes, these editions were often "[p]rinted upon wretched paper and marked by the most undistinguished press work" (*Confederate Belles-Lettres* 22). However, the Thackeray edition was a lavish endeavor by Confederate standards. See Oram; see also Snowden 23–26. Remarkably, these Confederate reprints did not lag all that far behind the original British publications. For instance, Ayres and Wade were able to publish their editions of *Darrell Markham; or The Captain of the Vulture* (1863) and *Eleanor's Victory* (1864) in the same calendar year as their respective London editions. This suggests a great deal about both the resourcefulness of Confederate publishers and the demand for foreign works even in a time of war.

5. Calling West and Johnston "undoubtedly" the leading Confederate publisher,

Harwell notes that the firm published a wide range of texts in addition to literary works: "military manuals and treatises, political tracts, biography, children's books, and even a cook book" (*Confederate Belles-Lettres* 20). Eaton (217), London (83), and Tebbel (474) all concur with Harwell's assessment. Contemporaneous southern accounts also praised the press widely and wildly. See, for instance, the March 1862 issue of the *Messenger* (34), esp. 207–8. In the February 1863 issue, the *SLM* noted that in the past year the firm had paid $15,000 to southern writers "more than *all* the publishers of the North ever paid any one year to Southern writers!" (37:118). See also Fahs 38.

6. On the immediate reception of the novel, both in France and beyond, see Bach; also Rosselet. The *SLM* published lengthy reviews of the first two volumes of the Confederate edition; see the July (37: 434–46) and August (37: 493–510) 1863 issues. Olin Moore suggests that the Richmond edition did in fact improve upon the Wilbour translation (see esp. 245–46), but that after page 49 it becomes "increasingly dependent on Wilbour's version" (246). For a perhaps apocryphal account of West and Johnston's tireless efforts to procure the French text, see Page 741; see also Tebbel 475.

7. At least one southern reader did complain. The *SLM* reviewer found these omissions and suppressions "deplorable" and urged West and Johnston "not to travel in the footsteps of Perugino or Harper & Brothers"—that is, to stop trafficking in "literary expurgations" (37 [July 1863]: 446; see also O. Moore 244–46). Moore suggests that paper shortages may have "resulted in longer and longer omissions" (246).

8. The *SLM*'s July 1863 "Notices of New Works" notes the "Tenth Thousand" copy of *Fantine* (448). The novel was a particular favorite of Confederate soldiers. One source notes that "few perfect copies were left after 1863. They were read to pieces by the soldiers" (qtd. in Rosselet 43). See also Kaser 18 and 37. For an early version of the *Les Misérables*/"Lee's Miserables" anecdote, see Devens 561–62. See also Rosselet 43; O. Moore 240; and Power passim. The final three volumes of the novel were much delayed, a fact that drew comment from the *SLM*. See the October 1863 issue, esp. 634. "A Note to the Public" in the Confederate edition of *Cosette* explains that scarcity of paper was to blame for the delay.

9. Indeed, this culture of reprinting was so pervasive that one Confederate author, Alexander St. Clair Abrams, complained about the difficulty of getting an original book published in the Confederacy "when the principal publishers of the South are so busily engaged in publishing works written in foreign parts, and which cost them nothing but the expense of publication, and the procuring of them through our blockaded ports" (182).

10. For a discussion of Evans's articles, see Fidler, "Augusta Evans Wilson as Confederate Propagandist"; Sofer 69–72; Homestead, *American* 202–6; and E. Moss 163–67. I am grateful to Lindsey Schell for her heroic attempts to track down these essays.

11. Evans echoes Poe again when she notes that "the fear of the sharp eyed critic has made British literature what it is." In fact, Evans was quite familiar with Poe's fiction, poetry, and criticism. See, for instance, *Macaria* 129 and 164.

12. Homestead rightly suggests that such a claim constitutes a "dominant version

of Confederate nationalism, which represented the Confederate nation as commercially disinterested, agrarian, and aristocratic in opposition to the commercially motivated, industrialized, and plebian 'Yankee' North" (*American* 210).

13. In the late 1850s, American literary nationalist rhetoric was perhaps appropriately drowned out by debates over the Dred Scott decision, concern about the Panic of 1857, and the increasingly loud rumblings of disunion. See Varon, esp. 273–304.

14. As Naomi Z. Sofer suggests, Evans here "both challenges her peers to escape the self-imposed provincial ghetto of Southern literature and announces her intention to devote her own energies to 'the building of a *national* literature'" (72). Yet, Sofer's "both-and" construction obscures the fact that these were, to Evans's mind at least, twinned efforts, with literary nationalism providing the very means for escape from said "ghetto." On the oppositional dynamics of the region-nation relationship, see Ayers et al., esp. 1–11; Davey; Duck, esp. 28–37; Greeson passim; and Fetterley and Pryse, esp. 1–33.

15. Unless otherwise noted, all citations to *Macaria* are to the edition published by West and Johnston in Richmond in 1864.

16. Writing in the late 1870s of the death of Lincoln, Whitman noted, "Then there is a cement to the whole people, subtler, more underlying, than any thing in written constitution, or courts or armies—namely, the cement of a death indentified thoroughly with that people, at its head, and for its sake. Strange, (is it not?) that battles, martyrs, agonies, blood, even assassination, should so condense—perhaps only really, lastingly condense—a Nationality" (1046). See also Faust, *Creation* 24–26.

17. In many ways *Macaria*'s dedication calls to mind the dedication of the first American novel, *The Power of Sympathy*, a text Evans would have known well. See Davidson 88–92.

18. On the back cover of the first volume of Hugo's *Les Misérables*, West and Johnston advertised *Macaria* in terms of both its excellence and its dedication: "This is the most brilliant and interesting novel ever written in the South. It is dedicated to the gallant army of the Confederate States."

19. Perhaps unsurprisingly, this ardent dedication appeared only in West and Johnston's wartime edition of the novel. The excision of the dedication is one of a handful of revisions that distinguish the novel's 1864 New York from its 1864 Richmond edition. For a too-brief discussion of these revisions, see Faust's introduction to her edition of *Macaria*, esp. xxviii.

20. Although W—— is the primary setting of the novel, some of the novel's action takes place in New York, where Irene Huntingdon is sent for boarding school and Electra Grey apprentices as a painter. In addition, Russell Aubrey and Electra Grey each spend time in Europe, and the novel's battle and hospital scenes take place in Virginia.

21. For Barthes, an emancipated signifier like "W——" "intercedes" into discourse by opening up the interpretative and perverse possibilities of a single letter as sign. See Barthes, *Roland Barthes* 63–64; D. A. Miller 18–28; and Masten. This sense of perverse interpretative possibility also brings to mind Deleuze and Guattari's discussion of minor literature and collective enunciation. See their treatment of the letter-sign *K* in Kafka's fiction, esp. 18. In a later passage, W—— is compared favorably to a re-

markably diverse and cosmopolitan set of localities: "Chili, England, Madagascar, Utah, or Burmah" (73).

22. See also *The Index* for 1 December 1864, esp. 764. Bakker goes on to suggest that the characters "all could be South Carolinians, or perhaps Louisianans" (141). However, internal evidence suggests that W—— is not in South Carolina. See 133, where the narrator differentiates between South Carolina and the state in which W—— resides. A reference to Virginia on page 137 further suggests that W—— was not a part of that Commonwealth. On page 133 the ordinance of secession for W——'s state is described as being signed "late in the afternoon of a winter day." South Carolina, Mississippi, Florida, Alabama, Georgia, Louisiana, and Texas all seceded from the Union in the winter of 1861–62.

23. On dissent and disunion in the Confederacy, see McCurry passim; Thomas, *Confederate Nation* esp. 244–57; Bynum passim; and Freehling passim.

24. Fidler finds the dissonance between *Macaria*'s strident dedication and the comparatively tepid twenty chapters that follow it so pronounced that he concludes it is only the last 120 pages of the novel that "fulfill the promise of the dedication" (*Augusta Evans Wilson* 108). See also Gardner 15; and Faust, *Mothers* 174–76.

25. By my count, the novel makes only two explicit references to the increasing sectional tension that characterized the 1840s and 1850s. On page 83 Irene is described as "gravely discussing the tariff question with Mr. Herbert Blackwell . . . and politely listening to his stereotyped reasoning." Yet no further details of the conversation are offered, and Irene is distracted from it by a "scrap of conversation at the opposite end of the table" regarding her forbidden love interest, Russell Aubrey. In addition, at the beginning of chapter 23, Evans makes a brief, ominous reference to the contentious election of James Buchanan. See 107–8. While her description certainly foreshadows the coming conflict, Evans quickly returns the reader to the novel's domestic plot.

26. See Faust, *Mothers* 175–77; and Gardner 273–74n27. See also the *Richmond Age* January 1865: 393.

27. In the 1896 edition, this caustic passage is omitted. See A. J. E. Wilson, *Macaria* 380. Given the glut of insistent cultural imperatives to reunite the United States following the war, the excision of such a pointed and virulently anti-Union statement is, perhaps, unremarkable. Amid the "mind-numbing" mantras and fiercely conciliatory culture of post-Reconstruction America, there was simply no place for such fractious rhetoric (Silber, *Romance* 1).

28. Evans later brags that her novel in progress is "dedicated to the Army of the Confederacy" (Sexton 56). For Beauregard's 24 March 1863 response, see U.S. War Department, *The War of the Rebellion* 688–89. That a wartime general would reply to this request—and reply in a little more than a week's time—is remarkable. Then again, Beauregard seems to have been quite taken with Evans, of whom he said, "[I]t would not do for me to see [her] too often . . . for I might forget 'home and country' in their hour of need and distress'" (qtd. in Gardner 273–74n27). See also Griffith; Fidler, *Augusta Evans Wilson* 94–95; and Sexton 43, 57–58.

29. The narrator refers to colonial revolutionaries as "the rebels" (147); later, Irene calls the American Civil War "Our Revolution" (181). On Confederate interest in the American Revolution see Thomas, *The Confederacy*; Faust, *Creation*, esp. 14; A. S.

Rubin, esp. 14–25; and Bonner, *Mastering*, esp. 255–64. Evans goes even further back in time, suggesting an affinity between the women of Carthage and the women of the Confederacy and comparing favorably Duvall's coded message to the "Talmudish Shemhamphorash" (147). Just one chapter later, Evans has Electra smuggle more Confederate "despatches" on the back of one of her paintings, a copy of Michelangelo's *Fates* (153–54).

30. See Bakker 141; Riepma 92; and Holstein 117. On debates in the Confederacy, see Durden passim; and B. Levine.

31. For an anatomy of Lost Cause ideology, see Nolan. On the willingness of both the South and the North to "shov[e] slavery under the rug" in the early months of the war, see McPherson, *Battle Cry* 311–12. This also calls to mind the decision of the editor of the Confederate *Les Misérables* to omit references to slavery. On slavery in Evans's wider oeuvre, see Fox-Genovese's introduction to Evans, *Beulah*, esp. xiii–xiv; Trubey; Entzminger, esp. 67; and Sofer, esp. 66.

32. Homestead argues persuasively that the delayed publication may in fact have helped it to become a "sensation" in the North. See "Publishing" 686.

33. The body of literature on gender and the American Civil War is enormous. Exemplary studies include McCurry; Rable, *Civil*; Samuels, esp. 81–98; Silber, *Gender*; Whites, *Civil* and *Gender*; and E. Young. Clinton and Silber's edited collections, *Divided Houses* and *Battle Scars*, also provide excellent starting points. For treatments of gender in *Macaria*, see Faust, *Mothers*, esp. 168–77, as well as the introduction to her 1992 edition of the novel; Sofer, esp. 65–104; and E. Moss, esp. 180–92 and 217–19. Unfortunately, much of the criticism of the novel gets bogged down in debates about its progressive politics and feminism, which, as the Romero epigraph suggests, often prove recursive. See Bakker, esp. 131 and 141; McCandless, "Concepts"; Gross; and Alder.

34. In one instance Irene sounds a great deal like a latter-day southern literary character, Scarlett O'Hara: "I would consent to die for my father to-morrow, if thereby I might make him happy; but I can not endure to live, and bring upon myself the curse of a loveless marriage; and, God is my witness, I never will!" (106). It is very likely that Margaret Mitchell knew and read *Macaria*. Indeed, Mitchell claimed Evans's subsequent hero St. Elmo as one of the models for Rhett Butler. See E. Young 258.

35. Later Irene takes a firm stance on marriage: "Father, let us understand each other fully. I speak deliberately and solemnly—I shall never marry." (125). In addition to those of Hugh and Russell, Irene also rejects the Reverend Harvey Young's proposal (106–7). Like Irene, Electra makes an early vow to remain single. After rejecting a marriage proposal from her mentor, Mr. Clifton, Electra says, "'Electra Grey will be carved on my tombstone'" (63). Although both women remain infatuated with Russell, neither marry in the course of the novel. For an illuminating discussion of the status of unmarried women in the Civil War–era South, see Gross. It is of note that, on the eve of the Civil War, Evans broke off her engagement to James Reed Spaulding because of his purported antisouthern, "*Black Republican*" politics (Sexton 23). Evans had met Spaulding, the editor of the *New York World*, in October 1859 through J. C. Derby. See Fidler, *Augusta Evans Wilson* 84–86; and Sexton 23–26.

36. Electra concludes, "I dedicate myself, my life, unreservedly to Art" (95). By fo-

cusing on Electra's twinned commitments to both art and nation, Naomi Z. Sofer provides the best sustained reading of this character and a very convincing interpretation of the novel. See 65–104.

37. Later Irene refuses an extravagant gift from her father in the hopes that he will gift her instead a plot of land for an orphan asylum. See 126–28. On Evans's own attempts to modestly influence Confederate legislation, see her correspondence with Senator J. L. M. Curry (Sexton 65–71). For less modest attempts, see Homestead, *American*, esp. 197–212. As Nina Silber has recently argued, such indirect influence was not unheard of in the Confederacy. See *Gender* 20. See also McCurry passim.

38. Similarly, the emergence of sectional strife emboldens Electra to disagree with Russell about the proper role of art in a republic. Among other things, she argues that "æsthetics, properly directed, is one of the most powerful engines of civilization" (94).

39. Irene believes that nursing is the "least the women of the land can do. . . . The call is imperative" (166). The war also draws Electra back from Europe; like Irene she soon commits to nursing—"true womanly work" (161). See J. Schultz passim.

40. See Faust, *This Republic* 2, 273–74n2; also Schantz.

41. Two additional examples of wartime "Womanly Usefulness" are cut from the 1896 edition: the comparisons of Emily Geiger and Bettie Duvall discussed above. Taken together, the excision of Irene and Electra's colloquy and the absence of these anecdotes speak to a deep cultural investment in the rewriting of the history of women's place in American Civil War efforts. Faust notes but does not discuss such revisions in the introduction to her edition of the novel. See esp. xxvii–xxix.

42. As Romero notes, the domestic novel provided a "particularly appropriate vehicle for what the age defined as women's proper exercise of power" (16). See also, Kelley passim. For an overview of reviews of *Macaria*, see Bernath 264–67.

43. As Nina Baym points out, withholding from a work of fiction the generic title "novel" was not unprecedented in mid-nineteenth-century American letters. See 270.

44. See also Gardner, who calls Evans, Sallie Rochester Ford, and Maria McIntosh "propagandists" (15). I prefer Elizabeth Fox-Genovese's more subtle suggestion that Evans "took second place to none as a southern *polemicist*" (Evans, *Beulah* xiii; emphasis mine). Given the inclusiveness of most definitions of *propaganda*, it seems possible that any nineteenth-century novel that undertook some form of cultural work could be deemed propaganda, since all literary discourse is predicated on, and achieved through, the manipulation of representations. See Jackall, esp. 13; and Lasswell et al., esp. 21. As Jane Tompkins has shown, many novels of the nineteenth century in particular aimed to "influence[e] human action," "redefine the social order," and "win the belief and influence the behavior of the widest possible audience" (xi). On actual existing Civil War–era propaganda, see Taylor 168.

45. Elizabeth Moss notes that "by integrating the substance of contemporary political debate into the very heart of her narrative, Evans necessarily altered the shape of the southern domestic novel" (186). See also Faust's introduction to the novel, esp. xv–xvi. On the pressures antebellum novelists were under to keep the political cordoned off from the domestic, see Baym, esp. 215. On the history of the relations be-

tween "the language of sexual relations" and "the language of politics" in domestic fiction, see Armstrong, esp. 3–5.

46. Romero goes on to caution that "by calling domesticity feminist we prepare ourselves for disappointment over its lack of radicalism at the same time that we obscure the interventionary value it did have" (20). Understood in these terms, *Macaria* may be considered what Susan K. Harris deems an "exploratory novel," a distinction Harris herself grants to Evans's 1867 bestseller, *St. Elmo* (33). See also LaCapra, esp. 14. Faust contends that the cultural work of the novel was to "'reorganize' the Confederate war effort 'from the woman's point of view'" (Evans, *Macaria* xvi). See also Bakker 132; Faust, *Mothers* 173; and Sofer 78.

Chapter Three. Southern Amaranths

1. Stephen Cushman agrees explicitly with Wilson. See 183. See also Walston 103; and Aaron 235. Ritchie D. Watson's over-the-top rhetoric extends Wilson's original metaphor: "The poetic landscape of the Civil War is a metaphorical wasteland, an artistic terrain of shocking banality" (202). One admirable exception to this dismissive and ahistorical critical practice is Faith Barrett and Cristanne Miller's innovative anthology *"Words for the Hour."* Barrett and Miller aim to "balance presentation of what a contemporary reader would have found in popular periodicals and newspapers with a generous selection of the work of major poets writing extensively in response to the war" (xvi). See also Pearce 234.

2. For instance, the last two decades have seen an outpouring of studies of Walt Whitman's *Drum-Taps* (1865), Herman Melville's *Battle-Pieces and Aspects of the War* (1866), and Emily Dickinson's wartime poetry. See Renker and Robillard; Barrett. With a few notable exceptions—William Moss in particular—recent work on Confederate poetry has proved similarly poetcentric, focusing on Henry Timrod, Paul Hamilton Hayne, Sidney Lanier, and Father Abram Joseph Ryan, among others. Such "recovery work"—North and South—has taken place within a broader renaissance of nineteenth-century American poetry criticism. For exemplary studies, see Bennett; Cavitch; V. Jackson; Loeffelholz; Richards, *Gender*; and Sorby.

3. See also Fahs 32–36; and Bernath 113.

4. Describing the resulting poetry as "overwhelming in sheer quantity" (3), William Moss goes on to note that while the North out-published the South by a "great ratio," the Confederacy "probably came closer to parity in war-poem production than in almost any other area" (13). On the popularity of Civil War poetry, see Buell; also C. Miller.

5. I am not the first to describe Civil War poetry's occasional character. See Walston, esp. 93–103; also Ellinger, esp. 17–19. On the diversity of Confederate poets, see Barrett and Miller, esp. xv; also Walston 93. In deference to this occasional character, the following pages largely ignore the best-known "Confederate" poets: Henry Timrod, Paul Hamilton Hayne, Sidney Lanier, and Father Abram Joseph Ryan. (I place "Confederate" in quotation marks because the majority of Lanier's and Ryan's poetry appeared in print after the war.) As this chapter demonstrates, these poets were

part and parcel of a diverse Confederate poetic culture, one that literary historians have not reckoned fully.

6. Elizabeth Renker and I develop this argument in our essay in the *Oxford History of Popular Print Culture*. On the complex dissemination and circulation of Confederate poems, see also W. Moss, esp. 28–29.

7. Alice Fahs observes that on the eve of the war, "most Americans related to their nation in profoundly localized and particularized ways" (11). In the Confederacy such localized and particularized relations continued to dominate throughout the war.

8. On Mary Boykin Chesnut's epic ambitions for her Civil War–era diary, see Stern.

9. In truth, we can also read the phrase "bordering on the doggerel" as a somewhat disingenuous confession. By 1862 Hewitt was an established and prolific poet, songwriter, and playwright. His composition "All Quiet Along the Potomac" would become one of the most popular songs of the war—on both sides of the Mason-Dixon line. In an elegant piece of irony, it was John Hill Hewitt who beat out Edgar Allan Poe in the 1833 *Baltimore Saturday Visitor* poetry competition.

10. As Alice Fahs has suggested, the performative nature of such rhetoric was a distinctive element of Confederate literary distinctiveness. See 9. For contemporaneous criticism of this poem, see Bernath 263–64.

11. On the Confederacy's imperial designs, see Guterl, esp. 54; and Levander. On the relations between epic poetry and empire, see Quint.

12. On flag culture in the Confederacy, see Bonner, *Colors*; and Fahs, esp. 61–92.

13. On Lincoln's wartime reputation in the Confederate South, see Trefousse passim; and Holzer, *Lincoln*, esp. 73–148. See also Schwartz, esp. 79–82. On Confederate caricatures of Lincoln, see Holzer, "Confederate Caricature."

14. At least one Confederate periodical found such representations of the First Family distasteful. See *The Index* 3 (24 September 1863): 347. Harwell described the poem as the "[m]ost pretentious of the Confederate anti-Lincoln publications" (S. F. Miller, *Ahab Lincoln* 4).

15. Keeping with the theme of Shakespearean tragedy, it is "Iago Seward" (19) who emerges as the villain on the pages: The Secretary of State plans to pin the two suicides on Jefferson Davis, whose rhetoric leads Lincoln to acknowledge his sins. The Davis that emerges from *Ahab Lincoln* is stately and forgiving—the hero of this several-hundred-line poem.

16. Not every Confederate poet addressed the Confederate national moment in such direct, all-encompassing ways. At least two poets worked the war into poetic collections begun before the secession of the southern states. Of the thirty-five poems in Theophilus Hunter Hill's *Hesper* (Raleigh: Strother and Marcom, 1861), only two, "Reveille" and "Tear Down that Flag!," address the Confederate national moment. Instead, Hill's poetry, which is deeply indebted to Poe and Keats, celebrates more mundane topics (for example, "Song of the Butterfly," "St. Valentine's Day," and "Taking a Snooze"). Nonetheless, *Hesper* gained fame as the first collection of poems copyrighted in the Confederate States, and in 1863 Raleigh's Branson, Farrar, and Company produced a second edition of the volume. Similarly, the anonymous, thirty-eight-page children's collection *For the Little Ones* (n.d.) makes only a handful

of direct references to the war, despite being dedicated "To the Little Girls and Boys of the Southern Confederacy" and intended to benefit soldiers' relief. For instance, "Willie's Political Alphabet" sings the alphabetic praises of "Beauregard, Bartow, Bethel and Bee," among others (32). And "Our Young Volunteer" documents a Confederate mother's attempt to "woo" her overly eager and precocious son "from your soldier life, / To *be a boy again!*" (23). On children's literature in the Confederate South, see Marten, esp. 31–67; and Fahs, esp. 256–86.

17. William Moss defines broadsides as any "unfolded single sheets printed on only one side" (31). James D. Sullivan defines broadsides more broadly as "*all* single, unbounded printed sheets" (12). He goes on to call distinctions among broadsides, broadsheets (which are printed on two sides), and pamphlets (which are folded to make four pages) "pedantic and trivial" (12). Most Confederate broadsides provide little to no publication information. As a result, in this chapter and the next, I refer readers to entries in Parrish and Willingham's bibliography of Confederate imprints (e.g., P&W 6578). Bibliographical information for broadsides not included in Parrish and Willingham appears in the list of works cited.

18. James D. Sullivan concurs, noting that Confederate broadsides "carried a greater burden . . . of nationalist aspirations" than their northern counterparts (19). See also Ellinger, who speculates that, after periodicals, broadsides were the second "most common" venue for publication of southern war poetry (18). Suffice it to say that Confederate broadsides return us to an earlier mode of circulation for poetry, one that dominated the English Renaissance and colonial period in America. On the broadside in Renaissance England, see Watt. On the history of broadsides in North America—which dates to the introduction of the printing press during the colonial period—see Cushing. On broadsides in the American Revolutionary War, see Berger; also Bailyn and Hench. For a useful synthesis of these histories, see J. D. Sullivan, esp. 12–20. At present Wake Forest University's Z. Smith Reynolds Library maintains an open-access digital archive of its extensive Confederate Broadside Poetry Collection (on which William Moss's print bibliography is based).

19. See Wood, esp. 80–81. Although Lincoln bore the brunt of such critiques, his cabinet members were also targets. "Great Cry and No Wool" (n.p.,[1861–65]), a broadside dated "Baltimore, *July* 2, 1861" and credited to "Barnstable," lampoons each member of Lincoln's cabinet, "the leading Black Republicans." Another broadside imagines "John Brown's Entrance Into Hell" (n.p.: n.d.) and the delight Satan feels at his presence. The twenty-stanza poem also notes Satan's anticipation of the arrival of Lincoln and his cabinet: "John at my left, Abe at my right, / We'll give the heavenly hosts a fight; / A triune group we then shall be, / Yes, three in one and one in three."

20. Bonner usefully reads this poem in relation to the Confederacy's "martial paternalism." See *Mastering*, esp. 273–85. Confederate broadside poems even responded to ongoing political debates. The poem "Niggers in Convention. Sumner's Speech" addresses discussions (largely broached by Senator Charles Sumner of Massachusetts) about the enlistment of freedmen in the Union Army. This dramatic monologue voices the views of an uneducated former slave as he addresses his "bredren." Although the speaker is alarmed by the prospect of having to fight "[j]ust in de front ob battle," he

also sees great potential in "nigger arming." This short poem evinces a great deal of anxiety about an armed black population, underscoring the purportedly duplicitous and violent nature of people of African descent.

21. For more on this "news-in-verse function," see Kurtz, esp. 187. On the social force of "flat, derivative, and conventional" poems and songs, see M. C. Cohen, esp. 271–72.

22. As with so many broadside poems, this version of "Beauregard at Manassas" varies significantly from other broadside versions of the poem (for example, P&W 6270–71; cf. Shepperson 123–24).

23. The poem was also published in the September 1861 number of the *SLM* (33: 169–70). See also Shepperson 126–32.

24. On the response to Jackson's death, see Faust, *This Republic* 154–56. Faust notes that "the combination of his legendary piety with his military successes rendered him the ideal embodiment of the Christian Soldier" (154). See also the broadside "Jackson Is Dead!," which opens with a scene of national mourning: "Jackson is dead! And the tears of a nation / Rise with the prayers of the millions that pray."

25. On the Confederate Constitution, see C. R. Lee passim; and De Rosa, esp. 38–56.

26. See Sheehan-Dean, esp. 39–62.

27. Another broadside poem, "The Last Request," claims to have been found "upon the body of a South Caroline Volunteer, after he was killed at the Battle of Dranesville, Dec. 20, 1861." The poem's speaker asks that if he should fall on the battlefields of Virginia he be taken home to South Carolina: "This is a noble State, and generous hearts are here, / To whisper kind and cheering words to the stranger volunteer, / But, if on Virginia's soil, I fall to rise no more, / Carry me back, carry me back to my own loved Carolina shore; / Oh! boys, carry me back. I'll ask no marble tomb. / But, lay me down in the sacred ground of my *own dear mountain home*" (P&W 6401). As the roll call poems suggest, border states were also well represented in these poems. "Maryland in Chains" (P&W 6606), or its variant "Maryland in Fetters" (P&W 6429), appeared in a number of broadside editions. "God help Kentucky!" (P&W 6334) was another widely reproduced poem.

28. This is in keeping with J. D. Sullivan's contention that the broadside has always served as an "American samizdat, produced and distributed beneath the surface of institutional and commercial publishing" (1). See also Loughran, esp. 1–32 and 161–221.

29. On the relative neglect of nineteenth-century newspaper verse in its original form, see Houston, who argues persuasively that we need to read newspaper poems "in relation to their original material context" (234).

30. Even the envious *SLM* had to admit as much: "A pictorial paper, started in this city not much more than a month ago, has already a circulation quadruple that obtained by THE MESSENGER after twenty seven years" (34 [October 1862]: 581). See also 34 (December 1862): 688. A few months later, the *SLM* described the *SIN*'s circulation as "something enormous for a paper of its class in the South" (37 [April 1863]: 252). The *SLM* then proceeded to belittle the quality of the *SIN*'s illustrations, a com-

mon and well-founded critique. See Vandiver 209; Neely, Holzer, and Boritt, esp. 23–30; Bryer and Schorr; and Binnington.

31. See Fahs 31; and Frost 214n1.

32. In a wonderful piece of chutzpah, this editorial rationale appears to have been lifted from a 4 July 1840 issue of the *New York Mirror* (18.2: 15).

33. See also Fahs 31–33; and Mott 2: 112.

34. On the newspaper exchange system, see Fahs, esp. 30–31. Richard Harwell considered the *SIN*'s roster to be inclusive of "the leading Southern authors" and the poetry of the *SIN* to be "the material which now stands up best" ("Confederate View" 53). See also Fahs 35; and Bernath, esp. 160–64. The *SIN* even ran a number of poetry contests during the war. One, for a poem to commemorate the new Richmond Theater, offered a remarkable three-hundred-dollar prize. Drawing inspiration from the 1812 Royal Theatre/Drury Lane prize competition (which Lord Byron won), the *SIN* asked, "But where is the Byron of our day or the man that can even imitate him successfully?" (3). Henry Timrod won the Richmond Theater competition. See 21 February 1863: 8.

35. As Neely, Holzer, and Boritt note, that inaugural illustration did not resemble Jackson. It is likely that the *SIN*'s illustrator was working from the wrong photographic image (110).

36. For contemporaneous accounts of the "elegiac character" of Confederate verse, see Simms, *War Poetry* vii; and Brock v–vi.

37. In truth, the *SIN* published poems that explicitly drew this connection. See for instance "I'm Thinking of Thee, Mary," a soldier's anxious address to his beloved, who may or may not have forgotten him while he is away at war: "Dost thou ever think of me, Mary, / When joy and mirth surround— / When music swells the heart, Mary, / With soul-inspiring sound?" (3 [23 January 1864]: 21).

38. Alas, Hayne did not have the space or inclination to sing the praises of his sister minstrels, as a note at the bottom of the expansive poem explains: "It was not possible, in accordance with the scope and design of this poem, to introduce the many gifted female poets of the South. Such an introduction would have extended the piece to an unreasonable length" (2 [4 July 1863]: 5).

39. On the relationship between literary canons and nationalism, see Jusdanis, *Belated*, esp. 49–87; and Corse, esp. 1–17 and 63–96. On "The Southern Lyre," see Harwell, "Confederate View."

40. The *SIN* published no small amount of literary criticism, including book reviews of Confederate editions of *Great Expectations* and *Tannhauser* (17 May 1863: 2); essays on "The Novel" (2 [24 July 1863]: 20) and "Yankee Literature" (2 [8 August 1863]: 36–37); and extensive coverage of the passing of William Makepeace Thackeray (3 [6 February 1864]: 33–34; 3 [14 May 1864]: 147).

41. The 1 November 1862 issue noted, "Though the *News* is but eight weeks old, we have lyrics enough, were they worthy of print, to supply the poet's corner for as many years" (3). See also the 10 January 1863 issue, esp. 3. The 25 April 1863 issue sighed similarly, "We are again besieged. . . . We did not establish our paper for the purpose of instructing young ladies and gentlemen in *Belles-Lettres*. Young people

should avoid the folly of supposing everything they write worthy of being printed" (7). On the function of literary criticism in the Confederacy, see Bernath, esp. 227–37.

42. As Fahs notes, the *SIN* seems to have catered to a broad audience. It would have needed to distinguish itself from the "more gentlemanly *Southern Literary Messenger*," which was also based in Richmond and had no truck with popular verse (33). See also Frost, esp. 86–88.

43. The Greek example was a recurring motif in the *SIN*. For instance, in an introduction to a revised version of his "Sketches in Greece," William Gilmore Simms noted similarities between the histories of Greece and the Confederate States. See 11 October 1862: 2.

44. My discussion of a locality effect is indebted to Barthes. See esp. his treatment of the "reality effect."

45. The Confederate forces at the Battle of Secessionville/James Island were made up of soldiers from South Carolina, North Carolina, and Georgia.

46. For a further discussion of the popular poetry anthology, see Hutchison and Renker, esp. 402–13. The most popular of these anthologies were (Father) Abram Joseph Ryan's *War Lyrics and Songs of the South* (1866); T. C. De Leon's *South Songs* (1866); William Gilmore Simms's *War Poetry of the South* (1867); Emily V. Mason's *The Southern Poems of the War* (1867); and Sallie Brock's *The Southern Amaranth* (1869). Many of these anthologies were both memorial and philanthropic, aiming to canonize the poetry of the Confederacy while raising funds for relief and memorial organizations. See Mason 7–8; Brock v–vi; and Ryan iii. Post-Reconstruction anthologies include Frank Moore's *Songs and Ballads of the Southern People, 1861–1865* (New York: D. Appleton, 1886); Charles W. Hubner's *War Poets of the South and Confederate Camp-Fire Songs* ([Atlanta?], 1896); Nora Fontaine Davidson's *Cullings from the Confederacy* (Washington: Rufus H. Darby Printing, 1903); and H. M. Wharton's *War Songs and Poems of the Southern Confederacy, 1861–1865* (Philadelphia: John C. Winston, 1904).

47. Shepperson's anthology drew on a previously assembled but unpublished collection of poems edited by W. S. Chase and John R. Thompson, suggesting that the process of anthologization began immediately following the secession of the southern states.

48. On the complexity of Simms's relationship to nationalism and the American Civil War see C. S. Watson, *From Nationalism*, esp. chaps. 9–10.

49. See, for instance, Frank Moore, who notes that his *Rebel Rhymes and Rhapsodies* were originally published "in the magazines and periodical literature of the South, while many are copies of ballad-sheets and songs circulated in the Rebel armies" (v). Similarly, Shepperson emphasizes the importance of newspapers to the distribution of Confederate verse. Worried that "the newspaper can give only an ephemeral life to 'thoughts that breathe and words that burn,'" the anthologist extends his macabre metaphor and suggests that his "book embalms if it does not immortalize" (3). Finally, Simms acknowledges the impossibility of representing fully the literary field he compasses, suggesting that anthologies of local literary cultures may be in order. See vii.

1. This anecdote is much loved and oft repeated in Lincoln lore. Tellingly, even anecdotes about "Dixie" give rise to variation and revision. See Sandburg 4: 207.

2. The ubiquity of popular song during the period has led one critic to conclude that the American Civil War was "certainly the singingest war in American history" (Pedersen 536). See Heaps and Heaps; Abel; and esp. Harwell, *Confederate Music* 5.

3. See also Williams 266. Following Simms, Williams reads these "folk-songs" as the "emotional literature" of the people, "the most genuine expression of the feelings and thoughts which filled their hearts and minds" (283). Editors, critics, and historians of the American Civil War have long conflated popular poetry and song. For instance, all of the anthologies discussed in chapter 3 include both poems and the lyrics to popular songs. This is exacerbated by the fact that the lyrics to popular songs often circulated without musical notation. Since both are forms of metered verse, it can be difficult to distinguish song lyrics from poetry on the printed page. More often than not it is only the through the explicit indication of an air, tune, or melody (for example, "Tune—Camptown Races") that we can identify song lyrics from this period. This is to say nothing of the complicated historical relationship between music and poetry. Winn offers an accessible introduction to the immense body of literature on this topic.

4. As Faust points out, music publishing (broadly considered) "outstripped every other area of southern publishing during the war, expanding dramatically in response to popular demand" (*Creation* 18). See also Harwell, who suggests that these conditions in fact help to explain the archive of Confederate imprints that survived the war (*Confederate Music* 4). See also Abel xvii.

5. See Abel, esp. 29. I remain skeptical about this "official" compositional history and songwriting credit, given Sacks and Sacks's provocative study of an African American claim to the song; Lott's celebrated explication of an ambivalent culture of "love and theft" at work in blackface minstrelsy; and conflicting contemporaneous accounts as to the source of the song's melody. See, for instance, *The Index* 1: 140; cf. Hewitt 11. Harwell, for one, acknowledges the likelihood that "Emmett's melody was of folk origin" (*Confederate Music* 50). See esp. 47–52.

6. Antebellum broadside song sheets of "Dixie" from Boston and Philadelphia also survive. See "Dixie's land" and "Dixey's Land. No. 2." As early as 1860, Daniel D. Emmett found himself ensnared in a drawn-out "war over Dixie," due in large part to his lack of business savvy and belated concern for copyright. See Nathan 269 and 288–89; and Emmett, "Away." See also Sacks and Sacks; and Lott passim. For an accessible, if ungenerous, history of these "wars," see Abel 43–49. Among other things, Abel finds Sacks and Sacks's argument "totally unconvincing" (49); I disagree. Nonetheless, Abel's chapter on "Dixie" offers a compelling but decidedly nonscholarly history of the song; we share many sources.

7. See for instance Abel 33–38; Nathan 274; and Silber and Silverman 50. On the quickstep variation, see Galbreath 20.

8. Sources proliferate: *Dixie* as a corruption of Mason-*Dixon* line; *Dixie* as a reference to a mythical, kind plantation holder named Dixy; *Dixie* as a nickname for a Dix, a ten-dollar bank note from New Orleans; *Dixie* as a professional jargon used by minstrel performers to refer to "the Negro." See Nathan 265; and Harwell, *Confederate Music* 44.

9. "Dixie" served as a campaign song for the 1860 Lincoln presidential campaign. See Bungay 66–67; also *Lincoln and Hamlin Songster* 34.

10. See Heaps and Heaps 48; and Dichter and Shapiro 48–49. On early lyrical variations, see Galbreath, esp. 14–19. Harwell also mentions several "local" "Dixie" parodies. See *Confederate Music* 42–44.

11. For an extended discussion of this dynamic, see my "Secret in Altered Lines."

12. For an important re-reading of "repeatable materiality," see Bhabha 22–24.

13. Louis C. Elson may not have been the only mid-nineteenth-century music aficionado to think so. Firth, Pond, and Company published an instrumental "Dixie's Land, with Brilliant Variations" in 1860. See also Jean Manns's rondo arrangement. For an explication of the formal elements of "Dixie," see Spaeth 142; and Nathan 248–50. According to several music critics, the song's "universal" appeal lies in its accessibility: Almost anyone could—and can—sing "Dixie." Spaeth notes that the range of the tune is an octave and a major third, a range generally "comfortable for the average voice" (143). This accessibility may be, in turn, the source of the phrase "whistling Dixie."

14. See K. Schultz 148–49. The most popular of these songs included "Gay and Happy," "The Happy Land of Canaan," "Yankee Doodle Dandy," "John Brown's Body," "Marseillaise Hymn," several Scots-Irish folk tunes, a series of blackface minstrel songs, and, of course, "Dixie." See Mahar; and Wiley, *Life of Billy Yank*, esp. 157–69, and *Life of Johnny Reb*, esp. 151–56. On the North and South sharing an "extensive prewar repertoire" of songs, see Moseley 45. Given their wild popularity during the war years, songsters in particular offer a surviving trace of the cultures of both musical performance and revisionism that produced so many versions of the "same" song. The history of the songster in America predates the Civil War by a generation or more. These collections of secular song lyrics saw wide use during the late eighteenth and early nineteenth centuries in political campaigns and clubs and as souvenirs of musical performances. Their small size and portability also made them particularly well-suited to military settings (K. Schultz 133). Kirsten Schultz counts at least five dozen unique editions of Confederate songsters, including *Hopkins' New-Orleans 5 Cent Song-Book* (New Orleans: J. Hopkins, 1861), *The Dixie Land Songster* (Augusta: Blackmar and Bro, 1863), and *The Jack Morgan Songster* (Raleigh: Branson and Farrar, 1864). *The Stonewall Song Book* (Richmond: West and Johnston, 1863) went through a remarkable twelve editions during the war (K. Schultz 164–68; cf. Parrish and Willingham 962).

15. Moseley also sees "significant differences" between the musical cultures of the Confederacy and the Union, calling the war a "conflict of cultures" (45).

16. Decrying the political convenience of instrumental versions of the song, Sacks and Sacks have taken Ken Burns to task for featuring a lyricless "Dixie" in his documentary series *The Civil War*. See 155.

17. For a catalog of such opinions, see *Joint Committee* 2 and Abel 34–36. For postwar opinions, see J. A. Simpson. *Songs of the South* and other southern songsters from the period did place "The Original Words" to "Dixie's Land" alongside multiple whitewashed, Confederate versions of the song (30).

18. T. C. De Leon suggests that the origins of Confederate songs were not all that important to auditors. He notes that they were "accepted greedily by ear, when they hit the popular fancy: but it was rare that any man, or woman, who whistled, sang, or recited them, paused one instant to sift either their origin, or what of meaning they had" (*Belles* 360).

19. Parrish and Willingham list four different versions of Pike's "Dixie." See 549. See also Galbreath 37–38. Abel also notes that Pike's "Dixie" became "Awake! To Arms in Texas!" See 305n35. On the importance of Pike's shift, see J. A. Simpson 39.

20. See Anderson's discussion of religious communities, esp. 12–19, as well as L. P. Simpson's treatment of the South as a "redemptive community," esp. 203. See also Faust, *Creation* 24–26.

21. Stanton's "Dixie" also circulated as the broadside "Awake in Dixie" (P&W 6562). See also "P.W.H.T.'s" "Southern Dixie," which is dedicated "To the Friends of States Rights" and bristles with patriotic pride: "Oh Dixie's Land's a Nation now, / Her sons no longer slaves" (P&W 7483: 2). Another Confederate nationalistic "Dixie" is Randal M. Weber's "We're All in Arms in Dixie" (P&W 7617). Dedicated "To the Friends of Dixie" and published by J. A. McClure of Nashville and Memphis, Weber's "Dixie" reiterates much of Pike and Stanton's rhetoric, while offering several innovations as well. Of particular note is the presence of "Old Abe," who, the song prophesizes, "we'll . . . slay" alongside his "Yankees."

22. As Basler notes, this paragraph was itself heavily revised. In one early draft the musical metaphor was much more explicit: "all the hearths in this broad continent of ours will yet . . . again harmonize in their ancient music" (Lincoln 4: 262).

23. See Faust, who argues persuasively that music was "the most striking example of the importance of southern orality in the creation of Confederate nationalism" (*Creation* 18). Tellingly, Butler also confiscated all of Blackmar's copyrights. See Harwell, *Confederate Music*, esp. "Copyright, C.S.A." 8–25.

24. Several sources suggest that Emmett, a fierce Unionist, came under fire for his purported southern sympathies. After all, he had written the de facto Confederate national anthem (Galbreath 20–21). T. C. De Leon describes Emmett as being deeply chagrinned by the Confederate appropriation of the song. Asked during the war if he was the author of "Dixie," Emmett is credited as saying, "'Yes: and if I had known to what use they were going to put my song, I will be damned if I'd have written it!'" (*Belles* 359).

25. For a discussion of popular consumption of wartime media, see Fahs passim; and Grover. On spectatorial knowingness, see Bailey.

26. See also the sheet music for A. W. Muzzy's "Dixie Unionized," which bears an endorsement from Lydia Sigourney. This Union "Dixie" opens with a direct engagement with the peculiar institution: "O! I'm glad I live in a land of freedom, / Where we have no slaves nor do we need them / Look away, look away, look away, to freedom's land" (2).

27. Cribbing the "Dixie boy/Uncle Sam" chorus from "Dixie for the Union" and large portions of the verses from "Dixie of Our Union," "Dixie's Land" is something of a composite text of Union "Dixies."

28. See also "Hurra for Our Union."

29. Both the English and American national "anthems" are, technically speaking, hymns.

30. As Donald Pease notes, "Transnational American Studies does not merely refer to the movement but also to the objects taken up for analysis and the means of analyzing them" (James xxx).

31. For John Carlos Rowe, such alternatives are at the heart of transnational cultural criticism, since such criticism "reveals how pervasively other societies, nations, and states were subordinated to the triumphalism of United States nationalism" ("Nineteenth-Century" 87). Rather gingerly, I want to include the Confederate States of America as one such "subordinated" nation, as a form of what Rowe calls "nineteenth-century alternative nationalisms"—no matter how unsavory the politics of such inclusion may prove, and in full view of the Confederacy's own imperial aspirations.

32. It is also to resist that most persistent of Civil War metaphors, "the house divided." See Anderson's too brief discussion of the American Civil War, esp. 201.

33. On the idiosyncratic models of proprietary authorship that attended "Dixie," see Spaeth 139; Sheerin 958; Sacks and Sacks 160; Nathan 287; and Lott passim. Harwell notes that music is often a transnational phenomenon. See his discussion of the difficulties of "attempts to nationalize a song or a composer" (*Confederate Music* 94). See also Galbreath, esp. 13–14.

Chapter Five. In Dreamland

1. Velazquez even describes Buford as an "irresistible lady-killer" (195). Elizabeth Young offers an elegant and convincing reading of the "protolesbian" aspects of the narrative (173) and of the ways cross-dressing "serves in this text as a metaphorical point of exchange for intersections between individual bodies and the national body politic" (156).

2. This is despite the heroic efforts of scholars such as Richard Hall, who concludes that "the evidence is increasing that her memoirs contain a basically true story" ("Loreta Janeta Velazquez" 230). See also *Patriots* 207–11; "Loreta Janeta Velazquez" 231–37; and *Women* 192–200. For a litany of skeptical readings of the narrative, see R. Hall, "Velazquez" 237–38; Blanton and Cook 197; and Alemán, *Woman* ix–xix. On the lack of evidence of Velazquez's pre-1876 existence, see Alemán, *Woman*, esp. xvi–xvii. Velazquez's publishers seem to have anticipated such skepticism. The Kelley broadside devotes a full page to "unsought testimonials" to Velazquez's character (4). Onetime U.S. naval officer C. J. Worthington edited *The Woman in Battle*. Scholars have not been able to determine the degree of Worthington's involvement in the composition of the narrative. See R. Hall, "Loreta Janeta Velazquez" 229; and Leonard 256.

3. This is a central tenet of much of the past three decades of autobiography criticism, which, inspired by a poststructuralist suspicion of authentic subjectivity, has

emphasized the performative aspects of autobiographical writing. As Jacques Derrida quipped, "[b]ut when you say he writes himself, you seem to assume that he already has his identity, that he is already himself" (88). Clay Lewis recommends that we examine all Civil War accounts "in the context of their composition, revision, and publication . . . [w]ithout checking our skepticism at the door" (272). I agree wholeheartedly. See also Elizabeth Young, who takes "the charge of 'fiction' as a point of departure for literary analysis rather than the cause for historical censure" (156).

4. Despite all her extraordinary adventures, Velazquez was described by the book's editor, C. J. Worthington, as "a typical Southern woman of the war period" (10). As Sylvia Hoffert notes, "[a]nyone who read her book can clearly see that there was nothing typical about Loreta Velazquez" (28).

5. David W. Blight suggests that "by 1880 American culture, especially the publishing industry and its growing legions of readers, began to welcome soldiers' stories" (170). See also 160–62. Similarly, Andrew C. Higgins notes that by the mid-1880s, the book-length Civil War memoir was "well established" as a genre (122). On the political climate during these years, see Blight, esp. 135–39. On the boom in histories produced during the war, see Fahs 287–310.

6. It is worth noting that the thumbnail literary-historical sketch offered by Fahs, Blight, and others—myself included—is at best impressionistic. In fact, a number of soldiers—both northern and southern—talked, wrote, and published about their wartime experiences during the immediate postwar period. Other early examples of Confederate postwar memoir include Harry Gilmor, *Four Years in the Saddle* (New York: Harper and Brothers, 1866); Heros von Boecke, *Memoirs of the Confederate War for Independence* (Edinburgh: William Blackwood and Sons, 1866); and John Esten Cooke, *Wearing of the Gray: Being Personal Portraits, Scenes and Adventures of the War* (New York: E. B. Treat, 1867).

7. The historiography on the Lost Cause is extensive. The best book-length studies remain Gaines M. Foster's and Charles Reagan Wilson's. The collection in which Nolan's "anatomy" appears, *The Myth of the Lost Cause and Civil War History*, is also instructive. For the literary culture of the Lost Cause, see Hobson 85–128. For the relationship between the Lost Cause and southern conservatism, see Poole. Historiographical debates about the Lost Cause as ideology have also enlivened the burgeoning field of Civil War memory studies. See especially Blair, *Cities*; Blight; Fahs and Waugh; G. W. Gallagher, *Lee*; Marshall; Neff; and N. Silber, *Romance*. On northern memory, see Jeffrey; and Griffin. On material memorial culture, see Savage; Mills and Simpson; and Janney. Anne Sarah Rubin's history of the Confederacy is particularly on point here, since she considers the "dreamland" period (that is, up to 1868) to be part of the history of the C.S.A. See esp. 190–200. Bernath draws a sharper distinction between Confederate and Lost Cause habits of mind. See esp. 291–99.

8. Velazquez repeatedly devalues the "manner" of her book. See especially her "Author's Prefatory Notice" (5–6). On Edmonds, see Teorey; on Greenhow and Boyd, see W. Sullivan. For incisive readings of Eggleston's, Taylor's, and Watkins's memoirs, see Higgins, who is particularly good on conflicts between Old and New Souths. On the Velazquez narrative's pulpiness and genre confusion, see Alemán, *Woman* xxiii.

9. See also 42 and 51. For a discussion of Velazquez's departure from the "Female

Warrior" tradition in nineteenth-century literature, see Blanton and Cook 178. For a perceptive discussion of the cultural work of Joan of Arc "as myth and legend," see Elshtain 173–77.

10. For a further discussion of Velazquez's motivations, see esp. 239; see also Leonard 260–63; and De Grave 97. On men's motivations for fighting the American Civil War, see McPherson, *For Cause*, esp. 12; also Sheehan-Dean. As we might expect, her first experiences on the battlefield force Velazquez to revise significantly her "Dreams of Delusion." See 128–29 and 145–46.

11. On Buford/Velazquez's plight as "the little independent lieutenant" (220), see 182–83, 186–87, 272–73, and 345. At one point Harry T. Buford is so frustrated by his lack of an official commission that he offers an officer five hundred dollars for his (96). See also Elshtain 173.

12. See also 108, 133, and 340–41. As Blanton and Cook suggest, such "restlessness, impulsiveness, and impatience were serious character flaws in a soldier, especially in an officer, and these traits impinged on her military career" (70). Jubal Early deemed such movements "simply incredible" (qtd. in Hoffert 26). Richard Hall, responding to Early's deep skepticism about the veracity of *The Woman in Battle*, admits that such independence would have been more or less unprecedented. See R. Hall, *Women* 211 and "Loreta Janeta Velazquez" 229.

13. See also 108 and 346–47. At the same time, Velazquez confesses that the fidelity of her narrative is undoubtedly compromised by the loss of her contemporaneous notes and the "treacherous" nature of memory (5).

14. In accounting for the failures of Confederate armies, Velazquez remains vague, citing "inefficiency somewhere . . . in the management of military affairs on our side" (277). See also 183–84.

15. Later she moderates such rhetoric, noting that the war brought her into contact "with all sorts of people—blackguards as well as gentlemen," and that she "had some pretty good opportunities for studying masculine character" (311).

16. Such counterfactual thinking is another trademark of the narrative. For instance, Velazquez claims to have had the opportunity to assassinate Ulysses Grant, which, needless to say, she did not take. This leads her to ask, "If I had fired, what would have been the consequences, so far as the results of the war were concerned?" (214). Later, Velazquez wonders "what might have happened" if the U.S. securities frauds with which she was involved had been found out. See 485.

17. On the reconstruction of postwar masculinity, see N. Silber, *Romance* passim; and Whites, *Gender Matters*, esp. 85–94. On the motivations behind Early's condemnation of the narrative, see Blanton and Cook, esp. 180–83; Alemán, *Woman* ix–xxvi; and E. Young 156, 158–60, 170, 178–80, and 192–94.

18. We might usefully compare this description of Lincoln to that of Jubal Early, who "regarded Abraham Lincoln, his counsellors and supporters, as the real traitors who had overthrown the constitution and government of the United States, and established in lieu thereof an odious despotism" (iii–iv). Velazquez seems aware of the incendiary nature of her comments, since she immediately clarifies her point: "My change of sentiment with regard to Mr. Lincoln . . . did not influence me in the least

with regard to my own opinions concerning the rights and wrongs of the contest between the North and the South" (142).

19. Compare this rhetoric to that of Sam R. Watkins. See esp., 233–36.

20. Of course, she also acknowledges that she is writing her memoir from memory, several years after the war; whether she had such awareness during the war is an open question.

21. In truth, both France and England needed cotton, "though not necessarily Confederate cotton" (Thomas, *Confederate Nation* 170). The history of Confederate diplomacy in Europe has been told many times. See esp. Owsley et al.; Hubbard; and H. Jones, *Blue and Gray*. As Thomas suggests, it can be characterized as "a series of dashed hopes—great expectations followed by greater frustrations" (*Confederate Nation* 169). See also Cullop 135. Thomas attributes such frustration to the one-dimensional nature of Confederate foreign policy, a policy "founded on righteousness and cotton [that] did not sufficiently impress Britain and France" (170). See also Dufour 272.

22. Kevin Willmott's 2004 film *C.S.A.: The Confederate States of America* offers a counterfactual narrative of Confederate victory in the Civil War—a victory due almost entirely to foreign intervention by France and England. Willmott's film, which uses as its narrative frame a faux British documentary, also underscores the internationalism of the American Civil War but through a fictitious alternative history. See also C. Gallagher.

23. Not surprisingly, the British government watched closely the U.S.-Canadian border, increasing its colonial garrisons throughout the war. See Winks, esp. 1–11. On the presence of Canada in hemispheric American studies, see Adams; also, Adams and Casteel.

24. See Mayers 79–89.

25. I should note that Velazquez is more forgiving of Cuban blockade-runners. See esp. 250. On the economic impact of the war, see Foner, esp. 18–34; P. O'Brien, 11–20; Ransom, 253–88; and Thornton and Ekelund, 88–103.

26. The narrative addresses slavery as a social institution only a few times. See esp. 367–68. We might usefully compare Velazquez's treatment of Bob to her manipulation of an "old negro woman" in order to cross Federal lines. Velazquez convinces the old woman that she is on an important mission for the Union, and that if the woman aids Velazquez, emancipation will surely follow shortly. See 131–32.

27. As Burnett notes, Hotze seems to have been "overly zealous in his subjective editing of the original—conveniently ignoring passages that distracted from his own beliefs" (5). Throughout his career Hotze maintained a "deep commitment to slavery," arguing that the institution was "to the positive good of both races" (Cullop 64). Oates notes that the waning days of the war revealed in full Hotze's racist and white supremacist leanings. For a superb account of Hotze's "racialist mission," see Bonner, "Slavery." See also R. J. C. Young, esp. 111–32.

28. To this end, Hotze used what we might call a viral or tangential model of influence. See United States Naval War Office 534. In this regard, *The Index* proved a remarkable success, attracting the support, readership, and services of many eminent

Londoners. It should also be noted that Hotze regularly reprinted unattributed articles from European journals in *The Index*. He was also not above placing his own work in foreign journals so that he could reprint them in *The Index* as evidence of broad international support for the Confederacy. See Marlin 61; and Georgini. On Hotze's "school of writers," see Dufour 279–80; and Oates 150.

29. See Dufour, esp. 287. Elsewhere, Hotze discussed the "tone of studied moderation" he maintained on the pages of *The Index*: "It was essential to avoid the great error of American journalism, that of mistaking forcible words for forcible ideas, and to draw a marked contrast between the Index and the popular idea of an American paper" (United States Naval War Office 661). For attacks on Hotze's "moderate" position by his fellow Confederate diplomats, see Cullop 53; and Dufour 282–83. For a critique of Hotze's heavy-handed editorial style, see former Paris correspondent Paul Pecquet du Bellet's memoir, esp. 41–43.

30. On Hotze's work in continental Europe, see Dufour 288–89. Oates claims that Hotze continued to write "almost a dozen articles a week" for several different British periodicals after founding *The Index* (144). Hotze's authorship of many of these pieces is unconfirmed, but he claimed to have written "virtually all the material on slavery" (Cullop 52).

31. Such aspirations echoed Hotze's editorial rationale: "To be cosmopolitan & yet to have a country, to be miscellaneous & yet to have an object; to be tolerant & yet not indifferent" (qtd. in Harwell, *Creed* 5).

32. As Homestead notes, "by passing an international copyright law, the Confederacy sharply and concretely differentiated its regulation of literary property and thus its literary culture from the North's." See *American* 195–96 and 198. As Homestead has demonstrated ably, Augusta Jane Evans was intimately involved in this legislation and the cause of Confederate copyright more broadly. See *American*, esp. 197–212.

33. The description by Owsley et al. of Hotze's comportment and skill has become canonical: "[A]s able as any agent who went abroad during the Civil War. He showed more insight into public opinion and tendencies than did either Mason or Slidell, and his fastidiousness, his deftness, and his lightness of touch in a delicate situation were remarkable. His resourcefulness had a masterly finesse that would have done honour to Cavour or Bismarck" (155). See also Confederate secretary of state Benjamin's 16 January 1863 letter to Hotze (United States Naval War Office 659–60); also Crook 148; and Dufour 267. Bonner calls Hotze "the most important Confederate propagandist in Europe"—before noting that *The Index* helped to spread scientific racism transatlantically ("Slavery" 290). See also Oates 142; Hubbard 99; and Burnett 1.

34. See Elizabeth Young's provocative reading of *The Woman in Battle* as a picaresque novel, esp. 160–61. Reading the multiple significations of the word *pass*, Young argues persuasively that Velazquez's "geographic movements between regions provide a metaphorical gloss on her oscillation between genders" (166). While I find Young's reading of the narrative very convincing, I am hesitant to turn those movements into a mere metaphorical gloss.

35. In truth, southerners had complex reasons for emigrating. As Foster notes, "[s]ome sought better economic opportunities, others could not face life in a society

with free blacks, and a few simply longed for adventure in a strange new land" (16). See also Griggs 1–4.

36. See 549. Despite Velazquez's recommendation, a Confederate colony was in fact set up in Venezuela. Hanna and Hanna describe the endeavor as "both unsuccessful and tragic" (20). There have been extensive studies of Confederate colonies in Venezuela (Hanna and Hanna), Mexico (Burden), Brazil (Harter; Griggs; Dawsey and Dawsey), Peru (Werlich), British Honduras (Simmons), and various provinces in Canada (Rescher). Several of these studies suggest that approximately ten thousand Confederates—"less than two-tenths of 1 percent of the white population of the South" (Foster 17)—went into exile in foreign lands (Foster 16–17; Hanna and Hanna 11; Dawsey and Dawsey 13). See Foster's compelling interpretation of the emigration movement, esp. 15–17.

37. It is worth noting that Pollard would later distance himself from these comments. See Maddex.

38. Velazquez does claim Cuban identity a handful of times in the narrative. See, for example, 502. However, she also aligns herself throughout the text with Spanish colonial rule. See 39–40 and 247. On her ambivalent desire for Cuban independence, see 248, and Alemán's superb discussion in *Woman* xxxiv–xxxv. After meeting with her, Jubal Early remained dubious about Velazquez's "Spanish birth or origin" (qtd. in E. Young 193). See also R. Hall, *Women* 211; also Alemán, "Crossing" 112 and 120–22.

39. For a discussion of Velazquez's "homelessness," see Alemán, *Woman* xxxvi; and "Crossing" 121–22. Alemán argues that the text "works to blur the ethnonational differences between Cuba and the South to enact a literary and historical merger between two geopolitical regions connected by a common history of slavery, a shared fiction of Old World white gentility, and a mutual enemy in Yankee economic and territorial expansion" ("Crossing" 113). See also Levander 827. I propose that the text enacts several mergers among several geopolitical regions.

40. Just ask Cleanth Brooks, one of Faulkner's most devoted readers. In a 1970 *Shenandoah* essay promisingly titled "The Poetry of Miss Rosa Coldfield," Brooks, too, excuses us from having to read this fugitive verse. He believes that Faulkner "wisely refused to provide the reader with any examples of her verse" since "it is all too easy to imagine the banal and hackneyed quality of Miss Rosa's verse tributes" to Confederate soldiers (199). Brooks holds that "Miss Rosa's real poetry" comes in her "long tirade against Thomas Sutpen which comprises nearly all of Chapter V" (199). He even goes so far as to read her prose for a "formalized accentual structure" (200). See also Roberts 164–65; Boone 319–21; Edenfield 60–61; and Mesquita 62–63. Recent critics have made convincing cases for Rosa's importance to the novel. See, for example, Sundquist, esp. 96–130; Wagner-Martin, esp. 2; Coleman, esp. 421; and Lazure, esp. 479. As P. Weinstein noted nearly two decades ago, this character has provided, among other things, "the occasion for the most spirited feminist commentary so far written on Faulkner" (21).

41. See also Muhlenfeld 179; Bakker 131; and Bernath 299. This habit of mind dates at least to the late nineteenth century. Writing in 1888 on the topic of "The

South as a Field for Fiction," Albion W. Tourgée suggested that readers should look to the post–Civil War generation for literary distinction. It would be "the children of soldiers and of slaves" who would "advance American literature to the very front rank" (413). This follows Tourgée's iconoclastic claim that by 1888 American literature had become "not only Southern in type, but distinctly Confederate in sympathy" (405). For a stirring critique of the domineering presence of Faulkner in southern studies, see Yaeger, esp. 96–97.

Works Cited

Aaron, Daniel. *The Unwritten War: American Writers and the Civil War*. New York: Knopf, 1973. Print.

Abel, E. Lawrence. *Singing the New Nation: How Music Shaped the Confederacy, 1861–1865*. Mechanicsburg: Stackpole Books, 2000. Print.

Abram, a Military Poem. Richmond: Macfarlane and Fergusson, 1863. Print.

Abrams, Alexander St. Clair. *The Trials of the Soldier's Wife*. Atlanta: Intelligencer Steam Power Presses, 1864. Print.

Adams, Rachel. *Continental Divides: Remapping the Cultures of North America*. Chicago: University of Chicago Press, 2009. Print.

Adams, Rachel, and Sarah Phillips Casteel, eds. *Canada and the Americas*. Special issue of *Comparative American Studies* 3.1 (2005). Print.

Adventures of the Marion Hornets, Co. H, 7th Regt. Fla. Vols. Knoxville, 1863. Print.

"Aera." *The Oxford English Dictionary*. Web. 21 February 2011.

Alder, Nancy. "Women's Rights in Three Novels by Augusta Jane Evans." *Synthesis* 1.2 (1995): 77–82. Print.

Alemán, Jesse, "Crossing the Mason-Dixon Line in Drag: The Narrative of Loreta Janeta Velazquez, Cuban Woman and Confederate Soldier." *Look Away! The U.S. South in New World Studies*. Ed. Jon Smith and Deborah N. Cohn. Durham: Duke University Press, 2004. 110–29. Print.

———, ed. *The Woman in Battle: The Civil War Narrative of Loreta Janeta Velazquez, Cuban Woman and Confederate Soldier*. Madison: University of Wisconsin Press, 2003. Print.

Allen, Hervey. *Israfel: The Life and Times of Edgar Allan Poe*. New York: George H. Doran, 1926. Print.

Allen, Michael L. *Poe and the British Magazine Tradition*. New York: Oxford University Press, 1969. Print.

Anderson, Benedict R. O. *Imagined Communities: Reflections on the Origin and Spread of Nationalism*. Rev. and extended ed. New York: Verso, 1991. Print.

"Apocalypse." *The Oxford English Dictionary*. Web. 21 February 2011.

Appadurai, Arjun. *Modernity at Large: Cultural Dimensions of Globalization*. Minneapolis: University of Minnesota Press, 1996. Print.

Armstrong, Nancy. *Desire and Domestic Fiction: A Political History of the Novel*. New York: Oxford University Press, 1987. Print.

Ayers, Edward L., et al. *All over the Map: Rethinking American Regions*. Baltimore: Johns Hopkins University Press, 1996. Print.

Bach, Max. "Critique et Politique: La Reception *Des Miserables* en 1862." *PMLA* 77.5 (1962): 595–608. Print.

Bailey, Peter. *Popular Culture and Performance in the Victorian City*. New York: Cambridge University Press, 1998. Print.

Bailyn, Bernard, and John B. Hench. *The Press and the American Revolution*. Worcester: American Antiquarian Society, 1980. Print.

Bakker, Jan. "Overlooked Progenitors: Independent Women and Southern Renaissance in Augusta Jane Evans Wilson's *Macaria; or, Altars of Sacrifice*." *Southern Quarterly* 25.2 (1987): 131–42. Print.

Balibar, Étienne, and Immanuel Maurice Wallerstein. *Race, Nation, Class: Ambiguous Identities*. New York: Verso, 1991. Print.

Barnstable, "Great Cry and No Wool." N.p., [1861–65]. Print.

Barrett, Faith. "Public Selves and Private Spheres: Studies of Emily Dickinson and the Civil War, 1984–2007." *Emily Dickinson Journal* 16.1 (2007): 92–104. Print.

Barrett, Faith, and Cristanne Miller, eds. *"Words for the Hour": A New Anthology of American Civil War Poetry*. Amherst: University of Massachusetts Press, 2005. Print.

Barthes, Roland. "The Reality Effect." *The Rustle of Language*. Ed. and trans. Richard Howard. New York: Macmillan, 1986. 141–48. Print.

———. *Roland Barthes*. 1977. Trans. Richard Howard. Berkeley: University of California Press, 1994. Print.

Baym, Nina. *Novels, Readers, and Reviewers: Responses to Fiction in Antebellum America*. Ithaca: Cornell University Press, 1984. Print.

Bell, Robert. "S. H. Goetzel, Publisher, Mobile, Alabama, 1857–1865." *The Book Club of California Quarterly News-Letter* 34.2 (1969): 27–32. Print.

Benjamin, Walter. *Illuminations*. Trans. Harry Zohn. Ed. Hannah Arendt. New York: Harcourt, 1968. Print.

Bennett, Paula Bernat. *Poets in the Public Sphere: The Emancipatory Project of American Women's Poetry, 1800–1900*. Princeton: Princeton University Press, 2003. Print.

Berger, Carl. *Broadsides and Bayonets: The Propaganda War of the American Revolution*. Philadelphia: University of Pennsylvania Press, 1961. Print.

Bernath, Michael T. *Confederate Minds: The Struggle for Intellectual Independence in the Civil War South*. Chapel Hill: University of North Carolina Press, 2010. Print.

Bhabha, Homi K. *The Location of Culture*. New York: Routledge, 1994. Print.

Bigelow, John. "The Confederate Diplomatists and Their Shirt of Nessus: A Chapter of Secret History." *The Century* 42.1 (1891): 113–21. Print.

Binnington, Ian. "Promoting the Confederate Nation: *The Southern Illustrated News* and the Civil War." *Virginia's Civil War.* Ed. Peter Wallenstein and Bertram Wyatt-Brown. Charlottesville: University of Virginia Press, 2005. 114–22. Print.

Birch, Edmund Pendleton. *The Devil's Visit to "Old Abe."* [La Grange?, Ga.], [1861?]. Print.

Blackwell, Robert. *Original Acrostics on All the States and Presidents of the United States, and Various Other Subjects, Religious, Political, and Personal.* Nashville, 1861. Print.

Blair, William Alan. *Cities of the Dead: Contesting the Memory of the Civil War in the South, 1865–1914.* Chapel Hill: University of North Carolina Press, 2004. Print.

———. *Virginia's Private War: Feeding Body and Soul in the Confederacy, 1861–1865.* New York: Oxford University Press, 1998. Print.

Blanton, DeAnne, and Lauren M. Cook. *They Fought Like Demons: Women Soldiers in the American Civil War.* Baton Rouge: Louisiana State University Press, 2002. Print.

Blight, David W. *Race and Reunion: The Civil War in American Memory.* Cambridge: Harvard University Press, 2001. Print.

Bonner, Robert E. *Colors and Blood: Flag Passions of the Confederate South.* Princeton: Princeton University Press, 2002. Print.

———. *Mastering America: Southern Slaveholders and the Crisis of American Nationhood.* New York: Cambridge University Press, 2009. Print.

———. "Slavery, Confederate Diplomacy, and the Racialist Mission of Henry Hotze." *Civil War History* 51.3 (2005): 288–316. Print.

Boone, Joseph Allen. *Libidinal Currents: Sexuality and the Shaping of Modernism.* Chicago: University of Chicago Press, 1998. Print.

Bourdieu, Pierre. *The Field of Cultural Production: Essays on Art and Literature.* Ed. Randal Johnson. New York: Columbia University Press, 1993. Print.

Brock, Sallie A., ed. *The Southern Amaranth. A Carefully Selected Collection of Poems Growing out of and in Reference to the Late War.* New York: G. S. Wilcox, 1869. Print.

Brooks, Cleanth. "The Poetry of Miss Rosa Coldfield." *Shenandoah* 21 (Spring 1970): 199–206. Print.

Brugger, Robert J. *Beverley Tucker: Heart over Head in the Old South.* Baltimore: Johns Hopkins University Press, 1978. Print.

Bryer, Morton, and Irwin Schorr. "*The Southern Illustrated News.*" *Civil War Times Illustrated* 38.1 (1999): 46–53. Print.

Budd, John. "Henry Timrod: Poetic Voice of Southern Nationalism." *Southern Studies* 20.4 (1981): 437–46. Print.

Buell, Lawrence. "American Civil War Poetry and the Meaning of Literary Commodification: Whitman, Melville, and Others." *Reciprocal Influences: Literary Production, Distribution, and Consumption in America.* Ed. Steven Fink and Susan S. Williams. Columbus: Ohio State University Press, 1999. 123–38. Print.

Bungay, G. W., ed. *The Bobolink Minstrel: or, Republican Songster for 1860.* New York: O. Hutchinson, 1860. Print.

Burden, Georgie. *Mexico: A Confederate Haven*. Boulder: John E. Burden, 2004. Print.

Burnett, Lonnie A., ed. *Henry Hotze, Confederate Propagandist: Selected Writings on Revolution, Recognition, and Race*. Tuscaloosa: University of Alabama Press, 2008. Print.

Bynum, Victoria E. *The Long Shadow of the Civil War: Southern Dissent and Its Legacies*. Chapel Hill: University of North Carolina Press, 2010. Print.

Cash, W. J. *The Mind of the South*. New York: A. A. Knopf, 1941. Print.

"Catalyst." *The Oxford English Dictionary*. Web. 21 February 2011.

Cavitch, Max. *American Elegy: The Poetry of Mourning from the Puritans to Whitman*. Minneapolis: University of Minnesota Press, 2007. Print.

Charvat, William. *The Profession of Authorship in America, 1800–1870: The Papers of William Charvat*. Ed. Matthew J. Bruccoli. Columbus: Ohio State University Press, 1968. Print.

Cheah, Pheng, and Bruce Robbins, eds. *Cosmopolitics: Thinking and Feeling Beyond the Nation*. Minneapolis: University of Minnesota Press, 1998. Print.

Clinton, Catherine, and Nina Silber, eds. *Battle Scars: Gender and Sexuality in the American Civil War*. New York: Oxford University Press, 2006. Print.

————, eds. *Divided Houses: Gender and the Civil War*. New York: Oxford University Press, 1992. Print.

Cohen, Leonard. *The Future*. Columbia Records, 1992. CD.

Cohen, Michael C. "Contraband Singing: Poems and Songs in Circulation during the Civil War." *American Literature* 82.2 (June 2010): 271–304. Print.

Coleman, Rosemary. "Family Ties: Generating Narratives in *Absalom, Absalom!*" *Mississippi Quarterly* 41.3 (1988): 421–31. Print.

"The Confederate Flag." N.p., [1861–65]. Print.

Corse, Sarah M. *Nationalism and Literature: The Politics of Culture in Canada and the United States*. New York: Cambridge University Press, 1997. Print.

Cowper, R. Lynden. *Confederate America*. Raleigh: Book and Job Office Steam Power Press Printers, 1864. Print.

Crandall, Marjorie, et al. *Confederate Imprints: A Check List Based Principally on the Collection of the Boston Athenaeum*. 2 vols. Boston: Boston Athenaeum, 1955. Print.

Craven, Avery. *The Growth of Southern Nationalism, 1848–1861*. Baton Rouge: Louisiana State University Press, 1953. Print.

Crook, D. P. *Diplomacy during the American Civil War*. New York: Wiley, 1975. Print.

Crosby, Frances J. *Dixie for the Union*. New York: Firth, Pond, 1861. Print.

C.S.A.: The Confederate States of America. Dir. Kevin Willmott. 2004. DVD.

Cullop, Charles P. *Confederate Propaganda in Europe, 1861–1865*. Coral Gables: University of Miami Press, 1969. Print.

Current-Garcia, Eugene. "Southern Literary Criticism and the Sectional Dilemma." *Journal of Southern History* 15.3 (1949): 325–41. Print.

Cushing, John D., ed. *More Early Massachusetts Broadsides: The First Century, 1639–1739*. Boston: Massachusetts Historical Society, 1981. Print.

Cushman, Stephen. "Poems of the Civil War, Past and Present." *Value and Vision in American Literature: Literary Essays in Honor of Ray Lewis White.* Ed. Joseph Candido and Charles H. Adams. Athens: Ohio University Press, 1999. 180–201. Print.

Davey, Frank. "Toward the Ends of Regionalism." *Textual Studies in Canada/ Etudes Textuelles au Canada* 9 (1997): 1–17. Print.

Davidson, Cathy A. *Revolution and the Word: The Rise of the Novel in America.* New York: Oxford University Press, 1986. Print.

Davis, Mary Elizabeth Moragne. *The British Partizan: A Tale of the Olden Time.* Macon: Burke, Boykin, 1864. Print.

Davis, William C. *Battle at Bull Run: A History of the First Major Campaign of the Civil War.* Garden City: Doubleday, 1977. Print.

Dawsey, C. B., and J. M. Dawsey. "The Context of Southern Emigration to Brazil." *The Confederados: Old South Immigrants in Brazil.* Ed. C. B. Dawsey and J. M. Dawsey. Tuscaloosa: University of Alabama Press, 1995. 11–23. Print.

Dayan, Joan. "Amorous Bondage: Poe, Ladies, and Slaves." *American Literature* 66.2 (1994): 239–73. Print.

———. "Poe, Persons, and Property." *American Literary History* 11.3 (1999): 405–25. Print.

De Forest, John William. *Miss Ravenel's Conversion from Secession to Loyalty.* New York: Harper and Brothers, 1867. Print.

De Grave, Kathleen. *Swindler, Spy, Rebel: The Confidence Woman in Nineteenth-Century America.* Columbia: University of Missouri Press, 1995. Print.

de Grazia, Margreta, and Peter Stallybrass. "The Materiality of the Shakespearean Text." *Shakespeare Quarterly* 44.3 (Autumn 1993): 255–83. Print.

De Leon, Edwin. *Secret History of Confederate Diplomacy Abroad.* Ed. William C. Davis. Lawrence: University Press of Kansas, 2005. Print.

De Leon, T. C. *Belles, Beaux and Brains of the Sixties.* New York: G. W. Dillingham, 1909. Print.

———, ed. *South Songs: From the Lays of Later Days.* New York: Bledock, 1866. Print.

De Man, Paul. *Blindness and Insight: Essays in the Rhetoric of Contemporary Criticism.* 2nd ed. Minneapolis: University of Minnesota Press, 1983. Print.

De Rosa, Marshall L. *The Confederate Constitution of 1861: An Inquiry into American Constitutionalism.* Columbia: University of Missouri Press, 1991. Print.

Deleuze, Gilles, and Félix Guattari. *Kafka: Toward a Minor Literature.* Trans. Dana Polan. Minneapolis: University of Minnesota Press, 1986. Print.

Derby, James Cephas. *Fifty Years among Authors, Books and Publishers.* New York: G. W. Carleton, 1884. Print.

Derrida, Jacques. *The Ear of the Other: Otobiography, Transference, Translation: Texts and Discussions with Jacques Derrida.* Ed. Christie McDonald et al. Lincoln: University of Nebraska Press, 1988. Print.

Desmos. *Old Toney and His Master, or, the Abolitionist and the Land-Pirate: Founded on Facts: A Tale of 1824–1827.* Nashville: Southwestern Publishing House, 1861. Print.

Detlefsen, Ellen Gay. "Printing in the Confederacy, 1861–1865: A Southern Industry in Wartime." Diss. Columbia University, 1975. Print.

Devens, R. M. *The Pictorial Book of Anecdotes and Incidents of the War of the Rebellion*. Philadelphia: Hartford, 1867. Web. 21 February 2011.

Dichter, Harry, and Elliott Shapiro, eds. *Handbook of Early American Sheet Music, 1768–1889*. New York: Dover, 1977. Print.

Diffley, Kathleen Elizabeth. *To Live and Die: Collected Stories of the Civil War, 1861–1876*. Durham: Duke University Press, 2002. Print.

————. *Where My Heart Is Turning Ever: Civil War Stories and Constitutional Reform, 1861–1876*. Athens: University of Georgia Press, 1992. Print.

"Dis-Union Dixie Land." Philadelphia: J. W. Du Bree, [1860–1865]. *American Memory*. Library of Congress. Web. 21 February 2011.

"Dixey's Land. No.2." Philadelphia: J. H. Johnson, [1860–1865]. *American Memory*. Library of Congress. Web. 21 February 2011.

"Dixie." *The Oxford English Dictionary*. Web. 21 February 2011.

"Dixie's land." Boston: Horace Partridge, [1860–1865]. *American Memory*. Library of Congress. Web. 21 February 2011.

"Dixie's Land." New Orleans: Hopkins, 1859. Print.

"Dixie's Land, No. 5." New York: J. Wrigley, [1860–1865]. *American Memory*. Library of Congress. Web. 21 February 2011.

"Dixie's Land, No. 6." New York: H. De Marsan, [1860–1865]. *American Song Sheets*. Duke University Library. Web. 21 February 2011.

"The Dixie of Our Union." New York: H. De Marsan, [1860–1865]. *American Memory*. Library of Congress. Web. 21 February 2011.

"The Dixie of Our Union." New York: J. Wrigley, [1860–1865]. *American Memory*. Library of Congress. Web. 21 February 2011.

Duck, Leigh Anne. *The Nation's Region: Southern Modernism, Segregation, and U.S. Nationalism*. Athens: University of Georgia Press, 2006. Print.

Dufour, Charles L. *Nine Men in Gray*. Garden City: Doubleday, 1963. Print.

Durden, Robert Franklin. *The Gray and the Black: The Confederate Debate on Emancipation*. Baton Rouge: Louisiana State University Press, 2000. Print.

Early, Jubal. *A Memoir of the Last Year of the War for Independence, in the Confederate States of America*. Lynchburg: Charles W. Button, 1867. Print.

Eaton, Clement. *A History of the Old South*. New York: Macmillan, 1949. Print.

Edenfield, Olivia Carr. "'Endure and Then Endure': Rosa Coldfield's Search for a Role in William Faulkner's *Absalom, Absalom!*" *Southern Literary Journal* 32.1 (1999): 57–68. Print.

Ellinger, Esther Parker. *The Southern War Poetry of the Civil War*. Hershey: The Hershey Press, 1918. Print.

Elshtain, Jean Bethke. *Women and War*. New York: Basic Books, 1987. Print.

Elson, Louis C. *The National Music of America, and Its Sources*. Boston: L. C. Page, 1900. Print.

Emmett, Daniel D. "'Away Down South in Dixie': The Story of Its Origin, as Told by Its Author, Dan. Emmett." *New York Clipper* 6 April 1872. Print.

————. *I Wish I Was in Dixie's Land*. New York: Firth, Pond, 1860. Print.

Entzminger, Betina. *The Belle Gone Bad: White Southern Women Writers and the Dark Seductress*. Baton Rouge: Louisiana State University Press, 2002. Print.

Erkkila, Betsy. "The Poetics of Whiteness: Poe and the Racial Imaginary." *Romancing the Shadow: Poe and Race*. Ed. J. Gerald Kennedy and Liliane Weissberg. Oxford: Oxford University Press, 2001. 41–74. Print.

Evans, Augusta J. *Beulah*. 1859. Ed. Elizabeth Fox-Genovese. Baton Rouge: Louisiana State University Press, 1992. Print.

———. *Macaria*. New York: John Bradburn, 1864. Print.

———. *Macaria; or, Altars of Sacrifice*. Richmond: West and Johnston, 1864. Print.

———. *Macaria; or, Altars of Sacrifice*. 1864. Ed. Drew Gilpin Faust. Baton Rouge: Louisiana State University Press, 1992. Print.

Fahs, Alice. *The Imagined Civil War: Popular Literature of the North and South, 1861–1865*. Chapel Hill: University of North Carolina Press, 2001. Print.

Fahs, Alice, and Joan Waugh, eds. *The Memory of the Civil War in American Culture*. Chapel Hill: University of North Carolina Press, 2004. Print.

Faulkner, William. *Absalom, Absalom!* 1936. New York: Vintage Books, 1990. Print.

Faust, Drew Gilpin. *The Creation of Confederate Nationalism: Ideology and Identity in the Civil War South*. Baton Rouge: Louisiana State University Press, 1988. Print.

———. *The Ideology of Slavery: Proslavery Thought in the Antebellum South, 1830–1860*. Baton Rouge: Louisiana State University Press, 1981. Print.

———. *Mothers of Invention: Women of the Slaveholding South in the American Civil War*. Chapel Hill: University of North Carolina Press, 1996. Print.

———. *A Sacred Circle: The Dilemma of the Intellectual in the Old South, 1840–1860*. Baltimore: Johns Hopkins University Press, 1977. Print.

———. *This Republic of Suffering: Death and the American Civil War*. New York: Alfred A. Knopf, 2008. Print.

Ferry, Anne. *Tradition and the Individual Poem: An Inquiry into Anthologies*. Stanford: Stanford University Press, 2001. Print.

Fetterley, Judith, and Marjorie Pryse. *Writing out of Place: Regionalism, Women, and American Literary Culture*. Urbana: University of Illinois Press, 2003. Print.

Fidler, William Perry. *Augusta Evans Wilson, 1835–1909*. Tuscaloosa: University of Alabama Press, 1951. Print.

———. "Augusta Evans Wilson as Confederate Propagandist." *Alabama Review* 2 (1949): 32–44. Print.

Fliegelman, Jay. "Anthologizing the Situation of American Literature." *American Literature* 65.2 (1993): 334–38. Print.

Flora, Joseph M., Lucinda Hardwick MacKethan, and Todd W. Taylor, eds. *The Companion to Southern Literature*. Baton Rouge: Louisiana State University Press, 2002. Print.

Foner, Eric. *Reconstruction: America's Unfinished Revolution, 1863–1877*. New York: Harper and Row, 1988. Print.

Ford, Sallie Rochester. *Raids and Romance of Morgan and His Men*. Mobile: S. H. Goetzel, 1863. Print.

For the Little Ones. Savannah: John M. Cooper, [1861–65]. Print.

Foster, Gaines M. *Ghosts of the Confederacy: Defeat, the Lost Cause, and the Emergence of the New South, 1865 to 1913*. New York: Oxford University Press, 1987. Print.

Foucault, Michel. *The Archaeology of Knowledge*. Trans. A. M. Sheridan Smith. London: Tavistock Publications, 1972. Print.

———. "What Is an Author?" *Aesthetics, Method, and Epistemology*. Vol. 2 of *Essential Works of Foucault, 1954–1984*. Ed. James D. Faubion. New York: New Press, 1998. 205–22. Print.

Frederick, John T. "American Literary Nationalism: The Process of Definition, 1825–1850." *Review of Politics* 21 (1959): 224–38. Print.

Freehling, William W. *The South vs. the South: How Anti-Confederate Southerners Shaped the Course of the Civil War*. New York: Oxford University Press, 2001. Print.

Freeman, Douglas Southall. *South to Posterity: An Introduction to the Writing of Confederate History*. 1939. Ed. Gary W. Gallagher. Baton Rouge: Louisiana State Press, 1998. Print.

Fritz, Karen E. *Voices in the Storm: Confederate Rhetoric, 1861–1865*. Denton: University of North Texas Press, 1999. Print.

Frost, Linda. *Never One Nation: Freaks, Savages, and Whiteness in U.S. Popular Culture, 1850–1877*. Minneapolis: University of Minnesota Press, 2005. Print.

Galbreath, Charles Burleigh. *Daniel Decatur Emmett, Author of "Dixie."* Columbus: Fred J. Heer, 1904. Print.

Gallagher, Catherine. "When Did the Confederate States of America Free the Slaves?" *Representations* 98 Spring (2007): 53–61. Print.

Gallagher, Gary W. *The Confederate War*. Cambridge: Harvard University Press, 1997. Print.

———. *Lee and His Generals in War and Memory*. Baton Rouge: Louisiana State University Press, 1998. Print.

Gallagher, Gary W., and Alan T. Nolan, eds. *The Myth of the Lost Cause and Civil War History*. Bloomington: Indiana University Press, 2000. Print.

Garber, Marjorie B. *A Manifesto for Literary Studies*. Seattle: University of Washington Press, 2003. Print.

Gardner, Sarah E. *Blood and Irony: Southern White Women's Narratives of the Civil War, 1861–1937*. Chapel Hill: University of North Carolina Press, 2003. Print.

Gellner, Ernest. *Nations and Nationalism*. Ithaca: Cornell University Press, 1983. Print.

Genette, Gerard. *Paratexts: Thresholds of Interpretation*. Trans. Jane E. Lewin. New York: Cambridge University Press, 1997. Print.

Georgini, Sara. "The Poetry of Taste and Power: Reading Southern Prospects and Literary Wants in the Confederate *Index*." Unpublished manuscript.

Giles, Paul. *Transatlantic Insurrections: British Culture and the Formation of American Literature, 1730–1860*. Philadelphia: University of Pennsylvania Press, 2001. Print.

———. "Transnationalism and Classic American Literature." *PMLA* 118.1 (2003): 62–77. Print.

Goddu, Teresa A. "The Ghost of Race: Edgar Allan Poe and the Southern Gothic." *Criticism and the Color Line: Desegregating American Literary Studies*. Ed. Henry B. Wonham. New Brunswick: Rutgers University Press, 1996. 230–50. Print.

Grant, Susan-Mary. *North over South: Northern Nationalism and American Identity in the Antebellum Era*. Lawrence: University Press of Kansas, 2000. Print.

Gray, Richard J. *Southern Aberrations: Writers of the American South and the Problem of Regionalism*. Baton Rouge: Louisiana State University Press, 2000. Print.

Greenfeld, Liah. *Nationalism: Five Roads to Modernity*. Cambridge: Harvard University Press, 1992. Print.

Greeson, Jennifer Rae. *Our South: Geographic Fantasy and the Rise of National Literature*. Cambridge: Harvard University Press, 2010. Print.

Griffin, Martin. *Ashes of the Mind: War and Memory in Northern Literature, 1865–1900*. Amherst: University of Massachusetts Press, 2009. Print.

Griffith, Ben W. "The Lady Novelist and the General: An Unpublished Letter from Augusta Evans to P. G. T. Beauregard." *Mississippi Quarterly* 1 (1957): 97–106. Print.

Griggs, William Clark. *The Elusive Eden: Frank McMullan's Confederate Colony in Brazil*. Austin: University of Texas Press, 1987. Print.

Grobe, Charles. *Dixie's Land, with Brilliant Variations*. New York: Firth, Pond, 1860. Print.

Gross, Jennifer Lynn. "'Lonely Lives Are Not Necessarily Joyless': Augusta Jane Evans's *Macaria* and the Creation of a Place for Single Womanhood in the Postwar South." *American Nineteenth-Century History* 2.1 (2001): 33–52. Print.

Grover, Jan Zita. "The First Living Room War: The Civil War in the Illustrated Press." *Afterimage* 11 (February 1984): 8–11. Print.

Guterl, Matthew Pratt. *American Mediterranean: Southern Slaveholders in the Age of Emancipation*. Cambridge: Harvard University Press, 2008. Print.

Gwin, Minrose. "The Silencing of Rosa Coldfield." *William Faulkner's* Absalom, Absalom!: *A Critical Casebook*. Ed. Fred Hobson. New York: Oxford University Press, 2003. 151–87. Print.

Hall, David D. *Cultures of Print: Essays in the History of the Book*. Amherst: University of Massachusetts Press, 1996. Print.

Hall, Richard. "Loreta Janeta Velazquez: Civil War Soldier and Spy." *Cubans in the Confederacy: José Agustín Quintero, Ambrosio José Gonzales, and Loreta Janeta Velazquez*. Ed. Phillip Thomas Tucker. Jefferson: McFarland, 2002. 225–39. Print.

———. *Patriots in Disguise: Women Warriors of the Civil War*. New York: Paragon House, 1993. Print.

———. *Women on the Civil War Battlefront*. Lawrence: University Press of Kansas, 2006. Print.

Hanna, Alfred Jackson, and Kathryn Abbey Hanna. *Confederate Exiles in Venezuela*. Tuscaloosa: Confederate Publishing, 1960. Print.

Harris, Susan K. *Nineteenth-Century American Women's Novels: Interpretative Strategies*. New York: Cambridge University Press, 1990. Print.

Harter, Eugene C. *The Lost Colony of the Confederacy*. Jackson: University Press of Mississippi, 1985. Print.

Harwell, Richard Barksdale. "Brief Candle: The Confederate Theatre." *The Publications of the American Antiquarian Society* 81.1 (1971): 41–160. Print.

———. *Confederate Belles-Lettres*. Hattiesburg: The Book Farm, 1941. Print.

———. *Confederate Music*. Chapel Hill: University of North Carolina Press, 1950. Print.

———. "A Confederate View of the Southern Poets." *American Literature* 24.1 (1952): 51–61. Print.

———. *The Creed of a Propagandist: Letter from a Confederate Editor*. Atlanta: Association for Education in Journalism, 1951. Print.

———. *In Tall Cotton: The Two Hundred Most Important Confederate Books for the Reader, Researcher, and Collector*. Austin: Jenkins Publishing, 1978. Print.

Harwell, Richard Barksdale, and Marjorie Crandall. *More Confederate Imprints*. Richmond: Virginia State Library, 1957. Print.

Heaps, Willard Allison, and Porter Warrington Heaps. *The Singing Sixties*. Norman: University of Oklahoma Press, 1960. Print.

Heartman, Charles F. *What Constitutes a Confederate Imprint?: Preliminary Suggestions for Bibliographers and Catalogers*. Hattiesburg: The Book Farm, 1939. Print.

Heisser, David C. R. "Bishop Lynch's People: Slaveholding by a South Carolina Prelate." *The South Carolina Historical Magazine* 102.3 (2001): 238–62. Print.

Hewitt, John Hill. *War: A Poem with Copious Notes, Founded on the Revolution of 1861–62*. Richmond: West and Johnston, 1862. Print.

Higgins, Andrew C. "Reconstructing Rebellion: The Politics of Narrative in the Confederate Memoir." *Mississippi Quarterly* 58.1–2 (2004): 119–39. Print.

Higonnet, Margaret R. "Civil Wars and Sexual Territories." *Arms and the Woman: War, Gender, and Literary Representation*. Ed. Helen Margaret Cooper, Adrienne Munich, and Susan Merrill Squier. Chapel Hill: University of North Carolina Press, 1989. 80–96. Print.

Hill, Theophilus Hunter. *Hesper, and Other Poems*. Raleigh: Strother and Marcom, 1861. Print.

———. *Hesper, and Other Poems*. 2nd ed. Raleigh: Branson, Farrar, 1863. Print.

Hobson, Fred C. *Tell about the South: The Southern Rage to Explain*. Baton Rouge: Louisiana State University Press, 1983. Print.

Hoffert, Sylvia D. "Madame Loreta Velazquez: Heroine or Hoaxer?" *Civil War Times Illustrated* 17.3 (1978): 24–31. Print.

Holland, Sharon P. "The Last Word on Racism: New Directions for a Critical Race Theory." *South Atlantic Quarterly* 104.3 (2005): 403–23. Print.

Holstein, Suzy Clarkson. "'Offering up Her Life': Confederate Women on the Altars of Sacrifice." *Southern Studies* 2.2 (1991): 113–30. Print.

Holzer, Harold. "Confederate Caricature of Abraham Lincoln." *Illinois Historical Journal* 80.1 (1987): 23–36. Print.

———. *Lincoln Seen and Heard*. Lawrence: University Press of Kansas, 2000. Print.

Homestead, Melissa J. *American Women Authors and Literary Property, 1822–1869*. New York: Cambridge University Press, 2005. Print.

————. "The Publishing History of Augusta Jane Evans's Confederate Novel *Macaria*: Unwriting Some Lost Cause Myths." *Mississippi Quarterly* 58.3–4 (2005): 665–702. Print.

Hood, John Bell. *Advance and Retreat. Personal Experiences in the United States and Confederate States Armies.* New Orleans: G. T. Beauregard, 1880. Print.

Houston, Natalie M. "Newspaper Poems: Material Texts in the Public Sphere." *Victorian Studies* 50.2 (2008): 233–42. Print.

Hubbard, Charles M. *The Burden of Confederate Diplomacy.* Knoxville: University of Tennessee Press, 1998. Print.

Hubbell, Jay B. "The Literary Apprenticeship of Edgar Allan Poe." *Southern Literary Journal* 2.1 (1969): 99–105. Print.

————. "Literary Nationalism in the Old South." *American Studies in Honor of William Kenneth Boyd.* Ed. David Kelly Jackson. Durham: Duke University Press, 1940. 175–220. Print.

————. *The South in American Literature, 1607–1900.* Durham: Duke University Press, 1954. Print.

Hugo, Victor. *Les Misérables.* 5 vols. Richmond: West and Johnston, 1863–64. Print.

"Hurra for Our Union." N.p., [1861–65]. *American Memory.* Library of Congress. Web. 21 February 2011.

Hutchison, Coleman. "Secret in Altered Lines: The Civil War Song in Manuscript, Print, and Performance Publics." *Cultural Narratives: Textuality and Performance in American Culture before 1900.* Ed. Sandra Gustafson and Caroline Sloat. Notre Dame: University of Notre Dame Press, 2010. 255–75. Print.

Hutchison, Coleman, and Elizabeth Renker. "Popular Poetry in Circulation." *U.S. Popular Print Culture 1860–1920.* Ed. Christine Bold. Vol. 6 of *The Oxford History of Popular Print Culture.* Ed. Gary Kelly. New York: Oxford University Press, 2011. 395–413. Print.

Hutchisson, James M. *Poe.* Jackson: University Press of Mississippi, 2005. Print.

"Independent." *The Oxford English Dictionary.* Web. 21 February 2011.

Inge, M. Thomas, ed. *Literature.* Vol. 7 of *The New Encyclopedia of Southern Culture.* Chapel Hill: University of North Carolina Press, 2008. Print.

Jackall, Robert. *Propaganda.* New York: New York University Press, 1995. Print.

Jackson, David Kelly. *Poe and the Southern Literary Messenger.* Richmond: Press of Dietz Printing, 1934. Print.

Jackson, Leon. *The Business of Letters: Authorial Economies in Antebellum America.* Stanford: Stanford University Press, 2008. Print.

Jackson, Virginia. *Dickinson's Misery: A Theory of Lyric Reading.* Princeton: Princeton University Press, 2005. Print.

"Jackson Is Dead!" N.p., [1861–65]. Print.

Jacobs, Robert D. "Campaign for a Southern Literature: *The Southern Literary Messenger.*" *Southern Literary Journal* 2.1 (1969): 66–98. Print.

James, C. L. R. *Mariners, Renegades, and Castaways: The Story of Herman Melville and the World We Live In.* 1953. Ed. Donald E. Pease. Hanover: Dartmouth College/University Press of New England, 2001. Print.

Janney, Caroline E. *Burying the Dead but Not the Past: Ladies' Memorial Associations and the Lost Cause*. Chapel Hill: University of North Carolina Press, 2008. Print.

"Jeff Davis Forever." N.p., [1861–65]. Print.

"Jeff Davis in the White House." N.p., [1861–65]. Print.

Jefferson, Thomas. *Notes on the State of Virginia*. 1787. Ed. William Harwood Peden. Chapel Hill: University of North Carolina Press, 1955. Print.

Jeffrey, Julie Roy. *Abolitionists Remember: Antislavery Autobiographies and the Unfinished Work of Emancipation*. Chapel Hill: University of North Carolina Press, 2008. Print.

"John Brown's Entrance into Hell." N.p., [1861–65]. Print.

Joint Committee Appointed to Consider and Report on a Selection of New Words for "Dixie." Opelika: n.p., 1905. Print.

Jones, Gavin. *Strange Talk: The Politics of Dialect Literature in Gilded Age America*. Berkeley: University of California Press, 1999. Print.

Jones, Howard. *Blue and Gray Diplomacy: A History of Union and Confederate Foreign Relations*. Chapel Hill: University of North Carolina Press, 2010. Print.

———. *Union in Peril: The Crisis over British Intervention in the Civil War*. Chapel Hill: University of North Carolina Press, 1992. Print.

Jordan-Lake, Joy. *Whitewashing Uncle Tom's Cabin: Nineteenth-Century Women Novelists Respond to Stowe*. Nashville: Vanderbilt University Press, 2005. Print.

Jusdanis, Gregory. *Belated Modernity and Aesthetic Culture: Inventing National Literature*. Minneapolis: University of Minnesota Press, 1991. Print.

———. *The Necessary Nation*. Princeton: Princeton University Press, 2001. Print.

Kaser, David. *Books and Libraries in Camp and Battle: The Civil War Experience*. Westport: Greenwood Press, 1984. Print.

Keckley, Elizabeth. *Behind the Scenes, or, Thirty Years a Slave and Four Years in the White House*. New York: G. W. Carlton, 1868. Print.

Kelley, Mary. *Private Woman, Public Stage: Literary Domesticity in Nineteenth-Century America*. 1984. Chapel Hill: University of North Carolina Press, 2002. Print.

Kennedy, J. Gerald. "'A Mania for Composition': Poe's Annus Mirabilis and the Violence of Nation Building." *American Literary History* 17.1 (2005): 1–35. Print.

Kerkering, John D. *The Poetics of National and Racial Identity in Nineteenth-Century American Literature*. New York: Cambridge University Press, 2003. Print.

King, Richard H. *A Southern Renaissance: The Cultural Awakening of the American South, 1930–1955*. New York: Oxford University Press, 1980. Print.

Klein, Stacey Jean. *Margaret Junkin Preston, Poet of the Confederacy: A Literary Life*. Columbia: University of South Carolina Press, 2007. Print.

Kolchin, Peter. *A Sphinx on the American Land: The Nineteenth-Century South in Comparative Perspective*. Baton Rouge: Louisiana State University Press, 2003. Print.

Kurtz, Richard L. "Occasional Verse as History." *North Carolina Literary Review* 5 (1996): 187–88. Print.

LaCapra, Dominick. *History, Politics, and the Novel*. Ithaca: Cornell University Press, 1987. Print.

Ladd, Barbara. *Nationalism and the Color Line in George W. Cable, Mark Twain, and William Faulkner*. Baton Rouge: Louisiana State University, 1996. Print.

Lasswell, Harold D., et al., eds. *Propaganda and Communication in World History*. Honolulu: University Press of Hawaii, 1979. Print.

Lays of the South: Verses Relative to the War between the Two Sections of the American States. Liverpool, 1864. Print.

Lazure, Erica Plouffe. "A Literary Motherhood: Rosa Coldfield's Design in *Absalom, Absalom!*" *Mississippi Quarterly* 62.3–4 (2009): 479–96. Print.

Lee, Charles Robert. *The Confederate Constitutions*. Chapel Hill: University of North Carolina Press, 1963. Print.

Lee, Maurice S. "Absolute Poe: His System of Transcendental Racism." *American Literature* 75.4 (2003): 751–81. Print.

Leonard, Elizabeth D. *All the Daring of the Soldier: Women of the Civil War Armies*. New York: W. W. Norton, 1999. Print.

Levander, Caroline. "Confederate Cuba." *American Literature* 78.4 (2006): 821–45. Print.

Levine, Bruce C. *Confederate Emancipation: Southern Plans to Free and Arm Slaves during the Civil War*. New York: Oxford University Press, 2006. Print.

Levine, Robert S. *Dislocating Race and Nation: Episodes in Nineteenth-Century American Literary Nationalism*. Chapel Hill: University of North Carolina Press, 2008. Print.

Lewis, Clay. "Confederate Testimony." *Sewanee Review* 108.2 (2000): 271–83. Print.

Lincoln, Abraham. *The Collected Works of Abraham Lincoln*. 9 vols. Ed. Roy P. Basler. New Brunswick: Rutgers University Press, 1953. Print.

The Lincoln and Hamlin Songster, or, the Continental Melodist. Philadelphia: Fisher and Brother, 1860. Print.

Loeffelholz, Mary. *From School to Salon: Reading Nineteenth-Century American Women's Poetry*. Princeton: Princeton University Press, 2004. Print.

London, Lawrence F. "Confederate Literature and its Publishers." *Studies in Southern History*. Ed. Joseph Sitterson. Chapel Hill: University of North Carolina Press, 1957. Print.

Lott, Eric. *Love and Theft: Blackface Minstrelsy and the American Working Class*. New York: Oxford University Press, 1993. Print.

Loughran, Trish. *The Republic in Print: Print Culture in the Age of U.S. Nation Building, 1770–1870*. New York: Columbia University Press, 2007. Print.

Maddex, Jack. *The Reconstruction of Edward A. Pollard: A Rebel's Conversion to Postbellum Unionism*. Chapel Hill: University of North Carolina Press, 1974. Print.

Mahar, William. "March to the Music: Twenty Top Hits of the Sixties." *Civil War Times Illustrated* 23.5 (1984): 13–14, 18, 41–45. Print.

Manns, Jean. *I Wish I Was in Dixie Land*. New York: Firth, Pond, 1860. Print.

Marlin, Randal. *Propaganda and the Ethics of Persuasion*. Orchard Park: Broadview Press, 2002. Print.

Marotti, Arthur F. *Manuscript, Print, and the English Renaissance Lyric*. Ithaca: Cornell University Press, 1995. Print.

Marshall, Anne E. *Creating a Confederate Kentucky: The Lost Cause and Civil War Memory in a Border State*. Chapel Hill: University of North Carolina Press, 2010. Print.

Marten, James Alan. *The Children's Civil War*. Chapel Hill: University of North Carolina Press, 1998. Print.

Mason, Emily Virginia, ed. *The Southern Poems of the War*. Baltimore: J. Murphy, 1867. Print.

Massey, Mary Elizabeth. *Ersatz in the Confederacy*. Columbia: University of South Carolina Press, 1952. Print.

Masten, Jeffrey. "Queer Philology." Unpublished manuscript.

Matthews, Brander. "The Songs of the War." *The Century* 34 (1886): 619–29. Print.

Mayers, Adam. *Dixie and the Dominion: Canada, the Confederacy, and the War for the Union*. Toronto: Dundurn Press, 2003. Print.

McCandless, Amy Thompson. "Augusta Jane Evans Wilson." *The History of Southern Women's Literature*. Ed. Carolyn Perry and Mary Louise Weaks. Baton Rouge: Louisiana State University Press, 2002. 150–55. Print.

———. "Concepts of Patriarchy in the Popular Novels of Antebellum Southern Women." *Studies in Popular Culture* 10.2 (1987): 1–16. Print.

McCardell, John. *The Idea of a Southern Nation: Southern Nationalists and Southern Nationalism, 1830–1860*. New York: Norton, 1979. Print.

McCurry, Stephanie. *Confederate Reckoning: Power and Politics in the Civil War South*. Cambridge: Harvard University Press, 2010. Print.

McDowell, Deborah E., and Arnold Rampersad, eds. *Slavery and the Literary Imagination*. Baltimore: Johns Hopkins University Press, 1989. Print.

McGill, Meredith L. *American Literature and the Culture of Reprinting, 1834–1853*. Philadelphia: University of Pennsylvania Press, 2003. Print.

———. "The Duplicity of the Pen." *Language Machines: Technologies of Literary and Cultural Production*. Ed. Jeffrey Masten, Peter Stallybrass, and Nancy Vickers. New York: Routledge, 1997. 39–71. Print.

McPherson, James M. *Battle Cry of Freedom: The Civil War Era*. New York: Oxford University Press, 1988. Print.

———. *For Cause and Comrades: Why Men Fought in the Civil War*. New York: Oxford University Press, 1997. Print.

Melville, Herman, *Moby-Dick; or, the Whale*. 1852. Ed. Harrison Hayford, Hershel Parker, and G. Thomas Tanselle. Evanston: Northwestern University Press, 1988. Print.

———. *White-Jacket, or, the World in a Man-of-War*. 1850. Ed. Harrison Hayford, Hershel Parker, and G. Thomas Tanselle. Evanston: Northwestern University Press, 2000. Print.

Mesquita, Paula Elyseu. "Daughters of Necessity, Mothers of Resource: White Women and the War in *Absalom, Absalom!*" *Faulkner and War: Faulkner and Yoknapatawpha, 2001*. Ed. Noel Polk and Ann J. Abadie. Jackson: University Press of Mississippi, 2004. 55–69. Print.

"Messenger." *The Oxford English Dictionary.* Web. 21 February 2011.

Miller, Cristanne. "Poetry, Society, and the American Civil War." *Walking on a Trail of Words: Essays in Honor of Professor Agnieszka Salska.* Ed. Jadwiga Maszewska and Zbigniew Maszewski. Poland: Wydawnictwo Uniwersytetu Lodzkiego, 2007. 103–15. Print.

Miller, D. A. *Bringing out Roland Barthes.* Berkeley: University of California Press, 1992. Print.

Miller, Stephen Franks. *Ahab Lincoln: A Tragedy of the Potomac.* 1861. Ed. Richard Barksdale Harwell. Chicago: Civil War Round Table, 1958. Print.

Mills, Cynthia, and Pamela H. Simpson. *Monuments to the Lost Cause: Women, Art, and the Landscapes of Southern Memory.* Knoxville: University of Tennessee Press, 2003. Print.

Moore, Frank, ed. *Rebel Rhymes and Rhapsodies.* New York: G. P. Putnam, 1864. Print.

Moore, Olin H. "Some Translations of *Les Misérables.*" *Modern Language Notes* 74.3 (1959): 240–46. Print.

Morrison, Toni. *Playing in the Dark: Whiteness and the Literary Imagination.* New York: Vintage, 1993. Print.

Moseley, Caroline. "Irrepressible Conflict: Differences between Northern and Southern Songs of the Civil War." *Journal of Popular Culture* 25.2 (1991): 45–56. Print.

Moss, Elizabeth. *Domestic Novelists in the Old South: Defenders of Southern Culture.* Baton Rouge: Louisiana State University Press, 1992. Print.

Moss, Sidney Phil. *Poe's Literary Battles: The Critic in the Context of His Literary Milieu.* Durham: Duke University Press, 1963. Print.

Moss, William. *Confederate Broadside Poems: An Annotated Descriptive Bibliography Based on the Collection of the Z. Smith Reynolds Library of Wake Forest University.* Westport: Meckler, 1988. Print.

Mott, Frank Luther. *A History of American Magazines.* 5 vols. Cambridge: Harvard University Press, 1957. Print.

Muhlenfeld, Elisabeth. "The Civil War and Authorship." Rubin et al., eds. 178–87. Print.

Muzzy, A. W. *Dixie Unionized.* New York: Firth, Pond, 1861. Print.

Nathan, Hans. *Dan Emmett and the Rise of Early Negro Minstrelsy.* Norman: University of Oklahoma Press, 1962. Print.

Neely, Mark E., Harold Holzer, and G. S. Boritt. *The Confederate Image: Prints of the Lost Cause.* Chapel Hill: University of North Carolina Press, 1987. Print.

Neff, John R. *Honoring the Civil War Dead: Commemoration and the Problem of Reconciliation.* Lawrence: University Press of Kansas, 2005. Print.

Nelson, Dana D. *National Manhood: Capitalist Citizenship and the Imagined Fraternity of White Men.* Durham: Duke University Press, 1998. Print.

Nichols, Shannon L. "Augusta Jane Evans Wilson (1835–1909)." *Nineteenth-Century American Women Writers: A Bio-Bibliographical Critical Sourcebook.* Ed. Denise D. Knight and Emmanuel S. Nelson. Westport: Greenwood, 1997. 479–83. Print.

"Niggers in Convention. Sumner's Speech." N.p., [1861–65]. Print.

Nolan, Alan T. "The Anatomy of the Myth." *The Myth of the Lost Cause and Civil War History*. Ed. Gary W. Gallagher and Alan T. Nolan. Bloomington: Indiana University Press, 2000. 11–34. Print.

Northrop, Claudian Bird. *Southern Odes*. Charleston: Harper and Calvo, Caloric Printers, 1861. Print.

Oates, Stephen B. "Henry Hotze: Confederate Agent Abroad." *The Historian* 27 (1965): 131–54. Print.

O'Brien, Michael. *Conjectures of Order: Intellectual Life and the American South, 1810–1860*. 2 vols. Chapel Hill: University of North Carolina Press, 2004. Print.

O'Brien, Patrick Karl. *The Economic Effects of the American Civil War*. Atlantic Highlands: Humanities Press International, 1988. Print.

"Occasional." *The Oxford English Dictionary*. Web. 21 February 2011.

"Oh! Abraham, Resign!" N.p., [1861–65]. Print.

Oram, Richard W. "The Confederate Thackeray: Evans and Cogswell's *The Adventures of Philip*." *American Book Collector* 4.4 (1983): 27–30. Print.

"Our Yankee Generals." New York: H. De Marsan, [1860–1865]. *American Memory*. Library of Congress. Web. 21 February 2011.

Owsley, Frank Lawrence, et al. *King Cotton Diplomacy: Foreign Relations of the Confederate States of America*. 3rd ed. Tuscaloosa: University of Alabama Press, 2008. Print.

Page, Thomas Nelson. "Literature in the South since the War." *Lippincott's Monthly Magazine* December 1891: 740–56. Print.

Parks, Edd Winfield, ed. *The Essays of Henry Timrod*. Athens: University of Georgia Press, 1942. Print.

Parks, Edd Winfield. *William Gilmore Simms as Literary Critic*. Athens: University of Georgia Press, 1961. Print.

Parks, Edd Winfield, and Aileen Wells Parks, eds. *The Collected Poems of Henry Timrod: A Variorum Edition*. Athens: University of Georgia Press, 1965. Print.

Parrington, Vernon Louis. *The Romantic Revolution in America, 1800–1860*. Vol. 2 of *Main Currents in American Thought*. 1927. Norman: University of Oklahoma Press, 1987. Print.

Parrish, T. Michael, and Robert M. Willingham Jr. *Confederate Imprints: A Bibliography of Southern Publications from Secession to Surrender*. Austin: Jenkins Publishing, 1987. Print.

"Patriotism." *The Oxford English Dictionary*. Web. 21 February 2011.

Pearce, Roy Harvey. *The Continuity of American Poetry*. Princeton: Princeton University Press, 1969. Print.

Pecquet du Bellet, Paul. *The Diplomacy of the Confederate Cabinet of Richmond and Its Agents Abroad*. Ed. William Stanley Hoole. Tuscaloosa: Confederate Publishing, 1963. Print.

Pedersen, E. Martin. "'The Music Changed at Fort Wagner': The Multicultural Impact of the Civil War on the English Language Music of the United States." *Red Badges of Courage: Wars and Conflicts in American Culture*. Ed. Biancamarie Pisapia, Ugo Rubeo, and Anna Scacchi. Rome, Italy: Bulzoni, 1998. 532–43. Print.

Perkins, David. *Is Literary History Possible?* Baltimore: Johns Hopkins University Press, 1992. Print.

Pike, Albert, and J. C. Viereck. *The War Song of Dixie*. New Orleans: P. P. Werlein and Halsey, 1861. Print.

"Polite." *The Oxford English Dictionary*. Web. 21 February 2011.

Pollard, Edward Alfred. *The Lost Cause: A New Southern History of the War of the Confederates*. New York: E. B. Treat, 1866. Print.

Pollin, Burton R., and Joseph V. Ridgely, eds. *Writings in the Southern Literary Messenger, Nonfictional Prose*. Vol. 5 of *The Collected Writings of Edgar Allan Poe*. New York: Gordian Press, 1997. Print.

Poole, W. Scott. *Never Surrender: Confederate Memory and Conservatism in the South Carolina Upcountry*. Athens: University of Georgia Press, 2004. Print.

"Popular." *The Oxford English Dictionary*. Web. 21 February 2011.

Potter, David Morris. *The South and the Sectional Conflict*. Baton Rouge: Louisiana State University Press, 1968. Print.

Power, J. Tracy. *Lee's Miserables: Life in the Army of Northern Virginia from the Wilderness to Appomattox*. Chapel Hill: University of North Carolina Press, 1998. Print.

Preston, Margaret Junkin. *Beechenbrook: A Rhyme of the War*. Richmond: J. W. Randolph, 1865. Print.

Quint, David. *Epic and Empire: Politics and Generic Form from Virgil to Milton*. Princeton: Princeton University Press, 1993. Print.

Rable, George C. *Civil Wars: Women and the Crisis of Southern Nationalism*. Urbana: University of Illinois Press, 1989. Print.

———. *The Confederate Republic: A Revolution against Politics*. Chapel Hill: University of North Carolina Press, 1994. Print.

Ransom, Roger L. *Conflict and Compromise: The Political Economy of Slavery, Emancipation, and the American Civil War*. New York: Cambridge University Press, 1989. Print.

"Rebel Gunpowder." N.p., [1861–65]. Print.

"Relic." *The Oxford English Dictionary*. Web. 21 February 2011.

Renker, Elizabeth, and Douglas Robillard, eds. *Melville the Poet*. Special issue of *Leviathan: A Journal of Melville Studies* 9.3 (2007). Print.

Rescher, Nicholas. *Niagara-on-the-Lake as a Confederate Refuge (1866–1869)*. Fox Chapel: NAP Publications, 2003. Print.

Richards, Eliza. *Gender and the Poetics of Reception in Poe's Circle*. New York: Cambridge University Press, 2004. Print.

———. "U.S. Civil War Print Culture and Popular Imagination." *American Literary History* 17.2 (2005): 349–59. Print.

Ridgely, Joseph V. "The Authorship of the 'Paulding-Drayton Review.'" *Poe Studies Association Newsletter* 20.2 (1992): 1–3, 6. Print.

———. *Nineteenth-Century Southern Literature*. Lexington: University Press of Kentucky, 1980. Print.

Riepma, Anne Sophie. *Fire and Fiction: Augusta Jane Evans in Context*. Amsterdam: Rodopi, 2000. Print.

Roberts, Diane. *Faulkner and Southern Womanhood*. Athens: University of Georgia Press, 1994. Print.

Roberts-Miller, Patricia. *Fanatical Schemes: Proslavery Rhetoric and the Tragedy of Consensus*. Tuscaloosa: University of Alabama Press, 2009. Print.

Romero, Lora. *Home Fronts: Domesticity and Its Critics in the Antebellum United States*. Durham: Duke University Press, 1997. Print.

Romine, Scott. *The Narrative Forms of Southern Community*. Baton Rouge: Louisiana State University Press, 1999. Print.

Rosenthal, Bernard. "Poe, Slavery, and the *Southern Literary Messenger*: A Reexamination." *Poe Studies* 7 (1974): 29–38. Print.

Rosselet, Jeanne. "First Reactions to *Les Misérables* in the United States." *Modern Language Notes* 67.1 (1952): 39–43. Print.

Rowe, John Carlos. "Nineteenth-Century United States Literary Culture and Transnationality." *PMLA* 118.1 (2003): 78–89. Print.

———. "Poe, Antebellum Slavery, and Modern Criticism." *Poe's Pym: Critical Explorations*. Ed. Richard Kopley. Durham: Duke University Press, 1992. 117–38. Print.

Royster, Charles. *The Destructive War: William Tecumseh Sherman, Stonewall Jackson, and the Americans*. New York: Knopf, 1991. Print.

Rubin, Anne Sarah. *A Shattered Nation: The Rise and Fall of the Confederacy, 1861–1868*. Chapel Hill: University of North Carolina Press, 2005. Print.

Rubin, Louis Decimus. *The Edge of the Swamp: A Study in the Literature and Society of the Old South*. Baton Rouge: Louisiana State University Press, 1989. Print.

Rubin, Louis Decimus, and C. Hugh Holman, eds. *Southern Literary Study: Problems and Possibilities*. Chapel Hill: University of North Carolina Press, 1975. Print.

Rubin, Louis Decimus, et al., eds. *The History of Southern Literature*. Baton Rouge: Louisiana State University Press, 1985. Print.

[Ryan, Abram Joseph, ed.]. *War Lyrics and Songs of the South*. N.p., 1866. Print.

Sacks, Howard L., and Judith R. Sacks. *Way up North in Dixie: A Black Family's Claim to the Confederate Anthem*. Washington: Smithsonian Institution, 1993. Print.

Samuels, Shirley. *Facing America: Iconography and the Civil War*. New York: Oxford University Press, 2004. Print.

Sandburg, Carl. *Abraham Lincoln, the War Years*. 4 vols. New York: Harcourt Brace, 1939. Print.

Savage, Kirk. *Standing Soldiers, Kneeling Slaves: Race, War, and Monument in Nineteenth-Century America*. Princeton: Princeton University Press, 1997. Print.

Schantz, Mark S. *Awaiting the Heavenly Country: The Civil War and America's Culture of Death*. Ithaca: Cornell University Press, 2008. Print.

Schivelbusch, Wolfgang. *The Culture of Defeat: On National Trauma, Mourning, and Recovery*. Trans. Jefferson Chase. New York: Metropolitan Books, 2003. Print.

Schultz, Jane E. *Women at the Front: Hospital Workers in Civil War America*. Chapel Hill: University of North Carolina Press, 2004. Print.

Schultz, Kirsten M. "The Production and Consumption of Confederate Songsters." *Bugle Resounding: Music and Musicians of the Civil War Era*. Ed. Bruce C. Kelley and Mark A. Snell. Columbia: University of Missouri Press, 2004. 133–68. Print.

Schwartz, Barry. *Abraham Lincoln and the Forge of National Memory*. Chicago: University of Chicago Press, 2000. Print.

Seals, A. B. *Rockford; a Romance*. Atlanta: Franklin Printing House, 1861. Print.

Sexton, Rebecca Grant. *A Southern Woman of Letters: The Correspondence of Augusta Jane Evans Wilson*. Columbia: University of South Carolina Press, 2002. Print.

Shakespeare, William. *The Complete Works*. Ed. Stanley W. Wells and Gary Taylor. New York: Oxford University Press, 1986. Print.

Sharkey, P. "Freedom's Guide." New York: J. Wrigley, [1860–1865]. *American Song Sheets*. Duke University Library. Web. 21 February 2011.

Sheehan-Dean, Aaron Charles. *Why Confederates Fought: Family and Nation in Civil War Virginia*. Chapel Hill: University of North Carolina Press, 2007. Print.

Sheerin, Robert. "'Dixie' and Its Author." *The Century* 50.6 (1895): 958–60. Print.

Shelton, William J. *Confederate Poems*. Lynchburg: Virginian Power Press Job Office, 1862. Print.

Shepperson, William G., ed. *War Songs of the South*. Richmond: West and Johnston, 1862. Print.

Silber, Irwin, and Jerry Silverman, eds. *Songs of the Civil War*. New York: Columbia University Press, 1960. Print.

Silber, Nina. *Gender and the Sectional Conflict*. Chapel Hill: University of North Carolina Press, 2008. Print.

———. *The Romance of Reunion: Northerners and the South, 1865–1900*. Chapel Hill: University of North Carolina Press, 1993. Print.

Silverman, Kenneth. *Edgar A. Poe: Mournful and Never-Ending Remembrance*. New York: HarperCollins, 1991.

Simmons, Donald C. *Confederate Settlements in British Honduras*. Jefferson: McFarland, 2001. Print.

Simms, William Gilmore, ed. *War Poetry of the South*. New York: Richardson, 1867. Print.

Simms, William Gilmore. *The Wigwam and the Cabin*. New and rev. ed. New York: Redfield, 1856. Print.

Simpson, John A. "Shall We Change the Words of Dixie?" *Southern Folklore Quarterly* 45 (1981): 19–40. Print.

Simpson, Lewis P. *The Man of Letters in New England and the South: Essays on the History of the Literary Vocation in America*. Baton Rouge: Louisiana State University Press, 1973. Print.

Sizer, Lyde Cullen. *The Political Work of Northern Women Writers and the Civil War, 1850–1872*. Chapel Hill: University of North Carolina Press, 2000. Print.

Skaggs, Merrill Maguire. "Varieties of Local Color." Rubin et al., eds. 219–27. Print.

Smith, Jon, and Deborah N. Cohn, eds. *Look Away! The U.S. South in New World Studies*. Durham: Duke University Press, 2004. Print.

Smith, William Russell. *The Royal Ape: A Dramatic Poem*. Richmond: West and Johnston, 1863. Print.

Snowden, Yates. *War-Time Publications (1861–1865) from the Press of Walker, Evans and Cogswell Co.* Charleston: Walker, Evans and Cogswell, 1922. Print.

Sofer, Naomi Z. *Making The "America of Art": Cultural Nationalism and Nineteenth-Century Women Writers*. Columbus: Ohio State University Press, 2005. Print.

"Song! Hail to the South." N.p., [1861–65]. Print.

Songs of the South. Richmond: J. W. Randolph, 1862. Print.

Sorby, Angela. *Schoolroom Poets: Childhood, Performance, and the Place of American Poetry, 1865–1917*. Durham: University of New Hampshire Press, 2005. Print.

"A Southern Scene." N.p., [1861–65]. Print.

Spaeth, Sigmund Gottfried. *A History of Popular Music in America*. New York: Random House, 1948. Print.

Spencer, Benjamin T. "A National Literature, 1837–1855." *American Literature* 8.2 (1936): 125–59. Print.

———. *The Quest for Nationality: An American Literary Campaign*. Syracuse: Syracuse University Press, 1957. Print.

Spivak, Gayatri C. *A Critique of Postcolonial Reason: Toward a History of the Vanishing Present*. Cambridge: Harvard University Press, 1999. Print.

Stampp, Kenneth M. *The Imperiled Union: Essays on the Background of the Civil War*. New York: Oxford University Press, 1980. Print.

Stanton, H. S. *Dixie War Song*. New Orleans: Blackmar and Bros., 1861. Print.

Stern, Julia A. *Mary Chesnut's Civil War Epic*. Chicago: University of Chicago Press, 2010. Print.

Stowe, Harriet Beecher. *Three Novels*. Ed. Kathryn Kish Sklar. New York: Library of America, 1982. Print.

Strauss, Jennifer. "Anthologies and Orthodoxies." *Australian Literary Studies* 13.1 (1987): 87–95. Print.

Sullivan, James D. *On the Walls and in the Streets: American Poetry Broadsides from the 1960s*. Urbana: University of Illinois Press, 1997. Print.

Sullivan, Walter. "Civil War Diaries and Memoirs." *The History of Southern Women's Literature*. Ed. Carolyn Perry and Mary Louise Weaks. Baton Rouge: Louisiana State University Press, 2002. 109–18. Print.

Sundquist, Eric J. *Faulkner: The House Divided*. Baltimore: Johns Hopkins University Press, 1983. Print.

Swain, Margie P. *Mara; or, A Romance of the War*. Selma: Mississippian Steam Book and Job Office, 1864. Print.

Sweet, Timothy. *Traces of War: Poetry, Photography, and the Crisis of the Union*. Baltimore: Johns Hopkins University Press, 1990. Print.

Tamarkin, Elisa. *Anglophilia: Deference, Devotion, and Antebellum America*. Chicago: University of Chicago Press, 2008. Print.

Tate, Allen. "The New Provincialism: With an Epilogue on the Southern Novel." *Virginia Quarterly Review* 21.2 (Spring 1945): 262–72. Print.

Taylor, Philip M. *Munitions of the Mind: A History of Propaganda from the Ancient World to the Present Era*. 3rd ed. New York: Manchester University Press, 2003. Print.

Tebbel, John William. *A History of Book Publishing in the United States*. New York: R. R. Bowker, 1972. Print.

Tennenhouse, Leonard. *The Importance of Feeling English: American Literature and the British Diaspora, 1750–1850.* Princeton: Princeton University Press, 2007. Print.

Teorey, Matthew. "Unmasking the Gentleman Soldier in the Memoirs of Two Cross-Dressing Female U.S. Civil War Soldiers." *War, Literature, and the Arts: An International Journal of the Humanities* 20.1–2 (2008): 74–93. Print.

Thomas, Dwight, and David Kelly Jackson. *The Poe Log: A Documentary Life of Edgar Allan Poe, 1809–1849.* Boston: G. K. Hall, 1987. Print.

Thomas, Emory M. *The Confederacy as a Revolutionary Experience.* 1971. Columbia: University of South Carolina Press, 1991. Print.

———. *The Confederate Nation, 1861–1865.* New York: Harper and Row, 1979. Print.

Thornton, Mark, and Robert B. Ekelund. *Tariffs, Blockades, and Inflation: The Economics of the Civil War.* Wilmington: SR Books, 2004. Print.

Tompkins, Jane P. *Sensational Designs: The Cultural Work of American Fiction, 1790–1860.* New York: Oxford University Press, 1986. Print.

Tourgée, Albion W. "The South as a Field for Fiction." *Forum* 6 (December 1888): 404–13. Print.

"The Traitors' Land." New York: H. De Marsan, [1860–1865.] *American Memory.* Library of Congress. Web. 21 February 2011.

Trefousse, Hans L. *"First among Equals": Abraham Lincoln's Reputation during His Administration.* New York: Fordham University Press, 2005. Print.

Trubey, Elizabeth Fekete. "Emancipating the Lettered Slave: Sentiment and Slavery in Augusta Evans's *St. Elmo.*" *American Literature* 77.1 (2005): 123–50. Print.

Tucker, Beverley D. *Nathaniel Beverley Tucker: Prophet of the Confederacy 1784–1851.* Tokyo: Nan'un-do, 1979. Print.

Tucker, Nathaniel Beverley. *A Key to the Disunion Conspiracy. The Partisan Leader.* New York: Rudd and Carleton, 1861. Print.

———. *The Partisan Leader.* Ed. Carl Bridenbaugh. New York: A. A. Knopf, 1933. Print.

———. *The Partisan Leader: A Novel and an Apocalypse of the Origin and Struggles of the Southern Confederacy.* Ed. Thomas Ware. Richmond: West and Johnston, 1862. Print.

———. *The Partisan Leader; a Tale of the Future.* Washington: [Duff Green, 1836]. Print.

———. *The Partisan Leader; a Tale of the Future.* Ed. C. Hugh Holman. Chapel Hill: University of North Carolina Press, 1971. Print.

Tucker, Phillip Thomas, ed. *Cubans in the Confederacy: José Agustín Quintero, Ambrosio José Gonzales, and Loreta Janeta Velazquez.* Jefferson: McFarland, 2002. Print.

[Turner, Joseph Addison.] *The Old Plantation: A Poem.* Turnworld [Plantation, Putnam County, Ga.]: Countryman Printers, 1862. Print.

United States. War Department. *The War of the Rebellion: A Compilation of the Official Records of the Union and Confederate Armies.* 1897. Ser. 1, Vol. 51 (Part 2). Web. 21 February 2011.

United States. Naval War Office. *Official Records of the Union and Confederate Navies in the War of the Rebellion*. 1922. Ser. 2, Vol. 3. Web. 21 February 2011.

"Utopia." *The Oxford English Dictionary*. Web. 21 February 2011.

Van Tuyll, Debra. "Essential Labor: Confederate Printers at Home and at War." *Journalism History* 31.2 (2005): 75–87. Print.

Vandiver, Frank Everson. *Their Tattered Flags: The Epic of the Confederacy*. New York: Harper's Magazine Press, 1970. Print.

Varon, Elizabeth R. *Disunion!: The Coming of the American Civil War, 1789–1859*. Chapel Hill: University of North Carolina Press, 2008. Print.

Velazquez, Loreta Janeta. *The Woman in Battle: A Narrative of the Exploits, Adventures, and Travels of Madame Loreta Janeta Velazquez, Otherwise Known as Lieutenant Harry T. Buford, Confederate States Army*. Richmond: Dustin, Gilman, 1876. Print.

Vollaro, Daniel R. "Lincoln, Stowe, and the 'Little Woman/Great War' Story: The Making, and Breaking, of a Great American Anecdote." *Journal of the Abraham Lincoln Association* 30.1 (2009): 30 pars. 12 August 2009. Web. 21 February 2011.

Waal, Carla. "The First Original Confederate Drama: *The Guerillas*." *Virginia Magazine of History and Biography* 70.4 (October 1962): 459–67. Print.

Wagner-Martin, Linda. "Rosa Coldfield as Daughter: Another of Faulkner's Lost Children." *Studies in American Fiction* 19.1 (1991): 1–13. Print.

Wakelyn, Jon L. *The Politics of a Literary Man: William Gilmore Simms*. Westport: Greenwood Press, 1973. Print.

Walston, Mark L. "Voices of the Holy War: Occasional Verse of the American Civil War." *Victorians Institute Journal* 15 (1987): 93–104. Print.

Watkins, Sam R. *1861 vs. 1882. "Co. Aytch," Maury Grays, First Tennessee Regiment; or, a Side Show of the Big Show*. Nashville: Cumberland Presbyterian Publishing House, 1882. Print.

Watson, Charles S. *From Nationalism to Secessionism: The Changing Fiction of William Gilmore Simms*. Westport: Greenwood Press, 1993. Print.

———. *The History of Southern Drama*. Lexington: University Press of Kentucky, 1997. Print.

———. "Simms's Review of *Uncle Tom's Cabin*." *American Literature* 48.3 (1976): 365–68. Print.

Watson, Ritchie Devon. *Normans and Saxons: Southern Race Mythology and the Intellectual History of the American Civil War*. Baton Rouge: Louisiana State University Press, 2008. Print.

Watt, Tessa. *Cheap Print and Popular Piety, 1550–1640*. New York: Cambridge University Press, 1991. Print.

Watts, Charles H., II. "Poe, Irving and the *Southern Literary Messenger*." *American Literature* 27 (1955): 249–51. Print.

Weber, Randal M. *We're All in Arms in Dixie*. Nashville: J. A. McClure, 1861. Print.

Weinstein, Cindy. "*Uncle Tom's Cabin* and the South." *The Cambridge Companion to Harriet Beecher Stowe*. Ed. Cindy Weinstein. New York: Cambridge University Press, 2004. 39–57. Print.

Weinstein, Philip M. *Faulkner's Subject: A Cosmos No One Owns.* New York: Cambridge University Press, 1992. Print.

"We're Marching Down to Dixie's Land." Philadelphia: Johnson, [1860–1865]. Web. *American Memory.* Library of Congress. Web. 21 February 2011.

Werlich, David P. *Admiral of the Amazon: John Randolph Tucker, His Confederate Colleagues, and Peru.* Charlottesville: University Press of Virginia, 1990. Print.

Whalen, Terence. "Average Racism: Poe, Slavery, and the Wages of Literary Nationalism." *Romancing the Shadow: Poe and Race.* Ed. Gerald Kennedy and Liliane Weissberg. New York: Oxford University Press, 2001. 3–40. Print.

———. *Edgar Allan Poe and the Masses: The Political Economy of Literature in Antebellum America.* Princeton: Princeton University Press, 1999. Print.

White, Richard Grant. *National Hymns: How They Are Written and How They Are Not Written.* New York: Rudd and Carleton, 1861. Print.

Whites, LeeAnn. *The Civil War as a Crisis in Gender: Augusta, Georgia, 1860–1890.* Athens: University of Georgia Press, 1995. Print.

———. *Gender Matters: Civil War, Reconstruction, and the Making of the New South.* New York: Palgrave Macmillan, 2005. Print.

Whitman, Walt. *Complete Poetry and Collected Prose.* Ed. Justin Kaplan. New York: Library of America, 1982. Print.

Wiley, Bell Irvin. *The Life of Billy Yank, the Common Soldier of the Union.* New York: Bobbs-Merrill, 1943. Print.

———. *The Life of Johnny Reb, the Common Soldier of the Confederacy.* New York: Bobbs-Merrill, 1943. Print.

Williams, Alfred M. "Folk-Songs of the Civil War." *Journal of American Folklore* 5.19 (October–December 1892): 265–83. Print.

Wilson, Augusta Jane Evans. *Macaria; or Altars of Sacrifice.* New York: G. W. Dillingham, 1896. Print.

Wilson, Charles Reagan. *Baptized in Blood: The Religion of the Lost Cause, 1865–1920.* 1980. Athens: University of Georgia Press, 2009. Print.

Wilson, Edmund. *Patriotic Gore: Studies in the Literature of the American Civil War.* New York: Oxford University Press, 1962. Print.

Winks, Robin W. *Canada and the United States: The Civil War Years.* Baltimore: Johns Hopkins, 1960. Print.

Winn, James Anderson. *Unsuspected Eloquence: A History of the Relations between Poetry and Music.* New Haven: Yale University Press, 1981. Print.

The Woman in Battle: A Narrative of the Exploits, Adventures, and Travels of Madame Loreta Janeta Velazquez. Advertisement. Philadelphia: H. W. Kelley, 1876. Print.

Wood, Marcus. *Blind Memory: Visual Representations of Slavery in England and America, 1780–1865.* New York: Manchester University Press, 2000. Print.

Yaeger, Patricia. *Dirt and Desire: Reconstructing Southern Women's Writing, 1930–1990.* Chicago: University of Chicago Press, 2000. Print.

Young, Elizabeth. *Disarming the Nation: Women's Writing and the American Civil War.* Chicago: University of Chicago Press, 1999. Print.

Young, Robert J. C. *Colonial Desire: Hybridity in Theory, Culture, and Race.* New York: Routledge, 1995. Print.

Zelinsky, Wilbur. *Nation into State: The Shifting Symbolic Foundations of American Nationalism.* Chapel Hill: University of North Carolina Press, 1988. Print.

Ziff, Larzer. *Literary Democracy: The Declaration of Cultural Independence in America, 1837–1861.* New York: Viking Press, 1981. Print.

Žižek, Slavoj. *Tarrying with the Negative: Kant, Hegel, and the Critique of Ideology.* Durham: Duke University Press, 1993. Print.

ethnicity, 10–11, 60, 84, 141, 156–57, 191–96 passim, 198–200, 212n19, 218n42, 218n44, 227–28n20
"Ethnogenesis" (Timrod), 4–14
Evans, Augusta Jane, 15–16, 63–98 passim; *Beulah*, 65, 76, 77–78, 80, 98; *Macaria*, 15–16, 63–65, 66, 67, 69, 74–98, 120, 194; "Northern Literature," 69–71; "Southern Literature," 71–74; *St. Elmo*, 64, 80, 225n46; *Vashti*, 80; on "Womanly Usefulness," 16, 65, 75, 83–84, 87–95 passim, 96
Evans, Mary (Margaret Stilling), 128

Fahs, Alice, 2, 14, 64, 176, 212n21, 213nn25–26, 226n7, 226n10, 229n34, 230n42, 235n6
Fane, Julian, 67; *Tannhauser* (with Bulwer-Lytton), 67, 229n40
Faulkner, William, 209n1, 239nn40–41; *Absalom, Absalom!* 200–203, 239n40
Faust, Drew Gilpin, 13, 92, 94, 95, 210n8, 221n19, 224n41, 225n46, 228n24, 231n4, 233n23
Fay, Theodore, 38, 216n19; *Norman Leslie*, 33–36
Ferry, Anne, 142
Feuillet, Octave, 67, 68
Féval, Paul, 67
Fidler, William Perry, 63, 69, 78–79, 80, 97, 222n24
First Year of the War, The (Pollard), 106
Firth, Pond, and Company, 146, 147, 153, 155, 156, 163, 232n13
Fisher, Philip, 170
Fliegelman, Jay, vii, 3, 98
"Florence Vane" (P. P. Cooke), 131
For the Little Ones, 226–27n16
Ford, Sallie Rochester, 219n2, 224n44; *Raids and Romance*, 66, 69, 81
Foster, Gaines, 198, 235n7, 238–39n35, 239n36
Foucault, Michel, 94, 151
Four Years in the Saddle (Gilmor), 235n6

Fox-Genovese, Elizabeth, 223n31, 224n44
France, 68, 186–88, 193, 197, 220n6, 237nn21–22
Frank Leslie's Illustrated Newspaper, 127
"Freedom's Guide" (Sharkey), 167
Freeman, Douglas Southall, 12
From Manassas to Appomattox (J. Longstreet), 178
Frost, Linda, 127
Fuller, Richard, 44
futurity, 1–2, 8–9, 18–62 passim, 66–67, 83, 94–95, 132–33, 177–78, 194, 200–203, 211n14, 219n48

Gallagher, Gary W., 3, 210nn7–8, 210n10, 235n7
Garber, Marjorie, 14
Gardner, Sarah E., 224n44
"Gay and Happy," 232n14
Geiger, Emily, 83, 224n41
Gellner, Ernest, 4, 211n16, 213n25
Genette, Gérard, 75, 76
George Balcombe (N. B. Tucker), 40–41, 59
Georgia Scenes (A. B. Longstreet), 38–39
"Georgia Volunteer, The," 123–24
Giles, Paul, 169–70, 213n23
Gilmor, Harry, 235n6
"God help Kentucky," 228n27
Godwin, William, 32–33
Goetzel, S. H., 67
Gone with the Wind (Mitchell), 223n34
Gorrell, Henry Clay, 120–21
Goulding, Francis Robert, 66
Grant, Anne, 217n27
Grant, Ulysses, 188, 236n16
Gray, Richard, 73
"Great Cry and No Wool" (Barnstable), 227n19
Great Expectations (Dickens), 67, 229n40
Great Panic of 1837, 31, 61

Jackson, Leon, 31, 34, 214n5, 215n18, 217n28

Jackson, Thomas Jonathan "Stonewall," 103, 106, 119–20, 128–29, 228n24, 229n35

"Jackson Is Dead!" 228n24

Jacobs, Robert D., 27, 28, 218n38, 218n43

"Jeff Davis in the White House," 117–18

Jefferson, Thomas, 71, 72; *Notes on the State of Virginia*, 28, 214n8

Jim Crow, 62

Joan of Arc, 180, 235–36n9

"John Brown's Body," 149–50, 232n14

"John Brown's Entrance Into Hell," 227n19

Johnson's Island, 189, 196

Johnston, Albert Sidney, 83

Johnston, Joseph E., 118; *Narrative of Military Operations*, 178

Jones, Gavin, 155, 156

Journal of a Residence on a Georgian Plantation (Kemble), 194

Jusdanis, Gregory, 7, 12, 20–21, 132, 133, 171, 210nn9–10

Keckley, Elizabeth, 151, 171; *Behind the Scenes*, 143–44

"Kelly's Irish Brigade," 124

Kemble, Fanny, 194

Kennedy, J. Gerald, 215n17

Kennedy, John Pendleton, 25, 31; *Horse-Shoe Robinson*, 38

Kerkering, John D., 215n12

Knox, William, 134

Kolchin, Peter, 212n19, 213n24

"Ladies of Richmond," 125

Lady Audley's Secret (Braddon), 194

Lafitte (Ingraham), 217n27

Lake Erie Conspiracy, 188–89, 196

Lanier, Sidney, 16, 142, 209n1, 225n2, 225–26n5

"Last Race of the Rail-Splitter, The," 114

"Last Request, The," 228n27

Lays of the South: Verses Relative to the War, 140

Lee, Robert E., 65, 69, 129, 143, 177, 188, 196

Levine, Robert, 20, 214n3, 214n11

Lewis, Clay, 234n3

Lincoln, Abraham, 46, 82, 84, 89, 162, 185, 217n33, 233n22; and anti-Lincoln sentiment, 110–18 passim, 128, 134, 161, 194, 226nn13–15, 227n19, 233n21, 236–37n18; and "Dixie," 143, 144, 148, 231n1, 232n9

Lincoln, Mary Todd, 111, 143

Lincoln, Robert, 111

Lincoln and Hamlin Songster, 232n9

"Lines on the Death of Lieut. Gen. T. J. Jackson C.S.A.," 119–20

"Lines on the Proclamation Issued by the Tyrant Lincoln, April First, 1863," 116, 128

"LINES Sacred to the Memory of Capt. Henry C. Gorrell of Greensboro', N.C.," 120–21

Linwoods, The (Sedgwick), 34, 35

"Literary Prospects of the South" (Simms), 211n16

Lives of the Necromancers (Godwin), 32–33

locality, 27–28, 32, 38–39, 41–42, 44–45, 58, 69–78 passim, 99–142 passim, 143–72 passim, 185, 226n7

London Index, 192

London Times, 56–57, 134

Longstreet, Augustus Baldwin: *Georgia Scenes*, 38–39; *Master William Mitten*, 66

Longstreet, James, 178

Lost Cause, 84, 85, 145, 156, 173–203 passim, 223n31, 235n7

Lost Cause, The (Pollard), 177–78, 198–99

Lott, Eric, 231nn5–6, 234n33

Lovejoy, Elijah P., 61

Lowell, James R., 194

Lynch, Patrick, 110
Lyons, Rachel, 80, 86

Macaria (A. J. Evans), 15–16, 63–65, 66,
  67, 69, 74–98, 120, 194
Madison, James, 71, 72
Mara (Swain), 105–6
Marotti, Arthur, 101
"Marseillaise Hymn," 232n14
"Maryland in Chains," 228n27
"Maryland in Fetters," 228n27
Mason, Emily V., 140, 142; *The
  Southern Poems of the War*, 230n46
Master William Mitten (A. B.
  Longstreet), 66
material shortages and scarcities, 2, 8,
  65–69, 80, 102, 113–14, 122, 124–25,
  131, 194, 219n2, 220n7
Matthews, Brander, 148–50; "The Songs
  of the War," 148–49
Mattson, Morris, 36; *Paul Ulric*, 36, 37
Maury, Matthew Fontaine, 43
McCabe, James Dabney, Jr.: *The Aid-
  De-Camp*, 66, 69; "Mississippians
  Never Surrender," 129
McCardell, John, 20, 27, 54, 55, 59,
  214n3, 214n5, 215n12
McCord, Louisa S., 217n34
McCrimmon, Mary A., 128, 129, 137
McCurry, Stephanie, 10, 213n24, 223n33
McPherson, James M., 82, 129, 176,
  223n31, 236n10
Melville, Herman, 50, 100; *Battle-
  Pieces and Aspects of the War*, 225n2;
  Moby-Dick, 75; *White-Jacket*, 48
*Memoir of the Last Year of the War for
  Independence, A* (Early), 178
"Memoir on Slavery" (Harper), 44
Memoirs of an American Lady
  (A. Grant), 217n27
Memoirs of Service Afloat (Semmes), 178
*Memoirs of the Confederate War for
  Independence* (von Boecke), 235n6
Miller, Cristanne, 225n1, 225n5

Miller, Stephen Franks, 112, 226n15
Millwood, Grace, 130
Milton, John, 134; *Paradise Lost*, 111
Minor, Benjamin Blake, 43–44, 45, 54,
  56, 217n30
Misérables, Les (Hugo), 68–69, 86,
  220n8, 221n18, 223n31; translated by
  Wilbour, 68, 220n6
"Miss Martineau on Slavery"
  (Simms), 44
*Miss Ravenel's Conversion from
  Secession to Loyalty* (De Forest), 77
"Mississippians Never Surrender"
  (McCabe), 129
Mistress and Maid (Craik), 67
Mitchell, Margaret, 184; *Gone with the
  Wind*, 223n34
Mobile Daily Advertiser, 69–74, 78
Mobile Register, 192
Moby-Dick (Melville), 75
Moore, Frank: *Rebel Rhymes and
  Rhapsodies*, 139, 230n49; *Songs
  and Ballads of the Southern People*,
  230n46
Moore, Olin, 220nn6–7
Moore, Thomas, 27, 134
*Moral and Intellectual Diversity of the
  Races, The* (trans. Hotze), 191–92
Morrison, Toni, 212n17
Mosby, John Singleton, 178
Mosby's War Reminiscences (Mosby), 178
Moseley, Caroline, 144, 232nn14–15
Moss, Elizabeth, 97, 98, 220n10, 223n33,
  224n45
Moss, Sidney, 33, 36, 216n19
Moss, William, 101, 114, 126, 225n2,
  225n4, 226n6, 227nn17–18
Mrs. Halliburton's Troubles (Wood), 68
Mühlbach, Luise (Clara Mundt), 67, 69
Muhlenfeld, Elisabeth, 1
Mundt, Clara (Luise Mühlbach), 67, 69
My Imprisonment (Greenhow), 179
"My Life Is like the Summer Rose"
  (Wilde), 131

The New Southern Studies

The Nation's Region: Southern Modernism, Segregation,
and U.S. Nationalism
by Leigh Anne Duck

Black Masculinity and the U.S. South: From Uncle Tom to Gangsta
by Riché Richardson

Grounded Globalism: How the U.S. South Embraces the World
by James L. Peacock

Disturbing Calculations: The Economics of Identity in Postcolonial
Southern Literature, 1912–2002
by Melanie R. Benson

American Cinema and the Southern Imaginary
edited by Deborah E. Barker and Kathryn McKee

Southern Civil Religions: Imagining the Good Society in the
Post-Reconstruction Era
by Arthur J. Remillard

Reconstructing the Native South: American Indian Literature and the
Lost Cause
by Melanie Benson Taylor

Apples and Ashes: Literature, Nationalism, and the Confederate States
of America
by Coleman Hutchison

Reading for the Body: The Recalcitrant Materiality of Southern Fiction,
1893–1985
by Jay Watson